THE
CISTERCIANS
IN MEDIEVAL ART

To all those
past and present
who have made this book possible.

THE
CISTERCIANS
IN MEDIEVAL ART

J A M E S   F R A N C E

CISTERCIAN PUBLICATIONS

First published in the United Kingdom in 1998 by
Sutton Publishing Limited · Phoenix Mill
Thrupp · Stroud · Gloucestershire · GL5 2BU

First published in the United States in 1998 by
CISTERCIAN PUBLICATIONS
Editorial Office: WMU Station,
Kalamazoo, Michigan 49008
Distribution: Saint Joseph's Abbey,
Spencer, Massachusetts 01562

ISBN 0 87907 870 7

Typeset in 10/14pt Sabon.
Typesetting and origination by
Sutton Publishing Limited.
Printed in Great Britain by
Butler & Tanner, Frome, Somerset.

CONTENTS

Map vi

Preface vii

CHAPTER ONE   Benedictine Roots   1
CHAPTER TWO   The New Monastery 12
CHAPTER THREE   'Four Branches from the Cistercian Root' . . 17
CHAPTER FOUR   St Bernard and the Cistercian Expansion . . 26
CHAPTER FIVE   More Cistercian Portraits 50
CHAPTER SIX   The Monastic Community 72
CHAPTER SEVEN   The Abbots 99
CHAPTER EIGHT   Lay Brothers 122
CHAPTER NINE   The Nuns 139
CHAPTER TEN   God's Work – *Opus Dei* 169
CHAPTER ELEVEN   Manual Labour – *Labor Manuum* 191
CHAPTER TWELVE   Sacred Reading – *Lectio Divina* 205
CHAPTER THIRTEEN   Edification, Entertainment, Exposure . .213

Notes 227

Glossary 243

List of Illustrations 245

Acknowledgements 261

Bibliography 263

Index 273

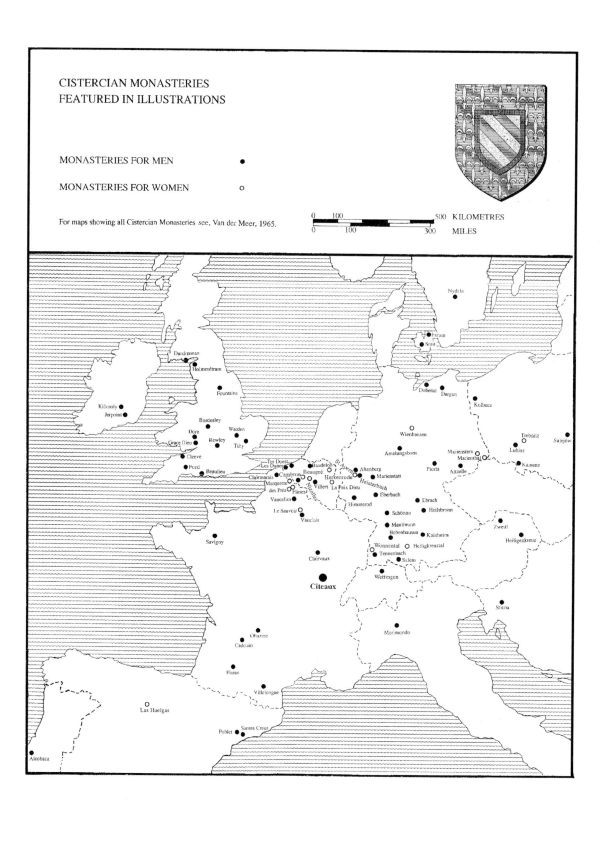

CISTERCIAN MONASTERIES
FEATURED IN ILLUSTRATIONS

MONASTERIES FOR MEN ●

MONASTERIES FOR WOMEN ○

For maps showing all Cistercian Monasteries see, Van der Meer, 1965.

100   500 KILOMETRES
100   300 MILES

PREFACE

'The Cistercians are a model for all monks, a mirror for the diligent, a spur to the indolent.'

William of Malmesbury[1]

These words by the English chronicler written nearly 900 years ago are among the first testimony we have of the nascent Cistercian family. Another early witness, the Benedictine monk Ordericus Vitalis, talks of a 'swarm of monks in their cowls spread over the whole earth'.[2] Nothing remains of the primitive huts they first occupied, but the construction of stone churches which Ordericus claimed 'they built with their own hands in lonely wooded places' began at Cîteaux in 1125–30, at Clairvaux in 1135, and at Fontenay in 1139.[3] Such scanty evidence that exists, both in the form of 'words' and 'stones' may, however, be supplemented by 'images', the earliest of which pre-date most of the literary, archaeological and architectural material and thus provide additional information of substantial value. Remarkably, the famous monastic work scenes in the Cîteaux manuscript of St Gregory the Great's *Moralia in Job*, were produced little more than a decade after the arrival of the monks (*see* 45, 134 & **colour plate 24**). Over and above their artistic merit they attest to a number of features which characterized the Cistercian reform: the importance of manual labour, the wooded location of many sites and the need for land clearance, the agrarian nature of their economy, and to the simplicity and poverty of their lives.

Recent decades have seen Cistercian studies advancing in almost geometric progression. A number of factors have contributed to this: the work of the Institute of Cistercian Studies at Western Michigan University, Kalamazoo, Michigan, and the many books put out by Cistercian Publications; the contribution of great scholars like Jean Leclercq and Louis J. Lekai; and the exhibitions, conferences and published papers in connection with the ninth centenary of the birth of St Bernard of Clairvaux in 1990. To these must be added the ever-increasing dialogue between diverse disciplines, each of which has its own special contribution to make and, as a result of which, more and more of the overall picture is being revealed. Having noted the importance of the images in the *Moralia* manuscript, I set out to examine the extent to which these and other medieval representations of monks and nuns in illuminated manuscripts, architectural sculpture, stained glass and paintings may add to our global understanding of Cistercian history.

I have not been concerned with artistic styles and forms – the proper preserve of the art historian upon which I am not qualified to encroach – but with seeing what a historian of monastic life can glean from the images that show the daily lives of monks and nuns, of their communities and leaders, of their spirituality, and of the way the Order developed in the course of the Middle Ages. There are examples of how the monks pictured themselves, as in the *Moralia* work scenes, of how they were viewed by others whom the monks commissioned, and of how they were seen by other outsiders, friends and foes. Many have not previously been reproduced. More often than not the images confirm what is already known from other sources, but as the lacunae are not the same in the visual as in the verbal material available, our overall understanding may be enhanced by a study of the pictorial evidence. Furthermore, viewed from a different perspective, new layers of meaning may be drawn from the visual sources. Iconography, for example, gives added meaning to our appreciation of the role of Cistercian nuns in the thirteenth-century religious women's movement in Flanders and the Rhineland, to the contribution of lay brothers, and to the European dimension of the Cistercian dispersion. The portraits of known Cistercians, however, leave as many gaps as they fill. They are inevitably heavily slanted to members of the Order who rose to positions of authority in the hierarchy of the Church and are not representative of all those who contributed most to the Order. I have, for example, been unable to find 'portraits' of monks like Gilbert of Hoyland, John of Ford, or Adam of Perseigne.

The iconography of St Bernard has already been well covered, particularly in a number of regional studies, and I have therefore limited myself to dealing with him only as a monk and abbot and not in his wider public role. The emphasis in most of the studies, however, is on the later and post-medieval material and, in a number of cases, the early images of Bernard have not been shown.[4] I have therefore concentrated on these, among them one from Bernard's lifetime which, although it was briefly noted by Jean Leclercq in 1955, is very little known (*see* **colour plate 7**), and two others from before his canonization in 1174 (*see* 7 & **colour plate 10**).

St Bernard's celebrated diatribe in his Apology to William of St Thierry against 'a fantastic conglomeration of beauty misbegotten and ugliness transmogrified',[5] although traditionally interpreted as directed against the excesses of Cluniac cloister carvings, has more recently been seen as aimed at the exuberance of the Cîteaux manuscript illuminations under Bernard's former abbot, Stephen Harding.[6] In Bernard's opinion, both types of decoration were inappropriate for monks on account of their extravagance and distractive influence. Legislation followed decreeing that manuscripts were to be in one colour and without illuminations, the glass white, and crosses and pictures were banned from the church.[7] The potency of abstract symbols as aids to contemplation had long been recognized and, under Bernard's influence, were universally adopted by the Cistercians: geometric patterns and interlace, sometimes accompanied by simple vegetative designs, became the tell-tale sign of Cistercian art. They decorated corbels, capitals and grisaille glass for which the Cistercian churches became famous, and adorned the modest initials in their manuscripts. In the words of a modern authority: 'Had it been fully implemented, the Cistercian church reform would have been one of the most radical manifestations of abstinence and restraint in history'.[8] But it was not to be.

The vehemence of Bernard's condemnation was in itself evidence of the strong appeal of representations of the human form and, paradoxically, Bernard himself possessed a lavishly illuminated Bible (admittedly not produced at Clairvaux, but a gift).[9] It seems equally strange that someone whose works were filled with such evocative imagery should have so fervently opposed its visual expression. The use of images as a spiritual aid, even in a monastic context, could not be resisted and, although the General Chapter attempted to enforce the legislation, it was soon a dead letter. At the end of the twelfth century the Cistercian Adam of Dore, whose views on art in the cloister coincided with Bernard's, drew up a programme of types and anti-types for the use of artists so that, if images could not be altogether banned, at least suitable ones might be chosen in preference to 'the double-headed eagles, four lions with one and the same head, centaurs with quivers, headless men grinning, the so-called logical chimaera, the fabled intrigues of the fox and cock, monks playing the pipe, and Boethius's ass and lyre'.[10] After a relatively short period conforming to Bernardine ideals, Cistercian manuscript illumination became indistinguishable from what could be found elsewhere. Architectural sculpture gradually abandoned the block-like capital in favour of foliate, animal and human representations. In the wake of the other art forms, Cistercian glass used coloured historiated images, first as devotional aids and later in narrative scenes.[11] These are the works from which images of monks and nuns in this study have been drawn and which add to our knowledge of Cistercian life through the medieval centuries.

The inclusion of examples from all over Europe has only been made possible through the assistance of many individuals and institutions, monasteries, libraries and museums. I am first and foremost grateful to all those who have provided me with photographs, details of which are acknowledged elsewhere. To some I am indebted for information and material relating to whole countries: to Dr Katerina Charvátová and Dr Zuzana Všečteková for the Czech Republic; to Revd Dr David H. Williams and Dr Krystyna Białoskórska for Poland; and to Dr Thomas Coomans who has been most helpful in drawing my attention to the Belgian sources. Others have provided invaluable help relating to individual monasteries: Dr Charlotte Ziegler on Zwettl, Austria; Fr Jesús M. Oliver OCist on Poblet, Catalonia; Wolfgang Brandis on Kloster Wienhausen, Germany; Ephorus Markus Henrich, Evangelisches Seminar Maulbronn, on Maulbronn, Germany; and Christine Kratzke on Dargun, Germany. To these I add Professor Marsha Dutton, Dr Terryl N. Kinder and Professor Nigel Palmer, who have pointed me to images of whose existence I would not otherwise have been aware. I have, as always, been greatly encouraged by the friendly interest and advice of Professor Brian McGuire. I owe an especial thanks to Professor Joseph V. Guerinot and Fr Hilary Costello OCSO for the many hours they have devoted to reading my manuscript. As a result of their wise suggestions, many improvements have been made, errors of fact and interpretation avoided, and further lapses forestalled. All remaining are my own – *mea culpa, mea culpa, mea maxima culpa.*

James France
Feast of St Benedict, 21 March 1997

CHAPTER ONE

BENEDICTINE ROOTS

'The monastic order, formerly dead, was revived: there [at Cîteaux] *the old ashes were poked; it was reformed by the grace of novelty, and by zeal it recovered its proper state . . . and the Rule of Benedict recovered in our times the truth of the letter.'*

Philip of Harvengt writing in the 1140s[1]

Tradition puts the foundation date of Cîteaux in 1098 on 21 March. The choice was no coincidence for on that day the feast of St Benedict was celebrated. It was only with hindsight that the event heralded the birth of the new religious body, for at the time the intention of Robert of Molesme and his twenty-one companions was merely to settle at a place of solitude where they could live a simpler life and provide their every need for themselves according to their reading of the Rule of St Benedict. In reading history in reverse it is only too easy, but a mistake, to see in the community that settled at Cîteaux the nascent Cistercian Order which was to eclipse all others. At the time the move represented only one of many attempts at monastic renewal and reform which were so characteristic of the late eleventh and early twelfth centuries.

The monks did not at first use the name of the heavily wooded place that they had been given, Cîteaux – described as 'a place of horror and vast solitude' in a text borrowed from Deuteronomy[2] – but chose to call it the 'New Monastery' – *Novum Monasterium*. The choice was apt, for here they wished to leave the 'old' ways of traditional monachism with its emphasis on the elaborate and time-consuming celebration of the liturgy into which Molesme had slipped and replace it with a 'new' interpretation of the Rule or rather a return to one based on the authentic sources – one which looked back not just to St Benedict but past him to the fathers of the desert, to the golden age of the early Church with its emphasis on communality, and beyond to the Garden of Eden.

Among early accounts the *Exordium Cistercii* gives the reason for the departure of the reforming party from Molesme:

They realized that, although life in that place was a godly and upright life, they observed the Rule they had vowed to keep in a way short of their desire and intention.[3]

The *Exordium Parvum* goes further. While still at Molesme Robert and his companions 'often spoke to each other, lamented, and were saddened by the transgression of the Rule of St Benedict, the Father of Monks'.[4] They promised to 'place their lives under the custody of the holy Rule of Father Benedict'.[5] In a letter the papal legate, Archbishop Hugh of Lyons, referred to their wish 'to adhere henceforth more strictly and more perfectly to the Rule of blessed Benedict, which so far you have observed poorly and neglectfully in that monastery'.[6]

Writing in 1130 the Norman monk, Orderic Vitalis, described the reforming community as endeavouring 'to carry out a literal observance of the Rule of St Benedict',[7] and he quotes Robert as saying to his monks,

> We have made our profession, my dear brothers, according to the Rule of our holy father Benedict, but it seems to me that we have not observed it in every point. We have many customs which are laid down there, and we carelessly overlook a number of its precepts. . . . I propose therefore that we should observe the Rule of St Benedict in everything, taking care not to turn aside either to the left or to the right.[8]

In the same way William of Malmesbury in his Chronicle asserts that they left Molesme as they were not able to follow 'the purity of the Rule',[9] and he pointed to the importance the Cistercians attached to this by saying, 'So intent are they on their Rule, that they think no jot or tittle of it should be disregarded'. This is what formed the basis of the revival noted by Harvengt in whose words, quoted above, 'the rule of Benedict recovered in our times the truth of the letter'.

The lesson of Molesme was remembered in the later move of the reforming party from the English abbey of St Mary's, York, which led to the foundation of Fountains as a Cistercian monastery. In a letter Archbishop Thurstan of York recalled

> what happened in the affair of the Molesme monks which is quite similar. The Cistercians went forth to establish and founded a most perfect way of life. . . . They faithfully undertook a renewal of the Holy Rule and a total living of it.[10]

As followers of the Rule the monks who settled at Cîteaux were true Benedictines. This description is, notwithstanding its accuracy, nevertheless normally reserved to describe the 'black' monks of the old dispensation. This is done so as to avoid confusion with those who adopted the evolving customs of Cîteaux who were later called 'white' monks. The resolve of the monks of Cîteaux to observe the precepts of the Rule more faithfully made their claim to the title of Benedictines the more authentic and one which has been and is shared by all subsequent Cistercians.

The Rule was one of the books which every Cistercian abbey was bound to possess. Every day one of its seventy-three chapters was read aloud, followed by

1 St Benedict and his Rule.

a commentary by the abbot. This reading gave its name to the room in which it took place, the chapter house, after the church the most important area in the abbey. The abbot's commentary was sometimes written down. This happened, for example, at Heilsbronn (Bavaria, Germany) under Abbot Ulrich Kötzler (1432–62) who wrote a commentary in two volumes in 1442 helped by two monks, Hermann von Kottenheim who was a former abbot of Ebrach (Franconia, Germany) and Johannes, a Polish monk who had visited Ebrach. The abbot is portrayed kneeling with another monk, both in black habits, before an initial *I(hesu)* made up of the figure of the Man of Sorrows, all within a red frame with a blue background.[11]

The iconography of St Benedict went back centuries.[12] The oldest representation is thought to be an eighth-century fresco in the catacomb of S. Ermete in Rome where Benedict is depicted with a short beard, wearing a black scapular and hood. The image underwent a considerable development in the tenth and eleventh centuries as exemplified by a fresco portrait in the chapel of St Benedict in Civate.[13] Here he displays an open book with the inscription *Ego sum Benedictus aba* ('I am abbot Benedict'). He is identified as a monk by his tonsure and as an abbot by the pastoral staff which had a curved end like all subsequent western croziers in contrast to earlier staffs which were indistinguishable from those of travellers or pilgrims.

Not surprisingly these images of St Benedict were later adopted and developed in Cistercian art, particularly in illuminated manuscripts. The commonest form is in the opening initial letter to the Prologue to the Rule *A(usculta o fili precepta magistri)* – 'Hearken, my son, to the precepts of the master and incline the ear of thy heart. . . .'[14]

The oldest is probably in a composite manuscript from the Austrian abbey of Zwettl from 1173 in which the Rule is preceded by a Calendar, Necrology and Martyrology.(1)[15] On a blue ground with a green outer frame, the initial is filled with interlacing tendrils and leaves. In a circular medallion above the *A* is a bust of St Benedict in a frontal position, nimbed and with a crozier passing through the fingers of his left hand with which he is at the same time blessing. Below are busts of three young monks, the two on the outside turned inwards, while the one in the centre faces forward, and with both hands he supports a scroll which envelops the initial.

In another composite manuscript, consisting of the Rule and a Martyrology, the initial *A(usculta)* is very similar both in shape and in the way the design is treated. Although produced in the famous scriptorium of the Benedictine abbey of Posa in the middle of the thirteenth century, it was made for the Cistercian abbey of Altzelle (Saxony, Germany) and is now in the library of the Cistercian nunnery of Marienthal.(2)[16] Benedict is shown tonsured with a green nimbus and in a greyish habit sitting on a folding stool with claw feet and hand grips with animal heads. In his left hand is a green book – the Rule – and his right hand is raised as if instructing a young monk in a blue-grey habit, squatting at his feet, on the obligations of the monastic life. The rest of the space within the initial is taken up with six coiled tendrils and leaves similar to those in the Zwettl illustration, and the dominant green and blue background, symbolic of the tension between the temptations of the world and the longing for heaven, are also reminiscent of the Austrian counterpart. The stepped frame following the outline of the letter and the way the initial spreads into the margin are characteristic of the Thuringian style of the Posa scriptorium.

2 St Benedict instructing a young monk.

Another manuscript of the Thuringian-Saxon school of illumination depicts St Benedict within the initial *O(s justi meditabitur)*.(3)[17] It is characterized by the same intertwining branches and acanthus leaves and the stepped outline of the initial as the Altzelle manuscript. Benedict is tonsured and bearded; with his left hand he holds a crozier and a scroll with the opening words of the Rule while his right hand is raised instructing a small young monk at his feet. This novice holds his own scroll which reads 'Speak, O Lord' (*Loquere Domine*) taken from 1 Kgs 3:9, 10. This manuscript is a Gradual from *c*. 1270 from the Silesian abbey of Kamenz (founded 1247), but it was probably written in the scriptorium of the mother-house of Lubiaz (Leubus, Silesia). A contemporary Gradual from the nunnery of Seligenthal (Bavaria, Germany) has Benedict in the same initial *O(s)* tonsured and in a black habit with a red book and nimbus, together with St Francis in a brown habit, his left hand raised and showing the stigmata, and a Cistercian nun in a greyish brown habit with white wimple and black veil.[18] In a mid-fourteenth-century Gradual from the nunnery of Wonnental (Bavaria, Germany), Benedict is again depicted within the initial *O(s)* on a gold ground with an abbot kneeling before him while two nuns kneel in the margin.[19]

3 St Benedict with a young disciple.

The Zwettl manuscript with the image of Benedict contains another historiated initial at the beginning of the first chapter of the Rule (**colour plate 1**):[20] *M(onachorum)* – 'There are evidently four kinds of monks'.[21] The middle of the *M* consists of a column which curls outwards terminating in two animal heads thus forming the letter. A castellated crossbar creates four sections within which are the busts of four monks. The two above are in a frontal position; the one on the right has a book in his left hand, his right hand is raised as if instructing another monk, the back of whose bald and tonsured head is just visible above the castellation. The two monks below are turned inwards, both with their hoods up. The four monks probably represent the four types described by St Benedict: Cenobites who live in monasteries under a rule and an abbot whom Benedict calls the 'strong race' for which he is providing, such as the Benedictines and Cistercians; Anchorites or Hermits who live without the help of others; Sarabaites who live in twos or threes without a shepherd or a Rule, whom Benedict describes as 'detestable'; and, the fourth class, Gyrovagues, who wander from place to place and whom Benedict considers even worse than the Sarabaites.

Since the upper right figure is holding a book he probably represents the Cenobites living under a Rule. If that is the case, the upper left figure may be a Hermit who fights against temptations on his own without the need of a Rule and, in the words of Benedict, 'with his hand and arm alone' (*sola manu vel brachio*), an expression which may explain why he is depicted with both hands raised. The two hooded monks below look rather miserable, and they probably represent Benedict's *bêtes noires*! The one on the left could be a Sarabaite since he has a tonsure by which, as the Rule says, his tonsure is a lie to the Lord. And finally, as Benedict puts the Gyrovagues in the last place, the wretched one on the right must belong to that genus.

4 St Benedict with his Rule.

In a Cistercian context St Benedict is also frequently represented within the initial *F(uit vir)*, the first antiphon of his feast on 21 March. The oldest is perhaps the one from Zwettl from the last quarter of the twelfth century.(4)[22] Here a bearded, tonsured and nimbed figure is shown standing behind the crossbar of the *F*. The crozier is at an angle with the crook leaning on his shoulder and the staff in front of the bar. In his right hand he holds an open Rule with the opening words of the Prologue: *Ausculta o fili*. . . . In another manuscript from the late thirteenth century belonging to the Silesian abbey of Lubiaz (Leubus) a nimbed monk (St Benedict) in a black habit carrying a crozier and book is shown with a disciple under two arcades within a square formed by the upper half of the *F*.[23] A similar composition is found in the manuscript known as the Osek Lectionary because it was deposited at this Bohemian abbey before the war, although it emanated from the Cistercian nunnery of Marienstern in Saxony.(5)[24] Within a square in the upper half of the initial *F(uit)* a nimbed St Benedict in a black cowl over a white tunic is seen instructing a group of four monks at his feet looking up at him. In his left hand Benedict holds a book – the Rule – to which he points with his right hand in a teaching gesture. One of his disciples has another copy of the Rule and indicates his concentration by pointing to this.

St Benedict is frequently portrayed together with St Bernard in Cistercian iconography. Together they not only symbolize the two great branches of the Benedictine family, but they also represent the Lawgiver and the Mystic, Moses and Elijah, who were present at the Transfiguration of the Lord, united in leading their disciples to the heights of the union of love. When linked to Benedict, Bernard is also shown as interpreting the Rule of the father of monks, and the book he is most frequently depicted carrying may safely be considered to represent the Rule upon which he based his own teaching. An exception may be when he is portrayed instructing a group of monks, when the book he is seen with may be either the Rule of one of his own works. An example of this is found in a full-page miniature in a fourteenth-century manuscript of William of Tournai's *Flores Sancti Bernardi*. Here the two saints are shown looking like identical twins, each depicted under an arcade with a crozier in the right hand and an open book in the left. Virtually the only difference is that St Benedict on the left is in a black habit while St Bernard is in white. The texts of the two books are Benedict's familiar opening words of the Rule while Bernard's, significantly, are those of his commentary on the Rule, the treatise, *On precepts and dispensation*.[25]

Bernard's role in such dual images is that of *alter Benedictus* – the 'other Benedict', as he was referred to by Burchard of Balerne.[26] St Gregory in his *Dialogues* had invested Benedict with the title *vir Dei* ('man of God'), traditionally conferred on prophets and patriarchs in the Old Testament and one later frequently bestowed on Bernard.[27] The two are seen together in a number of media. They are, for example, again depicted looking like twins in a carving on the end of one of the rows of oak choir stalls from *c.* 1310 in the abbey church of Doberan (Mecklenburg, Germany).(6)[28] In order to preserve the symmetry of the composition they each carry a crozier and a book but in opposite hands.

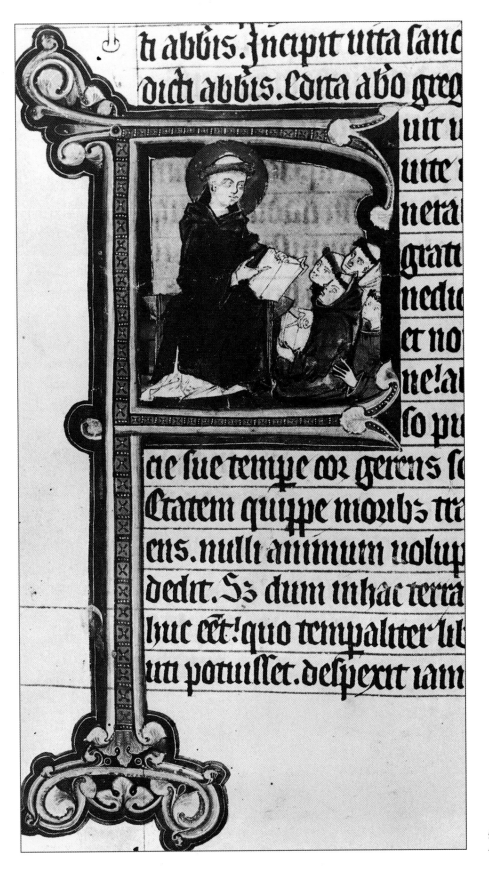

5 St Benedict teaching.

6 Carving of St Benedict
and St Bernard on choir
stalls.

A carving of them in limestone forms the capital of two slender columns in the cloister of the Portuguese nunnery of Celas.[29] Made during the reign of Alfonso III (1245–79) it shows Benedict on the left and Bernard on the right. The two saints are depicted in two adjacent pointed stained glass windows from *c.* 1340 in the upper cloister of the nunnery of Wienhausen (Celle, Germany) (**colour plates 2 & 3**).[30] The two are separated by a square panel above containing a biblical scene witnessed by a kneeling nun (*see* 98). Bernard is in a greyish blue habit, Benedict in greyish violet, each of them carrying a book in the right hand and a white crozier in the left.

The *Steps of Humility and Pride* is St Bernard's first written work, probably already composed in 1118/19.[31] It was undertaken at the request of one of his monks who wanted him to develop at greater length the sermons he had given to the community. In it he interprets the twelve steps of St Benedict in what is the heart of the Rule contained in its longest chapter, Chapter 7.[32] He does so in the light of his own experience, but instead of examining what happens on the way up he chooses to travel down in what has been described as a 'retro-tour of St Benedict's steps of humility, with all the fun that seeing things in reverse can bring'.[33]

The oldest collection of the works of St Bernard was compiled at the Benedictine abbey of Anchin (Nord, France) *c.* 1165, little more than a decade after his death. It consists of three volumes and was the work of one hand, the monk Siger, who is represented near the beginning in a large initial B(*ernardus abbas*).[34] Introducing Bernard's treatise on the twelve steps of humility is a large miniature extending the full length of the folio and forming the capital *I*. (7) It consists of a ladder, the one Jacob had dreamt of stretching from earth to heaven (Gen 28:12), a fragile connection on which the angels of God moved up and down, and a reminder that faith is a precarious commitment. Not only is it easy to fall off, but it is only possible to reach the summit one step at a time. In the words of Bernard: 'No one reaches the summit immediately: the top rung of the ladder is grasped by ascending, not by flying.'[35] This accords with the kernel of Benedict's teaching contained in the famous definition of the monastery as 'a school of the Lord's service',[36] heaven being the reward for a long apprenticeship of humility.

The two sides of the ladder, representing the body and the soul, are painted silver, while the twelve rungs, indicating the twelve degrees of humility, the stages on the road to salvation, are in gold. The angels on the left are ascending by humility, while those on the right are descending by self-exaltation. The angel on the highest rung carries a scroll with the inscription: 'I will place my seat to the north, and I will be like the most high.' (Is 14:13–14) The devil at the foot of the ladder has an axe in his right hand; with the other he grabs the hair of a falling angel. At the bottom Jacob is shown awaking within the top half of a semi-circle. He holds a scroll which reads, 'Truly this is a holy place'. (Gen 28:16) At the top, within the lower half of a semi-circle, Christ is depicted as the goal to be reached at the summit. He is shown blessing those who, having followed the *way*, have now reached the Truth. This very Benedictine theme occupied a central position

7 Jacob's Ladder with
St Benedict and St Bernard.

in the teaching of Bernard, and here Christ is flanked by two monks, Benedict in a brown habit seen writing his Rule and Bernard in a white habit carrying a book (either the Rule or his own treatise) in his right hand and a crozier in the left. Bernard is not shown nimbed but this is correct as the picture was painted some years before his canonization in 1174.

The same theme is repeated in a wall painting in the former refectory (now library) of the German nunnery of Seligenthal (Bavaria).[37] Two large figures of Benedict on the right and Bernard on the left, both nimbed and carrying croziers and in black and brown cowls respectively, stand on either side of a ladder with twelve rungs. This is surmounted by the monogram of Christ and a cross and supported at the top by an angel on each side. A diminutive nun in a grey habit and black veil is seen kneeling on the seventh rung. More than half way there she has made good progress, but she still has a fair way to go! The painting is thought to be from the late fifteenth century with later restoration in the seventeenth century.

CHAPTER TWO

THE NEW MONASTERY

'You should know that they come from a place which is called the New Monastery. They migrated to that place, after seceding from the community of Molesme with their abbot, in order to lead a stricter and more consecrated life according to the Rule of blessed Benedict. . . .'

Archbishop Hugh of Lyons to Pope Paschal II[1]

'The Cistercian Order had its beginning in the year 1098 under Father Robert.' These are the opening words of the inscription to the Foundation Wall Painting from 1424 in the church of Maulbronn in Württemberg.[2] They are repeated below the picture in the Dijon collection of privileges from 1491 (*see* 8). The words are historically incorrect on two counts and, furthermore, would not have made sense to the twenty-one monks under their abbot, Robert, who had left Molesme to settle at Cîteaux. First, the adjective Cistercian was meaningless as it was known as the New Monastery for a number of years and not as Cîteaux; it is so described in the *Exordium Parvum*, the *Charter of Charity*, and in the foundation charters of Pontigny and Morimond. An early use of the new name occurred in the bull of 1119 addressed to 'Stephen, abbot of the monastery of Cîteaux'.[3] Secondly, the intention was not to found a new 'Order' but merely to secure a place conducive to an ascetic life in poverty and solitude in keeping with the Rule. The fledgling Order can only be said to have had its beginning when Cîteaux found it necessary to found daughter-houses and draw up guidelines defining the relationship between these and Cîteaux, and guarantee unity of observance and discipline. Although the seed which was, in the words of Caesarius of Heisterbach, 'to grow and expand and to extend its branches from sea to sea' may be traced back to 1098, nothing could have been further from the minds of the monks who were struggling just to survive and within little more than a year, the role Robert played would have been denied by the monks he left behind at Cîteaux when he returned to Molesme.

With hindsight, however, the modest beginning was seen as heralding a major departure in monastic history. The event was recorded in numerous chronicles and not confined to Cistercian accounts. A fine example is found in the Chronicle of the English Benedictine Abbey of Rochester. Under 1098 it says: 'In this year the monastery of Cîteaux was founded' (**colour plate 4**). As an event of major importance, the entry is highlighted by a picture in the adjoining margin of a bust of a Cistercian monk in a pale brown habit with the hood over his tonsured and bearded head, over which the legend, 'The Monastery of Cîteaux founded', is repeated in red ink.

Before moving to Cîteaux Robert had experienced a chequered monastic career. Before joining the abbey of Moutier-la-Celle as a young monk, he had already relinquished or abandoned the office of superior four times: first as abbot of Saint-Michel-de-Tonnerre, then as prior of its dependent cell of Saint-Ayoul. While abbot of Molesme, which he had founded in 1075, he left to join a group of hermits at Aux near Riel-les-Eaux. Finally, he moved a fourth time when he left for Cîteaux. He subsequently made a fifth move by returning to Molesme.[4] His career reflects the state of turmoil characteristic of this period of monastic renewal. So great was the appeal of greater solitude and poverty than contemporary monasteries allowed that small groups of hermit-monks found themselves attracting large numbers of recruits and being showered with gifts of land by local nobles, to the point that within a few years the original character had changed and part of the community felt the need to make a new start. This is what had happened at Molesme. In the words of the *Exordium Cistercii*:

> Within a short time of its foundation God in his goodness enriched it with the gift of his graces, raised it to honour with the presence of distinguished men, and caused it to be as great in possessions as it was resplendent in virtues. But, because possessions and virtues are not usually steady companions, several members of the holy community . . . decided to pursue heavenly studies rather than to be entangled in earthly affairs.[5]

The struggle between those who wanted a stricter observance and those satisfied with prevailing Cluniac customs was acrimonious. According to the *Exordium Parvum*, one of the leaders of the reforming group, Alberic, who was to become prior at Cîteaux before succeeding Robert as abbot, had 'laboured much and for long for the brethren to move from Molesme to this place, for which endeavour he had to suffer many insults, prison and beatings'.[6]

After Robert's departure Molesme suffered a crisis of discipline and he was called back on papal orders at the request of the monks to resolve it. According to William of Malmesbury Robert was not reluctant to return for he 'could not well bear such continued scantiness of diet', and the monks at Molesme

> drew him back to the monastery, by his obedience to the pope, for such was their pretext: compelling him to a measure to which he was already extremely well-disposed. . . . He left the narrow confines of poverty, and resought his former magnificence.[7]

Allowance must of course be made for the fact that William was writing in praise of his fellow-countryman, Stephen Harding, but at the same time he may have based what he wrote on information he had obtained from Cîteaux. The papal legate's terms included permission for 'all those brethren of the New Monastery who will follow him when he leaves' to do so.[8] According to the *Exordium Parvum* 'he returned with a few monks who did not find the solitude to their liking'.[9] William of Malmesbury's version is that 'All followed him from Cîteaux, who had gone thither with him, except eight. These, few in number but great in virtue, appointed Alberic abbot, and Stephen prior.'[10] No wonder that the fledgling community which was left behind looked upon Robert's departure as a defection which put their survival at risk.

Their resentment expressed itself in their refusal to accord Robert the title of first abbot of Cîteaux. The *Exordium Parvum* has a chapter entitled, 'About the Election of Alberic, the First Abbot of the Monastery of Cîteaux'.[11] For a long time they erased Robert from their memory. Almost a century later the early negative assessment was perpetuated by Conrad of Eberbach in the *Exordium Magnum*. Here, too, Alberic is called the first abbot and Stephen Harding the second, and the *Moralia in Job* manuscript is said to have been completed 'in the time of Lord Stephen, second abbot of Cîteaux'.[12]

The rehabilitation of Robert came on the initiative of Molesme and not of Cîteaux. His *Life* was written and in 1220 the abbot of Molesme asked the abbot of Cîteaux to petition the pope to proceed with Robert's canonization.[13] Four years later the General Chapter ordered his feast to be observed throughout the Order, and Robert was finally acknowledged as 'the first abbot of Cîteaux'.[14]

Even though in the long run Robert was bound to be accorded his rightful place as the founding abbot of the New Monastery, for a long time an attempt was made to write him out of Cistercian history. In the same way he is also totally unrepresented in medieval Cistercian iconography: there was no need for statues of him, his feast day was not marked by historiated initials in illuminated manuscripts and he is not commemorated in stained glass.

A rare exception is the wood engraving in a collection of privileges from 1491 by Peter Meglinger, the first book printed in Dijon, *Collecta privilegiorum ordinis cisterciensis.* (8) Here the pope, wearing a cope and tiara, is seated on a throne flanked by two cardinals on either side. His right hand is raised in blessing, and with the other he hands a sealed bull to the members of the Order kneeling at his feet. The main characters are identified by the name inserted within each nimbus. Below the pope in the centre is a model of the church of Cîteaux with its coat of arms underneath it. It is held by Robert and Alberic who offer it up to the pope for his protection. In this way they are honoured as the joint founders of Cîteaux. Behind Robert is an abbess holding a crozier, a bearded lay brother, and a large number of monks. Behind Alberic is his successor, Stephen Harding, Saint Bernard and another group of monks. After nearly 300 years we have a representation of Robert which acknowledges his role in the Cistercian genesis. The legend referring to Robert as the founder of the Cistercian Order may be challenged, but a further inaccuracy has the effect of seriously undervaluing what was undoubtedly the main achievement of Alberic's abbacy. The most important event during the nine years of his rule (1099–1108) was the bull of protection he obtained from Paschal II, the so-called *Roman Privilege*, the first in a long succession of papal privileges which was in due

8 Pope handing the charter
to the Cistercian founding
fathers.

course to give them full exemption from episcopal jurisdiction.[15] Papal approval provided the security and confidence needed for further expansion. Alberic's abbacy was not spectacular compared with that of his successor, Stephen Harding, and in one exemplum collection he is forgotten altogether and Stephen is referred to as the first abbot of Cîteaux, Robert being ignored in the usual way.[16] Like Robert Alberic is barely acknowledged in medieval iconography, the only notable exception being the Meglinger woodcut in which he is depicted as the equal founder of Cîteaux with Robert.

The contrast between the impact of the two predecessors and Stephen Harding is vividly expressed in Cistercian iconography by a famous portrait of him painted during his lifetime, in about 1125, in itself a rare occurrence in the twelfth century: this, the earliest portrayal of a named Cistercian (**colour plate 5**) is a full-page miniature in a manuscript of a Commentary of Saint Jerome on Jeremiah, written and illuminated in the scriptorium of the Benedictine abbey of Saint-Vaast in Arras. It commemorates the spiritual association of Cîteaux with this black monk abbey concluded in about 1124 on Stephen's visit to Arras. St Stephen is shown on the right in a greyish blue habit, nimbed and tonsured and holding a crozier in his left hand; Abbot Henry of Saint-Vaast is on the left in a pale brown habit, also nimbed and tonsured, with a crozier in his right hand. They are identified by their names written in the margins along the two sides of the picture. They are both looking up at the figure of the crowned Virgin to whom they are offering models of their respective churches. Below is the kneeling figure of the scribe, Osbert, shown presenting the manuscript to Stephen who had ordered it for use at Cîteaux. The legend at the bottom of the page expresses Osbert's wish that as scribe of the book he should have eternal life as recompense.[17]

The miniature is ample evidence of the good relations that existed between Cîteaux and the black monks at a time when the Cistercians were not yet a serious threat to the Benedictines and prior to subsequent conflicts associated in particular with St Bernard.

One puzzling feature of the picture is that although it was painted during the lifetime of the two abbots they are both shown nimbed. It is the more surprising as St Bernard does not appear nimbed in the small number of pictures of him known to have been painted before his canonization in 1174, but he is almost always nimbed in subsequent representations. One can only speculate as to the reason for this anomaly, but it may be analogous to the way Bernard's sainthood was anticipated by the *Life* that was begun during his lifetime and which, in the custom of the time, was the dossier that the later canonization depended upon, or the way in which he was, for example, described as *sanctissimus vir* (most holy man) and *vir Dei* (man of God) by Burchard of Balerne.[18] Perhaps a similar accolade was intended by investing Stephen with a nimbus. The very high esteem in which Stephen was held is further attested by the way in which he was referred to by Pope Calixtus II as 'venerable', a style of address usually reserved for bishops and which is most unexpected when used in referring to a little-known abbot of a relatively recent foundation.[19]

CHAPTER THREE

'FOUR BRANCHES FROM THE CISTERCIAN ROOT'

'O Cîteaux, how great is thy house, how fruitful in sons, how great in tongues, how glorious in people. Lift up your eyes and see these people gathered together, they have come to you, the profession of one life is a sign with you of a diversity of tongues, and of every kind the religious gathered together represent the miracle of Pentecost in the sending forth of the Holy Spirit.'

Richard, archbishop of Canterbury, 1173–84[1]

The Book of Revelation was one of the richest springs to feed the fertile imagination of medieval artists and writers. It formed the subject of numerous paintings, sculptures and stained glass as well as a long line of literary works going back to Bede.[2]

One of the most popular of these was the *Commentary on the Apocalypse* written by the Franciscan friar Alexander, *c*. 1243, in his native Saxony.[3] The Apocolypse is seen as prefiguring key events in the life of the Church, and its theme was the struggle between good and evil. The villains are identified in chronological order down to the reign of Frederick II (elected German king 1212 and crowned emperor 1220). They include emperors, heretics, Saracens and finally Frederick himself in conflict with the papacy.[4]

Benedictine monks are featured in the eight extant manuscripts of Alexander's *Commentary*, five of them illustrated,[5] and the climax is reached in his own time when the Heavenly Jerusalem is identified with the coming of the friars. One manuscript, written in the third quarter of the thirteenth century, has both a fuller text and more pictures than do the others.[6] In it is a lucid description of the foundation of Cîteaux, the early growth of the Cistercian Order, the role of St Bernard, and the apogee of the Order, reached at the election of Bernard's disciple, Bernard Paganelli, to the papacy as Eugenius III.[7] Alexander records how

> some were sent to Clairvaux, others to the house of La Ferté, the third to the place called Morimond, the fourth to Pontigny. The whole Order grew up from these four branches produced from the Cistercian root.

The short account is illustrated by a unique picture which covers the full width of the folio including the margins. (**colour plate 6**). It brilliantly encapsulates the key features of the genesis of the Cistercian Order and contains, as in a nutshell, the essence of the heroic saga transmitted in the early Cistercian texts. The subject of the picture is explained in brief notes added in the margins on either side above the picture.[8] The note on the left reads,

> Here is the monastery of Cîteaux whose brothers are engaged in manual labour and whose abbot of the same place sent four abbots with a group of brothers to different places. One of these was blessed Bernard who was sent to Clairvaux.

The figure on the far left, although not named, represents Stephen Harding, the Englishman who became the third abbot of Cîteaux. During his abbacy the Cistercian Order may be said to have been founded by the sending out of new daughter-abbeys.[9] The foundation document of the first daughter of Cîteaux, La Ferté, states that after fifteen years (this is in 1113), 'the number of brethren at Cîteaux was such that neither the existing estates were sufficient to support them, nor could the place where they lived conveniently accommodate them'.[10]

The circumstances making it necessary for a group of monks to be separated from the others in body if not in spirit arose with increasing frequency and herein lay the genesis of the Cistercian family. The following year (1114) saw the foundation of Pontigny, followed a year later by Clairvaux and Morimond. These were the four monasteries referred to in the note. They became known as the 'elder daughters' of Cîteaux and enjoyed a special status within the Order whereby each, together with Cîteaux, headed a 'filiation' or 'line' which made up the Cistercian family. According to the *Charter of Charity* each abbey was to be visited annually by the abbot of its mother-house. Thus Cîteaux was charged with the visitation of the four and they, in turn, were to visit Cîteaux and were jointly empowered to admonish or depose her abbot.[11] Furthermore, all abbots were to meet annually at Cîteaux for General Chapter. The machinery which was to ensure the future well-being and cohesion of abbeys was in place, and we can now speak of the Cistercians as an 'Order'. The *Charter of Charity* has been described as a masterpiece, 'one of the small group of documents that have influenced, in the course of the Church's history, the constitutional history of all religious bodies subsequent to their composition'.[12] Constitutional provisions may at first glance seem prosaic and unexciting, but on reflection we realize that Stephen's foresight in defining the relationship between the mother-abbey and the first offshoots, and subsequently between all Cistercian houses, was prophetic. The twin planks of visitation and annual General Chapter provided the abbot of Cîteaux with the means to be effectively able to exercise his *cura animarum* over the Cistercian family and thereby guarantee the desired degree of uniformity.[13] Uniformity in all essentials was seen by Stephen as indispensable to the bond of charity which was to bind all monasteries together.

In the *Apocalypse* picture Stephen is shown standing between two pillars under a trifoliate arch surmounted by a domed tower. The whiteness of his habit is accentuated by a blue outline; his hands are raised in acknowledgement of the group of monks kneeling before him under a roof upon which a white dove is perched. The monk nearest to Stephen is in a grey habit, the one behind in a pale brown habit. Between them is the head of a third monk, and above the three the tops of a further four heads or more may be seen. These are the abbots sent by Stephen to found new houses. As there are more than the four senior abbots mentioned they may represent the heads of the numerous monasteries that were settled during Stephen's abbacy.

The middle of the picture features six figures engaged in manual labour. The centrality of this scene and the comment in the margin underline the importance attached to manual labour by the white monks.

The explanatory note in the right margin reads, 'Here are the four monasteries built by the four abbots sent from Cîteaux, that is St Bernard's place Clairvaux, the house of La Ferté, Morimond, and Pontigny. From these four houses the whole Cistercian Order was spread.'[15]

Four tonsured monks, each holding a book, are depicted within four niches under trifoliate, circular and pointed arches separated by coloured columns and surmounted by domes and towers, each in a different design and colour. They represent the founding abbots of the four 'elder daughters' referred to in the text who are known by name. In addition to St Bernard who is mentioned, these are: Bernard of La Ferté, Hugh of Mâcon, first abbot of Pontigny and later bishop of Auxerre, and Arnold of Morimond, a native of Cologne who is thought to have entered Cîteaux at the same time as Bernard.[16] Each of the four is in a habit of a different colour: from the left, white with blue outline, grey, pale brown and greyish brown. The second from the left is bearded and may therefore represent Bernard who, according to tradition, had a short beard.

The architectural features are similar to those depicted throughout the manuscript. They bear no relationship to the size of the figures, nor is there any resemblance to the architectural style of the early Cistercians. The difference in design and colour as well as the variety in the habits serves to emphasize the distinctive place of each of the filiations. Situated south, north-west, north and north-east of Cîteaux, the four proto-abbeys laid the geographical framework of the Order, each with its principal sphere of influence. As a result of their wide dispersion each of the 'four branches' inevitably acquired a character of its own which was accentuated with the passage of time.[17] This is powerfully expressed by the nuances in the picture.

The special place of the four elder daughters was mentioned by Caesarius of Heisterbach in his *Dialogue on Miracles*:

From this time forward that vine of the Lord Sabaoth began to grow and expand and to extend its branches from sea to sea till the earth was filled with the fullness of it. La Ferté, Pontigny, Clairvaux, Morimond were its first offshoots, whose abbots became of so great importance that together they made a visitation of their father the abbot of Cîteaux and are in turn visited by him one by one.[18]

9 Pope handing bulls to two abbots.

A picture at the beginning of a mid-fourteenth century manuscript of a *Book of Cistercian Privileges* illustrates the way in which the vine began to grow. (**9**) In a miniature the width of the folio a mitred pope, wearing a chasuble and maniple and seated on a bench backed by a drape decorated with fleurs-de-lys, is shown handing a sealed bull to each of two kneeling abbots. The abbots are accompanied by three other abbots carrying croziers and by a number of monks. The quality of the work compares most unfavourably with that with which the Cîteaux scriptorium was associated in earlier times.

Two possibilities present themselves in determining the identity of the figures featured in the scene. It may represent the model upon which the picture in the privilege collection of Peter Meglinger was based (*see* 8) and depicting Robert of Molesme, Alberic, Stephen Harding and Bernard, plus a fifth unknown abbot.[19] Another explanation, however, is more likely. The pope shown is almost certainly Lucius III (1181–5) who in 1184 granted the Cistercians the important bull *Monasticae sinceritas disciplinae*, giving them immunity from excommunication, one of the most important privileges in a long succession freeing them from episcopal jurisdiction.[20] The five abbots depicted may therefore be identified as those of Cîteaux and the four elder daughters, La Ferté, Pontigny, Clairvaux and Morimond.

The crucial role Stephen played in the formative years of the Order is here seen in perspective. Just as Robert of Molesme was the founder of Cîteaux, Stephen may be considered the founder of the Cistercian Order: during his abbacy the first foundations were made and the constitutional framework laid that guaranteed further expansion; it also ensured the remarkable degree of unity that characterized the Cistercian family. Conrad of Eberbach devotes eleven chapters to Stephen in the *Exordium Magnum* and sums him up as the 'leader and standard-bearer of the most valiant champions of Christ'.[21] By the time of his death in 1134 more than seventy-five abbeys had been founded. Bernard's charisma and his impact upon the affairs of all Christendom have tended to overshadow the essential groundwork done by Stephen Harding. Without this the phenomenal further growth attributed to the reputation of Bernard could not have taken place.

David Knowles wrote that there are men in history, among whom he lists St Bernard, along with Cicero, Augustine, Anselm, Lincoln and Newman, whose personality and charm reveal themselves in every word they wrote or spoke, and others whose charm and power were felt by their contemporaries in their influence and achievements but whose 'surviving words are not conductors of the magnetic spark'.[22] He might have put Stephen Harding among the latter. Unlike Bernard, Stephen left few writings behind, and his life's work was confined to the cloister of Cîteaux and the small group of daughter-houses. The difference in their personalities explains the quite disproportionately extensive coverage of Bernard in Cistercian history and the relative neglect of Stephen, a disparity amply reflected in Cistercian iconography. A close attention to and careful scrutiny of the few pictures that do exist of Stephen help to redress the bias. Typically, it is Bernard and not Stephen who is mentioned by name in the explanatory note to the *Apocalypse* picture, but more important is what is shown: Bernard kneeling in submission to his abbot Stephen, to whom he owes his appointment to Clairvaux. The same deference is seen in a number of the Bernard cycles, both in scenes of Bernard being received at Cîteaux by Stephen and of his being handed the abbatial staff of Clairvaux at the hands of Stephen (*see* for example, 22). These pictures help to restore the proper balance in evaluating the contributions of the two men respectively.

Stephen's role in the monastic formation of Bernard is acknowledged by Conrad of Eberbach who celebrates Stephen's humility and describes him as 'the father in holy religion of our most blessed father Bernard. This perfect master deserved to have a very perfect disciple.'[23] A further remarkable example – a story in Herbert of Clairvaux's *Book of Wonderful Happenings* which is repeated in the *Exordium Magnum* – forcefully makes the point that, like all other young novices, Bernard had a great deal to learn and that he owed his spiritual development to the guidance of the older and more experienced Stephen.[24] As a novice Bernard once failed to recite the seven penitential psalms he had promised to say daily after Compline for the repose of the soul of his mother. His youthful negligence was noted by Stephen Harding who reprimanded him and Bernard, confessing his transgression, threw himself at Stephen's feet. Stephen had taught him a lesson 'for he was found to be more solicitous in both private and public observances'. The admission that Bernard was in any way flawed was quite contrary to the usual hagiographical convention, and the purpose of it would seem to be to enhance the stature of Stephen rather than to detract from that of Bernard.

10 St Stephen Harding
reprimands St Bernard.

The episode was considered to have been sufficiently important for its inclusion in two Bernard cycles in stained glass, those from the cloisters of Altenberg and its dependent women's house of St Apern in Cologne, both from the same Cologne workshop from 1505–20 and *c.* 1525 respectively.[25] Although the design, colouring and size of the panels are very similar, their composition is quite different, an interesting indication of the importance of the input of the commissioning monastery and of the different briefs given to the glaziers.

The Altenberg panel (**10**) – one of some ninety of which sixty-eight are still in existence in twelve different locations – contains three scenes with one frame in which the story unfurls in three consecutive episodes, an old device known from the eleventh-century cycle of St Benedict and St Maur from Monte Cassino and later commonly used to illustrate the *Lives* of saints based on legends rooted in literary and oral tradition.[26] The unfolding in time is handled by a sequence in which the chief character reappears in a succession of scenes. The viewers' ability to understand the story is aided by the use of scrolls with text as well as an abbreviated version of the whole story at the foot of the panel. We have here a medieval forerunner to the strip cartoon in which scrolls or banderoles have been replaced by 'bubbles'.

In the middle of the panel, Bernard is praying in a distant dark church before the Blessed Sacrament, seen through an arched window. The banderole, which reads 'O Lord, do not reprove me in your anger' (Ps. 6:1), tells us that he is reciting one of the penitential psalms for his mother. On the left he is sitting with a closed psalter on his knee. The scroll reads, 'O Bernard, O Bernard, why have you come here?' A fellow monk looks at him, his left hand over his breast indicating his inability to help. On the right comes the climax when Stephen asks him, 'Brother Bernard, what are you doing leaving aside those psalms you should have said today, or whom have you delegated to say them?' Bernard kneels down before his abbot, his hands over his face in shame and begging for pardon. He exclaims, 'O Lord, my God, how has this matter come out in the open which was known to my conscience alone?'

The same story is depicted in a single scene in the St Apern panel, one of the original fifty-four which adorned the cloister of the nuns who moved to Cologne in 1476, and of which eight are now in Cologne Cathedral (see 46). The gist of it is given in the text below – almost the same as that on the Altenberg panel – and culminating in the words taken from Herbert of Clairvaux: ' . . . he blushed throwing himself at his feet and asked for pardon confessing his negligence.' Here Bernard is reprimanded publicly in the presence of six other novices, all of them identifiable as such by the mantle worn by novices as opposed to the monastic cowl. Stephen, wearing a cowl, is seated in the centre in what looks like the chapter house, his gaze directed at Bernard who is identified by the nimbus. Significantly, although Stephen is the central figure depicted in a position of authority, he is not nimbed.

The pictorial representation of the birth of the Order in the *Apocalypse* manuscript may be looked upon as a graphic counterpart to the literary genre known as foundation narratives. The primary purpose of each was didactic, to impress the viewer with the spiritual power of the white monks and inspire him to emulate the holy lives and follow the example of the founding fathers. The *Exordium Parvum*, the Cîteaux foundation history, promised that those who did so would 'repose happily in eternal rest'.[27] The artist was depicting events that had taken place more than a century earlier, and objective impartial historicity was not his primary concern. Several inaccuracies are apparent. First, the abbots sent out by Stephen Harding would not have been kneeling before him at the same time: the foundations were made over a number of years. Second, because of the prestige of St Bernard, Clairvaux is mentioned first whereas in fact it was the youngest of the four daughters, and Morimond and Pontigny are also listed in the wrong chronological order. Third, Morimond was only granted the status of 'elder daughter' in 1163 as a reward for having been responsible for more foundations than any of the others with the exception of Clairvaux.[28] It is therefore wrong to treat it in the same way as the others at the time of its foundation. Such errors do not detract, however, from the primary purpose of the illustration, which was to impart spiritual truth. As with the foundation narratives, factual accuracy was subservient to the forging of a Cistercian mythology which would influence future attitudes. In terms of the information

11 Marienstatt foundation panel.

the picture imparts it is a masterpiece of Cistercian iconography, and is the more remarkable on account of its origin outside the Order.

There are two remarkable examples of pictorial foundation narratives. One, from Marienstatt in the Rhineland dated 1324, consists of two large panels painted on parchment mounted on wood. (11) In each corner of one are medallions containing the symbols of the Evangelists, and in the other those of Old Testament Prophets. Between these each border consists of ten framed squares, altogether forty per panel, within each of which are almost identical half-figures of abbots with a crozier in the left hand and a book (the Rule) in the right, and all are looking inwards. The space taken up by the first two squares in the first panel contains no portraits (this panel therefore only has thirty-eight squares) but instead contains the following text: 'In the present picture you will see and discover all the abbots who have ruled in the old monastery and in this place.' The names of the abbots have been entered under each picture and, remarkably, kept up to date until into the seventeenth century. Altogether forty-two names are entered, thus completing the thirty-eight squares in the first panel and with four names inserted in the second. These 'portraits' are a pictorial equivalent to the thumbnail sketches which were a common ingredient of foundation narratives.[29] The purpose of including them was the same: to commemorate the abbots, to stimulate veneration for past leaders and to inculcate a sense of pride in those who had held positions of responsibility.

The central portion of the first panel is framed by two columns supporting a trifoliate arch. Two thirds of the space is taken up by a crowned and nimbed Virgin with the Cross-nimbed Child on her knees and holding a model of the church of Marienstatt in her right hand. To her right, in liturgical vestments, is Archbishop Henry of Cologne (1306–32) mitred with a crozier in the left hand, his right hand raised in blessing. On the left is Abbot Wiegand of Marienstatt, who commissioned the pictures to commemorate the consecration of the enlarged abbey church in 1324. He is dressed in a brown habit over which he wears a brown cloak lined in red and fastened with a metal buckle. In his left hand he holds a crozier and his right hand is raised in blessing. A small figure in a red habit kneeling at his feet may represent the abbey's founder, Henry of Sayn or, more likely, the artist who painted the panels.[30] In the space created on each side by the pointed Gothic arch, two angels on clouds swing censers in honour of the Virgin. Below the central scene, the community is represented in a strip the width of the panel. This consists of twenty-six kneeling figures, thirteen on each side, and consisting of seven cowled and tonsured monks behind whom are six bearded lay brothers wearing mantles. All of them face towards the Virgin and below them runs the Latin text of the foundation history of Marienstatt.

The second panel consists of a crucifixion scene surrounded by the instruments of Christ's Passion – the *Arma Christi* – with a continuation of the foundation history beneath it. Although the purpose of the panels was undoubtedly didactic, their original location in the abbey is not known.

The other narrative foundation picture is a large wall painting in the church of Maulbronn in Württemberg dated to 1424.[31] Kneeling at the feet of a seated Virgin and Child are the two joint founders, Bishop Günther of Speyer and the knight, Walter of Lomersheim, shown carrying a model of the church which they are presenting to Mary. On the right Walter appears again. He has laid down his sword and is shown kneeling before the abbot who carries a crozier supported on his left shoulder and bends down to welcome Walter into the community. A monk on the side has a habit ready for Walter's clothing. A brief text refers to the foundation in 1138, to Walter making his profession to Abbot Dieter, and to the painting of the picture in 1424 under Abbot Albert, during whose abbacy the nave and aisles were completed.

CHAPTER FOUR

ST BERNARD AND THE CISTERCIAN EXPANSION

'From this last [Clairvaux] *rose Bernard, and began to shine among, or rather above, the rest, like Lucifer among the stars of night.'*

Walter Map, *The Courtiers' Trifles*[1]

'You were the strongest and most splendid pillar of the church, a mighty trumpet of God, the sweet organ of the Holy Spirit whose presence was to councils what the sun is to the heavens, whose absence left assemblies lifeless and dumb.'

Geoffrey of Auxerre, *Vita Prima* [2]

'The devil appeared to him in the likeness of a black monk saying to him: "Father, What are you doing? I have come from a distant land to see you, and here you are polishing your boots. You should not be doing this, but you should let your servants and ministers do it for you." The man of God replied: "I haven't got any servants, and I do not want ever to have any. I have sons whom I have begotten for Christ through the Gospel. They minister to me with great charity and meekness, and I love them in the truth and I teach them the way to the kingdom of heaven." '

John the Hermit, *Vita Quarta* [3]

Few, if any, medieval figures have been so extensively or as variously portrayed as St Bernard. As the earlier medieval period, marked by the anonymity of artists, thought of as craftsmen on a par with scribes or carpenters, gave way to the named practitioners of 'high art', St Bernard formed a subject much in demand among their patrons. Among the famous artists who depicted him can be listed Fra Angelico da Fiesole (1387–1455), Filippo Lippi (1406–69), Filippino Lippi (1457–1504), Jean Fouquet (*c.* 1416–80), Perugino (*c.* 1450–1523), Hans Holbein (1497–1543), El Greco (Domenico Theocópuli) (1541–1614), Francisco Ribalta (1550–1628), Bartolomé Estebán Murillo (1618–82) and Francisco de Goya (1746–1828).[4] As we shall see, there is no reason to doubt that the earlier unnamed artists who had portrayed Bernard were as accomplished as these later masters.

The courtier and cleric Walter Map's satirical comment on St Bernard quoted above forms part of his invective directed at the Cistercians.[5] While recognizing Bernard's undoubted stature as a commanding perhaps even domineering figure, who towered above his contemporaries on the strength of his personality, Map also draws attention to the complex and enigmatic side of his character. Bernard was himself only too aware of the tensions created by the inconsistency between his monastic profession and his activity in the world, which, it has been estimated, caused him to be away from his monastery more than a third of his time.[6] He made frequent references to the pain this caused him, and he likened himself to an 'unfledged nestling', exposed to winds and tempests.[7] In another letter he pleaded to be relieved from non-monastic duties, 'may it please you to bid the noisy and importunate frogs keep to their holes and remain contented with their ponds'.[8] There was a serious conflict between life in the cloister and his involvement in the affairs of church and state – papal schism, contested episcopal elections, preaching crusade, defending orthodoxy and countering Catharism. All this Bernard acknowledged when he gave himself the well-known title, 'chimaera of my age', for having 'kept the habit of a monk but long ago abandoned the life', but he still justified his involvement as in obedience to a higher authority and in the interest of the welfare of the Church.[9]

It is interesting that Bernard should have chosen the title of the fire-breathing monster of Greek mythology whose body was made up of three parts from different animals. Three elements may be identified in the iconography of Bernard, not always in isolation, but often overlapping; the monastic, the miraculous and the politico-religious. The emphasis on Bernard as the leader of Western Christendom which characterizes much of the written work on him is also reflected in late medieval Bernardine iconography. Take, for example, what is perhaps the most comprehensive medieval cycle, the early sixteenth-century stained glass from the cloister at Altenberg. Of the sixty-two panels that include representations of Bernard, thirty-three depict his activities away from Clairvaux, fifteen miracles and visions, and fourteen his monastic life. In other words, as much weight is placed on what he achieved outside the cloister as on his role as a monk and thaumaturge.

He influenced the course of events as much by his writings as by his travels and sermons. This side of Bernard's life is encapsulated in one of the Altenberg panels. (12) Bernard is the central figure behind a table on which are a number of his books, sermons and letters. He is surrounded by the recipients, first and foremost Pope Eugenius III, a former disciple from Clairvaux, to whom he is handing his treatise *On Consideration*. A scroll above St Bernard has him saying to the pope, 'Expel simony from the Church', to which the pope's reply on another scroll is, 'Expel slothfulness from the Cloister'. Others around the table receiving Bernard's books and advice are, on one side, a bishop, a cardinal, an abbot and, on the other, a king, some noblemen and two kneeling Templars. The inscription below reads, 'He wrote many books, sermons, and 350 letters, to four popes, cardinals, bishops, kings, princes, abbots, and many others'.

Crenas unidio imptas et midhat unidio e axma multehabur unidio et lumt petdut t kipt mitos
libros fermions et quis et ad e fintos politices tradmales quos teges pumps abbos et plus alios.

12 St Bernard and the recipents of his books and letters.

Bernard the miracle worker and mystic given to having visions came to dominate his iconography in the late Middle Ages and especially in the centuries that followed. Four principal themes emerged which were variously distributed at different periods and in different countries: Bernard's encounter with the devil, the Embrace of Christ (*Amplexus*), Bernard receiving Mary's Milk (the *Lactatio* or Lactation), and the related Vision of Mary (*Doctrina*).

The portrait presented in the *Vita Prima* by Bernard's close friend and collaborator, William of St Thierry, and by his secretary and travel companion, Geoffrey of Auxerre, although coloured by the conventions of medieval hagiography, was nevertheless based on first-hand knowledge and personal closeness to Bernard and reveals human qualities often lacking in later versions. This picture is reinforced by a look at his own writings, especially his letters. Later in the twelfth and early in the thirteenth centuries a number of miracle stories and *exempla* were gathered together to form collections, the most famous of which was Herbert of Clairvaux's *Liber Miraculorum* and the *Exordium Magnum* by Conrad of Eberbach.[10] Notwithstanding that they deal with visions and miracles, Bernard emerges as an abbot deeply concerned for the welfare of his monks, always reassuring and trusting in God's mercy.

Stories of demons abound in early Cistercian texts. Their evil is directed at all Christians, but monks are at greater risk than anyone else.[11] St Bernard was no exception and a number of his encounters with demons are recorded. The devil came in many guises: in the one quoted above, Bernard's biographer

appropriately chose to portray the devil as a black monk, referring of course not
to the colour of his skin but of his habit, and thus alluding to the rivalry between
Cistercians and Benedictines immortalized in the best known of all Bernard's
treatises, the *Apologia*, and later in works like the *Exordium Magnum*. In this
passage the devil got nowhere with Bernard and he transformed himself into the
likeness of a small animal and vanished.[12] One story has Bernard being tempted
by the devil,[13] and in another Bernard challenges the devil and defeats him,
'leaving the enemy completely confounded, he left the gathering and the man of
God came to himself'.[14]

13 Abbot (St Bernard?)
with the devil on a chain.

Bernard's victory over the devil gave rise to one of the late medieval examples
of Bernardine iconography, the saint holding the devil on a chain, a theme
perhaps derived from the angel in the Apocalypse who held the key of the abyss
and with a great chain in his hand took hold of the dragon serpent.[15] A fifteenth-
century carving in the cloister at Cadouin (Dordogne) has a monk holding a
staff, the top of which is broken off but which was probably a crozier and is
therefore likely to represent St Bernard. He holds a long chain at the end of
which stands a horned devil of approximately the same height as Bernard. (**13**)

One of the legends which found its way into the iconography of Bernard was a
late medieval story of how he forced the devil to disclose the nine verses from the
psalms which would save the soul of anyone who recited them daily.[16] The devil
informed Bernard that he knew the nine verses but would not divulge them.
When Bernard decided to recite the whole psalter every day the devil relented,
fearing that even greater spiritual advantage might thus be gained. The scene is
depicted in the lower half of Jean Fouquet's full-page miniature in the Hours of
Etienne Chevalier (*see* 50). A brown horned devil with a tail and bat-like wings
creeps up behind Bernard, interrupting him while reading the psalms. Bernard
turns round and with his left index finger he points to an open psalter on the
desk before him.

Of the four iconographical topoi the earliest and the one which was to colour
the late medieval tradition of Bernard was that of Christ's Embrace. The story is
found first in Herbert's *Liber Miraculorum* from the 1170s and is repeated in the
Exordium Magnum at the turn of the thirteenth century.[17] Abbot Menard of
Mores, the story goes, had heard that a monk had once found Bernard in the
church praying alone when Christ on the Cross appeared to him. When Bernard
kissed the Cross, Christ removed His arms from the Cross, bent down and
embraced Bernard. The motif was ubiquitous in the iconography of Bernard. It
appears in German paintings in the fifteenth century,[18] forms part of the Altenberg
cycle,[19] was widespread in Spain in the sixteenth and seventeenth centuries[20] but
was never popular in Italy.[21] The earliest known representation occurs in a
Gradual from the women's abbey of Wonnental in Breisgau, Baden, from the first
half of the fourteenth century. (**14**) It appears within a filigree initial O(*scintillans
sidus celi*), itself decorated with four intertwining hybrids one of which appears to
be a hooded monk. Bernard is kneeling before Christ who, partially descended
from the Cross, is embracing him. A smaller kneeling monk with hands folded in
prayer may represent the monk who witnessed the vision in the original story.

14 Christ embracing
St Bernard.

Among many later embellishments to the Bernard tradition which obscure the
picture of him given in the *Vita Prima*, much the most widespread, and the one
which more than any other helped to foster popular devotion to the saint, was the
Lactatio.[22] The earliest pictorial example is found in the Templars' church in
Palma, Majorca. It forms one of the four scenes flanking the central figure of
Bernard the abbot with crozier and book.[23] The first known literary reference to
the miracle occurs in a manuscript of Christian instruction, an *exemplum* collection
entitled *Ci nous dit* from the opening words written between 1313 and 1330 by a
mendicant friar.[24] In the tradition of *exemplum* stories elements of this can be
traced back to twelfth-century sources.[25] Written in the vernacular, it contains four
illustrations, each with two scenes, one of them featuring the lactation, the only
one of the four Majorca scenes not drawn from the *Vita Prima*. The theme gained
in popularity so rapidly that it has been described as 'a veritable scene-attribute of

Bernard', as it were his hallmark.[26] It was especially widespread in Spain and France. In the late Middle Ages representations frequently included a scroll with St Bernard addressing Mary with the words *Monstra te esse Matrem* ('Show us that you are our Mother') taken from the Marian hymn, 'Hail, star of the sea'.[27]

In Italy, to which the lactation story did not spread, the knowledge and skill to preach and write was transmitted to Bernard by Mary in a parallel but less physical variant beginning in the fourteenth century. In this, known as the *Doctrina*, Mary appears to Bernard who is seated at his desk writing. The gestures of both figures indicate the dialogue between them which inspires Bernard in his work. Physical nurture is replaced by the verbal and intellectual. The most famous examples are the paintings on wood of Filippo Lippi and his son Filippino Lippi.[28]

The iconography of the lactation, like that of the *Amplexus*, was part of the popular religious culture of the later Middle Ages. Such images were designed to stimulate the emotions and, with their emphasis on physicality and overtones of sentimentality and kitsch, they were far removed from the simplicity and purity of early Cistercian spirituality. Gone is the Bernard we know from the twelfth century, now replaced with an overlay of subjective devotion appealing to an individual response instead of to the solidarity of the monastic community with its saintly abbot. The material was made up of anecdotal accounts, stories of wonders and of apparitions. Such images abound in Books of Hours and small *Andachtsbilder* for private devotion. They expressed graphically the cult of Mary, so strongly influenced by Bernard and the Cistercians. They also served to keep the memory of Bernard alive, but they seem far removed from our perception of Bernard the monk and abbot and are therefore outside the scope of this study.

Bernard's public role also came to colour much of his iconography with Baroque images of Bernard the thaumaturge dominating later representations, often pushing Bernard the monk into the background. But this had not always been the case.[29]

His life is well documented and includes a description of what he looked like by one of those who knew him best, his secretary and biographer, Geoffrey of Auxerre. Such literary portraits from the Middle Ages are rare and this one has greatly influenced the iconographical tradition. Geoffrey describes both Bernard's physique and the way it was shaped by his inner qualities and delicate health:

A certain refinement in his appearance was spiritual rather than physical. His face shone brightly in a way that was not earthly but heavenly. His eyes revealed an angelic purity and a dove-like simplicity radiated from him. His inner beauty was so great that it revealed itself clearly in his outward appearance. He had an air of complete inner purity full of grace. His body was very thin, and he seemed gaunt with a complexion so pale that there was hardly any colour on his cheeks. . . . His hair was a light auburn. His beard was reddish, and towards the end of his life flecked with white. He was of average, or perhaps a little above average, height. He was like something precious contained in a fragile vessel, a vessel at times almost broken. He was afflicted with various debilitating infirmities.[30]

15 *Vera Effigies* of
St Bernard.

To this may be added the observation of Bernard's other biographer, William of
St Thierry, according to whom 'he had a pleasant face, was good-looking, even
elegant'.[31] These literary portraits gave birth to one strand which, after a long
chain of intervening examples, developed into the *Vera Effigies* (True Likeness)
portraits that came to be commonly displayed in abbeys in the sixteenth and
seventeenth centuries. The prototype for these pictures was a bust which once
hung in the monks' refectory at Clairvaux and which has assumed the grandiose
title of *Vera Effigies*.[32] (15) This picture had an immense influence on the way
Bernard has subsequently been represented. Painted in oil on wood within an
oval medallion, St Bernard appears much as he was described by Geoffrey of
Auxerre, with a thin face and pale complexion, hair and beard whitish and with

a meditative expression. The inscription around the edge reads, 'St Bernard first abbot of the archabbey of Clairvaux'. His head is inclined to the right, he has a large cranium emphasizing his great mental powers, and there are two gaps in his monastic crown or tonsure with a small tuft of hair in the centre. This small feature, in itself quite unimportant, nevertheless appears in too many Bernardine portraits for it to be a coincidence and it seems to have been one of the physical characteristics which came to make up his attributes, much as the beard was.[33] This has not previously been observed and, although it is only a tiny detail, it points to a common source for a good deal of the iconography of Bernard. At times it even provides us with the only feature which enables us to identify Bernard positively. In the carving of St Bernard and St Benedict on the oak choir stalls at Doberan, for example, both are nimbed, both carry croziers and books, and being carved in natural wood it is not possible to distinguish the colour of their habits, usually the only way of telling them apart (see 6). Only the tiny detail of the central tuft of hair enables us to ascertain that St Bernard is the figure on the right.

The evolution of the *Vera Effigies* has been traced back to the statue of St Bernard which was later placed on his tomb in the church at Clairvaux. This is either the late fourteenth-century statue (see 25) – one of the first representations of Bernard in sculpture – or one on which this surviving statue is modelled. It corresponds exactly to a description of the one that adorned Bernard's tomb and shows him with his head inclined to the right, as was common in later representations, and with the central tuft of hair. Sculptures were prohibited in early Cistercian legislation and for a long time this restriction was strictly adhered to and there were no statues in their churches, not even of St Bernard.[34] One of the earliest examples of a deviation from this is a statue of St Bernard in red limestone from about 1350, above the celebrants' *sedilia* at Amelungsborn in Lower Saxony. (**16**)

There were two other links in the *Vera Effigies* chain. One was a silver-gilt bust-reliquary made on the orders of Abbot Jean d'Aizanville of Clairvaux (1330–45). The Austrian monk Joseph Meglinger saw it in 1667 and was struck by its resemblance to Geoffrey of Auxerre's literary portrait.[35] The other was a silver-gilt statue which, like the reliquary, perished during the French Revolution, and was the paradigm for paintings which found their way to six different Austrian abbeys including Heiligenkreuz and Zwettl.[36]

Although it is much earlier than the paintings in the Austrian abbeys and unconnected with the chain between the *Vita Prima* description and the *Vera Effigies*, and therefore almost certainly a coincidence, the remarkable likeness between a portrait of Bernard in a Zwettl manuscript from 1175–6 and the *Vera Effigies* is striking. (**17**) A nimbed St Bernard is portrayed in the initial *T(e igitur)* in a Missal at the beginning of the canon of the Mass as the celebrant dressed in an alb, chasuble and stole, standing before an altar. His right hand is raised in blessing a chalice which he holds in his left hand, and the hand of God appears from above in benediction. It is one of the earlier representations of St Bernard from just after his canonization and is a rare example of him portrayed as a priest.

16 A statue of St Bernard.

In the *Vera Effigies* we can identify Bernard by his tuft of hair, while other distinguishing traits rely on the more usual and traditional attributes according to the conventions of the iconography of saints.[37] Some of these – the ones relating to the themes of *Amplexus*, *Lactatio*, *Doctrina* and Bernard's encounters with the devil – have already been referred to. Other later medieval signals include a beehive for the sweetness of the teaching of the *Doctor Mellifluus* (honey-tongued teacher), a mitre or five mitres on the ground denoting his refusal of five bishoprics,[38] and a small, usually white, dog, alluding to a dream his mother had while expecting him, according to which she would give birth to a puppy who would 'become the guardian of God's household' and 'bark on its behalf at the enemies of the faith'.[39] But the main properties to look for in identifying Bernard, and the only ones needed for all early representations, are those which refer to him as a monk: the habit, usually but not always white, and tonsure; as an abbot: the crozier and book (the Rule) and, rarely, and only in the later Middle Ages, the mitre;[40] and as a saint: the nimbus.

Two of Bernard's letters refer to the theft of his seal by one of his secretaries, Nicholas. Because of this he had a new one made which, he says, contained both my 'image and name'.[41] Matrices of two seals bearing the figure of an abbot identified by the inscription as Bernard used to be considered the earliest representations of Bernard and the only ones from his lifetime, but they have since been shown to have been made in the seventeenth or eighteenth century.[42] That being so, it is sometimes claimed that no image of Bernard produced during his lifetime has been preserved, remarkable considering that we have a full-page miniature of St Stephen Harding painted in 1124 during the lifetime of Bernard's abbot at Cîteaux[43] (*see* **colour plate 5**).

This is in fact not so. St Bernard is depicted in a manuscript of his first treatise, *The Steps of Humility*, a pastoral work in which Bernard the monk is addressing his fellow monks on monastic virtues. He wrote it before 1124[44] at the request of one of the first monks of Clairvaux, Godfrey, who later became prior and bishop of Langres (1138–63) (**colour plate 7**). This manuscript dates from before 1135 and was written at the Benedictine abbey of St Augustine at Canterbury. It is evidence of the popularity and early dispersion of Bernard's writings even outside the Order. This little-known earliest image of Bernard has him sitting at a desk writing within the initial *R(ogasti)*, the opening of the preface in which he states how he came to write it: 'You asked me, Brother Godfrey, to write out at greater length the sermons I gave to the brethren on the Steps of Humility'.[45] Bernard is shown against a gold background as a young tonsured monk. In his left hand he holds a knife used to sharpen the pen, erase errors and steady the parchment. This is placed on the book before him, and his right hand is raised in blessing, clear evidence that we have St Bernard here and not the scribe of the manuscript. The letter is in red, blue and green ink, the lower half consisting of intertwining green and blue foliage with one complete dragon and the heads of two others. Bernard is not shown carrying a crozier, but there is nothing unusual in this as the crozier is often missing when he is engaged in an activity where this would not be appropriate as, for example,

17 St Bernard celebrating
Mass.

when saying Mass (*see* 17) or writing or teaching (*see* 19) although it is
sometimes propped up against a chair or lectern (*see* **colour plate 9**).

Although this is the only known image from St Bernard's lifetime, there are
others from between his death in 1153 and canonization in 1174 as well as a few
more from before the end of the twelfth century. One of the earliest is in a

manuscript of *The Steps of Humility*, also from a Benedictine abbey – Anchin in northern France. Bernard appears together with St Benedict on either side of Christ at the head of Jacob's ladder (*see* 7). In another little known representation, also from Anchin, and also written before his canonization, he is shown tonsured and in a grey cowl and pale brown tunic with the letter ordering Aelred of Rievaulx to write his *Mirror of Charity* (*see* **colour plate 10**).

Other early pictures of St Bernard nearly always show him in his key monastic role of writer and teacher. Bernard the teacher is shown alone, nimbed and carrying a simple crozier in the prologue to an antiphonary from the Austrian abbey of Heiligenkreuz from the turn of the thirteenth century.[46] He appears as teacher and abbot with a group of his monks in a manuscript dated *c.* 1180 from the German Benedictine abbey of Liesborn (*see* 67). Contemporary with this is a portrait of Bernard writing at a desk with head bowed, pen in the right hand and knife in the left, in what is an early French manuscript of his sermons in the vernacular.[47]

These early examples may be compared with later ones. In a composite French manuscript of unknown provenance from the second half of the thirteenth century containing the Rule of St Benedict and St Bernard's 'On Precept and Dispensation' (*De praecepto et dispensacione*), there is a diminutive historiated initial *D(omino)* at the opening of St Bernard's treatise (**colour plate 8**). The letter contains the nimbed and tonsured figure of Bernard in a white habit. He is sitting at a desk on which is an open book in which he is writing. He holds a knife in his left hand and instead of a pen in his right hand, he raises this in blessing in exactly the same way as in the earliest example from Canterbury (*see* **colour plate 7**). Very close to his face is the beak of a white bird as if feeding him with the words which he is writing down. In the iconography of the saints the dove was the attribute of the Evangelists and the Doctors of the Church into whose ear the Paraclete was speaking, Bernard being thus represented as a new Evangelist.[48] The source may also be sought in William of St Thierry's description in the *Vita Prima* of Bernard's charisms which included those of wisdom and knowledge, which William drew from St Paul's famous reference to the gifts of the Spirit.[49] A very similar image is found as one of a number of scenes in a full-page miniature in a Table of Virtues from an early English thirteenth-century manuscript from Abbey Dore.[50] It is a bust of an abbot within a circular medallion. Very close to his face, in the same position as in the French example, is an almost identical head of a bird, the rest of whose body is outside the medallion and which this time is cross-nimbed to indicate that it is the Holy Spirit.

The so-called *Hedwig Codex* (*see* 95 and 96), the pictorial biography of St Hedwig of Andechs, Duchess of Silesia, completed in 1353, also contains the Sermons of St Bernard with a number of illustrations. One folio has two scenes with St Bernard. Above, a nimbed and tonsured Bernard in a brownish habit is shown writing at an adjustable desk against which his crozier is leaning. (**18**) The inscription in red ink above reads, 'Bernard, abbot of Clairvaux, is writing a sermon on the gospel passage "An angel was sent".[51] Below, again nimbed and

18 St Bernard writing and teaching his monks.

carrying a crozier, Bernard is pointing to an open book which he holds in his left hand while addressing five monks at his feet. The monks' habits are greyish blue, Bernard's brownish. Two of them have their hoods partially over their heads, one is pointing to Bernard and another looking at him attentively. The inscription in red reads, 'Here he reads the homily to his most beloved brethren'.

A similar scene is depicted in the Lectionary from Marienstern in Saxony from c. 1280. (19) Within the initial A(c) a nimbed Bernard, this time without crozier, is pointing to an open book which he holds in his left hand. Below six tonsured monks are sitting, three of them looking up and concentrating on what Bernard is saying; on the left one of them is writing in a book, on the right another with his hood up is writing on a scroll, and in the middle between the two writing monks the sixth monk is assisting them by holding an inkwell in one hand and a knife in the other.

As is to be expected early representations of St Bernard are also to be found in manuscripts of his Life, the *Vita Prima*. He is featured in a miniature in a late twelfth-century manuscript at the opening of the text alongside the paragraph in red ink announcing the beginning of the work by William of St Thierry. (**20**) Here he is tonsured but with longish hair, nimbed, with a crozier in his left hand and

19 St Bernard teaching monks.

20 St Bernard the teacher.

his right hand raised in a teaching mode with the index finger pointing. Unusually, he is dressed in eucharistic vestments of alb, blue chasuble with white spots and gold stole.

One of the best known images of Bernard is in a composite manuscript from the Austrian Zwettl dated from about 1189 which contains the *Vita Prima* and is roughly contemporary with the English manuscript. (**21**) In the upper half of the initial *B(ernhardus)* – the opening which goes on to announce his birth at Châtillon in Burgundy of illustrious parents – is a half figure of a youthful Bernard in a frontal position, nimbed and tonsured, holding a simple crozier in

21 St Bernard and William of St Thierry.

22 Stephen Harding commissions Bernard to found Clairvaux.

his right hand, his left hand raised in blessing. In the lower half a tonsured monk sits on a stool writing at a desk, a pen in his right hand and a knife in his left. The initial is in reddish brown ink, the figures the same and in black. This is almost certainly meant to represent the author of the first part of the *Vita Prima*, William of St Thierry, and as such is the only early medieval portrait of Bernard's great friend and biographer.

Among later medieval narrative pictures are a number of scenes from Bernard's life as a monk. His entry to Cîteaux is represented in a number of Bernard cycles, for example those from Altenberg and Zwettl.[52] After only a couple of years Stephen Harding commissioned Bernard to found a new monastery, Clairvaux, at the very early age of twenty-five. The scene is also depicted in one of the Altenberg glass panels. (**22**) Stephen Harding is shown at the gate of Cîteaux in a white habit, nimbed, and carrying a crozier. Bernard kneels before his abbot who hands him a crozier, the symbol of his authority as abbot of a new convent, some of whose members stand behind Bernard. On the right some lay workers are seen in the process of building the new monastery. The inscription below describes the scene and is taken almost verbatim from the *Vita Prima*.

Another scene in stained glass, this one from the women's abbey of St Apern in Cologne, shows St Bernard on his sick bed surrounded by the community. (**23**) Nimbed he lies on a bed with his hands folded and his eyes closed. To remove

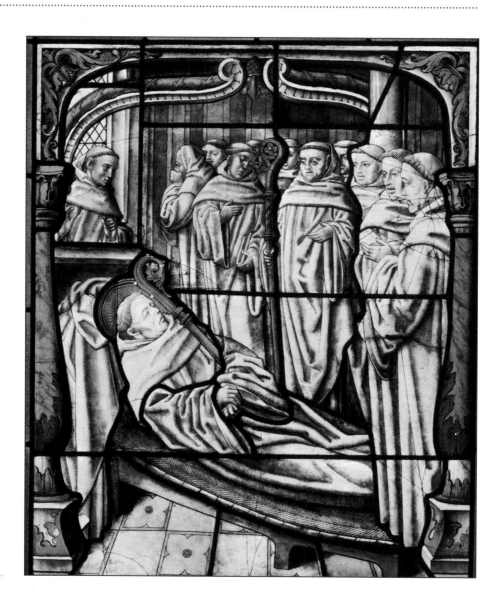

23 St Bernard on his sick bed.

any doubt as to the identification, he has a crozier under his arm. The episode is described by William of St Thierry, relating that Bernard

> once felt sick and as it were a river of phlegm flowed constantly from his mouth. Exhausted in body his strength began to fail. After some time his condition became so severe that his sons and his friends came together to perform the last rites.[53]

Among these a Cistercian abbot in a white habit and carrying a crozier is depicted in the centre of the scene. William says that he himself was present but neither as the black monk abbot of St Thierry nor as the simple Cistercian monk he became at Signy in 1135 can the abbot represent him, unless, of course, the artist was unaware of the finer points of habit and history, which is quite possible. A monk on the left with his hood over his head holds his hands to his mouth and nose as if the smell is overpowering. There is an almost identical panel made in the same Cologne workshop which used to adorn the Altenberg cloister.[54]

The burial of St Bernard is depicted in a thirteenth-century manuscript of his Sermons from the Benedictine abbey of St Martin des Champs in Paris. (24) Within the initial *H(odie)* a bearded, tonsured but not nimbed Bernard is placed in a tomb by two prelates wearing red vestments with white spots and greyish pallia with white crosses. Bernard is wearing eucharistic vestments – a white chasuble above a pale blue alb. Above him are two rows of three tonsured monks each carrying candles and the two front ones swinging round white censers above the tomb. The scene accords with Geoffrey of Auxerre's description of Bernard's burial:

24 The burial of St Bernard.

> After the sacrifice of the Mass was over they celebrated Mass for two more days and continually recited the psalms. They then committed the most pure balsam into its vessel, and in a stone they placed the most precious jewel.[55]

Another important theme in Bernardine iconography is of the saint as a founder, first and foremost of Clairvaux, but subsequently as the initiator of a larger number of monasteries than perhaps any other single person before or since. Images of him carrying the model of a church refer to him in this role. The most famous is a late fourteenth-century statue which may have adorned Bernard's tomb at Clairvaux. (25) He is dressed in a cowl with the hood partially pulled over his head, which is inclined, but exposing the distinctive central tuft of the tonsure. In his left hand he holds a model of a church. The lower part of the crozier is visible on his right; the upper part together with most of the right arm is missing.

The growth of the Clairvaux family of monasteries during Bernard's lifetime, an era dominated by his work and personality, was little short of miraculous. Only three years after Clairvaux itself was founded a group of monks was sent out to settle at Troisfontaines (Marne) and a year later another group founded Fontenay (Côte-d'Or).[56] In the same way as the growth in numbers had originally necessitated the separation of a convent of monks from Cîteaux to establish the first daughter-house of La Ferté, the pressure of numbers resulting from an influx of recruits made the setting up of new monasteries inevitable. The *Exordium Magnum* tells us that there were at one time ninety novices at Clairvaux.[57] No less than sixty-eight daughter houses were founded in Bernard's lifetime. Eventually the Clairvaux filiation reached a total of 356 monasteries, as compared with 109 under Cîteaux and 214 under Morimond.

Clairvaux did not rely on local recruitment alone for its early growth. Its fame attracted many from far and wide, some of whom later returned to their native lands to found new monasteries. Among these, for example, were William, the first abbot of Rievaulx in England, and Henry Murdac, abbot of Fountains and archbishop of York.[58] Other monasteries sprang up in the wake of Bernard's travels throughout France and the Low Countries, Germany and Italy. The *Vita*

25 St Bernard as the
founder of Clairvaux.

Prima records that his magnetism was such that 'mothers hid their sons and
wives their husbands' when Bernard was around and, according to Walter Map,
he 'used to have carts driven round through the town and castles, in which to
carry off his converts to the cloister'.[59] Yet others were the outcome of Bernard's
friendship with churchmen like St Malachy who brought the Cistercians to
Ireland and whose biographer Bernard became, and Archbishop Eskil of Lund,
who was influential in the spread of the Order in Scandinavia.

In the words of David Knowles, the year 1147 marked 'in many ways the apogee of the new order considered as a force working upon the Church and society'.[60] The General Chapter was attended by the Cistercian pope himself, who in the same year had consecrated the church of Fontenay. Two years earlier Bernard had been amazed when his former disciple, Bernardo Pignatelli, had been elected pope on the same day as the death of his predecessor.[61] In writing to congratulate the new pope, St Bernard was able to say 'my son Bernard has been promoted to be my father Eugenius'. Bernard reminded Eugenius that it was he who 'begot you in the Gospel' and that the pope is 'not to be served, but to serve'. He goes on by describing the election as God 'raising up the poor man out of the dust, the beggar from his dung-hill to sit among princes and reach the honour of a throne'.[62] Here St Bernard already adopts the tone which he was to develop in his famous treatise on the duties of a pontiff, 'On Consideration' (De consideratione). Many centuries later a successor of Eugenius, Pope John XXIII, used to have this read to him at mealtimes and described it as,

> nothing more suitable and useful for a poor Pope like myself, and for any Pope at any time. Certain things which did not redound to the honour of the Roman clergy in the twelfth century still survive to-day. Therefore 'one must watch and correct', and bear in patience.[63]

A native of Pisa, Eugenius became a monk at Clairvaux and then returned to Italy to found the abbey of St Vincenzo and St Anastasio outside Rome. As pope he devoted himself to raising clerical and monastic standards and he never discarded his Cistercian habit or mitigated his monastic lifestyle. Although he had been nurtured by St Bernard, as pope he was scrupulous in acting independently.

Eugenius is portrayed together with St Bernard in a late twelfth or early thirteenth-century manuscript from the German abbey of Kaisheim which contains the De consideratione. (26) It is introduced by a full-page ink drawing in brown, green and red which contains a good deal of text, some of it on scrolls. In the upper half Mary is enthroned with the Child and flanked by two named noblewomen, benefactresses of Kaisheim, who are kneeling. Below them two bearded figures, dressed in robes like Roman togas with headdresses resembling primitive mitres, are sitting on stools under two round arches supported by columns surmounted by capitals. The two figures are identified by the names next to their heads as Eugenius on the left and Bernard on the right. The legend above St Bernard around the arch reads, 'This is Abbot Bernard redolent with the lovely perfume of his works and the rich fragrance of his virtue'. The scroll which he holds proclaims that he is handing his treatise to the pope, 'O, Eugenius, as pope you are a father and not a son, receive this writing and listen to an old man'. The legend above Eugenius reads, 'Here is the chief prince of the Church yet a pupil of Clairvaux who, listening intently, takes in what Bernard is writing to him', and the scroll held by Eugenius proclaims, 'Wonderful harpist of the Holy Spirit singing songs of wisdom, I drink attentively from the pleasing goblet of your words'.

26 St Bernard and Pope
Eugenius III.

The drawing, although artistically highly accomplished, is nevertheless rare in
its complexity for a work from a Cistercian scriptorium. The representation of
Bernard is most unusual in that he is not shown with any of his traditional
attributes. He does not appear in the distinctive monastic cowl, he is not nimbed
and he does not carry a crozier or a book. He is normally never depicted wearing
a headdress except a simple skullcap or, in much later representations, very
occasionally a mitre. We are able to identify him and Eugenius only by the text.

Fifty-one abbeys were added to the Cistercian Order in 1147, its *annus mirabilis*. Of these, most belonged to the affiliation of Savigny which in that year merged with the Cistercians and their many daughter-houses. Among them were eleven abbeys in England that already existed before the absorption and included Furness, founded in 1123, five years before the first Cistercian house, Waverley in Surrey.[64]

Another smaller group of monasteries that centred on Obazine was also received into the Order at the 1147 General Chapter. Founded by St Stephen of Obazine, this was one of the many small groups of eremetical origin which gradually absorbed cenobitic elements and developed into monastic communities; these were popular in southern France and Italy around the time of the foundation of Cîteaux. A magnificent monument to Stephen was placed in the church in about 1280. (27) His effigy in high relief is surmounted by a slanting roof consisting of six trifoliate arcades each containing a group of figures: on the left the Virgin and Child are enthroned, then, kneeling before them, Stephen is accompanied by the abbots of his daughter-houses all of whom were received into the Order with Obazine, all of them carrying croziers. Four more arcades follow, each containing representatives of the different elements of which the community was composed – monks, lay brothers, sisters from the nearby nunnery of Coyroux affiliated to Obazine, and lay workers shown with their sheep (*see also* 77 and 93).

The meteoric rise in the number of monasteries in the first half century owed a great deal to the personality of St Bernard. It had in many ways been too rapid. The end of an era came with the death of both Bernard and Eugenius III in 1153, but the dangers inherent in the lead up to what David Knowles describes as the 'summer solstice of Cistercian growth'[65] had already been recognized in the previous year when the General Chapter had prohibited the future foundation or incorporation of new houses.[66] Although the statute proved impossible to enforce, the rate of growth was dramatically reduced. At the same time,

27 Tomb of St Stephen of Obazine.

established houses enjoyed a growing prosperity. This, with an increasing number of privileges bestowed on the Order – such as exemption from the jurisdiction of the local diocesan and freedom from paying tithes – inevitably led to a relaxation of the early austerity. Writing at the turn of the thirteenth century Conrad of Eberbach admits to a certain falling off from the enthusiasm of the first decades. He writes with some nostalgia about the simplicity and purity of

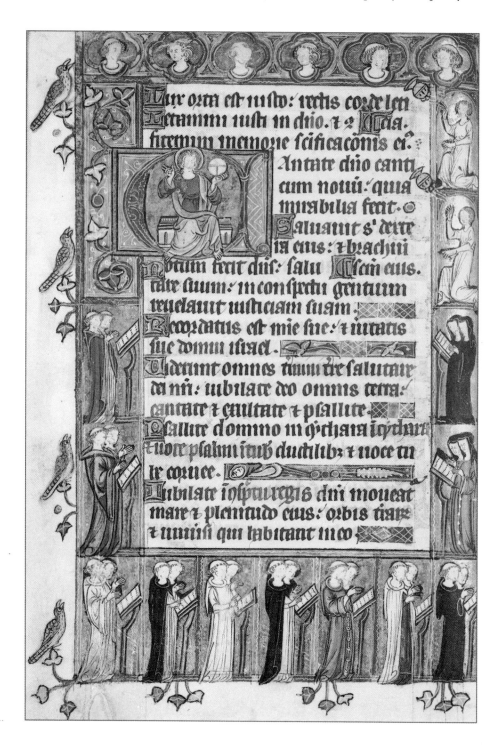

28 Psalter showing members of diverse religious orders.

the primitive evangelical spirit of the days of the founding fathers. He encapsulates this by describing Clairvaux in Bernard's lifetime as the golden age which was succeeded by the present iron age.[67]

The greatest challenge to the unquestioned position of moral leadership the Cistercians had taken throughout the twelfth century came in the thirteenth century with the rise of a new type of religious life – the mendicant friars. From then on the Cistercians no longer held their former impregnable position on centre stage, and they had to reconcile themselves to sharing the limelight with the friars. The mendicants' life seemed in many ways more in tune with the changing and increasingly urban world. The point is graphically made by an illuminated page in an English psalter which contains a rare illustration of members of diverse religious orders. (28) Within the initial C(antate domino) at the opening of Psalm 97, Christ in Majesty is depicted holding an orb in his left hand, his right hand raised in blessing. The top border consists of six busts in quatrefoils. The others are made up of sections containing pairs of singing figures standing before identical lecterns with open books and painted against a gold background. Anti-clockwise from the left these represent clerics in red copes; Benedictines in dark grey cowls; Cistercians in white cowls; Augustinian canons (?); Premonstratensians in white tunics and scapulars but without cowls; Dominicans; Franciscans in grey habits with white cords; Carmelites in white over black habits and Austin friars in black. Then in the right-hand border and facing the other way, there follow Franciscan nuns in grey habits with white cords; Benedictine nuns in black habits and finally two acolytes in albs kneeling and swinging censers. The religious are arranged in order of seniority: first the monks, the Benedictines before the Cistercians, then the canons regular, and finally the friars. Although made for use in the Exeter diocese, the manuscript is thought to have come from an Oxford workshop, and all the orders shown, with the exception of the Premonstratensians, were represented in or around the city, the Cistercians by Rewley Abbey, the Order's house of studies.

As we have seen, the almost infinite variety of representations of St Bernard across medieval time and space served to cater for a monastic as well as a lay audience in an ever-evolving religious climate. The development of a different cult of the saint is also reflected in the iconographical treatment of him. There was a discernible change in the way Bernard was portrayed from the twelfth century to the later Middle Ages. At first he is seen as a monastic figure catering for the needs of his community and the wider Cistercian family. This picture is based largely on what we hear in the *Vita Prima*, and especially in the first book by William of St Thierry. Later pictures owe a great deal to stories that cannot be traced back to the early Cistercian years but are more in tune with new devotional trends. He is no longer solely Cistercian property, and his image is adapted in a way that meant he could now be shared by a much wider non-monastic public.

CHAPTER FIVE

MORE CISTERCIAN PORTRAITS

'Lanterns shining in a dark place.'

Orderic Vitalis, *c.* 1135[1]

'The church of Cîteaux has flourished widely through the earth, and, gathering from all sides the most gracious flowers of the world, it has taken them into itself and transformed them by some mutation into the flowers of celestial paradise.'

Gilbert Foliot, m. Cluny, abb. Gloucester,
bp.Hereford (1148–63), bp. London (1163–87)[2]

'Shining through the mist like the morning star, the holy Cistercian Order fights in the Church militant by work and example. By the exercise of holy contemplation and the merit of innocent life, it fervently strives to scale the heights with Mary. It strives to conform itself to the work of the anxious Martha through the exercise of praiseworthy deeds and assiduous concern for pious works.'

Pope Benedict XII, *Fulgens sicut stella*, 1335[3]

HENRY MURDAC (d. 1153)

In the career of Henry Murdac we have the clearest imaginable evidence of the strength and magnetism of St Bernard's personality, of his singleness of purpose and of his extraordinary ability to enforce his will. Henry Murdac was born into a wealthy Yorkshire family and had entered the service of Archbishop Thurstan of York, the friend of the Cistercians at Rievaulx and Fountains, as a teacher and master. The call of the cloister and the further three steps in his career he owed entirely to the initiative of Bernard. Like a number of other Englishmen, among whom was William, the first abbot of Rievaulx, Henry had come under the spell of Bernard and entered Clairvaux.

In a forceful letter St Bernard had exhorted Henry to join him in the 'school of piety of which Jesus is the master', which, in a famous passage, Bernard contrasts with Henry's 'water from the clouds of the sky' (Ps 17:12) – a reference to his book-learning:

Believe me who have experience, you will find much more labouring amongst the woods than you ever will amongst books. Woods and stones will teach you what you can never hear from any master. Do you imagine you cannot suck honey from the rocks and oil from the hardest stone; that the mountains do not drop sweetness and the hills flow with milk and honey; that the valleys are not filled with corn? [4]

A postscript to the letter reveals that two English monks at Clairvaux, who appear to have been Henry's pupils at York, must have spoken so highly of their former master that Bernard decided to headhunt him. Henry responded and entered what the Rule describes as a 'school of the Lord's service'.[5]

Bernard's instinct proved to be right. Within a few years Henry was sent with a group of monks from Clairvaux to found Vauclair (Aisne) in 1134. When in 1143 the second abbot of Fountains, Richard, who had been one of the monks who left St Mary's, York, to enter Cistercian life, died on a visit to Clairvaux, Bernard wrote to the prior and convent at Fountains that he would send Henry 'who would be very useful to you in the present business' to oversee the election of a successor, and he urged them to receive him with the 'honour he deserves, and listen to him in all things'.[6] Notwithstanding that freedom in abbatial elections was a cornerstone of Cistercian practice, Bernard's intervention left the Fountains community with no alternative but to elect Henry. That this was Bernard's desired objective is revealed by a letter he wrote to Henry at the same time charging him to accept if elected.[7]

Fountains had originated as a breakaway group of Benedictine monks from York, and in choosing to send Henry there Bernard knew that any remnants there might still be of old black monk customs would be removed and replaced with the more severe Clairvaux observance. Under Henry's stern and forceful leadership Fountains prospered and, very much like its mother-house, Clairvaux, attracted a large number of recruits and became one of the most prolific houses, eventually the head of a family of fourteen monasteries.[8] No less than five of these were founded during Henry's abbacy, one of them, Lyse, the first Cistercian abbey in northern Scandinavia.

Henry's combative spirit and his total dedication to Cistercian support for the Gregorian reform policy, favouring free elections and the highest possible spiritual calibre of candidates, explains the prominent part he played in opposition to William Fitzherbert's claim to the archbishopric of York.[9] The Cistercian case against Fitzherbert rested on their view that he owed his promotion to the king, whose nephew he was, as well as on his reputation for unchaste living; on both counts he was deemed an unsuitable candidate for the second highest office in the English church.

With the accession to the papacy of Eugenius III, St Bernard's disciple and Henry Murdac's friend and fellow-religious from their days at Clairvaux, the tireless campaign that had been waged under Bernard's leadership finally paid off. William was deposed and the part Henry Murdac had played was rewarded by a party of William's supporters who sacked the abbey and reduced it to ruins.[10]

The election that followed was disputed, but in the end Henry Murdac was chosen and his election confirmed by Eugenius III at whose hands he was consecrated on 7 December 1147. William's cause was still upheld by the king and opposition to Henry in York remained strong. He was obliged to reside in Ripon not far from Fountains in whose affairs he continued to take an active interest. He was eventually enthroned in 1151, and in his two remaining years in office he initiated a policy of monastic reform among the Augustinians in his diocese. As a bishop he continued to lead the austere life of a monk. The Fountains chronicler characterized him as 'a man of high principles, invincible in the cause of justice'.[11]

After Henry's death William was restored to his see. One of his first acts on his return in 1154 was to visit Fountains and make his peace with the Cistercians, but shortly afterwards he died having supposedly been poisoned. Miracles were reported and the abbots of Rievaulx and Fountains were appointed by Honorius III to enquire into his life and in 1227 he was canonized. In *c.* 1423 the great St William window, one of the finest produced by the York school of glass painting, was installed in the north window of the east transept of York Minster. This consists of 105 panels depicting William's life, death and miracles, and, paradoxically, one of them depicts Henry Murdac on his deathbed. (**29**) He is shown lying on a bed with his head on a pillow. He is identified as a bishop by the mitre, and, significantly, he is surrounded by five distressed-looking

29 Monks at the deathbed of Archbishop Henry Murdac of York.

Cistercian monks in white cowls with their hoods over their heads. The one nearest to Henry has his right hand on Henry's chest and his left on his face. The scene is not correct historically as he died at Sherburn, but it conveys the importance he attached to his Cistercian roots, and the devotion to him of his former sons. He died on 14 October 1153, two months after St Bernard and three months after Eugenius III. Writing at the beginning of the thirteenth century the Fountains chronicler classed him with his two distinguished fellow Cistercians as 'guardians of the Lord's flock, columns of the Lord's house, and lights of the world'.[12]

AELRED OF RIEVAULX (1110–67)

The picture of Aelred of Rievaulx which has often been described as the only extant medieval representation of the Cistercian abbot and spiritual writer appears in a twelfth-century manuscript. Written at the French Benedictine abbey of Anchin (Nord), it appropriately contains his first work, the *Speculum Caritatis* or *Mirror of Charity*.[13] This he began in 1142 when he had just been appointed novice master, a position he held for one year only, after which he was chosen to be the abbot of Revesby, the new daughter-house of Rievaulx. In 1147 Aelred returned to Rievaulx as abbot. It was the same year in which Henry Murdac, whom Aelred revered and whose cross he kept in later years among the small number of devotional objects in his cell, became archbishop of York.[14]

Aelred's disciple and biographer, Walter Daniel, described the *Mirror of Charity* as 'in my judgment the best of all his works' which 'in three books . . . contains as good a picture of the love of God and one's neighbour as a man can see of himself in a mirror'.[15] Walter Daniel's assessment is one that is shared and reiterated by a number of modern Aelred scholars.[16]

Aelred is depicted as a young-looking monk in a white cowl with his tonsured head partially covered by the hood. He is sitting within the initial *U(ere)* (or *Vere*), the opening word of the Prologue on humility which echoes that of Bernard.[17] The seated figure holding a long scroll is identified by the words above his head, *Ailred mo(nachus)*. Above the initial the words *INCIPIT PROLOGUS*, with alternate letters in red and green, tell us that the Prologue to the work follows.

The picture has always been reproduced on its own,[18] as it were *in vacuo*. Yet, its true iconographic significance is revealed only when seen in the context of its position on the parchment folio and in relation to the historiated initial on the facing folio and the placement of this (**colour plate 10**). The first thing that strikes one as being unusual is that the picture of Aelred is half way down the page on the far right. The three letters following the initial *U*, which complete the opening word, have had to be relegated to the line below the initial. Only thus could the artist achieve the proper balance between this and the picture on the previous folio.

Aelred is facing left, his eyes directed upwards towards the figure on the opposite folio contained within the initial *E(st)*, the opening word of St Bernard's letter to Aelred, 'The great virtue of the saints is humility, but a sincere and discreet humility'.[19] These were the words that Aelred took up at the beginning of his Prologue. The figure on the left folio is St Bernard who is depicted facing inwards and looking down at Aelred on the opposite folio in an exchange of glances.[20] Bernard sits within the golden initial with a pastoral staff in his right hand. In his left hand he has a scroll and two fingers are raised in blessing. The scroll probably holds the text of his letter, while Aelred's scroll represents either the same letter from Bernard or his own work which follows. Bernard is tonsured and, in the tradition of the *Vita Prima*, lightly bearded. His cowl is light grey with the hood perched at the back of his head, and the tunic below is pale brown. Most unusually Bernard is not shown nimbed which suggests that the manuscript pre-dates his canonization in 1174.

As we have seen, Bernard dominates Cistercian iconography. The rarity of a medieval representation of Aelred in contrast to the myriad pictures of the abbot of Clairvaux makes it tempting to concentrate on him and cut Bernard out, but Bernard's role in Aelred's career, as in so many other spheres, was central, and to do so would be to distort the story and render the picture out of focus and incomplete.

In 1141–2 at the age of thirty-two Aelred was sent on a mission to Rome in connection with the disputed election at York. On the way he met St Bernard on whom he made a powerful impression. In Bernard's letter to Aelred he ordered him to write something to help assuage the fears of those embarking upon a monastic career.[21] Bernard reveals that Aelred had advanced the customary excuse of unworthiness, stating that he was 'ignorant of grammar . . . almost illiterate', a wild exaggeration, and that he had 'come to the desert, not from the schools, but from the kitchen', a reference to his service as steward at the court of King David of Scotland. Aelred's plea had the opposite effect of its purported intention: in Bernard's words his excuses 'serve rather to inflame than extinguish the spark of my desire, because knowledge that comes from the school of the Holy Spirit rather than the schools of rhetoric will savour all the sweeter to me'. For Aelred would 'be able to strike something out of those rocks that you have not got by your own wits from the bookshelves of the schoolmen, and that you will have experienced sometimes under the shade of the tree during the heats of midday what you would never have learned in the schools'. Bernard's wish expresses what was in fact to be Aelred's genius: his ability to draw on his own experience for the benefit of his novices, and, later as abbot, for the whole community in his care.

Bernard acknowledged the humility contained in Aelred's excuse, but he may have harboured the thought he had expressed in a letter to another abbot: 'Barren modesty is not acceptable nor is humility praiseworthy when it is not in accordance with the facts.'[22] To get his way Bernard invoked the primacy of obedience as laid down in the Rule when he asked Aelred, 'Where is the humility in refusing to consent to my wishes?'

As a concession to Aelred's feelings Bernard ordered that his letter be placed at the beginning of the work, and he even gave it its title 'so that whatever in the

1 St Benedict's four kinds of monks from a manuscript of his Rule, dated 1173, from Zwettl, Austria.

2 St Benedict in a window dated *c.* 1340 from the upper cloister at Wienhausen, Germany.

3 St Bernard facing St Benedict in the Wienhausen cloister.

4 Bust of a Cistercian monk in the margin of the Rochester Chronicle, adjoining the entry announcing the foundation of Cîteaux in 1098.

5 St Stephen Harding and the Benedictine abbot of St Vaast presenting their churches to the Virgin. The kneeling scribe Osbert offers up his manuscript written c. 1125.

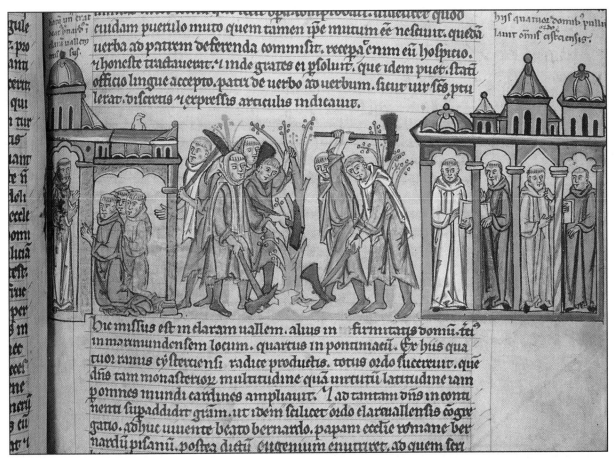

6 On the left St Stephen Harding commissions a group of kneeling monks to found new monasteries. On the right the abbots of La Ferté, Clairvaux (St Bernard), Pontigny and Morimond – the 'Four Branches from the Cistercian Root' – are within their respective churches. The group of working monks in the middle testify to the centrality of manual labour in the Cistercian reform.

Bodl. 530. [E.1.1.N.]

OGASTMEFR:G 22

Qvatm' ea que de gdib' humilita
uf corā frib' locut' fuerā. pleniori
t tractatu differere. Cui tue petu
oni digne ut dignū erat. & uolenf
satiffacere. & timenf n̄ poffe. euan
glia con'ilii memor. n̄ pri' fateor
incipe aufuf sū. q̄ sedenf coputa
ui. si sufficerent sūpo' ad pfia
endū. Cū aū caritā forā hunc
misiffet timore: q in timebā illudi de ope n̄ consūmando. subitur̄t
ali' timor de contrio q cepi timere qui piculū de gtā si pfeaiffe.

7 The earliest known image of St Bernard and the only one from his lifetime. Sitting before an open book within the opening initial of his first treatise, *The Steps of Humility*, his right hand is raised in blessing, his left hand holds a knife. From the Benedictine abbey of St Augustine, Canterbury.

8 A diminutive St Bernard within the opening initial of his treatise, 'On Precept and Dispensation'. He is seated writing, inspired by the Holy Spirit in the form of a bird's head. From a French thirteenth-century manuscript.

De diuisis diebz spiritalibz.
De diuisis saprbz.
De diuisis genibz spirituum.
De diuisis opracionibz uocis diuine in
    cis in anima.
De diuisis nominibz dei.
De diuisis saprbz dī.
De diuisis modis quibz se habet filiū
    ad partem.
Quod pr̄ ⁊ filius ⁊ sp̄c sc̄s ⁊ sc̄i angeli
    residerant ī sumacionē nr̄am.

Quod anime scōr̄ desiderant re-
    cipere corpora sua.
De diuersis impletionibz anime
    ⁊ corporis in futuro.
Expliciunt capitula libri certini.
Sequitur ternariꝰ sac̄ modis q̄st ipō.
De quibz hic tractus libr̄ ē ī spc̄ualī.
Par est ī sibis to odorferris op̄ labor.
Sempr̄ gerit flores leornardi nobilis.

9 A thirteenth-century pen and ink drawing of a tonsured and bearded St Bernard writing, inspired by
the hand of God. Two young pupils are at his feet, and his crozier leans against his chair.

INCIPT EPL'A EIVS
DAM AD AILRED
IN SEQVENTI OPERE

EST QDM SCO VIRTVS
p maxima humilitas: sed si uera.
sed si discreta. Neq; enim humilitas
in parte constituenda est mendacij,
nec inobedientiæ sacrilegio conser-
uanda. Rogaui frinitatem tuã. immo precepi. immo sub attestatione
diuini nominis adiutaui. ut michi
pauca quedam scriberes. inter que
etiam quozdam querimonijs qui de
remissiorib; ad arciora nituntur ob-
uiates. Non dampno. non reprehendo
excusationem: sed prsus obstinatione
accuso. fuerit humilitatis excusasse:
sed nunqd humilitatis est ñ obedire.
nunqd humilitatis est ñ acquiescere.
Immo quasi peccatum ariolandi est
repugnare. & quasi scelus ydolatrie
nolle acquiescere. Sed clamas femine
os humeros graui sarcinæ subducen-

dos: cautius q; onus oblatum ñ subire.
quam sub fasce cum subieris ruere. Sic
g' graue qd iubeo. sic arduum. sic im-
possibile. Sed nec sic excusationem ha-
bes. Persisto in sentencia mea. preptum
ingemino. Quid facies: Nonne is in
cuius uerba iurasti sciat inq't iunioz
hoc sibi expedire. & confidens de adiu-
torio dei obediat: fecisti utiq; quantũ
debuisti. si non plus quam debuisti:
quousq; licuit pcessisti. Causas tue im-
possibilitatis ostendisti. dicens te min
grammaticum. immo pene illitera-
tum. qui de coquinis non de scolis ad
heremum ueneris: ubi inter rupes &
montes agrestis & rusticus uictitas.
p diurno pane in secuti desudes &
malleo. ubi magis discis silere quam
loqui. ubi sub habitu paupum pisca-
toz. coturnus ñ admittitur oratoru.
Accipio gratissime excusationem tuã.
qua desiderij mei scintillam augeri
potius sentio quã extingui: cũ dulcius
michi debeat sapere si id pferas quod
non in cuilibet grammatici. s; in scola
didiceris spc sci. cum forte thesaurum
ob id habeas in uase fictili. ut sublimi-
tas sit uirtutis di. & non ex te. Id quoq;
quam iocundum qd quodam presagio
futuroz de coquina sis trãslatus ad
heremũ: cui forte ad horam in regia
domo carnalium ciboz fuit credita
dispensatio: ut aliquando in domo regis nri spiritalib; spiritalia coparares:
ac cibo uerbi di esurientes reficeres.
S; nec ardua montiũ. nec aspera ru-
pium. nec uallium concaua phorresco
cum in dieb; istis montes stillent dul-

10 A twelfth-century manuscript of St Aelred's *Mirror of Charity*. On the left St Bernard is seated within the opening initial of his letter to Aelred that he is shown holding and in which he instructs Aelred to write the treatise. Lower down in the right folio the young Aelred is depicted in the opening

cedinem. &'colles fluant lac &'mel. in quib; ualles abundant frumento. in quib; sugitur mel de petra oleumq; de saxo durissimo. &'in rupib; &'in montib; sunt pascue ouium xpi. Yn de arbitror qd malleo illo tuo aliqd tibi de rupib; illis excuderis. qd saga citate ingenii de magistror scriniis non tulisses. &'n nunquam tale aliqd in meridiano feruore sub umbris ar borum senseris. quale nunquam didi cisses in scolis. Non tibi g non t. sed nomini eius da glam. qui n solum de lacu miserie &'luto fecis. de psti bulo mortis &'sceno turpitudinis eri puit. despatum. s; &'memoriam fa ciens mirabilium suor misericors &' miserator dns. ad peccator spem cu mulatius erigenda. illuminauit ce cum. indoctum erudiuit. docuit im pitum. Proinde cum id qd exigeris. tuum n esse norit omis q te nouit. cur erubescis. cur trepidas. cur dissi mulas. cur ad eius uocis impium q dedit. renuis erogare qd dedit. An psumptionis nota. ut aliquor formi das inuidiam. Quasi aliqd utile qs unquam sine inuidia sepserit. aut pre sumptionis possis argui q monachus abbati parueris. Precipio itaq; in no mine ihu xpi. &'in spu di nri. qua tenus ea que tibi diuturna medita tione nota sunt. de excellentia carita tis. de fructu eius. de ordine ei. stilo adnotare non differas. ut &'quid sit caritas. &'quanta in ei possessione ha beat dulcedo. quanta in cupiditate que ei contraria est sentiat oppressio.

quam n ipsam dulcedine caritatis minuat ut qdam putant. s; potius augeat hominis exterioris afflictio. postremo. qualis in eius exhibitione sit habenda discretio. in ipso ope tuo quasi in quodam speculo agnoscam? Verum ut pudori tuo parcatur. hec ipsa epla in fronte opis psigat. ut qcqd in speculo caritatis. hoc enim libro nomen imponim? lectori dis plicuerit. non t qui parueris. sed michi qui inuitum coegerim im putetur. Vale in xpo dilecte frater.

EXPLICT: EPLA.
INCIPIT: PROLOG.

ERE SCOR VERA &'discreta humilitas uirtus est. mea autem &'mei similiu defect uirtutis. Ve qua ppha. Vide hum litatem meam &'eripe me. Neq; eni a uirtute aliqua se eripi postula bat. aut de humilitate extollebat. s; deiectioni sue subuentionem im plorabat. Quam miseram humili

initial of the prologue of his work, looking up at his mentor. In his hands he holds either Bernard's letter or his own manuscript.

11 Christ the Good Shepherd holding his pastoral staff and his good line of sheep. On the right is an abbot with the negligent line of goats. From a manuscript of Hugh de Fouilloy's *Shepherds and Sheep* from Clairmarais, France.

12 In a magnificent full-page miniature, Abbot Robert of Clairmarais presents a manuscript he commissioned to the Virgin.

Mirror of Charity (for that is the name I give it) should displease the reader shall be imputed to me who have commanded it and not to you who have obeyed by writing it'.

This explains the inclusion of Bernard's letter in the Anchin manuscript and gives meaning to the two pictures and their relative positions facing each other. Bernard is shown in a position of authority as the great abbot of Clairvaux ordering a subordinate, the young monk of an English daughter-house, to write a treatise.

It may be invidious to compare Aelred with Bernard, and yet he has been called 'Bernard of the North'.[23] Bernard's dynamic personality meant that his influence was felt in every corner of Christendom, while Aelred's much gentler nature resulted in his sphere of activity being largely confined to northern England and to a lesser extent to the rest of Britain. But similarities there certainly were; they both wrote spiritual treatises, homilies and letters, they both headed important abbeys with large numbers of monks (the numbers at Rievaulx were said to have doubled under Aelred to 640 monks, lay brothers, and hired labourers so that the church was 'crowded with the brethren like bees in a hive')[24] as well as daughter-houses, they were both involved with contentious episcopal elections, they arbitrated in disputes involving religious houses, and they played a part in the papal schism between the anti-pope Victor IV (Octavian) and the great friend of the Cistercians, Alexander III (Aelred is said to have been responsible for rallying Henry II to the side of Alexander).[25] In one respect, however, they differed sharply: in addition to his spiritual treatises Aelred was the author of historical works, an activity which was not consistent with Cistercian custom and practice and of which Bernard would almost certainly not have approved.[26]

Aelred's historical interest and sense of national consciousness and pride were grounded in his sensitivity to the currents in a country recently ravaged by civil war. A new society was emerging out of the political antagonism of the English and their new Norman masters, while at the same time the wind of change occasioned by the Gregorian reform was disturbing the cosy ways of an ecclesiastical backwater. Although much of Aelred's historical work is hagiographical and didactic, it nevertheless reflects national history and deals with issues far removed from his Cistercian interests. On account of this it has been said that 'Aelred belongs to the Northumbrian rather than the Cistercian school'.[27] This applies most particularly to his account of the Battle of the Standard between the Scots and the English, an important event which took place in 1138 not far from Rievaulx in which he had a particular personal interest. He tackled the subject with courage, for he was close to both protagonists, his old master, King David of Scotland, and his friend and patron, Walter Espec, the founder of Rievaulx. Aelred's scapegoats were the dreaded barbarian Picts of Galloway, and his lesson the futility of war.[28]

Aelred's last historical work was the *Life of Edward the Confessor*.[29] The cult of Edward had been growing gradually since his death in 1066 and his cause was championed by Aelred's kinsman, Abbot Laurence of Westminster, who secured his canonization in 1161 – a fitting reward for Henry II's support of the pope in the schism as well as a boost to the king's prestige. Laurence commissioned Aelred to write a new *Life* of Edward to celebrate the solemn translation of the saint's remains to a new shrine in Westminster Abbey on 13 October 1163.[30] At this Aelred is said to have presented his new *Life* to the king and to have preached the sermon.[31] Like the ceremony, Aelred's work was a powerful symbol and celebration of the peace that had descended on the country and the Church, a sign of the reconciliation of the English and the Normans. In a letter of dedication to the king, Aelred refers to Henry as the cornerstone which bound together the two walls of the English and Norman race.[32]

Among the many manuscripts of the *Life* two new representations of Aelred have recently been identified in a fourteenth-century version of the *Life of Edward King and Confessor* (*Vita Sancti Edwardi Regis et Confessoris*).[33]

The first historiated initial *M(ultis)* which appears at the beginning of the Prologue is straightforward. (30) It features a kneeling monk in a dark brown cowl in the centre (Aelred), holding a long scroll. He is depicted handing his

30 St Aelred the historian kneeling before King Henry II.

work to a crowned king (Henry II) in a blue garment who is sitting on a throne. Behind Aelred is a mitred figure (Abbot Laurence) carrying a crozier in his left hand and with his right hand raised in blessing. Although this is a traditional presentation portrayal it differs from most as it represents an event which took place on a particular day, the day of Edward's translation when Aelred preached and presented the king with his *Life*.

The meaning of the second initial *G(loriosi)* on the reverse of the same folio (not illustrated here) is more difficult to interpret.[34] With this the *Life* itself begins. Aelred is again shown kneeling, this time before a standing crowned king who holds out his right hand above Aelred's head. A ring is placed on his head by a nimbed figure with a pilgrim's hat standing behind Aelred: this figure represents John the Evangelist. Ambiguously, this second scene contains two levels of meaning, with Aelred seen with both Henry II and Edward, or rather with Henry as the new Edward. The scene refers to the story told by Aelred in the *Life* of how the king received back from St John the ring which he had given to a poor pilgrim, not knowing that the man was John himself. The story became well known and determined the iconography of Edward.

The artist has perfectly captured the message Aelred wished to convey, that of Henry as the impersonation of Edward. The link with Anglo-Saxon England gave legitimacy to the Norman successors while at the same time strengthening the king's position by identifying him as the heir of Edward's sanctity, symbolized by the receipt of the Evangelist's ring.

Since the identification of these two historiated initials from the *Life of Edward the Confessor*, we now have pictures of Aelred dating from the early period of his monastic career and from towards the end of his life, and representing the two products of his authorship, his spiritual writings and his historical works: the young novice-master author of the *Mirror of Charity* painted either during his lifetime or, if not, shortly afterwards, and the mature historian and royal biographer as seen by an artist approximately two centuries later.

OTTO OF FREISING (*c.* 1110–58)

Unlike Aelred, Otto of Freising is remembered not chiefly as a monk, still less as a spiritual writer, but almost exclusively as a distinguished historian. Another facet distinguishes him from Aelred and almost all contemporary fellow Cistercians: he was never close to St Bernard, did not come under his influence, and in fact criticized him for his stand against Gilbert de la Porée and Abelard under whom Otto had studied in Paris.

Otto was among the first Cistercian recruits to come from the highest level of society. A member of the great German princely Babenberg family, he was the son of Duke Leopold III of Austria, and through his mother the grandson of Emperor Henry IV; he was the half-brother of Conrad III and the maternal uncle of Frederick Barbarossa. Others of royal blood were to follow him into the cloister: Henry of France, brother of Louis VII, entered Clairvaux and subsequently became bishop of Beauvais and archbishop of Rheims, and a number of royal princes joined the Cistercian lay brotherhood.[35]

When Otto entered Morimond in 1133 with fourteen other young German noblemen, it had a similar, if less spectacular, effect on the growth of this branch of the Cistercian family as had the arrival of St Bernard and his thirty companions at Cîteaux some twenty years earlier. It initiated the rapid spread of the Morimond filiation which had already reached German territory with the foundation of Kamp in 1123, Ebrach in 1127, and Altenberg and Heiligenkreuz in 1133. It was to penetrate further into central and eastern Europe, and was surpassed only by the filiation of Clairvaux in the total number of monasteries founded. Otto became abbot in his mid-twenties – at about the same age as St Bernard – but in 1138 after a brief abbacy he was elected bishop of Freising where he remained in office until his death in 1158. This is how Alberic of Trois Fontaines describes his rapid promotion: 'Otto, noble by birth and monk of Morimond, was one day elected abbot of this monastery, and the following day named bishop of Freising, for he was the half-brother of the emperor Conrad.'[36]

As a bishop Otto was not himself active in the spread of the Cistercian Order in the way that Bernard was or that Bernard's friends, Malachy in Ireland or Eskil in Scandinavia were, nor was he able, on account of his family connections, to take the traditional Cistercian side in the tug of war between church and state. Yet he was in every way an exemplary monastic bishop; like Henry Murdac living an austere life, he was solicitous for the welfare of his clergy, built parish churches, and generally attended to the spiritual and material welfare of his diocese, but it was chiefly as a historian that he acquired a reputation. His *Two Cities*, inspired by St Augustine's *City of God*, recounts the struggle between good and evil in chronicle form down to 1146, but his major work was his biography of his uncle, *The Deeds of Frederick Barbarossa*.[37]

Although remembered as a historian, Otto never lost his attachment to his own monastic past. He was on his way to the General Chapter at Cîteaux when he was taken ill at his old abbey of Morimond where he died and was buried. He was accompanied by his secretary Rahewin who tells how before dying Otto entrusted *The Deeds* 'to pious and learned men, that if he seemed to have said anything in favour of the views of Master Gilbert which might offend anyone, it might be corrected in accordance with their decision, and he declared himself to be an adherent of the Catholic faith in accordance with the rule of the Holy Roman – and truly universal – Church'.[38] He was evidently concerned that his reputation should not be tarnished by the position he had taken in the theological debate in opposition to Bernard.[39] He had earlier claimed that St Bernard may have been deceived for 'that holy and wise men, hampered by corruptible flesh, are frequently deceived in such matters is proved by both modern and ancient examples'.[40]

Otto is portrayed in his seal dated 1158 seated on a faldstool, a common way of representing bishops. He is bare-headed and clearly tonsured, wears a chasuble and carries a crozier in the right hand and a book in the left.[41] The stained glass in the

31 Otto of Freising, monk and bishop.

late thirteenth-century lavatorium at the Austrian abbey of Heiligenkreuz, a daughter-house of Morimond, portrays members of the Babenberg family, including Otto of Freising. (31) Otto's Cistercian past is emphasized by showing him in the white Cistercian cowl. He is mitred and carries a crozier and a book in his left hand; his right hand is raised in blessing. His exalted position is underlined by portraying him as a mature bearded person. The legend surrounding his figure tells us that he was the son of Leopold who became a Cistercian monk and bishop of Freising.

BALDWIN OF FORD (d. 1190)

It is hard to know what to make of Baldwin. The contradictory evidence of the contemporary sources has inevitably coloured the evaluation of modern scholars.[42] Gerald of Wales, who knew him well, described him as learned and religious and remembered him for his kindness, but at the same time it is from his pen that we have the well-known verdict on Baldwin: 'He was a better simple monk than abbot, a better abbot than bishop, and a better bishop than archbishop.' In much the same way Urban III described him as 'the most fervent monk, the zealous abbot, the lukewarm bishop, the careless archbishop'. The eminent historian Stubbs referred to him as 'a Cistercian of the best sort, a man who lived but little for the world, and that to make it better', but the same authority accused Baldwin of 'errors of temper, harshness, arbitrary severity, and want of tact, of which he cannot be acquitted'.

Unlike Otto of Freising and so many of the Cistercians who later in their career served the wider Church as bishops, Baldwin was of humble origin. He distinguished himself as a canonist and became archdeacon of Exeter, but in about 1169 he renounced the prospects he had for a career in the Church and entered the neighbouring abbey of Ford, founded in 1136 as the second daughter-house of the first Cistercian abbey in England, Waverley. After a few years he was elected abbot, but in 1180 he became bishop of Worcester and four years later archbishop of Canterbury after an acrimonious disputed election.[43] His years at Canterbury were marked by the usual strained relations that existed between bishops of monastic sees and their chapters, owing to their different interests and the restricted freedom of action of both sides. In this case the situation was no doubt exacerbated by Baldwin's outlook as a clerk and training as a canonist as well as by his Cistercian background. For his part, being used to the simpler style of the white monks, he was no doubt offended by the privilege and lavish living of the Canterbury black monks. The conflict came to a head when a challenge was presented by the secular clergy to the monks to found a college for secular clerks nearby, and by Baldwin's high-handed treatment of the monks in holding them captive within the monastic precinct and suspending all liturgical services. The climax was reached when he installed an unworthy candidate as the head of the monastery. After the death of Henry II a compromise was reached and Baldwin left for the Holy Land on crusade. There he died at Acre in 1190.

Like Otto of Freising, Baldwin's monastic career was relatively short and although they both undoubtedly cherished the Cistercian ideals by which they had chosen to live in making their profession, neither of them was a monk for long enough to be primarily moulded by their monastic formation. Yet Baldwin did most of his writing during his time at Ford. He is remembered for a number of treatises and sermons, but his best known work is *On the Sacrament of the Altar* (*De sacramento altaris*).[44] Although the treatise was written at Ford, Baldwin is depicted as an archbishop at the opening of this work in a late twelfth or early thirteenth-century manuscript from the Benedictine abbey of Christ Church, Canterbury. (**32**) Within the initial *A(mantissimo)* he is shown as the author of the work; he is bearded, sitting on a stool and writing with pen and knife in his hands, wearing a mitre, with a pale blue pallium over a pink chasuble and green dalmatic and alb, all on a gold background.

32 Baldwin of Ford, Archbishop of Canterbury.

ST WILLIAM OF BOURGES (d. 1209)

William de Donjeon or Berruyer belonged to the family of the counts of Nevers.[45] He became a canon at Soissons but soon decided to enter Grandmont (Haute Vienne), the mother-abbey of the austere hermit order of that name. A serious conflict there between the monks and lay brothers led to the departure of a large number of monks, many of whom found refuge in other monasteries, notably Cistercian.[46] Among them was William who entered Pontigny (Yonne) where he became prior. He was then successively abbot of Fontainejean (Loiret) and, from 1187, of the royal foundation of Chaalis (Oise), founded in 1136 from Pontigny, before being elected archbishop of Bourges in 1200.

As archbishop he continued to live as a simple monk. His insistence on maintaining the highest standards brought him into conflict with the clergy of the cathedral. In total conformity with Cistercian policy, his unflinching loyalty to the papacy also led to strained relations with the French king. The old dispute at Grandmont had not been resolved, and when the pope was brought in to attempt a solution he called upon William to visit Grandmont, but William was not able to bring the parties together.[47] William died in 1209 as he was about to join the crusade against the Albigensians. He was canonized in 1218 by Honorius III as one of only three members of the Order for whom there is any record of official canonization. In the same year the General Chapter ordered the celebration of his feast on 10 January with two masses, and in 1261 his name was added to the litany of saints recited by the Order.[48]

It was during William's period in office that the cathedral in Bourges was rebuilt, the magnificent church which we now know and which contains some of the finest medieval stained glass anywhere. When the church was completed in 1218 William's relics were placed in a shrine behind the high altar following his canonization. This was commissioned by his great-niece, Mathilde de Courtenai, Countess of Nevers. The glass in the apse was installed shortly afterwards. It consists of three groups: the high windows of the choir feature prophets and apostles; the lower windows of the second ambulatory consist of a series of legends with the lives of the saints in the radiating chapels; while, in between, the first ambulatory windows are devoted to the holy bishops of Bourges, starting at the north with St Ursin and finishing with St William, the last of the seventeen bishops venerated as saints. Another of William's predecessors, Garin, had also come from Pontigny where he had been abbot from 1165 to 1174.

The image of William is contained within a pointed window. (33) He is nimbed, wears a chasuble with pallium over it and a mitre. He holds a crozier in his left hand, his right hand is raised in blessing. Below him is the kneeling figure of his great-niece identified by the inscription *Matildis Com.*

William was still remembered with pride at his old monastery of Chaalis. A fine pointed oval abbatial seal, known to have belonged to Abbot Gautier de Comte, who ruled from 1373 to 1379, shows as the central figure an abbot carrying a crozier and flanked by two smaller figures, that of a crowned Mary and Child on one side, and a mitred archbishop on the other.[49] We know that he

33 St William of Bourges.

is an archbishop because, instead of holding a crozier he carries a cross-staff, the iconographical attribute of an archbishop.[50] From the same atelier, and possibly from the same hand, comes a round conventual seal. Framed within a double arcade are an image of the Virgin and Child on one side and that of an archbishop, again mitred and carrying a cross-staff, on the other.[51] On this seal he is described by the initials *S G*, Saint Guillaume, the abbot's sainted predecessor from Bourges, the subject of both seals. William was also commemorated by a statue from 1515 on the west front of the cathedral by the sculptor Marsault Paule, but this was destroyed during the Wars of Religion.

FOLQUET OF MARSEILLE (*c.* 1155–1231)

In monastic parlance the word 'conversion' has the very specific meaning of entering religious life, seen as a transformation or turning around, in distinction to the more general connotation of the word as a change from a reckless to a righteous way of life. The entry of Folquet of Marseille to the Provençal abbey of Le Thoronet (Var) may be said to have encompassed both forms of conversion.

Born into a family of wealthy Genoese merchants Folquet (or Fulk) grew up in Marseille.[52] His reputation as a composer and performer of songs devoted to courtly love and crusading chivalry spread throughout southern France. As a troubadour he enjoyed the adulation showered upon him at many leading courts, including those of King Alphonsus II of Aragon, Count Raymond VI of Toulouse, William VIII of Montpellier and Richard I of England. His songs gradually took on a more religious tone, but all his poetic activity came to an end in about 1195 when he entered Le Thoronet. Although the active role he later played in the Albigensian crusade must have enhanced his reputation as the writer of troubadour lyric, he always showed great remorse whenever he was reminded of his past. He is said to have fasted on bread and water if he heard one of his songs performed.[53] As was quite normal at the time, the fact that he was married was no obstacle, as his wife became a Cistercian nun at the same time. Folquet was elected abbot in about 1201, and in 1205 he became bishop of Toulouse.

The Cistercians were the principal agents of the papacy in the promotion of and even active participation in the crusades to the Holy Land.[54] St Bernard had played an important part in the early stages, and Otto of Freising and Baldwin of Ford were among the many Cistercians associated with the movement. The role played by the Cistercians in combating the heterodox beliefs which were rapidly spreading in southern France is equally well documented, and again the original impetus was given by St Bernard.

A prominent part in the campaign against the Albigensians had already been played by the abbot of Clairvaux, Henry de Marcy, who in 1179 was appointed cardinal bishop of Albano and took charge of the mission,[55] and by St William's predecessor at Bourges, Garin, a former abbot of Pontigny.[56] In 1203 Peter of Castelnau, a monk of Fontfroide (Aude), was appointed legate, and Abbot Guy of Vaux-de-Cernay (Seine-et-Oise) also played an active part and later became bishop of Carcassonne. But the most famous of all was the abbot of Cîteaux, Arnold Amaury, a former abbot of the Catalonian monastery of Poblet and of Grandselve (Haute-Garonne), who was entrusted with the Albigensian mission in 1204. For it he enlisted the help of twelve Cistercian fellow abbots. He was rewarded with the archbishopric of Narbonne in 1212. He is perhaps best remembered for an alleged utterance which, unsurpassed in its sheer cold-blooded cruelty, found its way into Caesarius of Heisterbach's *Dialogue on Miracles* and has, not surprisingly, been retold *ad nauseam*. When consulted about the dilemma that arose after the capture of Béziers in 1209 when the crusaders found it impossible to distinguish heretics from others and therefore did not know whom to kill, Arnold is reputed to have said, 'Kill them all, the Lord knows them that are his', echoing the words of St Paul![57]

St Bernard had already described the leader of the heretics as 'a ravening wolf in the guise of a sheep', and, following a visit to the south of France, he remarked on the lamentable religious state there as 'Churches without people, people without priests, priests without the reverence due to them, and Christians without Christ'.[58] The Cistercian chronicler of the crusade, Peter of Vaux-de-Cernay, a nephew of Abbot Guy, was forced to admit that, in spite of their false teachings, the heretics by and large led more virtuous lives than many of those who professed to be Christians.[59] At Toulouse the bishop was deposed by the pope for having squandered the revenue of the church. As his successor, Folquet was faced with a church depleted of resources in a city at the very heart of the heresy and under the control of its leader, Count Raymond. The assassination of Peter of Castelnau in 1208 was followed by more than a decade of bloody war conducted against the Albigensians by Simon de Montfort under the spiritual leadership of Arnold Amaury and the group of Cistercian bishops including Folquet who, after Simon de Montfort took possession of Toulouse in 1215, was eventually able to exercise his ministry in his episcopal city. After the long war he brought in the Dominicans to help him, and, as a further measure in the eradication of heresy, he was also instrumental in establishing the university of Toulouse. The inaugural address was given by another former *trouvère* turned Cistercian, Hélinand, prior of Froidmont (Oise).[60] Folquet died in 1231 and was buried at the abbey of Grandselve near the tomb of a nobleman who had become a monk there, the grandfather of William VIII of Montpellier for whom Folquet had sung.

Folquet was the only troubadour to have found his way into Dante's *Divine Comedy* where, referred to as Folco, he is placed in Heaven (*Paradiso* 9). A number of his love songs and crusading lyrics have survived. They have the pride of place in a late thirteenth-century manuscript from northern Italy, probably from Padua, in which thirty-seven of the seventy-seven marginal images refer to him. In some of these he is depicted as the amorous troubadour offering his lady a gift or kneeling at her feet, in others his patrons are portrayed, but the one with which his songs open is a historiated initial containing a portrait of Folquet as bishop. (34) He is shown in liturgical vestments, mitred, and holding a crozier in his right hand across his body.

34 Folquet of Marseille.

POPE BENEDICT XII (*c.* 1285–1342)

Jacques Fournier was a native of the county of Foix in southern France. He became a monk at Boulbonne (Haute-Garonne) but then moved to Fontfroide (Aude) where his uncle was abbot. He was sent to Paris where he distinguished himself as a learned theologian before being elected abbot of Fontfroide. In 1317 he became bishop of Pamiers where he was noted as a skilful inquisitor, and in 1326 be moved to Mirepoix as bishop. The following year he was made a cardinal, and was often called the white cardinal because he kept his Cistercian habit. Finally, he was elected pope in 1334 and took the name Benedict XII, only the second and last Cistercian to have occupied the papal throne.[61]

His monastic and scholastic background, followed by a relatively short rule of two small remote dioceses, would not seem to have equipped him adequately for the highest office, but he was a superb administrator and turned out to be one of the great reforming popes. He set out to remove some of the worst ills that beset the church. He began with the curia in Avignon. He sent the many bishops and priests jockeying for positions at the curia back to their dioceses and parishes to look after the people entrusted to their care. He did away with the abuses of nepotism and the commendatory system, but he is perhaps best known for his reform of the religious orders, issuing a series of constitutions. He had already made an attempt at reforming his own Cistercians before being elected, but this had been thwarted by the abbot of Chaalis.[62] Once elected he naturally began with the Cistercians to whom he addressed the bull *Fulgens sicut stella* on 12 July 1335, less than a year after his election, and produced in consultation with the senior abbots of Cîteaux, La Ferté, Clairvaux and Morimond.[63] This was followed by similar constitutions for the Benedictines, Franciscans and Augustinians.

The opening words of the Cistercian constitution, also known as the *Benedictina* after its author – 'Shining through the mist like the morning star, the holy Cistercian Order fights in the Church militant by work and example' – diplomatically but erroneously suggest that all was well with the Order. But a look at the detailed provisions contained in its fifty-seven articles reveals a very different picture.[64] Benedict wisely judged that the proper administration of the monastic finances was a precondition for a more all-embracing and lasting reform, and the first part of the document is devoted to fiscal reorganization. Then follow provisions for the governance of the Order, for attendance at General Chapter and for regular visitation, for the observance of regulations on diet and clothing. Finally, and perhaps of the greatest importance, was the regulation of the studies of members of the Order which took up approximately a third of the constitution. To Benedict's mind the well-being of the Order depended on an improvement in the educational standard of monks. In a changing world the Cistercians no longer took a place at the centre of the stage but had to share the limelight with the newer orders, and the quality of education assumed a more important role. All monasteries of a certain size were required to send monks to the pope's old college, St Bernard's in Paris, which was to serve the whole Order, or to one of the regional houses of study at Oxford, Toulouse, Marseille, Salamanca, Bologna or Metz.

35 Pope Benedict XII.

The many references in subsequent General Chapter statutes to the topics covered by the *Benedictina*, and their frequent repetition, indicate that its provisions were by no means always or everywhere observed.[65] The traumas of the fourteenth century – wars, famine, pestilence and schism – all added to the forces of disintegration which affected society as a whole throughout Europe and from which the Cistercians were not immune. The inevitable weakening of ties between individual abbeys and their mother-houses and daughter-houses, and of the whole Order with Cîteaux, made the effective enforcement of Benedict XII's reforming regulations at times difficult and, across the frontiers of countries at war, impossible. His was, however, the only serious attempt at reform, and even if further decline could not be halted, the many later references to the constitution are evidence of its importance in providing a yardstick against which the spiritual health of the Order could be measured.

From the very beginning of his pontificate Benedict XII showed a keen interest in the restoration of St Peter's basilica, then in a serious state of decay. In fact, had he not acted, it is likely that it might not have been saved. His intervention was rewarded by placing a marble effigy of the pope below the entrance to the nave. (**35**) It was commissioned in 1341 by Pierre Laurent, the *Altararius* of St Peter's and a former canon of Arras who left behind an account of the restoration from which progress of the work may still be followed in great detail. More than a bust or half-figure, it shows Benedict from his thighs upwards. The inscription states that the pope renewed the roof of the basilica in 1341 and that the figure was made by Paul of Siena. Benedict is depicted wearing the double crowned papal tiara, which was later to develop into the triple crown. His right hand is raised in blessing and in his left hand he holds the keys of Peter, the symbol of his office. His face is full, even rather fat, and clean-shaven, corresponding to the description of his biographers. It was originally painted red and gold, and it was later moved to the crypt of the basilica.

GUILLAUME DE DEGULLEVILLE (*c.* 1295–*c.* 1360)

A native of Normandy, Guillaume de Degulleville was an almost exact contemporary of Benedict XII and may even have been a student in Paris at the same time. Unlike the future pope, however, he was not already a monk, but was professed at Chaalis (Oise), a daughter-house of Pontigny, shortly after his studies. He later served as prior there. He is best known for his allegorical poem in French, *The Pilgrimage of the Life of Man* (*Le Pèlerinage de la Vie Humaine*) written in 1330.[66] Although he is not widely known now, he was probably the most popular of all Cistercian writers in the later Middle Ages with the exception of St Bernard. The *Pèlerinage* was immensely influential and appeared in numerous recensions and translations into many foreign languages in the century after it was written.[67] The motif itself – that of the symbolic pilgrimage with the narrator as the pilgrim – was immensely popular throughout the fourteenth century and beyond. In addition to the *Pèlerinage*, other famous pilgrimage poems of the time, in which the figures of the poets were present in their work, include Dante's *Divine Comedy*, Langland's *Piers Plowman* and Chaucer's *Canterbury Tales*.[68] Chaucer is known to have used Degulleville in his *ABC*. The first three stanzas of this are a translation of Guillaume's *Prayer to a Virgin* written in 1330, each stanza beginning with one of the first three letters of the alphabet. John Bunyan is also thought to have been influenced by Degulleville in his *Pilgrim's Progress*.[69]

Guillaume's *Pèlerinage* takes the form of a dream in which the pilgrim is the Cistercian monk himself. He has as his guide a beautiful woman, Grace Dieu, who brings him to her house, the Church, to prepare him for the journey in which he encounters wild beasts representing the seven deadly sins. With these he grapples before reaching the ship which, through storm and mutiny, was to take him to Jerusalem. Just before reaching his destination he dies, at which point he is awakened by the bell summoning him to matins. In a later *Pèlerinage de l'Ame* (*Pilgrimage of the Soul*) which he composed in 1355–8 he travels to Purgatory, then enters Paradise, but a sudden burst of light from on high wakes him up.

The physical city of Jerusalem as a figure of the Celestial City, and the experience of pilgrims on their journey as a symbol of man's progress to salvation, were concepts that fired the imagination of men well acquainted with stories of earthly pilgrimages and crusades. The reader could identify with the physical experience and readily absorb the spiritual significance.

Although a monk, Guillaume is not generally regarded as a monastic writer. He was not writing primarily for a monastic audience, but the major themes he developed – those of the struggle between good and evil, and of life as a journey in which, through spiritual progress, the pilgrim reaches the heavenly Jerusalem – were deeply rooted in scriptural and monastic teaching. These were topics with which St Bernard was often preoccupied. For him the Cistercian life itself was an image of life in paradise – the *paradisus claustralis* – and superior to the earthly journey to Jerusalem. In a letter, Bernard described the decision of a young English canon to become a monk at Clairvaux when he interrupted his intended pilgrimage to the Holy Land as a 'short cut': 'He crossed "the vast ocean stretching wide on every hand" with a favourable wind in a very short time, and he has now cast anchor on the shores for which he was making. . . . He is no longer an inquisitive onlooker, but a devout inhabitant and an enrolled citizen of Jerusalem.'[70] Guillaume alludes to the problems which beset the Cistercian Order and which caused his contemporary Cistercian, Benedict XII, to initiate his reform programme. He condemned the avarice of many of its members. The pilgrim found the ship 'Religion' (the monastic order), storm-tossed by the winds of pride, in total ruin on account of the collapse of the commandments and observances which had held it together.[71]

One French manuscript of the *Pèlerinage* from *c*. 1390 contains an interesting and amusing pictorial commentary on the means whereby Benedictine monks and Franciscan friars reach their heavenly destination. St Benedict and St Francis are depicted side by side on the top of a high wall surrounding Jerusalem.[72] On the left St Benedict is welcoming a group of his sons to join him by helping them to climb up a long ladder leaning against the wall. On the right St Francis is

36 Guillaume de
Degullville.

being joined by his friars who reach him by the harder way of climbing up a
knotted rope, an allusion to the knotted cord of their habit. Sadly, there is no
record of how the Cistercians were to get to Jerusalem or of who would be there
to greet them! The manuscript was intended for a Benedictine monk of a noble
family, but it later belonged to the Duke of Burgundy, Philip the Good.[73]
Profusely illustrated, with 114 miniatures, it is the finest copy of all the
manuscripts of the *Pèlerinage* that have survived. One large miniature shows
Guillaume preaching to a crowned king, Charles VI of France (?), and a large

audience of disparate figures, some distracted by the royal presence while others are gazing up at the preacher who manages to hold their attention. (36) The scene is set in a magnificent vaulted chamber with Guillaume high up on a pulpit decorated with fleurs-de-lys. The faces of the figures are most expressive and original, so much so that it has been said that they would be at home in the works of Bosch or Bruegel.[74] Other images of Guillaume in the same manuscript include his vision of the Doctors of the Church teaching the people from the top of the ramparts of a city, his meeting with Grace Dieu, and, at the opening of the poem, lying asleep on a bed.[75] A similar picture is found in one of the many other manuscripts of his work in which Guillaume is featured, a French fourteenth-century manuscript. He is portrayed lying on a bed facing a mirror in which the wall and turrets of Jerusalem appear.[76] The same manuscript contains a picture of Guillaume kneeling before Mary and Child, and in yet another he is depicted with Satan as a fisher of souls.

The *Pèlerinage* was translated into English by John Lydgate, a Benedictine monk of Bury St Edmunds, a famous poet in his own right who in his lifetime and after his death was ranked among the greatest English poets, almost in the same class as Chaucer.[77] The frontispiece of one of his manuscripts consists of a full-page drawing in brown pen and ink.[78] It shows Guillaume tonsured and in his white Cistercian habit kneeling beside Lydgate who, also kneeling, is portrayed in a fleece coat with a pilgrim's hat, bag and staff. They are both kneeling before Lydgate's noble patron, the Earl of Salisbury, to whom he hands his translation of Guillaume's poem.

CHAPTER SIX

THE MONASTIC COMMUNITY

COWLED AND TONSURED

'. . . the apparel oft proclaims the man'

William Shakespeare

'For their name arose from the fact that, as angels might be, they were clothed in undyed wool spun and woven from the pure fleece of the sheep. So named and garbed and gathered like flocks of sea-gulls, they shine as they walk with the whiteness of snow.'

Walter Daniel[1]

The monk may be defined by his cowl and his tonsure. In a letter Aelred's biographer, Walter Daniel, says, 'I wear the habit of a monk, I am tonsured, I am cowled'.[2] Yet only one short statement in the early Cistercian texts refers to their clothing: Chapter 11 of the *Exordium Cistercii* entitled 'On Clothing' lays down that it 'shall be basic and inexpensive, without drawers, as the Rule prescribes . . .'[3]

The brevity of this directive and its avoidance of detail as regards the requirements of dress is totally consistent with Benedict's general guidelines in Chapter 55 of the Rule on 'The Clothes and Shoes of the Brethren'.[4] Here he enumerates rather than defines the monastic habit. It is to consist of two robes or tunics, two cowls (thick and woolly in winter, but thin or worn in summer), to allow for a change at night and for having these garments washed, one scapular for work, and shoes and stockings for the feet. Monks who were sent on a journey were to be issued with a habit of higher quality than normal and were also to be allowed the use of drawers. The only other stipulation was that their clothes should be inexpensive and that in cold districts they would need more clothing, and in warmer districts less.

The origin of what evolved as the western monastic habit goes back to Roman times and beyond.[5] The tunic was the standard Roman garment while the *cuculla* (cowl) was originally a simply sewn pointed headcover to act as protection

against the rain and the heat of the sun. It was worn by the poorest members of
society and especially by slaves. When attached to a garment covering the rest of
the body it became known as *vestis cum cuculla* (robe with cowl) which in time
became abbreviated to *cuculla* (cowl), in other words the cowl as later worn by
monks as well as by many others.

The scapular was a long piece of cloth slightly wider in the middle where there
was an opening for the head. Worn over the head it extended, front and back, to
below the knees. The extra width covered the shoulders, and it was fitted with a
hood. A belt, to which a knife was attached, was worn over the scapular and the
tunic. The scapular was worn for work as a protection for the tunic, very much
like an apron but narrower.

It has been argued that monastic and secular dress were originally the same
and that they only gradually evolved in different directions.[6] According to this
theory, the statement in Chapter 58 of the Rule that when the novice at his
reception is 'stripped of his own clothes which he is wearing and dressed in the
clothes of the monastery',[7] this does not refer to a change of style and colour of
dress. The significance of the act is symbolic in that the novice exchanges his
own (very likely more elegant) clothes for poor garments. From now on he will
wear the clothes he has been issued with rather than those he had himself
chosen and thus submit himself in obedience to the authority of the abbot. It
seems unlikely, however, even allowing for the fact that the monastic habit had
its origin in secular dress and for Benedict's scant regard for the minutiae of
regulations on dress, that symbolism alone formed the basis of the clothing of
novices which was a sacred rite celebrated in the oratory in the presence of all
and 'before God and his Saints'.[8] The habit was a sign of belonging to the
'house of God' at the same time as being a consecration to God in poverty and
humility.

In the course of the centuries a distinctive monastic habit had emerged and,
although the early Cistercians were not very explicit in their view of what this
should consist, they were clear as to what they found unacceptable in the
clothing of their monastic contemporaries. The fact that their only positive
statement on dress was couched in general terms, and that they avoided detailed
regulations, is all of a piece with what Benedict lays down on the subject, as well
as being in line with their desire to follow what 'the Rule prescribes'. But their
negative attitude to current monastic fashion (together with dietary regulations)
forms an important part in their conflict with the Cluniacs and is commented on
in all the important texts relating to the controversy – the clash between the new
and the old visions of the monastic life.

According to the *Exordium Parvum*

they rejected what was contrary to the Rule, namely capacious cowls with
wide sleeves (*frocci*) and furs, as well as shirts of fine linen, drawers and
ample hoods with capes (*caputia*) . . . and everything else which was against
the purity of the Rule. . . . In this way, having put off the old man, they
rejoiced in putting on the new.[9]

The *froccus* which the Cistercians rejected was the cowl which in the course of time had become very ample with long full sleeves and a copious hood, made of cloth of high quality. In the words of Bernard:

> Knight and monk today cut cloak and cowl from one bolt. There isn't a secular dignitary – no, not even the king, not the emperor himself – who would turn up his nose at our clothing, provided cut and style were adapted to his use. . . . Soft clothing is a sign of moral flabbiness.[10]

Another development had taken place: the cowl had been divided into two garments, the sleeved robe itself and the separate hood attached to a cape (*caputium*) covering the shoulders. It may be recognized by the distinctive horizontal line across the chest separating the two halves. The simple Cistercian cowl was a reaction against the opulence of the Cluniac model. It called for less cloth and was therefore cheaper to produce. The *Exordium Magnum* asserts that the motive for the change was the love of poverty.[11]

This uncompromising rejection of luxurious trappings found expression in St Bernard's famous letter to his nephew, Robert, who had abandoned the austerities of life at Clairvaux in favour of the easier life at Cluny.[12] In it Bernard asked:

> Does salvation rest rather in soft raiment and high living than in frugal fare and moderate clothing? If warm and comfortable furs, if fine and precious cloth, if long sleeves and ample hoods, if dainty coverlets and soft woollen shirts make a saint, why do I delay and not follow you at once? But these things are comforts for the weak, not the arms of fighting men. They who wear soft raiment are in king's houses.

Bernard says that Robert dreaded the clothes at Clairvaux as 'too cold in winter and too hot in summer'.[13] He devotes a whole chapter to the subject in his *Apologia: On Costly and Ostentatious Clothing*.[14] According to this,

> to-day's religious is less concerned with keeping out the cold than with cutting a good figure; so he is after refinement rather than serviceability, not the cheapest article, as the Rule prescribes, but the one that can be displayed to best advantage.

Referring to apostolic times he says, 'I do not think that they would have bothered overmuch with the quality, colour and style of their clothes', contrasting this with the current practice of matching the quality of a knight's attire.

The oldest picture of the primitive Cistercian cowl is of the monk prostrate at the feet of an angel, begging to be inscribed in the tablets of heaven held in the angel's left hand while his right hand is raised in blessing. (37) The main part of the initial *Q(uamvis)* at the beginning of Book 11 of Gregory's *Moralia* is ingeniously formed by the angel's body on the left and a wing on the right, while the tail consists of the prostrate monk. The same form of primitive cowl is featured in all other early pictures of Cistercian monks. Among them are two of St Bernard, one showing him writing and teaching, and the other just teaching. Both the saint and his disciples are shown in the early Cistercian cowl. In one of them, an early thirteenth-century pen and ink drawing, a tonsured and bearded Bernard is seen sitting in a chair with a high back against which his crozier is leaning. He is writing in a book placed on a lectern with his right hand and in his left hand he holds a knife.(colour plate 9) His two pupils, one of them with a book in his hands, are depicted very much smaller – a reflection of their relative status – and the hand appearing from a cloud indicates that his writing is inspired by God. The other is a late thirteenth-century historiated initial from an Italian manuscript which features Bernard, again bearded and tonsured, his right hand raised instructing two monks kneeling at his feet.[15] Unusually, in neither picture is St Bernard nimbed.[16] A late example of the same primitive style of cowl is from the far-flung Danish abbey of Sorø where a monk in a white cowl is featured in a wall painting on a pillar in the nave of the abbey church. (38) It dates from *c.* 1410–25 and is the only example of a Cistercian monk in what was a favourite form of church decoration in southern Scandinavia in the later Middle Ages.

38 Wall painting of Cistercian monk.

What emerges clearly from all this is the insistence of the Cistercians on poverty in dress. This is graphically borne out in the scenes of monks at work in Gregory's *Moralia* (*see* 45, 134 and **colour plate 24**). In all of these the sleeves and bottoms of both tunics and scapulars are frayed and worn, thus conforming to Bernard's dictum that he and his monks were clothed in 'rags and tatters', a claim which gave rise to Bernard being included among the wolf-monks in the satirical beast-epic, *Ysengrinus*, under the title of 'that rag-wearer from Clairvaux'.[17] Bernard says of his nephew, Robert, that when he left Clairvaux 'he was taken out of his rough, threadbare, and soiled habit', and also that he left his 'coarse habit for soft raiment'.[18] One of Bernard's novices, Peter de Roya, seeing the monks at work, referred in admiration to 'their uncared-for persons, their ill-arranged and common clothes'.[19]

Two curious anecdotes in the *Book of Miracles* by Herbert of Clairvaux reveal that small pieces of cloth were kept to patch up worn habits. At the same time they indicate the way in which daily life was circumscribed by petty regulations. The first tells of a monk who saw an unclean spirit in the form of an ape sitting on a perch near where his old and torn scapular was hanging. A small piece of cloth had recently been sewn in without permission, the effect of which was that the monk was vexed as the unclean spirit caressed the patch, frequently kissing it and even licking it with his tongue.[20] The other story is of a young monk who took a small piece of cloth in order to repair his robe and hid this secretly in his bed without permission. When he later tried to find it and failed, he was stricken in conscience and went to confession. Later, when he was

37 Monk (Stephen
Harding?) at the feet of an
angel.

washing in the kitchen, the small piece of cloth dropped down from the air and
fell into his hands.[21] In a poem written at the beginning of the thirteenth century
entitled *Of the White Order and the Black*, Matthew of Rievaulx lists among
the mortifications of the Cistercian life, 'the clothes which we wear are heavy
and cause us trouble'.[22]

Apart from simplicity and poverty the only other stipulation regarding
clothing was that the Cistercians dispense with the use of drawers, except when
travelling away from the monastery. Not surprisingly, this attracted the attention
of some contemporary commentators and fuelled the imagination of the satirists.
Sometimes the comment was good-humoured, not unlike the old jokes about
what the Scots wear under their kilts. The satirical poet, Nigel Wireker, a

Benedictine from Canterbury, in his *Mirror of Fools*, put this question into the mouth of his embarrassed Cistercian: 'What shall I do when the wind blows from the south and suddenly bares my posterior?'[23] In contrast, the arch-critic of the Cistercians, Walter Map, as a loyal monk of the old dispensation, defends the use of drawers as 'approved by every other order'.[24] He cannot resist the implied slur in the statement that drawers hide

> that which is better hid, 'tis Venus' privy seal, her barrier against publicity. A reason why the Cistercians do not use them was given me by some one, namely, to preserve coolness in that part of the body, lest sudden heats provoke unchastity.

He then tells an amusing tale of a white monk who, seeing the king (Henry II) come riding by accompanied by an abbot, fell in front of the king's horse just as a high wind blew his habit over his head 'so that the poor man was candidly exposed to the unwilling eyes of the lord king'. The king pretended not to have seen anything, but the abbot said, *sotto voce*, 'A curse on this bare-bottom piety'. Walter Map's own comment was that the poor monk 'would have got up again with more dignity had he had his breeches on'.

As part of the general relaxation of early austerity and one of the symptoms of the later decline, the Cistercian habit was to undergo a development similar to that which had taken place in pre-Cistercian days. The simple cowl was gradually replaced by a two-piece garment in the Cluniac style. It appears already to have been introduced at Beaulieu in England by the late thirteenth century. The Account Book dated *c.* 1270 lists both cowls and *caputia* (hoods with capes) as well as scapulars and cloaks (for novices and lay brothers).[25] It adds that the porter must distribute a quantity of these used garments to the poor on the feast of All Saints, an indication that they must have been in a usable condition and capable of being worn by the poor after the monks had discarded them.

At La Ferté the abbots buried in the chapter house up until 1387 are said to have been portrayed in the old cowl with hood attached while a grave from 1419 shows an abbot in the new style cowl with detachable hood and cape, indicating that the change must have occurred sometime between these two dates.[26] An earlier and less exaggerated version of this style is found in a historiated initial from the Polish abbey of Mogila from the second half of the fourteenth century.[27] In this neither the robe nor the sleeves are yet as capacious as they were later to become. A further development, yet more liberal in the cut of the cowl, with wider sleeves and again with the separate hood and cape, may be seen in numerous later medieval representations of monks, as for example in a manuscript from *c.* 1500 from the Belgian abbey of Baudeloo[28] (**39**). In an architectural setting a nimbed Bernard, open book in his left hand, crozier in the right, is surrounded by a kneeling abbot of Baudeloo also carrying a crozier. Behind the abbot are two monks, and on the other side four, all of them with their hands folded in prayer.

39 St Bernard with
disciples.

The style of cowl represented in these examples was almost universally
adopted from the fifteenth century onwards and remained the norm until the
French Revolution and the subsequent secularization in Germany, and it is still in
use in some houses of one of the two branches of the Cistercian Order, the
Common Observance.

There is no reference in the Rule to the colour of the monastic habit, and it
therefore comes as no surprise that there is no mention in the early Cistercian
texts of the change from the black, which had in the course of time been adopted
by the Benedictines, to white. Just as Benedict was indifferent to colour, so the
Cistercians were not preoccupied by the issue. To them it was not colour but cost
that mattered. The question was in fact first raised by writers outside the Order.

The earliest known reference to the adoption of white clothing by the Cistercians comes in a letter of Peter the Venerable, abbot of Cluny, to Bernard written in the early 1120s.[29] Trying to be tactful he says that 'there is no difference between the white and the black or any other flock. They are under the guidance of the same good shepherd and He has shown His concern for the flock of many colours.'[30] He perceives the difference in colour as being symbolic of the chasm between the two branches of the monastic family:

A different colour, diverse dwelling, dissimilar usages go to meet the beloved. They militate against unity. The white [monk] beholds the black and looks in wonder as if he were a monster. The black looks at the white in amazement as if he were an unfashioned freak.[31]

The change in the colour of the habit must have been effected soon after the foundation of Cîteaux, for the monk shown in the beautiful initial Q(uamvis) prostrate before an angel, from the *Moralia* manuscript completed by 1111, is quite clearly clothed in a white cowl (*see* 37).

According to legend the Cistercians owed the colour of their habit to the intervention of the Virgin who is said to have appeared to Alberic and miraculously changed the habit from black to white, in memory of which the Order celebrated the feast of the descent of Mary on 5 August.[32] In spite of the assertion by the seventeenth-century historian of the Order, Henriquez, that the miracle was described by 'many writers of great authority', there is no trace of the tradition in the early writers, and it appears to have its origin in the late fifteenth century.[33]

Writing in 1135 Ordericus Vitalis says of the Cistercian habit that they 'dispense with breeches and lambskins . . . and wear no dyed garments', and that

they specially favour white in their habit and thereby seem remarkable and conspicuous to others. Black represents humility in many places in Holy Scripture; therefore up to now monks in their devotion have chosen to wear that colour.[34]

Writing a little later Philip of Harvengt repeated that the Cistercians did not use dyed wool to make their garments,[35] and Walter Map repeated it again:

The white monks wear the woven wool just as the sheep did, innocent of dye, and though they taunt the black monks for their lambskins, they themselves were provided in equally good measure with numbers of comfortable habits, such as would become costly scarlet for the delight of kings and princes if they were not snatched from the dyers' hands.[36]

Before entering Rievaulx Aelred had heard tell of

> wonderful men, famous adepts in the religious life, white monks by name
> and white also in vesture. For their name arose from the fact that, as the
> angels might be, they were clothed in undyed wool spun and woven from
> the pure fleece of the sheep.[37]

The reason for the change was purely economic. Undyed wool was cheaper and
facilitated the manufacture of the habits in the monastery. The use of dyed wool
was specifically prohibited by the General Chapter in 1181 in these words: 'Dyed
and modish wools are utterly excluded from our Order.'[38] Ideally each monastery
would keep sheep, spin the yarn and weave the cloth, finish it and make the
garments.[39] In this way their desire for self-sufficiency would be fulfilled and the
brethren supplied with cheap garments made of ordinary materials.

As sheep and wool come in many shades, ranging from a natural white to a
creamy yellow, pale brown or grey to a reddish brown or darkish brown, so
garments made of undyed and unbleached cloth took on a wide spectrum of
colour from near-white to a dark brown. Ordericus Vitalis recognized that their
garments were not always white when he said that the Cistercians are 'clothed in
white or other distinctive habits'.[40] The ambiguity of colour was confirmed by
Benedict XII in 1335 in his Constitution *Fulgens sicut stella* which prescribed
white or brown as the colour of the habit.[41] There are many monks depicted
wearing grey or brown habits. They include all the pictures of monks at work in
the early Cîteaux *Moralia* manuscripts including the famous one of the monk at
the bottom of the large initial *I(ntellectus)* which forms the very lifelike tree
which he is in the process of felling (*see* 45). He is wearing a brown tunic with a
lighter brown scapular and a belt.[42] Examples of a darker brown may be seen in
the pictures of Caesarius of Heisterbach (*see* 47 and 48) and of the scribe from
the Kamp Bible of 1312 (*see* **colour plate 25**), while Aelred is portrayed in a very
dark brown, almost black, cowl (*see* 30). Grey is represented in the picture of
Gisilbertus from Eberbach (*see* **colour plate 22**) and its use is even more
widespread in the habits of Cistercian nuns.

Not surprisingly the Cistercians were sometimes known as 'grey monks', a
description more accurate than the more frequently used 'white monks' with its
detergent whiter-than-white connotations! It occurs in the twelfth-century text
Dialogue between a Cluniac and a Cistercian used by the Cluniac in accusing the
Cistercians: 'the grey monks are always on the move.'[43] The conflict between the
Benedictines in Schleswig and the Cistercians of Guldholm (*Aurea Insula*) in
Denmark, which led to physical violence, is graphically described in a classic
example of the Benedictine/Cistercian polemic: 'The black rise up against the
grey, monks against monks.'[44]

The symbolism of the contrast between the 'white monks' and the 'black'
provided the Cistercians with a useful weapon in their controversies; the
Cistercians came to use the colour to represent the light of reform and virtue in
contrast with the powers of darkness and decay. The difference in colour was

40 St Bernard with his
monks at Clairvaux.

seized upon by both sides in their polemics. To Peter the Venerable black
represented humility and the Cistercians' choice of white was an example of
haughtiness, while blackness to Bernard was a figure of sin and moral depravity.
In the *Dialogue between a Cluniac and a Cistercian* the Cistercian asserts that
the monk's life can be compared to that of an angel and that it is therefore fitting
that they should wear white. He adds that there is another sacred symbol in their

cowl, namely that it is their cross, 'a terrible sign to the powers of darkness'.[45] The symbolism of colour was acknowledged in subsequent statutes of the General Chapter. In 1312 it was said that the 'white habit has been adopted by the first fathers . . . it represents the contemplative life and interior purity', and this was repeated, almost verbatim, in 1350.[46]

Whereas the Cistercians changed the colour of the tunic and the cowl, they retained the darker scapular. At first this was normally brown, as may be seen in the early Cîteaux illuminations, but eventually it became universally black and remains so to this day. Cistercians are normally portrayed in medieval art wearing the cowl, and representations of them in white tunics and black scapulars are rare until the late Middle Ages. As one would expect, they are usually featured in scenes of monks at work, such as harvesting at Clairvaux and Zwettl (*see* 136 and 135) or building their monasteries, as at Maulbronn (*see* 148). An exception is the famous picture by Jean Fouquet in the *Hours of Etienne Chevalier* from the second half of the fifteenth century of St Bernard instructing his monks (*see* 50). One would have expected them to have been wearing their cowls in this scene, as Cistercians did in church and chapter and at meals, but they are shown in white tunics and black scapulars. The reason may be that the artist as a secular was unacquainted with Cistercian practice. A wonderfully inaccurate and idealized miniature in the fifteenth-century Burgundy Chronicle, which portrays the entry of St Bernard and his companions to Clairvaux on 15 June 1115, provides us with another example. (**40**) Behind a nimbed Bernard carrying a golden crozier and an absurdly large group of monks, all in white tunics and black scapulars, is an enormous edifice, reminiscent more of the church that was finally built there, or, with its four huge towers, perhaps even more of the sumptuous church at Cluny, than the modest wooden buildings that would have been there upon their arrival.[47] The scapular is seen to have undergone a similar development as the cowl. It is longer than in earlier days and now consists of two garments: the longer scapular itself and the hood and cape covering the shoulders.

Polonius may have been right when he asserts that 'the apparel oft proclaims the man', but a proverb nevertheless emerged among the monks to the effect that 'the habit does not make a monk'.[48] This accords with St Benedict's choice of image in the first chapter of the Rule in describing those monks whose actions conform to the standards of the world. For Benedict it is their tonsure which above all else distinguishes monks from all other men and makes worldly monks 'liars before God'.[49]

The point is pithily and humorously made in an early fourteenth-century carving of a small naked monk on a capital in the cloister of Maulbronn in Württemberg. (**41**) To us this may seem to be a flippant way of treating the subject, but to medieval man, for whom the dividing line between the sacred and the profane was not as sharply drawn, it would have appeared quite natural. In a lighthearted and amusing comment on monastic life the sculptor has chosen to show the monk sitting on a bunch of grapes while helping himself to a grape

41 Carving of a naked monk.

from another bunch, the only feature indicating his holy state being the unmistakable tonsure.

The tonsure is the cutting or shaving of hair after a particular fashion as a sign of belonging to the service of God. The loss of hair signifies an act of deprivation and renunciation; it is the symbol of a penitential life, a form of consecration. The earliest form probably only consisted of a close shave all over and although it was monastic in its origin, it was gradually extended to the rest of the clerical order. The Cistercian in the *Dialogue between a Cluniac and a Cistercian* made the point that monks also belonged to the clerical order when he said, 'all tonsured monks are clerics'.[50]

42 Carving of a monk's head, Tilty.

The monastic tonsure was also known as the monastic crown or *corona* as it represented Christ's crown of thorns or His royal priesthood. It consisted of a narrow horizontal band of hair approximately one inch wide, thus forming a circle around the head above the ears with the rest of the head shaven. This form of tonsure may be seen in a great number of examples, and its presence provides us with the clearest and safest evidence of the identity of monks as opposed to both laymen and lay brothers. It is the one seen in most portrayals of monks, as for example in most of the foregoing illustrations and in the earliest Cîteaux representations. Often the tonsure is the only feature which allows us to identify a figure as a monk. One of many examples of this is a crudely sculpted head of a monk on a corbel on the side of the sedilia in the fourteenth-century gatehouse chapel (*capella ad portas*) at Tilty in Essex – virtually all that remains of this little known Cistercian monastery. (**42**) Another is a carving of a head on each end of a red sandstone block from Holmcultram in Cumbria. (**43**) It dates from the turn of the sixteenth century, and has the inscription, 'Chamber erected this building, and covered it with lead'.[51] The actual building referred to is not known, but Abbot Robert Chamber is known to have built the porch to the church in 1507.

There is, however, also another form of tonsure, the use of which was widespread in the twelfth and thirteenth centuries but may also be seen in later examples. This consisted of shaving a large circular area at the top of the head but leaving the hair unevenly longish at the back and above the temples, and cannot therefore be described as a true crown. It already occurs in one of the early Cîteaux pictures, the one depicting two monks folding linen forming the initial *M*, and in the picture of Stephen Harding offering the church of Cîteaux to Mary (*see* **colour plate 5**). All monks featured in the twelfth and thirteenth-century manuscripts from Heiligenkreuz, Zwettl, Rein and Sittich, and all those depicted on Hugh of Fouilloy's *Wheels of True and False Religion*, belong to this type.[52] One of the examples from Heiligenkreuz is contained in an initial *M* in a Psalter from the first quarter of the thirteenth century. (**44**) Two monks with this form of tonsure, one of them bearded, are shown kneeling at the feet of St Peter and St Paul with Christ in the middle, His right hand raised in blessing. A later example of this type of tonsure is the monk from the Danish abbey of Sorø (see **38**).

43 Carving of a monk's head, Holmcultram.

44 Historiated initial from a
psalter.

PROFESSED AND CLOISTERED

*'When a whole year had passed by in the cell where the tyros of Christ are
proven, he [St Aelred of Rievaulx] made formal profession, written by his
own hand, to his vow before the altar in the church in the presence of all,
as the blessed Benedict commands. There he is vested in the sacred robe,
that is the habit sanctified by the Abbot's blessing, and henceforth is
regarded as a member of the monastic body.'*

Walter Daniel[53]

*'He who is in the world let him flee to the cloister there to conduct his
business, and he who is in the cloister let him not be idle or waste his time
through despondency as the lazy and good for nothing servant.'*

St Bernard[54]

In his chapter on 'The Order for the Reception of Brethren', St Benedict
insists that only those who are persistent in their attempts to enter a
monastery be admitted and that they should spend four days in the guest-
house before being taken to the chapter house.[55] Here the candidate would be
asked by the abbot what he wanted, to which he replied 'God's mercy and
yours'.[56] The abbot would then point out the severity of the Rule following
which the candidate was expected freely to consent to keeping it all. After the
ceremony had been repeated three times he was taken to the novitiate – the
cella novitiorum – which was normally situated at the south end of the east
range, there to spend his year of probation.[57] Here the novices slept, ate, and
studied.

At first novices continued to wear their secular clothing and had no special
habit. This accords with the Rule which states that only at profession is the
novice 'stripped of his own clothes which he is wearing'.[58] Evidence that this still
applied in St Bernard's lifetime is given in the letter he wrote to his nephew,
Robert:

You were tried in all patience for a year according to the Rule, living
perseveringly and without complaint. After the year had passed you, of
your own free will, made your profession and then, for the first time,
you put off the attire of the world and were clothed in the habit of
Religion.[59]

Further evidence that novices did not at first have their own habit is contained in
the famous picture in the Cîteaux *Moralia* manuscript of the large initial
I(ntellectus) representing a tree which is in the process of being felled. (45) At the
bottom of the tree is a tonsured monk wearing a very threadbare tunic and
scapular in two shades of brown. He is vigorously attacking the trunk with an
axe. The lighter but more dangerous work of lopping branches at the top of
the tree is performed by a young man with long neat hair and wearing an

elegant bright red tunic and immaculate shoes.[60] He is too well-dressed to be one of the hired labourers whom the Cistercians employed from the earliest days, and is undoubtedly a young nobleman and therefore the earliest representation of a Cistercian novice.

The novices were expected to perform the same manual labour as the monks. Much of the hard work in the fields and in the forests or on buildings would have been unfamiliar to many of the young men of noble birth who entered in the early days. St Bernard knew what it was like not to have the skill or strength to play his part at harvest time. He was ordered to rest, but he was reduced to tears at the thought that he was not able to contribute his fair share of the work. He fell on his knees, his prayers were answered and, we are told, he became a very good harvester (*see* 135 and 136).[61] Bernard was said never to spare himself any hardship as a novice, and his already frail health soon deteriorated. In later years his advice to those who were impatient to enter the monastery was:

> If you are in a hurry to come to what lies within, before you enter you must leave outside the bodies which you have brought from the world, for only hearts and minds may come in, since the flesh will not help you.[62]

45 Monk and novice felling a tree.

From the second half of the twelfth century, that is from the earliest known redaction of the *Ecclesiastica Officia* in which Cistercian daily life was regulated in the minutest detail, novices were required to wear 'the same habit as the monks except for what is the special monastic item', in other words excepting the cowl.[63] This meant the same tunic and scapular, but instead of the cowl they had a sleeveless mantle with hood or pelisse (*cappam et mantellam vel pelles habeat*). No colour is specified and there is no mention of a ceremony of blessing such as was provided for in the post-medieval clothing ceremony,[64] but the tunic

Singrellus seruus dei | bernardus ásteram ali quiđ uemillet šper in | corde· et· in· ore· habebat· folitus ni· ᵥ·ᵥ erat·
nouimus rôndie pro | amma tuis fue šepē plalmos dire quos ai | die· quadâ· poſt· ðpleroĩ· ichoans ſᵨdiſſe· ab·
abbate steplō dm | hᵇᵉlꝰ ralbiut pradanlque aĩ pedes tuis | et· neḡligentiam· rõufitens· uemam poꝛtulauit·

46 St Bernard reprimanded
by St Stephen Harding.

and mantle were normally the same as that of the monks, that is white. Just as
the monastic cowl with hood attached was later replaced by two separate
garments, the mantle with hood worn by novices became a detachable hood and
cape and a separate mantle. This development may be seen in the glass panel
from St Apern in Cologne which shows St Bernard as a novice being
reprimanded by his abbot, Stephen Harding, for neglecting his prayers. (46) He
is shown together with six other novices, all of them wearing the mantle with
detachable hood and cape while the abbot is depicted in a cowl, also with
separate hood and cape.

The novices were placed in the care of the novice master who was responsible
for their formation. The importance attached to this office may be seen from the
fact that he is mentioned in the list of the monastery's officers in the *Ecclesiastica
Officia* immediately after the abbot, the prior and the sub-prior. A chapter

entitled 'Concerning the Novice Master' outlines his duties.[65] As with all
teaching, its quality determined that of its outcome; the choice of novice master
was all-important as is testified by the high point that was reached when Aelred
of Rievaulx was appointed by his abbot:

> It was then that the lord William put him in charge of the novices, to make
> them worthy vessels of God and acceptable to the Order and even examples
> of perfection to those who truly yearn to excel as patterns of goodness. This
> he did and made good monks of them; some are still alive to testify, as
> much by the sweetness of their character as by the living voice to his
> praiseworthy industry. Their manner of life is such that they seem to bear
> blossoms more dazzling white than the white flowers about them and reveal
> a yet greater loveliness of incomparable grace.[66]

One of the best-known masters of novices was Caesarius of Heisterbach who in
the first quarter of the thirteenth century wrote the Dialogue on Miracles – the
Dialogus Miraculorum – so called because it takes the form of a dialogue
between him and a novice, although it is in fact more of a monologue with the
novice acting as little more than a foil to Caesarius. It is a collection of 746
popular *exempla* or short stories based on a living oral tradition, drawn from a
wide area and largely, though not exclusively, of monastic content.[67] Their
purpose was to extol the beauty of virtues and castigate the abomination of
vices, and his audience was the novices entrusted to his care and those of other
Cistercian houses that were acquainted with his work.

One of these was the abbey of Altenberg in the Rhineland which owned a
manuscript of his work copied out in the early fourteenth century and containing
the only known two portraits of Caesarius. Within the initial C*(olligite
fragmenta)* from the Prologue of the *Dialogue on Miracles*, a tonsured Caesarius
in a dark brown habit sits at a desk with an open book (probably the Rule) in
front of him to which he is pointing. Sitting at his feet is a small figure in a white
habit whom Caesarius is teaching. (**47**) In the other picture, from the beginning
of the first chapter in which he records the foundation of the Cistercian Order,
Caesarius is seen – also contained within an initial C*(upiens)* – kneeling with his
hands folded in prayer, beseeching to be granted the grace to undertake his work.
His gaze is directed upwards to a cross-nimbed and bearded head of Christ
looking down at him. (**48**)

Caesarius knew the power of good stories and the importance of retaining the
attention of his audience. He tells of how his own abbot had to endure the
monks falling asleep during his sermons in the chapter house. He discovered the
remedy by beginning a tale with the words 'there was once a king named Alfred',
realizing to his chagrin the greater impact of a secular story against the soporific
effect of his usual sermonizing.[68]

Novices feature in a number of Caesarius's stories. One tells of a vagabond
whose motive in entering Clairvaux was to steal the treasury of the church.[69]
Having failed, he proceeded to profession thinking that he would have easier

47 Caesarius of
Heisterbach as master of
novices.

48 Caesarius of
Heisterbach kneeling
before Christ.

access to the chalices, but in the course of time he repented and eventually rose
to become prior.

Exemplum stories were designed to engender in the novices a strong sense of
Cistercian identity, and a favourite theme was the privileged position of the
Cistercian Order. Caesarius tells of how he had heard from a Benedictine abbot
that one of his monks who had died had appeared to two confrères and told
them about the Cistercians in heaven that 'their reward is greatest and they shine
as the sun in the realm of the sky'.[70] We find a similar stress on reputation in
stories about the temptation of novices to leave the Order in other *exempla*
collections. In the Book of Visions and Miracles compiled under Prior John of
Clairvaux (1171–79) a novice is tempted to return to his former life as a secular
canon but is persuaded to stay by his master. One night he had a vision that at
the Last Judgment the Cistercians were to be given pride of place in heaven but
that when he tried to join them he was prevented by a branch of a tree in which
his feet had got entangled.[71] Another version appears in a collection from
Beaupré: a novice is again tempted to leave his community but changes his mind
when he discovers the exalted place of the Cistercians in heaven. This time he is
kept away by a host of angels who tell him that he is not one of them. Another
Beaupré story tells of a novice who is sent home to try to overcome his father's
opposition to his becoming a monk.[72] There are two devils sitting on the top of
the local church, but when he returns to the monastery he finds to his horror that
it is surrounded by a swarm of devils. At this he takes fright and returns home,
but when the abbot explains to him that all the troops were needed to besiege a
powerful fortress, he understands and returns to the monastery.

These examples of the Cistercian sense of superiority were typical of the early
days of the Order. The spiritual power of the Cistercians is a theme that recurs
frequently in their early literature. It sometimes reached pathological heights; the
most extreme of all was the assertion by Conrad of Eberbach that even Judas could
have been saved had he joined the Order and come to Clairvaux.[73] Another example
is found in the extravagant claim by Gilbert of Hoyland that 'it is better to be a
weak monk than a secular who is doing good'![74] This display of an unshakable faith
in the rightness of their cause goes a long way to explain their early success in
recruitment which was responsible for the meteoric growth of the Order.[75] In the
same way later attacks of self-doubt reflect the declining fortunes of the Order.

After a year in the novitiate came the solemn profession. The novice was called
into the chapter house where, in the presence of the entire community, he
disposed of his worldly possessions. Following this he received the tonsure from
the abbot and his hair was burnt by the sacristan in a piscina used for this
purpose.[76] Proceeding to the church for Mass the novice made the three monastic
vows of stability, conversion of life and obedience.[77] This took the form of a
written petition in his own hand if he could write, or written for him to which he
affixed his mark, and which he then placed on the altar. On his knees the novice
implored pardon repeating three times: 'Support me as you have promised, and I
shall live, do not disappoint me of my hope.' (Ps. 118:116) He then prostrated
himself at the abbot's feet and afterwards at all those present, asking them to

omo s bnarbe jefe refofirare uno ome chi rra morto

umus Bernar ... o ... glournali

49 Profession of novices by St Bernard.

pray for him. The abbot then blessed the cowl, sprinkling it with holy water, removed the novice's secular clothes and replaced them with the monastic dress. The novice was now a full member of the community and took his place in the choir. The Creed was said and the Mass continued.

In an Italian retable of an altar of St Bernard from *c.* 1430, the central figure of the saint is flanked by three scenes from his life on each side. One of these shows him receiving the cowl at the hands of Stephen Harding.[78] He is already wearing the tunic and scapular which he had worn as a novice, and he is now having the cowl placed over his head. One of nine scenes from his life in an Italian fresco from the second half of the fifteenth century shows St Bernard, nimbed and tonsured and with a long beard, clearly placing the hood and cape part of the cowl over the head of a kneeling novice who has already been invested with the other part of the garment. (**49**) Bernard is assisted by a monk who holds an open book while another monk is helping the next novice out of his secular clothes and a third novice waits his turn. The three young men may represent the three Paris students who entered Clairvaux after a sermon Bernard preached at the invitation of the bishop of Senlis.[79]

Having left the novitiate, the newly professed monk now shared all the other buildings which were basic to the monastic life and which were all directly accessible from the cloister. The innermost *claustrum* – literally a lock or a bolt, a door that shuts up a place – was the exclusive preserve of the monks. Normally situated south of the church, it consisted of four ranges arranged in a square or near-square around an open garth.[80] They were connected by covered and arcaded ambulatories supported by columns, often arranged in pairs.

If the church was the heart of the monastery, the cloister formed the main artery which gave access to all the other essential buildings. They are listed in clockwise sequence in the *Ecclesiastica Officia* in connection with the route the Sunday procession of their blessing with water should take after leaving the church: chapter house, parlour, dormitory, latrines, warming room, refectory, kitchen and cellar.[81] In addition to acting as a first-class circulation system the cloister also provided the monastery with a generous well-lit workspace where the monks could read and study, and perform a multitude of tasks.

In his Rule St Benedict enumerated what he describes as 'the tools of the spiritual craft' and he goes on to say, 'Now the workshop where we shall diligently execute all these tasks, is the enclosure of the monastery'.[82] The cloister was an ideal space for spiritual meditation. It was frequently referred to as 'paradise' (*paradisus claustralis*), an earthly Jerusalem in which the monk had a foretaste of his ultimate destiny. Thus Bernard referred to it as 'truly a paradise, a city surrounded and defended with a wall of discipline, containing a boundless superabundance of most precious commodities'.[83] The contrast between the serenity of the cloister and the dark world outside was a topic that had long been dear to monastic writers. According to Peter of Celle 'the cloister lies on the border of angelic purity and earthly contamination'.[84] Union with God in prayer in the cloister is infinitely preferable to the cares of this life. The almost magnetic attraction of the cloister was alluded to by Matthew of Rievaulx when he said that 'work draws us outside, the reins of the cloister pull us back'.[85]

The other image is that of the 'garden of delights' – the *hortus deliciarum* – which is associated with Mary, the garden enclosed; with Christ, the flower of the precious garden; and is closely related to the topos of Ecclesia in the Song of Songs.[86] The garden is also where the creative and redemptive power of God – the sowing, germination and fruition – is enacted. In a fit of hyperbole Conrad of Eberbach combines the two images when describing the cloister as 'the garden of delights as well as the paradise of the Lord'.[87]

The east range contained the sacristy, *armarium* (book cupboard or book room), chapter house, parlour and monks' day room on the ground floor, with the dormitory occupying the full length of the floor above. Next to the church the most important room in a monastery was the chapter house. Helinand of Froidmont eulogized it in these words:

> No place is holier than the chapter house, no place more worthy of reverence, no place more remote from the devil, no place nearer to God. For there the devil loses all that he might gain elsewhere, and there God regains in obedience whatever he might lose elsewhere through negligence or contempt.[88]

50 St Bernard in the
Chapter House.

The community met in the chapter house daily after Mass, the abbot
presiding. The monks sat in order of seniority, based on their date of profession,
on wooden or stone benches ranged along the wall facing the entrance and the
two side walls. A chapter of the Rule of St Benedict was read and commented
upon from which the room took its name. On certain days the abbot gave a
sermon. This was followed by business matters and the distribution of tasks, and
it concluded with the public confession and imposition of penances. The election
of abbot and the nomination of officers also took place in the chapter house.

The chapter house was an imposing vaulted chamber, the vaults resting on anything from one to six columns depending on the size of the house and the number of monks to be accommodated.[89] In the picture by Jean Fouquet of St Bernard preaching to his monks the chapter house at Clairvaux is shown with six vaults supported by two columns. (50) It is one of a series of illustrations which is considered among the masterpieces of fifteenth-century painting by a master who had been greatly inspired by his visit to Italy. Bernard is seen standing at a lectern, listing the points on his fingers in what may be one of his sermons on the Song of Songs. The monks are listening to him with varying degrees of attention, some expressing their agreement by raising their hands, others listening carefully while holding their hands or folding their arms, while one or two appear relatively disinterested. Another chapter house scene has Bernard seated on a massive chair addressing a group of ten monks, sitting on benches with five on each side. (51) It is from one of the early sixteenth-century glass panels from Altenberg. Bernard is nimbed, carries a crozier in his right hand and has a book on his lap. He is shown preaching his third sermon on the feast of St Peter and St Paul.[90] The power of his message is expressed by his seat floating above the floor, held up by two small angels dressed in red and blue respectively. The lower part of their garments protrude in front of the abbot's chair and trail along the floor which is covered in typically Cistercian patterned tiles. Bernard and his monks are tonsured and, more correctly than in the Jean Fouquet picture, are wearing white cowls.

As was only fitting the founding abbots of Cîteaux, Alberic and Stephen Harding, were buried in a key position, at the junction of the north and east

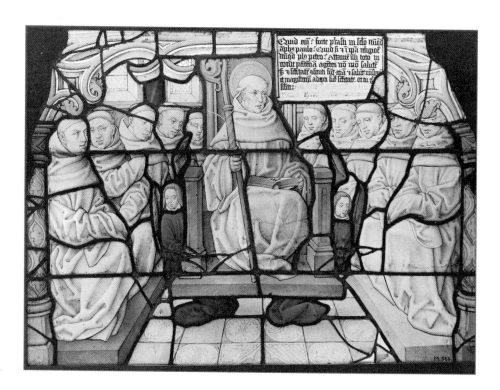

51 St Bernard preaches to the convent.

cloister galleries next to and at right angles to the door into the church. Their tombs were set in a twin niche containing an altar upon which the cloister lamp was placed and above which was an image of Our Lady of Cîteaux. Opposite it, years later, was laid the erudite and saintly lay brother, Alan of Lille. This place of honour was chosen as a constant reminder to the monks of their holy forebears whose remains they passed on their way in and out of the choir at the time of the offices. The example was followed at Preuilly, founded in 1118 as the fifth daughter-house of Cîteaux. There the first abbot, Artaud, was buried in the same position, as were the first three abbots at the German abbey of Eberbach.[91]

In other abbeys a smaller niche containing the cloister lamp was often located in the same position, between the *armarium* and the door into the church. Its light enabled the monks to select their books and helped them to find their way to their stalls. Such a niche originally existed at Villers in Brabant, but it was later removed to give way to a still deeper niche to contain the remains, not of a founder or principal benefactor or even of an abbot, but of one of its illustrious sons, Gobert of Aspremont, a simple monk who was never even ordained. (52) He was a nobleman born in 1187, who after a long military career entered the novitiate at Villers in middle age. Here he never held a position of responsibility and, in order to emphasize his humility, the author of his *Life* recounts that 'he was not skilled in the Latin idiom and did not have the mind of a cleric'.[92] He died in 1263, after which a marble effigy was erected within a niche surmounted by a large rose window into the south transept of the church and contained

52 Tomb of Blessed Gobert d'Aspremont.

within a high Gothic arch. The figure of Gobert, tonsured and wearing a cowl, lies under a trifoliate canopy with his hands folded and his feet resting on a lion. He was counted as one of the saints of the Order. It was said that in the seventeenth century the monks still bowed their heads in reverence whenever they passed.[93] The effigy was reconstituted in 1929 by a direct descendent of Gobert, from numerous fragments which had been preserved in the stone store in the former monastic brewery.

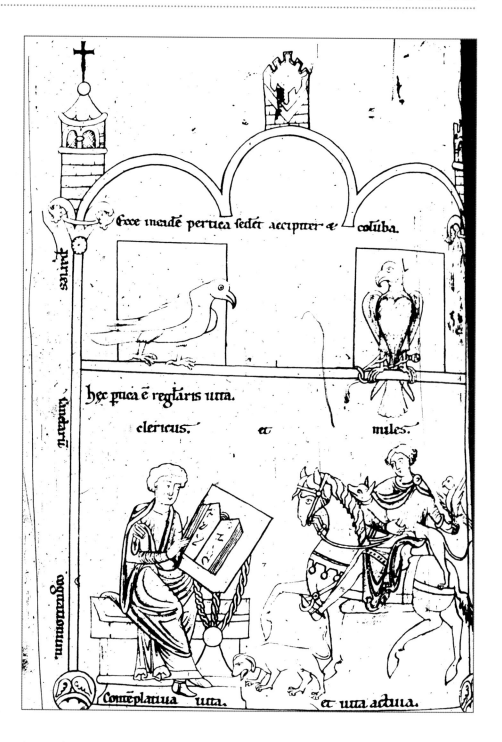

53 The contemplative and the active life.

Monks were normally buried in the cemetery north of the church and it was most unusual for their graves to be within the church or monastic buildings. Yet, although Gobert's monument was exceptional, it was not unique. At Longpont the remains of the almost contemporary Jean de Montmirail were transferred to the church where a magnificent mausoleum was constructed.[94] The monument consisted of two effigies which at ground level shows him as an armed knight and above this, on a stone table, in the Cistercian habit.

This double effigy is evidence of the strong tradition of Cistercian recruitment from among the military classes. This also found expression in frequent references to the contrast between the service performed by the knight in the world and the monks' service of Christ in the cloister.[95] It gave rise to the commonly articulated idea of the monk as the soldier of Christ – *miles Christi* – an idea found in the Rule in several places, most notably in the Prologue that speaks of the 'fight for the true King, Christ' with 'the strong and glorious weapons of obedience'. It was a notion readily understood by Cistercian recruits.

The contrast between these two services is conveyed graphically and with great clarity in a full-page miniature in red, black and brown ink at the opening of Hugh of Fouilloy's *Aviary*, one of his allegorical treatises. (53) In a manuscript from the first half of the thirteenth century from the Austrian abbey of Heiligenkreuz a seated monk, representing the contemplative life (*vita contemplativa*), is juxtaposed to a soldier on horseback representing the active life (*vita activa*). While the monk reads from a book placed on a lectern, the soldier holds a falcon in one hand and has one hound with him on the horse and another on the ground. Above the monk a dove sits on a perch described as 'the perch of regular life' and above the knight is a falcon. They are portrayed within a frame the sides of which are referred to as 'a wall of holy thoughts' and 'a wall of good deeds' surmounted by a church tower with a cross on the monk's side and a castellated turret with another falcon on the knight's side.

The north gallery of the cloister adjacent to the church was also known as the collation gallery, so called because here the community met daily between Vespers and Compline to listen to the *Collationes* of St John Cassian (d. 435) or a reading from one of the other Desert Fathers.[96] The procedure was laid down in the *Ecclesiastica Officia*, and the light meal that followed took its name from this gathering.[97] In a number of abbeys a stone bench along the wall to the church, and sometimes along both sides, provided seating for the monks. Such benches are found, for example, at Le Thoronet, La Clarté Dieu, Theuley, Fossanova and Santes Creus.[98] The most elaborate of all, however, occurs at Cadouin (Dordogne) where the north, east and south cloister galleries were rebuilt in two phases under Abbot Peter de Gaing (1455–75) and his nephew of the same name (1475–1504) and embellished by the same sculptors who had worked on the cloister of Cahors Cathedral. In the middle of the stone seating is an impressive abbot's throne surmounted by the abbey's arms. Facing this on the other side of the gallery is the reader's stone seat. Above and to the left of the throne is a carving of a kneeling abbot with a crozier, his hands folded in prayer. He is followed by five other monks, also kneeling and issuing from a doorway in a turret. (54) The abbot can be identified as Peter de Gaing by the arms at his feet. This part of the cloister was rebuilt under him in 1468.

54 Abbot of Cadouin and his monks.

The cloister gallery opposite the collation walk – usually the south gallery – contained the refectory whose size and architectural loftiness indicated its importance in the daily life of the monastery. Cistercian refectories were often at right angles to the cloister, thus overcoming the limitation of space imposed by refectories running parallel to it and enabling large communities to be

55 Corbel of monk with flask of wine.

56 Corbel of monk breaking bread.

57 Corbel of monk eating

accommodated. On one side was the warming house or calefactory, originally the only heated room in the monastery, and to the west was the kitchen, conveniently placed between the monks' and the lay brothers' refectories both of which it served.

The subject of diet formed an important part of all monastic codes. It was regulated in the minutest detail and the degree of strictness in the observance of the rules was one of the main yardsticks in determining the spiritual well-being of a monastery. St Benedict devoted three chapters to the subject, and these formed the basis for the Cistercian legislation.[99] He prescribed abstinence from meat, and moderation and frugality were to be observed in all ways.

The dangers inherent in the failure to comply were very early recognized. St Bernard drew attention to them when he said,

> Wine and white bread, honey-wine and pittances, benefit the body not the soul. The soul is not fattened out of frying pans! Many monks in Egypt served God for a long time without fish. Pepper, ginger, cummin, sage, and all the thousand other spices may please the palate, but they inflame lust.

Hard work, he claimed, restores the flavour to plain food:

> Vegetables, beans, roots, and bread and water may be poor fare for one living at his ease, but hard work soon makes them taste delicious.[100]

Here St Bernard is referring to bodily nourishment, but he also frequently used references to food and drink allegorically, both in a general sense and, more specifically, to refer to the Eucharist.

A number of cloister carvings relating to food and drink reminded the monks who passed them of the virtues of temperance and mortification, of the dangers inherent in their abuse, as well as of the spiritual truths which they symbolized. Among the many fine fourteenth-century carvings in the cloister at the Spanish abbey of Santes Creus, many of them by the English master sculptor Reinard Fonell, are two corbels with figures of monks. One of them is dressed in a tunic and scapular and holds a flask of wine in his left hand. (55) The other, with his hood over his head as was the custom during meals, is breaking bread. (56) A corbel in the cloister of Cadouin from the second half of the fifteenth century also features a bust of a monk with the hood over his head (57). He is shown eating, perhaps a warning to the community of the dangers of greed. On the side is a banderole but the inscription is missing.

The observance of the early restrictions both as regards the consumption of meat and the quantity and range of foods was gradually slackened, not least as the result of the introduction of 'pittances', extra portions of food and drink granted by benefactors in exchange for prayers and anniversary Masses and, most of all, for grants of burial within the precincts.[101] Attempts by the General Chapter and by Pope Benedict XII in his 1335 Constitution *Fulgens sicut stella* to stem the development and return to the earlier simplicity were by and large unsuccessful. Much of the later medieval invective that was directed at the Cistercians focused on what was seen as their greed and gluttony.

In a post-medieval example, the intrepid English traveller William Beckford described the great Portuguese abbey of Alcobaça in the eighteenth century as 'the most distinguished temple of gluttony in all Europe'. Writing in 1834–5 of the journey he made in 1794 he recounts how

> On one side, loads of game and venison were heaped up; on the other, vegetables and fruit in endless variety. Beyond a long line of stoves extended a row of ovens, and close to them hillocks of wheaten flour whiter than snow, rocks of sugar, jars of the purest oil, and pastry in vast abundance, which a numerous tribe of lay brothers and their attendants were rolling out and puffing up into a hundred different shapes, singing all the while as blithely as larks in a corn-field. . . . The banquet itself consisted of not only the most excellent usual fare, but rarities and delicacies of past seasons and distant countries; exquisite sausages, potted lampreys, strange messes from the Brazils, and others still stranger from China (edible birds' nests and sharks' fins), dressed after the latest mode of Macao by a Chinese lay brother. Confectionery and fruits were out of the question here; they awaited us in an adjoining still more spacious and sumptuous apartment, to which we retired from the effluvia of viands and sauces.[102]

After making full allowance for exaggeration, and bearing in mind that Beckford was describing the fare served to distinguished guests and not to the monks themselves, this example of extreme indulgence nevertheless makes it clear that we are light years from the days when St Benedict decreed that 'frugality shall be observed in all circumstances'.[103] A late medieval painting which shows three well-fed monks from Alcobaça suggests that the point had already been reached when Cistercians in Portugal were enjoying a standard of living equalled only by a small number of the most privileged persons in the world around them, as has been shown to have been the case in German and Austrian abbeys.[104] Ostentatious eating, and especially the consumption of foreign food which was one of the features of pittances, gave the monks, as members of the ruling classes, their chief opportunity to display their superiority. The

58 Three monks from Alcobaça.

painting, a detail of one panel of six which form the altar of St Vincent (58), was painted in 1465–7 by Nuno Goncalves, painter to King Alfonso V, when Portugal was at the zenith of its maritime power. The Alcobaça monks are shown

59 Monk being given tonsure.

as members of the privileged classes paying homage to the saint in the company of Henry the Navigator and the young Infanta John (later John II).

Before meals the monks washed themselves in a lavabo or *lavatorium* which consisted either of a water basin built into the wall in the cloister beside the refectory or of a fountain contained in a separate building adjoining the cloister, opposite the entrance to the refectory. It was used for all kinds of washing, including that of clothes. An initial *M(os)* in the Cîteaux *Moralia* shows two monks folding linen.[105] Shaving also took place in the cloister near the lavabo. Although the tonsure was originally administered by the abbot at the ceremony of profession, it was renewed at the shaving which originally took place seven times a year on stated days when, according to the *Ecclesiastica Officia*, 'the shaving of the crown must be thorough, the tonsure being above the ears'.[106] By 1257 this had been increased to twenty-six times a year.[107] Detailed regulations governed the procedure. The abbot or prior chose the day and one of the monks was appointed to prepare and sharpen the scissors and razors. It was to be carried out by whoever was chosen and no one could refuse. A picture of this routine is found in the margin of an early thirteenth-century manuscript from the English abbey of Dore. (**59**)

CHAPTER SEVEN

THE ABBOTS

'To rule over them you have appointed this your sinful servant. My God, you know my folly and my weakness is not hidden from you, which is why, dear Lord, I do not ask for gold or silver or precious stones, but for wisdom that I may rule over your people.'

St Aelred of Rievaulx, *Pastoral Prayer*[1]

'He [St Stephen Harding] was a pastor of great humility, not interested in worldly things. He hated all display of pride. This is sufficiently indicated by his pastoral staff which he used to carry in procession on feast days and which seems to be not dissimilar to the common staffs which old men and the sick lean on. On account of the reverence due to so great a father who was much esteemed, it is until this day kept in a cabinet at Cîteaux.'

Conrad of Eberbach, *Exordium Magnum*[2]

That the quality of leadership in any human organization percolates right through to its most junior members and has a decisive effect on the well-being of all is a truism. This is as much true of religious communities as it is of any other groups. It was recognized by St Benedict, and that is why he devoted so much space to the office of abbot in his Rule, four chapters in all.[3] Immediately after his definition of the four kinds of monks, Benedict describes the kind of man the abbot should be. He is 'the representative of Christ in the monastery' and his function is to teach. He 'ought to rule with a twofold teaching . . . by deeds and by words, but by deeds rather than words'. The illuminator of one of the early manuscripts of the Rule from the Austrian abbey of Zwettl has highlighted the importance of this chapter by portraying St Benedict in the initial *A(bbas)*, the opening word of the second chapter.[4] The upper half of the letter has a bust of a nimbed St Benedict in a frontal position. The space below is taken up with coiled tendrils and leaves. The dominant colours are blue and green. It is similar both in composition and colour to the larger initial *A(usculta)* with which the Rule begins (*see 1*).

In the first chapter of the Rule Benedict distinguished between those monks who live under a rule and an abbot and those who live without a shepherd and in their own sheepfold.[5] When defining the qualities of leadership required, Benedict developed the theme of the abbot as shepherd. In following the example of the

Good Shepherd (Luke 15:4–5) the abbot must be flexible and adaptable, and he is to realize that 'what he has undertaken is the charge of weakly souls, and not a tyranny over the strong'. Benedict reiterates this in a later chapter saying, 'let him act with prudent moderation, lest being too zealous in removing the rust he break the vessel . . . let him so temper all things that the strong may still have something to long after, and the weak may not draw back in alarm'.[6] The pastoral theme was the inspiration behind the short treatise *Shepherds and Sheep* by the twelfth-century Augustinian, Hugh de Fouilloy, which, like his other works, was usually illustrated with a drawing and which was particularly popular among the Cistercians.[7] The oldest surviving example and the first in a series of large miniatures is from the Flemish abbey of Les Dunes and is dated *c.* 1190–1200.[8] An almost identical copy belonged to the important abbey of Clairmarais (Pas-de-Calais), founded in 1140 as a daughter of Clairvaux, and there are two further examples, the provenance of which is not known.[9] The Clairmarais copy is a full-page miniature depicting on the left a nimbed and bearded Christ the Good Shepherd holding the top of a pastoral staff, the bottom end of which is grasped on the right by a tonsured and bearded figure in a very dark brown almost black habit, the unworthy shepherd (**colour plate 11**). Christ holds a staff surmounted by a cross in his right hand. Below him is the good line consisting of a ram, ewes and lambs, all bluish, guarded by an alert shepherd holding on a leash a standing dog who is barking and equally attentive. On the right, below the abbot, is the bad line of billy goat, nanny goats, kids and the negligent shepherd in a rose tunic and green hose, asleep and accompanied by a sitting dog, drowsy and silent. The figures and animals on the two sides are facing inwards, and the whole is framed by a blue, rose and orange patterned border.

The same favourite medieval theme of the contrast between good and evil was also used by Hugh de Fouilloy in his *Wheels of Religion* of which there are more extant illustrated copies than there are of the *Shepherds and Sheep*.[10] Hugh adapted the ancient tradition of the Wheel of Fortune, usually depicting the transient nature of the rule of kings – their rise to power, its exercise in office, and their fall from grace – to reflect on the vicissitudes of the office of abbot. The dangers inherent in the abbot's heavy responsibility are referred to time and again in the Rule. Seven times St Benedict reminds the abbot that he will one day have to give account of his stewardship. The burden of the office is clearly expressed in the *Wheels*. Pairs of full-page miniatures with identical diagrams centred on the wheel with the figural images and the text express the difference between false and true religion. Characteristic of de Fouilloy's work is the way in which the images and the text complement each other and are of equal weight in transmitting their lesson. Such illustrations are included in the two manuscripts from Les Dunes and Clairmarais which also contains the *Shepherds*, and among other Cistercian abbeys which owned the work were the Austrian Heiligenkreuz and Zwettl, Buildwas in England, the Belgian abbey Aulne, and Clairvaux.[11] In the early thirteenth-century manuscript of the *Wheels of True and False Religion* from Heiligenkreuz the wheels in the two drawings consist of six concentric circles which, with their spokes, contain the names of the virtues and vices and which, like the four borders of the folio containing more text, are drawn in red ink. The four tonsured and cowled figures around the four sides of the wheels are drawn in brown ink in both pictures. The wheel of *True Religion* depicts, from the left clockwise, a monk about to be elected on account of his virtue, at the top the good abbot with his staff sitting in 'dignity but with charity' and 'as the judge but not wanting to be powerful', then through humility relinquishing office and finally, at the bottom, 'he sits in poverty but with joy', reading a book.[12] In the wheel of *False Religion*, described as the wheel of the hypocrite, he is shown, from the left, climbing through ambition, ruling in splendour, falling head downwards through negligence, and finally sitting in shame, his head bowed and supported by his hand. (60)

The pastoral nature of the abbatial office is symbolized by the staff or crozier with which abbots were invested at their blessing by the bishop and which was the emblem *par excellence* of their authority. As we have seen, St Bernard is practically always portrayed holding his pastoral staff and Cistercian iconography abounds with pictures of abbots denoted by the crozier. According to the *Exordium Cistercii*, when Robert of Molesme and his companions began to transform the solitude they had found into an abbey, Robert 'received the care of the monks and the shepherd's staff from the bishop of the diocese'.[13] The way in which the early simple staff developed into the elaborately decorated and finally sometimes even jewel-encrusted crozier of the later Middle Ages tells us a good deal about the way in which the exercise of abbatial authority changed over the centuries, and this is well documented in Cistercian iconography. When Conrad of Eberbach commented on the simplicity and almost plainness of Stephen Harding's pastoral staff a century later he was clearly contrasting this with the more intricate designs that were becoming the fashion in the early thirteenth century and which were eventually to end in the ornate versions of the late Middle Ages and Renaissance. The importance of his observation was the way in which the design of the crozier signified a lessening of the early austerity and fervour. This development ran counter to both St Bernard's major objections of what is appropriate for monks: its ostentation and appeal to the senses, and its unnecessary expense.

At first the abbot's staff was, as Stephen Harding's, a simple wooden shepherd's crook. Soon a plain spherical knob was added between the curved crook-head and the straight staff, allowing the crozier to be made in two halves and of two different materials. This is how the pastoral staff is depicted in all early illustrations, for example St Benedict's in the Zwettl Lectionary from 1173 (*see* 4), St Bernard's in the Aelred manuscript from about the same time (*see* **colour plate 10**), the one in the Zwettl *Vita Prima* from the beginning of the thirteenth century (*see* 21), and in the Gradual from the Silesian abbey of Kamenz (*see* 3). It also appears in one of the earliest representations of an abbot who can be identified by name, that of Folknand (1150–80) of the Slovenian abbey of Stična (Sittich, or Sitticum in Latin). (61) He is depicted in a manuscript of St Augustine's *City of God* dated *c.* 1180 in a frontal, formal image within the initial O formed by two dragons, a warning of the dangers inherent in his position. He is seated on a decorated stone bench covered with a patterned

61 Abbot Folknand of Stična.

60 The Wheel of False Religion.

cushion, tonsured and with a droopy moustache. He holds the simple staff in his right hand across the body. In his left hand is an open book with the inscription, 'As his earthly life was about to come to an end, Folknand, the Catholic citizen, ordered this book to be written for the common use of the community'.

The primitive pastoral staff remained in use in many places even after the more complex designs had evolved. A remarkable example comes from the Norman monastery of Savigny. A sadly neglected ruin is all that remains of this great abbey, but in the nearby parish church a fine late thirteenth-century or early fourteenth-century effigy of an abbot is preserved in high relief. (62) A tonsured and cowled figure with his hands folded in prayer and a primitive crook

62 Tombstone of an abbot of Savigny.

63 Carving of an abbot, Kilcooly.

with a plain curved volute or head and circular knob held under his arm is lying under a canopy, his head resting on a cushion supported by two angels.

The rudimentary staff is found in an even later example from Ireland. Next to a doorway that was built between the transept and the sacristy as part of the reconstruction of Kilcooly in the second half of the fifteenth century is the carving of an abbot in low relief. (63) Set in a square frame below but not in alignment with a floriated and pinnacled arch, is a figure in liturgical vestments in a frontal position, with the simple crook in his right hand and a book in his left. This may well be Abbot Philip O'Molwanayn who rebuilt the monastery after its destruction in 1445 and whose grave slab in low relief is preserved in the church. There he is depicted under a shield containing the instruments of Christ's Passion in a chasuble of the same design as in the wall carving and also with the stole and maniple showing.[14] He is also carrying a crozier and a book, but the crozier is of a more advanced design with a number of leaves almost filling the space enclosed by the head. Philip died in 1463 and the inscription around his tomb tells us why he was considered worthy of these two fine memorials: 'Here lies Philip O Molwanayn, formerly abbot of this house, together with his parents, who performed many good works both spiritual and temporal.'[15]

64 Carving of an abbot, Jerpoint.

The next small development in the design of the pastoral staff was the appearance of a simple foliate ending of the crook, often in the form of a trefoil. This may, for example, be seen in the croziers carried by St Benedict and St Bernard in the carving on the choir stalls of Doberan in Mecklenburg from *c.* 1310 (*see* 6). It also appears with a figure which has been variously referred to as a bishop and an abbot in one of the many carvings from the late fourteenth-century cloister of the Irish abbey of Jerpoint. (64)[16] The figure on the reverse side of the 'dumb-bell' piers has been described as an abbot – leading to the conclusion that the other must be a bishop – but it almost certainly represents a lay brother (*see* 85). The croziered figure, however, is clearly tonsured and as he is not wearing a mitre, with which bishops are normally portrayed, he must be an abbot, quite possibly one who played a part in the building of the monastery, as was also the case at Kilkooly and at many other monasteries. He is arrayed in amice, chasuble, stole and maniple over an alb. His right hand is raised in blessing and he carries an out-turned foliate crozier in the left.

In another traditional portrayal an abbot is depicted with a crozier of floriate design, where the crook terminates in two trefoils. In a magnificent full-page miniature Abbot Robert of Béthune of Clairmarais (Pas-de-Calais) (1254–68) presents the manuscript he had commissioned of Richard of Saint-Laurent's *Of Charity and Other Virtues* to a standing Virgin, nimbed and crowned and carrying the cross-nimbed Child (**colour plate 12**). Each figure appears within an elegant trifoliate arch supported by slender columns surmounted by long thin crocketed pinnacles which rise beyond the golden decorated border within which the scene is framed. The figures are identified by the inscriptions beneath each: *Sancta Maria virgo virginum regina* and *Robertus abbas de Claromarisco* respectively. Robert is tonsured, has a grey beard and wears a brownish grey cowl. The long crozier rests at an angle against his body while he holds the book up to the Virgin with both hands. Above him the hand of God comes out of a cloud in blessing. The difference in status between the two figures is highlighted by the smaller scale of the abbot, accentuated by his kneeling, and further emphasized by Mary being depicted against a gold background while Robert is against one of pale brown.

A further development was the foliate, usually trefoil, crozier with leaves not just within the volute but also having buds or crockets on the outside of the crook. Examples of this are numerous and include the croziers of the abbots in the Cîteaux miniature of the pope granting them privileges (*see* 9), of St Bernard (*see* 18), and that of Abbot de Gaing from the cloister at Cadouin (Dordogne) (*see* 54).[17] Another is that on the incised grave slab of Abbot William Halforde of Bordesley (1445–60) who, however, only died in 1490 according to the inscription. (**65**) The stone is now in the parish church of Hinton-on-the-Green, Worcestershire, a long way from his monastery. It may either have been moved there after the Reformation for a reason which is not known, or he may have come to live there in retirement at the manor which belonged to the Benedictine monks of Gloucester. A further example of a trefoil crozier comes from a primitive incised grave slab from Jerpoint in Ireland. This example even has a series of full trefoils on the outside of the volute as well as a trefoil within.[18]

A still later type of crozier not only has carvings on the inside of the volute and exterior crockets, but the simple circular knob was replaced by a more substantial elongated section separating the crook from the staff. This was usually of an architectural design and made of gilt metal with the staff also occasionally decorated. A crozier of this kind may be seen in the representation of an abbot in stained glass in the parish church of Old Warden in Bedfordshire. (**66**) The easternmost window in the nave consists of two main lights with the abbot on the left facing the figure of St Martha in the right-hand light. He is depicted in a white habit under a canopy, his hands clasped in prayer and with a long crozier at an angle over his left shoulder. The crozier is of the later design and is executed in yellow stain to indicate that it is made of gilt metal. The border consists of the repeated letter W in white, and the scroll identifies the abbot as Walter Clifton of Warden whose exact dates are not known, but whose predecessor and successor are known in 1365 and 1397 respectively. The glass was designed for its present position in a church which was appropriated to the abbey in 1376. The head is not original which explains why he is not tonsured.

Late medieval croziers were often fitted with a cloth known as the *sudarium* or *vexillum*. This was attached to the top and had the dual function of protecting it

65 Grave slab of Abbot
William Halforde of
Bordesley.

66 Abbot Walter Clifton of
Warden.

67 St Bernard with six monks.

against the tarnishing caused by perspiration and of avoiding the cold touch of metal. It may, for example, be seen on St Bernard's crozier in the sixteenth-century glass from Herkenrode (*see* 112).

The crozier symbolized the abbot's supreme authority over the monks in his care. To him they owed total obedience and made their vow of stability. An expression of this dependence is found in a historiated initial *V(obis fratres)* in a manuscript of Bernard's Sermons on the Song of Songs from the German Benedictine abbey of Liesborn. (**67**) It contains one of the oldest representations of Bernard, dated to shortly after his canonization in 1174, as he is nimbed, and is proof of the early dispersion of his writings even outside the Order. The initial at the opening of the text is formed by a dragon which, together with images of smaller animals, is contained within a red and blue frame. At the top the bust of a nimbed figure with a simple pastoral staff in his left hand is identified by the inscription *Bernardus abbas*. His right hand holds a curved scroll across his body which reads, 'Obey them that have the rule over you' (Hebrews 13:17), a quotation which found its way into his work three times.[19] The dictate is addressed to the six monks contained within the circle formed by the dragon's tail who are looking up at St Bernard in awe.

If the pastoral staff was an emblem of the abbot's spiritual authority, then the abbatial seal represented his temporal rule. It provided him with the means whereby he administered the monastery's business. The possession of crozier and seal was what distinguished the abbot from the monks in his care. Aptitude for promoting the material well-being of a monastery, and ability as an administrator were important attributes for an abbot. His seal was the tool he employed in authenticating all official transactions, and the importance attached to this is reflected in the detailed provisions in the statutes of the General Chapter as to its design and use.[20] In contrast to the Benedictines, the Cistercians did not at first have a common or conventual seal alongside the abbatial seal. The greater authority vested in the Cistercian abbot as the sole user and guardian of the only official seal matrix made it that much more important to guard against misuse. In 1200 the General Chapter, referring to a 'certain discord in the seals of the Order', felt obliged to remind abbots of the only two acceptable varieties of design: that of a simple effigy with a pastoral staff, or an abbreviated version without effigy but with a robed arm grasping a staff.[21] These are the well known Cistercian types that occur in the twelfth and thirteenth centuries. Simplicity in design was matched by modesty in size by comparison with other monastic seals. In shape most abbatial seals were a pointed oval arrived at by the intersection of two segments of a circle and known as *vesica piscis*, derived from the most ancient Christian emblem.

One of the oldest figural abbatial seals is that used by the abbots of Les Dunes in Flanders in the second half of the twelfth century, of which there is a fine surviving copy from 1171. (68) The abbot is seated on a bench in a formal frontal position wearing a cowl, his authority denoted by the book (the Rule) and the simple pastoral staff in his hands. Conforming to early practice he is not named, the inscription merely states that it is the seal of the abbot of Les Dunes: SIGILLUM ABBATIS DE DUNIS.

In an attempt to counter the opportunities for abuse inherent in the abbot's sole possession and use of a seal, Benedict XII instituted a conventual seal for the Cistercians in his reform constitution *Fulgens sicut stella* of 1335. This second seal was to be round, made of copper, and bear the image of the Virgin Mary.[22] Although the abbot continued to have his own seal, the new seals reaffirmed the composite authority of the community indicated in their legends, which referred to the seals as belonging to abbot and convent. The system of visitation had always provided the Cistercians with a means by which the arbitrary rule of abbots could be controlled, but by the fourteenth century this had become less

68 Abbatial seal from Les Dunes.

effective with the loosening of ties between abbeys on account of the turbulent times. From now on the community was to share with the abbot the administration of the monastic assets, thus providing a safeguard against autocratic rule. Another innovation was that in future, for greater security, the abbatial seal was to carry the abbot's name.[23]

Change had already been heralded in England in 1307 by the Statute of Carlisle whereby all Cistercian and Premonstratensian houses were in future to have a common seal in the custody of the prior and four trusted members of the convent.[24] Whereas the motivation behind Benedict XII's provision was religious – that of tightening up on monastic discipline – that of the English measure was purely political and economic, an attempt at breaking the allegiance of English monasteries to their French mother-houses and preventing money from leaving the country.

A common seal from Rievaulx in Yorkshire from 1315, between the time of the Statute of Carlisle and the Cistercian reform, described in the legend as that of 'the abbot and convent of St Mary of Rievaulx', shows an abbot in liturgical vestments in the centre under a trifoliate arch supported by columns and surmounted by pinnacles and a smaller image of a seated crowned Virgin and Child under another trifoliate arch. The abbot is flanked by two monks on either side, also under arches.[25] This departure from the purism of earlier seals and especially the introduction of elaborate architectural settings was typical of Cistercian seals of the fourteenth century and later.

Although most conventual seals conformed to the required circular Marian design, new oval matrices were not uncommon.[26] One most unusual example survives in a late thirteenth or early fourteenth-century pointed oval abbatial seal matrix which, following either the Statute of Carlisle (1307) or *Fulgens sicut stella* (1335), was converted for use as a common seal by the simple addition of the words ET CONVENTUS to the legend. (69) It has a tonsured abbot in eucharistic vestments holding a staff and book. It comes from the small Welsh abbey of Grace Dieu in Gwent and is evidence of an ingenious way of conforming with the new requirement and yet not having to incur the expense of having a new matrix engraved.

The ethos of simplicity and restraint which had been the hallmark of the Order for its first century and which had found expression in the style of the primitive pastoral staff and abbot's seal was also to inform that of the funerary monuments of its abbots. In fact, there seems to have been a connection between the design of abbatial seals and tomb sculpture and their development.[27] Seal design led the way with figural images already in use in the middle of the twelfth century. These were not adopted on abbot's tomb slabs until 1220–30.[28]

The earliest grave slabs were mere plain grave covers, often tapered like coffins, and sometimes incised with the primitive pastoral staff to denote the status of the person commemorated. There is an example of this from Byland in Yorkshire with a simple trefoil in the head of the staff.[29] The same may be seen at Vaux de Cernay (Seine-et-Oise) but with an inscription of the abbot's name, Thibault (+ 1247).[30] Another development was the staff grasped by a robed arm

69 Abbatial/common seal from Grace Dieu.

expressing the authority of the abbot and conforming to the standard design of abbatial seals. Examples of this motif were found at Flaxley in Gloucestershire and at the Irish abbey of Boyle.[31]

According to Cistercian custom, abbots were buried in the chapter house. Although this practice was not universally followed – burials also took place in the cloister and sometimes in the church – it was nevertheless very common throughout Europe, and it was ratified by the General Chapter in 1180.[32] It was in the chapter house that the abbot exercised his authority and it was deemed the most appropriate location for a memorial denoting the status of the office held, at the same time acting as an appeal for the prayers of the community gathered there daily.

The restraint shown by the Cistercians in the design of tomb sculpture was not only dictated by their preference for simplicity but was equally demanded by the practical need of having unimpeded passage across the chapter house floor. The General Chapter found it necessary to remind monasteries of this three times within a few years (in 1191, 1194 and 1202), evidence that the practice was not always adhered to.[33] As with the design of seals, there was a gradual relaxation of the early austerity. The plain slabs with pastoral staffs were replaced by simple incised figural representations of abbots with inscriptions. These gave way to more ambitious versions with the figures usually in Mass vestments and contained within elaborate imaginary ecclesiastical structures. Many were inlaid with engraved brasses such as may be seen from the indents still in remote ruins, as at Fountains, Byland and Jervaulx in Yorkshire.[34] The two-dimensional funerary portraits were replaced by ones in low relief, probably the kind of which the General Chapter had disapproved.

This model was, for example, adopted at the wealthy Catalan abbey of Poblet where eleven abbatial tomb slabs in low relief are preserved in the chapter house, ranging in date from 1312 to 1623. Among them is that of Abbot Domenec Porta (+1526). (70) They all have cowls with ample sleeves dangling down to their knees and crossed so that the right sleeve falls on the left and vice versa. The crozier is held under the right arm and goes across to the left foot. The similarity of design over such a long timespan is interesting in that it shows how successive stone masons have copied earlier models generation after generation and not felt the need to put their own artistic stamp on their work.

A remarkable series of primitive incised slabs covering the period 1336 to 1491 have been preserved at Dargun in Mecklenburg.[35] As at Poblet, the design is remarkably static and uniform over this long timespan. A style was developed which successive generations of craftsmen were happy to follow. The facial features of Johann of Rostock (+1336) and Gregor of Rostock (+1381) are virtually identical; they are shown in the same position and each carries a simple crozier with trefoils in the heads. The double grave of Abbot von Attendorne (+1367) and Hermann of Riga (+1369) follows a similar pattern, but in an elaborate setting under arches and with a more decorative border.[36] Double graves are known from a number of other Cistercian monasteries. In a thirteenth-century example from the chapter house of Disibodenberg in Germany this is indicated by placing two

70 Tomb of Abbot
Domenec Porta of Poblet.

71 Gravestone of Abbot
Johann Becker of Dargun.

pastoral staffs of the primitive type side by side and with the heads turned outwards. The strength of tradition may also be seen here, for the same design, by now generally outmoded, was repeated more than a century later in the double grave of Abbots Dietmar and Johannes who died in 1403 and 1404 respectively.[37] Other double graves include an indent with two abbots at Byland in Yorkshire, and the grave stone of Godefroid of Arenberg (+1484) and Nicolas of Villers (+1504) from the Belgian abbey of Orval who are depicted mitred. In their position, dress and facial features they are like the Dargun example, depicted as if they were twins.[38] The same is the case with another example from Dargun, also a double grave depicting two identical figures, one of whom according to the inscription is Abbot Johann Becker (1475–91), who was responsible for completing the rebuilding of the church and monastic buildings in 1479. (71) The left-hand border is blank, awaiting an inscription for an abbot to be buried sometime in the future, someone who, although not known, was already depicted on the stone. This, and the way in which abbots were identically portrayed, both one generation after the next, and in double monuments, indicates that the engravers and sculptors made no attempt at achieving a likeness of their subjects but merely set out to represent them by the emblems of their office and left the identification to the inscription. Genuine portraiture in the modern sense, investing the subjects with individual character, was unknown until the late Middle Ages, and in most cases the craftsman would not have been acquainted with their subjects.

72 Effigy of the abbot of Dundrennan.

Cistercian funerary monuments only rarely progressed from the 'picturesque' to the 'statuesque', from low relief to high relief. When this happened, they were raised above the ground and one could no longer walk over them. Examples of such three-dimensional monuments that have already been mentioned are those of St Stephen of Obazine (see 27), Blessed Gobert of Villers (see 52), and Abbess Jeanne de Flandre (see 103). A fine and rare example of a sculptural representation of a Cistercian is that of a thirteenth-century recumbent figure of an abbot from the Scottish abbey of Dundrennan in Galloway. (72) The carving of the folds in his ample cowl with wide sleeves has been beautifully rendered. The simple crozier with trefoil leaf in the head lies diagonally across his body with the crook turned inwards and is held low down by the left hand. His right hand is on his breast and, unusually, he is not carrying a book. Beside his head is a rose. Of greatest interest, however, are the two details which, in a pictorial form, tell a story parallel to the brief thumbnail sketches of abbots usually contained in monastic chronicles. Below his neck on the left side a small dagger penetrates the breast, suggesting that the abbot, whose identity is not known, met a violent end. His feet stand on a small half-naked figure of a layman showing a wound in the abdomen from which a loop of intestine protrudes, and the pointed ferrule of the abbot's crozier rests on his head. This probably depicts the assassin and testifies to the dangers inherent in holding office in turbulent times.

Although abbots were usually elected for life, resignations were relatively common among the Cistercians. For example, the average term of office for the first century and a half was only seven years, both at Cîteaux and at Clairvaux. The Dundrennan effigy gives ample evidence of why an abbot might wish to resign. Another reason included the recognition by some that the gift of spiritual leadership was not always matched by the necessary administrative ability. Others shunned the limelight into which they were inevitably drawn by virtue of their office and longed to resume the life of an ordinary monk which they had originally chosen. Yet other resignations were occasioned by the instinctive feeling of inadequacy, misplaced or justified, or nostalgia for the house of profession to which they wished to return. Reference to abbatial resignation may be seen in the design of two grave slabs. Johann Billerbeck of Dargun (1336–49) ruled after Johann of Rostock whose slab is of the figural variety. Billerbeck's was of the earlier staff and arm type. His decision to resign is indicated by showing the staff broken in two places below the arm, with the three separate parts arranged in a zigzag fashion.[39] The other is from the very large matrix of a brass of Abbot Thomas Swinton of Fountains who resigned in 1478. The brass insets are missing, but the outline of the abbot's figure with a mitre and crozier under a canopy between two shields and with pinnacles, and the band around the border for the inscription and with corner roundels, can be clearly seen. The way in which his mitre is placed above and not on his head is thought to indicate the fact that he resigned.[40]

In the later Middle Ages the abbots emerged as powerful prelates almost on a par with bishops. It was generally a period of decline from which the Cistercians did not escape. The earlier austerity was replaced by a life of ease and plenty, of prosperity and even of luxury. From being the spiritual father of his monks, the abbot gradually emerged as a *grand seigneur*. His withdrawal from the common dormitory, where his place had traditionally been nearest to the night stairs, was rapidly followed by his retreat from the refectory and less frequent attendance in choir. A house was built for his own use where he could entertain distinguished guests in the same style he himself experienced when he was entertained by them. The emergence of a separate household with servants was perceived as a necessity for the head of a great abbey. As a notable landowner socially on a par with his lay counterparts, he adopted a style of life comparable to that of the gentry. Abbots had gradually come to enjoy privileges of exemption from episcopal jurisdiction and, as an outward sign of their status, their position received papal recognition by grants of *pontificalia*, whereby they were given the right to use a number of episcopal *insignia* and vestments which had formerly been forbidden, and they assumed many of the powers normally reserved to bishops.[41] Although many Benedictine abbots had long enjoyed such privileges, they were first granted to Cistercian abbots in the fourteenth century. *Pontificalia* were granted in 1336–7 to the Catalan abbeys of Santes Creus and Poblet, paradoxically only a year after Benedict XII's reform constitution, one of whose aims had been to curb the powers of abbots. It is no coincidence that these were the first, for they were both royal foundations patronized by the house of

73 Carving of monks on the tomb of Joana d'Ampurias.

Aragon. Both contained royal palaces and their abbots had a long tradition of royal service, three of the Poblet abbots having served as presidents of the *Generalitat* (the government of Catalonia). Peter the Great (+1285) was buried at Santes Creus, and eight of the thirteen kings of Aragon and Counts of Barcelona, from Raymond Berenguer IV to Ferdinand the Catholic (1479–1516), were buried at Poblet.[42]

The original grant of *pontificalia* was made at the beginning of the reign of one of the greatest monarchs, Peter the Ceremonious (1336–87). He erected a magnificent tomb to his daughter, Joana d'Ampurias. Although her effigy is not original, the carving on the side of her tomb is well preserved and much of its polychrome can still be seen. (73) Here we see the display of splendour associated with the pontifical liturgy. The central figure is that of the abbot as celebrant wearing a mitre and cope. He is attended by a deacon and sub-deacon, one carrying the abbot's crozier and the other an open service book. In front of the abbot is a grenial veil which he holds, assisted by the deacons. This was a cloth placed on the lap when sitting to protect the costly vestments and prevent them from being soiled by the hands. Other monks carry an aspergillum and censer and incense boat.

The continued connection of Poblet with the royal house is evidenced by the sumptuously illuminated Breviary of Martin of Aragon (1396–1410), a bibliophile and the last king of Aragon of the Catalan line. This masterpiece of fifteenth-century Catalan illumination is a rare example of a medieval manuscript which can be perfectly dated and localized. In a letter of 17 February 1398 the king wrote to the abbot giving his precise liturgical requests as to its contents. Another letter acknowledged the abbot's reply and notes with pleasure that the work had been put in hand and promises the abbot that more parchment would be sent. The manuscript was written from 1398 and decorated by Domingo Crespi, the illuminator, in *c.* 1403. It formed part of the library of Martin's successor, his great-nephew Alphonsus the Magnanimous (1416–58), who added the Office of St George on the last blank folio in *c.* 1420, including a miniature of the saint and an image of himself within the opening initial *G(eorgi miles)*. (74) The king is portrayed wearing a gold crown and a grey belted tunic, squatting on a red cushion and reading from an open book held by one of two monks in white habits with their hoods over their heads.

Grants of *pontificalia* were received by the Swabian abbey of Salem in 1373, by Clairvaux and Les Dunes in 1376, but Cîteaux itself was not invested until 1380.[43] Only a few years later Abbot James of Flavigny of Cîteaux is depicted mitred on his seal dated 1397.[44]

74 King Alphonse of Aragon with Cistercian monks.

13 Abbot Stantenat of Salem (1494–1510) entertained by musicians on a boat outing on Lake Constance.

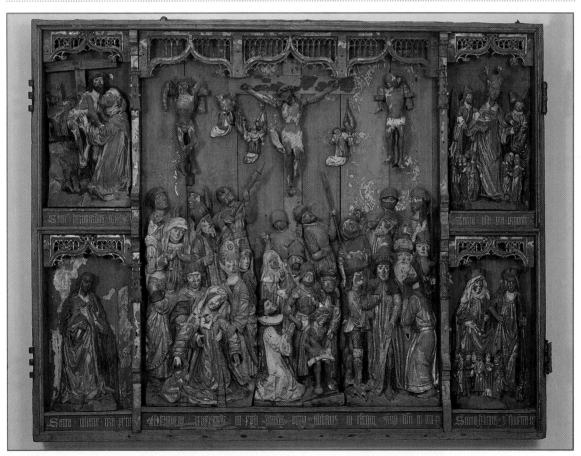

14 Retable from the Danish abbey of Esrum commissioned in 1496 by Abbot Peder Andersen, who is shown kneeling in the centre under the Crucifix. After the Reformation his identity was disguised by turning him into a Lutheran pastor.

15 Late thirteenth-century stained glass of a lay brother kneeling before Mary and Child, from the cloister of Wettingen, Switzerland.

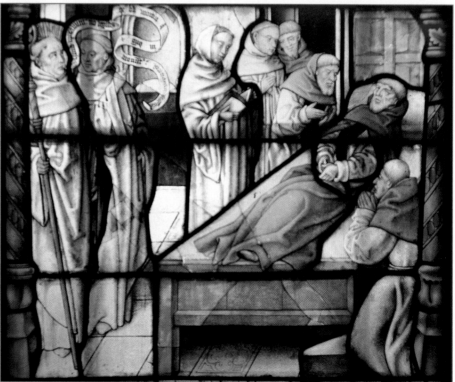

16 Early sixteenth-century stained glass from the cloister of Altenburg, Germany, depicting St Bernard at the deathbed of a lay brother.

17 A rare picture of a seated nun writing, a pen in her right hand and a knife in her left. Probably from a nunnery in the Rhineland.

18 St Bernard and a nun at the foot of the Cross. The expressive figures and the torrents of blood are in keeping with the devotion to the Passion which characterized the spirituality of medieval Cistercian nuns.

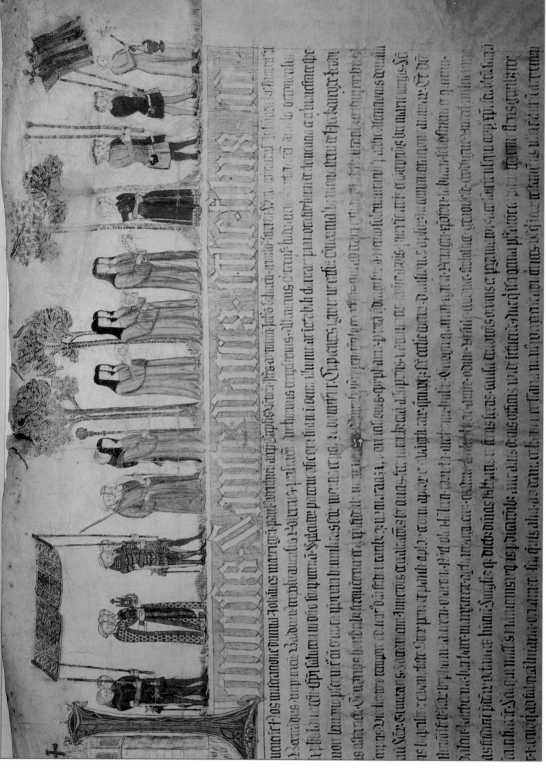

19 A procession of the community of nuns from Herkenrode, Belgium. The picture highlights the nuns' dependence on men: young acolytes, the provost accompanying the abbess, lay brothers, the laymen carrying the baldachin and chaplains. From a 1363 papal Indulgence.

20 Cistercian monk at the organ. From the Beaupré
Antiphonary.

21 Historiated initial with a priest celebrating Mass and a *schola* of
monks sharing a *Gradual*. From a Gradual dated 1268 from
Zwettl, Austria.

22 Presentation image of the scribe Gisilbertus from Eberbach, Germany, kneeling before the Virgin. The words in the margin are those of the Salutation of the Angel, of another prayer, and of a short exchange between the Virgin and Child. From a canon law manuscript dated *c.* 1330.

23 The opening folio of the Property Register of Tennenbach, Germany, from 1341–7. The upper initial contains a representation of the Trinity with the kneeling figures of St Benedict and St Bernard. The lower initial has the kneeling abbot, Johannes Zeulin, and the three figures represent the seated cellarer (Johannes Meiger) facing a lay brother and a peasant with a stick.

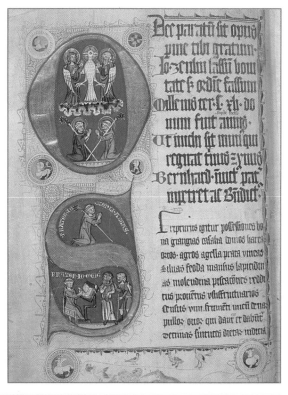

24 Two monks splitting a log – one of the famous Cîteaux work scenes from the manuscript of *Moralia in Job*, completed in 1111.

25 The scribe Rutger from Kamp, Germany, writing his Bible in 1312. He is seated on a high chair with a pen in his right hand and a knife in his left, writing on a removeable board supported by a hinged rod. On the side of his seat are two ink horns for black and red ink.

26 A humorous self-portrait of the scribe Sifridus Vitulus (meaning 'calf' in Latin) from Ebrach, Germany, depicting himself with the head of a calf. A hybrid creature at his feet hands him an ink horn.

Two images – one in an illuminated manuscript and one a portrait – provide us with conclusive evidence of the exalted social status of late medieval Cistercian abbots. An Alsatian monk, Amandus Schäffer, who himself later became abbot, copied and illuminated a richly decorated Breviary in two volumes for the abbot of Salem, Johannes Stantenat (1471–94). Begun during his abbacy, it was completed in that of his successor, Johannes Scharpffer (1494–1510). One folio contains Stantenat's coat of arms with that of St Bernard and surmounted by a mitre.[45] The same is featured again in a miniature depicting an idyllic summer afternoon boat trip in the lower half of the folio containing the liturgy for Trinity Sunday (**colour plate 13**). The coat of arms appears on the richly decorated canopy over the abbot's punt-like boat propelled by a standing oarsman at the bow. A corpulent abbot sits protected from the sun under a canopy with a small dog on his lap. He is accompanied by one of his monks in a white tunic and black scapular with the hood over his head, and a servant is retrieving a flask from the water where the drink has been cooling. Two musicians are entertaining the abbot on this outing on nearby Lake Constance.

The other image is a portrait of the thirteenth abbot of Les Dunes, Christiaan de Hondt, which forms the right-hand panel of a diptych painted in 1499 by the Bruges Master. It is an example of the typical Flemish donor portraits which characterized the devotional art of the fifteenth century and which, like the Books of Hours of the same period, were important status symbols. (75) The abbot is portrayed in a fine chamber kneeling on a padded prie-dieu. He is dressed in an elegantly arranged and very full white cowl, a white skullcap and with white gloves on his hands that are folded in prayer and display his abbatial ring. Before him is an open book on a cushion and at his feet a small dog is curled up (possibly alluding to his name which means dog in Flemish). A bejewelled silk mitre – a *mitra pretiosa* as used in solemn liturgical functions – rests on a pillow next to it. His costly crozier leans against the wall next to an elegant fireplace in which a fire is burning.

Many of the later medieval abbots were commemorated for their contribution to the fabric of their abbeys. In England, the greatest was probably Marmaduke Huby of Fountains (1495–1526) who has been called 'the last of his race'.[46] He was the commissary of the abbot of Cîteaux and advanced the cause of higher learning among the Cistercians by helping to build the College of St Bernard at Oxford, but he is perhaps best known for building the great tower at Fountains. He made sure that his memory would remain alive by the way in which this and other monuments for which he was responsible were marked with his initials and arms. Extensive repair work had already been undertaken by his predecessor, John Darnton (1479–95), for the church had long been neglected and was in a serious state of disrepair. Many new windows were inserted, buttresses built and a new timber roof installed. Large cracks in two window heads were ingeniously filled with carved stones. One of these represents an angel bearing a scroll inscribed *Anno Domini 1483*. The other, in the south wall of the Nine Altars' Chapel, bears testimony to the fact that they were inserted by Abbot Darnton. On the inside an angel holding a shield is surmounted by the mitred head of an

75 Abbot Christiaan de
Hondt of Les Dunes.

abbot. (76) On the outside is the bust of an angel holding a tun with the syllable 'Darn' carved in raised letters – a pun on the abbot's name – while above is an eagle, an allusion to his Christian name. Between them is the legend *Benedicite fontes Domino.*

Similar late medieval monuments by abbots to their own achievements are known from elsewhere. At Pforta (or Schulpforte) in Thuringia the last but one abbot, Peter (1516–33) built a column with a square upper part containing four carvings.[47] He had it erected just outside the monastery's gatehouse where it would be seen by the maximum number of people. It was an appeal for the prayers of the faithful in countering the increasing heresy in the region. Three of the carvings represented the Crucifixion, Mary, John the Baptist, while the fourth contained an image of the abbot himself.

In Denmark many monasteries enjoyed an Indian summer in the period that preceded the final eclipse. A period of prosperity, marked by a growth in their landed property and by extensive building activity, followed the decline of the fourteenth century. Many of the abbots were able administrators.[48] Among them was Peder Andersen of Esrum, founded by St Bernard's friend, Archbishop Eskil of Lund. He is commemorated in the great carved wooden retable from the abbey church which he commissioned in 1496 (**colour plate 14**). Only fragments of the two pairs of hinged wings have been preserved, but the *corpus* is intact. The legend at its base reads 'In memory of the reverend father in Christ Abbot Peder of Esrum the year 1496'. The central scene of the Crucifixion is flanked by two side panels with saints on each side. The top left is that of Christ descending from the Cross to embrace the kneeling figure of St Bernard – the *Amplexus* much favoured by the Cistercians – with the inscription 'St Bernard pray for us'. The prominent kneeling figure in the centre of the retable, his hands clasped in prayer, and looking up at the Cross, is that of the abbot himself, now well disguised. After the Reformation the retable was given to the church of St Olav in Elsinore. To protect the religious susceptibilities of the Protestant faithful, the tonsured figure of the abbot in the Cistercian cowl was transformed (by means of adding small pieces carved in soft wood) into that of a Lutheran pastor in the characteristic large ruff and now wearing a red and gold chasuble over the cowl, the tonsure replaced by a good crop of hair.

76 Carving of the head of Abbot John Darnton of Fountains.

CHAPTER EIGHT

LAY BROTHERS

'Deputed to ploughs and mattocks'

Burchard of Balerne, *c.* 1160[1]

The institution of the lay brotherhood was not original to the Cistercians. It was a distinctive feature of the monastic reform of the late eleventh century and had already been introduced at Camaldoli, Vallombrosa, Fonte Avellana and Hirsau, and the Carthusians also adopted it at their foundation in 1084. The Cistercians, however, developed it to its fullest extent so as to become a model for subsequent Orders.[2]

Although the monks themselves were expected to undertake work in the fields, they soon discovered that they were not able to achieve complete self-sufficiency by the work of their own hands alone. The earliest pictures in Gregory's *Moralia*, completed at Cîteaux in 1111, show exclusively monks at work and no lay brothers (*see* 134 and **colour plate 24**), but within a short time the problem was exacerbated by the acquisition of lands sufficiently far removed from Cîteaux to prevent the monks from cultivating them without neglecting their all-important choir duties.[3] To enable the monks to reside in the cloister as the Rule demanded and still cultivate scattered fields, they introduced *conversi* or lay brothers. In the words of the *Exordium Parvum*:

> It was then that they decided, with the bishop's permission, to take in bearded lay-brothers, whom they would treat as themselves in life and death – the status of monk apart – and also hired men, because without such backing they did not see how they could fully observe, day and night, the precepts of the Rule.[4]

Considering their lowly status it is surprising to find lay brothers extensively represented in medieval art. A look at the way in which they are depicted gives us an insight into their contribution to Cistercian history. The first way is the easiest to understand: they are portrayed as members of the wider Cistercian family.

Perhaps the finest example of this is the monument to Stephen of Obazine (*see* 27). One of the trifoliate arcades on the slanting roof contains carvings of lay brothers while abbots, monks, nuns and lay workers are represented in the

77 Lay brothers on the tomb of St Stephen of Obazine.

others. (77) The arcades on the other side contain the same groups, but on the Day of Judgment. While there are twenty-five members of the Order on one side, only twenty-three of these are counted out at the gate of heaven – two choir monks and a nun are missing, while all the lay brothers have made it! The lay brothers are wearing a belted tunic with tight sleeves and a long cloak over it, and *not* a sleeved cowl which is the distinctive garment of the monks. Their dress is similar to that of contemporary peasants but longer.

A fine example of lay brothers depicted as members of a Cistercian community comes from the German abbey of Marienstatt. In the large foundation panel painted in 1324 the community is represented by twenty-six kneeling figures in a strip across the width of the panel below the central scene of the Virgin and Child (see 11). Twelve of these – the last six figures on each side – are clearly bearded with fringed hair and wearing mantles and represent lay brothers taking their place behind the fourteen tonsured and cowled monks.

The *conversi* represented a new form of religious life. Monks were clerics and therefore tonsured, distinguished by wearing the monastic cowl and bound to the choral recitation of the Divine Office, while lay brothers were, as the name implies, lay. At the same time they were religious as they were under the same three vows – obedience, conversion of life and stability – as the monks and enjoyed the same privileges but were dedicated to manual labour. They were barred from the cloister – the special domain of monks – and had their own choir in the western end of the nave and their own quarters, refectory with dormitory above, in the west range. Sometimes there was a lane the length of the range and parallel to the cloister which gave them access to the church.[5] Their introduction occasioned a radical change in the traditional monastic plan. In the words of Idung of Prüfening the Cistercians now had 'two monasteries within the precinct of the monastery, one of lay brothers and another of clerics'.[6]

Bearded, they were also known as *barbati*, thus identifying them as laymen and distinguishing them from monks who were clean-shaven. Normally their beards were trimmed and their necks and temples shaven, leaving them with the distinctive fringe in a pudding-bowl style as seen in the group of *conversi* depicted on the Obazine tomb and on later illustrations.

In *c.* 1160 Abbot Burchard of Bellevaux, a former monk of Clairvaux and abbot of Balerne (and therefore more commonly known as Burchard of Balerne), wrote a curious but humorous treatise addressed to the lay brothers of the daughter-house of Rosières entitled an *Apology concerning Beards*.[7] He wrote it to make amends for the way in which he had severely criticized the lay brothers for their disorderly behaviour and incontinent lives. In it he discusses the different kinds of beards, and whether to have beards or not. On the difference between monks and lay brothers he has this to say:

> Observe finally, that beards are not convenient for the office of the altar, which is ours, but that beards are not inconvenient but well suited for agriculture, which is your office. . . . It would be unsuitable for beards to hang over books and chalices and we without beards therefore are engaged around the altars and chalices; you who have beards are deputed to ploughs and mattocks.[8]

Other portrayals of lay brothers as members of the Order pinpoint their subservient role. The woodcut in the Cîteaux collection of privileges shows the founding fathers with a large number of monks (see 8). Behind St Robert the nuns are represented by a solitary abbess and the lay brothers by a token brother.

Quam tibi Cisterci placeat sanctissimus ordo.
Hęc nobis primum ostensio facta probat:
Ergo tuo maneat semp sub numine tutus,
Deditus ante alios Virgo beata tibi.

78 Our Lady protecting the
Cistercian Order.

The commonest form of showing *conversi* as members of the Cistercian family,
however, is in images of Our Lady of Mercy – what the Germans call
Schutzmantelmadonna – that is Our Lady of the Protecting Mantle, based on a
popular story by Caesarius of Heisterbach from the early thirteenth century. In a
vision a terrified monk who could find no Cistercian in heaven was comforted

79 Our Lady of Mercy with Cistercian monks and *conversi*.

when Mary opened her cloak and revealed an 'innumerable multitude of monks, *lay brothers*, and nuns' of the Order.[9] While no *conversi* are portrayed in the most famous version of all – the sixteenth-century painting by Jean de Bellegambe with nuns on one side and St Bernard with his monks on the other (*see* 130) – in another woodcut in the Cîteaux collection of privileges the 'innumerable multitude' is represented by nuns on one side and monks under their abbot on the other, whereas the lay brothers are again represented by a solitary figure. (78) The lay brothers in both woodcuts are bearded and have the distinctive fringed hair.

However, in one of the oldest versions of Our Lady of Mercy from the Silesian abbey of Lubiaz (Leubus) dated *c.* 1320 (79), within the initial *G(audeamus)* and under a trifoliate arcade, Mary holds her cloak open, revealing four tonsured monks on one side and four bearded lay brothers with the usual fringed hair on the other.[10]

In another fine example, a carving in limewood by Michel Erhart from *c.* 1502–4 for the altarpiece at Kaisheim in Bavaria, a lay brother in a brown habit is featured on each side behind two hooded monks in white habits sheltering under Mary's cloak. The original polychrome may have been by Holbein, but, sadly, the figure was destroyed in the bombing of Berlin in 1945.[11]

Whereas only abbots were normally buried in the chapter house, monks and lay brothers were laid to rest in simple unmarked graves in the cemetery usually situated north of the church. There are only a handful of exceptions as regards ordinary monks, attributed to their reputed sanctity or powerful connections. It therefore comes as a surprise to learn that there were at least four effigies of lay brothers – one still in existence, two known from eighteenth-century prints, and one only from a literary source. They each throw light on different aspects of the life of lay brothers.

The first – the one still in existence – is perhaps the most expected in that it highlights

80 Effigy of a lay brother from Poblet.

the considerable contribution of lay brothers to the agricultural economy. It is an effigy in low relief of Brother William Tost who died in 1366 at the Catalonian abbey of Poblet and was buried in a prominent position which the monks would have passed daily in the east cloister gallery next to the day stairs to the monks' dormitory. (80) On the wall above is a contemporary epitaph in Catalan and Latin which reads: 'Here lies Brother William Tost who in asking for justice and in the defence of the forests of Poblet was put to death by the men of Prades. May his soul rest in peace. Amen.'

81 Lay brother Konrad
Teufel from Ebrach.

That his achievement merited the almost unique honour of a monument in the cloister is evidence of the importance the monks attached to safeguarding their territorial rights and the seriousness of some of the conflicts with their neighbours. We know nothing of the merits of this particular case, but one cannot help wondering whether it might not be one of those when they were defending rights which were questionable, such as had from the early days given the monks a reputation for avarice. At any rate, we have here an example of a lay brother who, being in the frontline, lost his life. On the granges and in the forests lay brothers were the butt for the grievances, justifiable or not, of neighbouring peasants.

The second and third grave monuments – the ones only known from eighteenth-century engravings – tell us that although the overwhelming majority of lay brothers were recruited from the peasantry, there were some very notable exceptions. The gravestone of Brother Konrad Zeuffel provides an obvious example. (81) He was buried at Ebrach in Franconia in 1348 near the entrance to the new sacristy which had been endowed by his kinsmen, the two brothers Zeuffel belonging to a patrician family from Würzburg.[12] Next to him lies his mother, Matilda, referred to as *maxima benefactor*. Among earlier examples were one of St Bernard's uncles, Milo, lord of Montbard, who became a lay brother at Cîteaux; Alexander, prince of Scotland who entered Foigny (Aisne) as a lay brother; and Salamon, prince of Austria, who entered Heiligenkreuz.[13] Another was Pons, a knight and the hermit founder of Silvanès (Aveyron) who, having handed his monastery over to the Cistercians, secured the election of one of his community as abbot and himself remained a lay brother for the rest of his life.[14]

Numerous knights and learned clerics chose to become lay brothers rather than monks. Caesarius refers to some of these, including Liffard who chose to tend the pigs of his monastery. Some chose out of humility to conceal their identity. Among them was Alan of Lille, a noted Paris master known as *doctor universalis* and famous for his theological treatises and poetic works, who retired to Cîteaux and spent his remaining days looking after sheep.[15] He died in 1203 and was buried in a place of honour in the cloister near the door to the church facing the tombs of the founding abbots, Alberic and Stephen Harding. The monument was sculpted in 1482 on the orders of Abbot Jean de Cirey. It is known from a poor engraving in which Alan is portrayed with sheep at his feet representing his life as a simple brother while the books above his head refer to his past career.

Among other exceptional examples of lay brothers who were not illiterate was the scribe Henry under whose leadership an important scriptorium was established at the Flemish abbey of Ter Doest in the second half of the thirteenth century.[16] He is thought to have learned his craft before joining the Order and may have done so in the workshop of the Counts of Flanders at Bruges. Among his known works are a large Bible in four volumes and a manuscript of St Augustine. He included an amusing caricature of himself in an inscription which reads: 'Brother Henry, lay brother of Ter Doest wrote this book. Pray for him.'(82)

Septum' est dñu requies his rite pactis.

Hunc libru scripsit frat henricus. o. de thosa

orate p eo

82 A caricature of Henry, lay brother scribe from Ter Doest.

The fourth effigy – the one known from a literary source – testifies to the important part lay brothers played in the building of Cistercian monasteries (*see* 149). It is that of a lay brother from the Frisian abbey of Aduard who was buried in the church as a reward for his part in building the church on the model of Clairvaux following a visit there in 1224.[17] The bricks used were transported from the abbey's own kiln to the building site by a human chain of lay brothers.

In the middle of a page in the Account Book of the English abbey of Beaulieu there is a drawing in brown ink of a bearded *conversus* with the usual fringe.[18] (83) Most of the seventy-five leaves of the manuscript have large holes where numerous drawings have been cut out. Only six leaves have escaped mutilation, leaving only three surviving drawings, two of which have been partly cut away, and an inferior drawing by another hand of a monk in the lower margin. The figure of the lay brother is complete, but part of the drawing to the right is missing. The post behind the figure and the beam above are similar to those of one of the other drawings which shows two lay workers in a fulling mill[19] and, as the text next to the figure refers to 'Brother J keeper of the wool-store and wardrobe' we may conclude that this is he, and that what he is carrying over his shoulder is either a sack of wool or some cloth. Another scene in the same manuscript shows two men cutting what is either cloth or parchment with scissors.[20] Although the heads have been cut away, the treatment of the tunic of one of them and the fact that he is drawn in brown ink while the other figure is orange suggests that this has represented another lay brother.

Although they were granted full rights as members of the Order it was not possible to disguise the fact that lay brothers were by the very nature of their original introduction inferior in rank to the monks. They were there as auxiliaries to the monks, in the words of Burchard, 'Deputed for ploughs and mattocks'. The vast majority were recruited from among the illiterate rural poor,

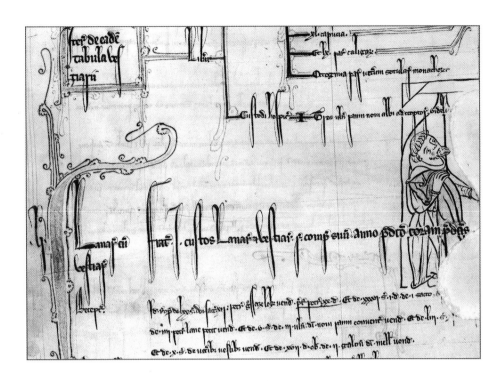

83 A lay brother from
Beaulieu.

mostly born and brought up in the neighbourhood of their abbey, and therefore belonged to a lower social class than the monks. The dangers inherent in this disparity were acknowledged by Stephen Harding in the preamble to the *Usus Conversorum*, the document regulating their lives. In it he states that the simpler and unlettered lay brothers have the more need for help, and that some abbots are inclined to neglect them and to demand too much from them.[21] According to a critic of the Cistercians, Walter Map, the lay brothers were exploited by the monks, 'for the basest and most menial cares, or for women's work, such as milking and so on, they employ no one but their own lay brethren'.[22]

At first they outnumbered the monks, often by two to one as at Vaucelles (Nord), sometimes by three to one as at Villers (Brabant) around the middle of the thirteenth century.[23] According to Caesarius of Heisterbach many of them first entered after they had enjoyed the world and spent their wealth, thus concealing their need with the mantle of piety and making of necessity a virtue! Speaking of Eberbach, Hildegard of Bingen wrote:

> The Cistercians draw another class of men to themselves, whom they call conversi, of whom very many do not convert themselves to God in their habits because they love perversity rather than uprightness . . . most of them labour neither day or night since they serve perfectly neither God nor the world. . . .[24]

The ambiguity of their status and the distinction between them and the monks inevitably led to tension which was bound sooner or later to break out in open revolt. Satirical writers saw them as marginal men – neither monks nor peasants, members of the sergeant class, the *feldwebel* – rather dim, cringing to their superiors of whom they are afraid, blown up by their own importance and tyrannizing those beneath them. Such a picture is of course a caricature but like most satire, it contains a grain of truth.[25] Revolts against their second-class status were numerous: twenty between 1168 and 1200, and thirty in the thirteenth century.[26] Statutes refer to incidents like burying a lay brother alive, cutting off the nose of a monk and murdering an abbot!

The most famous was a conspiracy at Schönau under Abbot Godfrey (1182–92) known as the Boot Uprising. It is recorded in great detail in the *Exordium Magnum* and illustrated in a cycle of three sixteenth-century line drawings.[27]

Abbot Godfrey had tried to abolish an old custom of issuing boots annually. (84) This naturally met with the fiercest opposition from the lay brothers who

CONTEMNVNT VETERES CONVERSI SVMERE BOTOS
QVOS ABBS POENA GODEFRIDVS CORRIPIT ACRI.

84 Lay brothers at Schönau disobey their abbot.

wore out their boots more quickly than the monks. On the left the abbot is shown with the monks on one side and the *conversi* on the other. While the monk on the left accepts the old boots from the abbot kneeling, the spokesman for the lay brothers on the right refuses them. On the right of the picture the abbot is seen in the chapter house threatening to punish them, while the devil is sitting on the shoulder of the lay brother.

The leader of the conspiracy, referred to as *non conversus sed perversus* planned that when all the brothers had returned from the granges for the Christmas vigil they should invade the monks' dormitory and cut the monks' boots to pieces. Another picture shows the plan being hatched, the devil presiding.[28] The inscription reads: 'The brothers conspire to harm the monks, but God prevents the plot as the conspirator dies.'

One of the many carvings in the late fourteenth-century cloister of Jerpoint in Ireland probably represents a lay brother who may have been remembered for his part in its construction. (85) It is located on one of the dumb-bell piers, so called because of the shape in section of the two colonnettes joined by a flat plate.[29] This is the earliest known example of this distinctive feature of Irish cloister design, known from at least eight other Irish abbeys. The carving shows a bearded figure with what seems to be a fringe and not a tonsure who wears a tunic and scapular belted with a hooded cloak over it. His right hand is raised, and in his left hand he carries a staff and a Pater Noster (an early form of the rosary). Because the figure on the other side has been wrongly identified as a bishop, this figure has been called an abbot, the staff being considered a crozier. Although the staff has a crook this is very small and, unlike the more usual crozier held by the figure on the other side, it is totally without embellishment. Furthermore, the head of the crook is turned inwards which is most unusual, and the staff may therefore be seen as a true shepherd's crook which it would be quite normal for a lay brother to carry. One scholar calls him St Bernard, while another refers to him as a monk or possibly St Dominic.[30] Both habit and hair style, however, point to him being a lay brother.

Stories of lay brothers abound in Cistercian literature: more than thirty in the *Exordium Magnum*, and eighty in the *Dialogus Miraculorum* are devoted to them.[31] Many refer to the heroic and saintly lives of brothers whose simple faith and dedication to duty witnessed to the cardinal monastic virtues of humility and obedience and were an example to the monks. Others are known from a number of Lives, like those of Arnulf of Villers who foresaw troubled times ahead for the Church, Peter who was famed for his extreme austerity and Simon of Aulne who was endowed with the gift of clairvoyance.[32] Conrad of Eberbach tells of their simple devotions, of visions and dreams. A brother on one of Clairvaux's granges was helped by Christ to drive his oxen;[33] another saw Christ on the cross, and still others saw doves and angels.

An unusual story is illustrated in the picture cycle of the Life of St Hedwig (+1243), the founder of Trebnitz, commissioned by one of her descendants in 1353. (86) On one occasion the saint was not satisfied with attending only one Mass, and she therefore ordered her chaplain to fetch another priest. Her

85 Carving of a lay
brother.

chaplain was anxious to comply with her wishes, but as he was unable to find a
priest he tricked her by presenting her with a Cistercian lay brother who
happened to be on business at the court, probably from the neighbouring abbey
of Lubiaz (Leubus). Hedwig, realizing that he was not a priest, said to her
chaplain, 'God forgive you for having deceived me'. The picture shows the

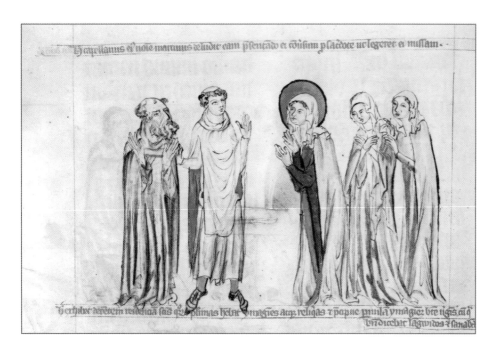

86   Lay brother with St Hedwig.

bearded and balding lay brother in a long cloak on the left being presented by the tonsured chaplain to Hedwig accompanied by two ladies. The caption reads, 'Here her chaplain named Martin tricks her by presenting a lay brother to her as if he were a priest who would read Mass for her.'

Many of the stories refer to temptations and the activities of the devil, often in the disguise of an animal like a lion, bear, serpent or ape. In another case – from the late thirteenth-century choir stalls in the north German abbey of Doberan – a small creature with a tail is significantly wearing as headgear the heraldic bull's head of Mecklenburg, a symbol of the Wendish pagans. (87) Facing him is a bearded lay brother, wearing a cloak with his hood over his head but with the distinctive fringe clearly showing. The scroll in Latin reads, 'What are you doing here, brother? Follow me – you will find no evil in me, horrid beast!' Above the figures are beautifully carved intertwining maple and oak branches and leaves. Maple stands for Mary, and oak for faithfulness – by turning to Mary the lay brother withstands the temptation and remains true to his vocation. The carving was at the western gable end of one of the two rows of twenty-six stalls in the lay brothers' choir and would have been seen as a warning by all the brothers as they entered the church.

A more explicit Marian theme is contained in a magnificent small stained glass window from the cloister of the Swiss abbey of Wettingen which is almost exactly contemporary with the Doberan carving (**colour plate 15**). It is star-shaped with six points, five of them containing palm leaves while the sixth in the lower left-hand point has a figure looking up to the central figures of Mary and Child contained within a circular red medallion. Mary is shown turned sideways, her head slightly bowed, looking down in tenderness on her Son who is standing on her knees. The sensitivity of the scene is redolent of the Cistercian cult of

87 Lay brother from
Doberan with the devil.

Mary and in contrast to more severe earlier portrayals of Mary as the Queen of
Heaven shown in a majestic frontal position. The kneeling figure has been
variously described as a monk, an abbot and St Bernard, but he is quite clearly a
lay brother – bearded, with fringed hair, and wearing a cloak with a tunic
underneath. The wrong identification may have been caused by the side of the
Virgin's seat being mistaken for a crozier.[34]

Another figure kneeling before Mary, his hands raised in prayer and his gaze directed at her as in the Wettingen glass, is in an antiphonary from the Austrian abbey of Heiligenkreuz. (88) Above his head is the name 'Wernardus', and, above this, a scroll which reads 'Mary, pray for me'. He has traditionally been identified as Werner who was abbot from 1207 to 1228 but, having studied a number of representations of lay brothers, I think there can be little doubt that we have here another lay brother. He is bearded, has the traditional fringe and not a tonsure, is wearing a belted tunic with tight sleeves and not a cowl, the distinctive monastic garment in which abbots are normally portraited, and, most tellingly, he is not

88 Lay brother kneeling before Mary.

carrying a crozier. Either his name was also Werner, or the name may have been inserted later erroneously to designate the abbot of that name.

We have in these images a parallel to the many literary references to the devotion of Cistercian *conversi* to Mary. Among these was, for example, Henry of Himmerod who saw Mary enter the infirmary and go among the sick and bless them. He also saw her one day entering the lay brothers' choir, stopping before the devout but quickly passing the lukewarm and those who were asleep.[35] One of the best-known stories concerns a simple brother who, being prevented from returning to the abbey from the grange for the vigil of the Assumption as he could not leave his sheep, turned towards the church and repeated the angelic salutation with such fervour that God made this known to Bernard, who used it in his sermon on the feast day for the edification of the monks as an example of the importance of obedience.[36]

On another occasion Bernard visited a lay brother on his deathbed.[37] He told him to have courage, but, realizing that the brother's confidence was excessive, felt bound to chastise him, saying,

> Are you not that miserable wretch who, leaving the world more from necessity than from the fear of God, at length obtained admission? Poor and miserable as you were, I took you in, fed and clothed you . . . even made you a brother to the wise and noble amongst us.

The brother then told Bernard the secret of his confidence, which he said he had learnt from Bernard,

> that the kingdom of God cannot be acquired by nobility of blood or be earthly riches, but solely by the virtue of obedience.

Bernard was overjoyed at hearing this and later preached a sermon on his life urging the community to follow the example of the lay brother.

This story in the *Exordium Magnum* is depicted in one of the seventy panels from the beginning of the sixteenth century which formed part of the Bernard cycle formerly in the cloister of Altenberg in Germany. Bernard is seen talking to a monk on the left (**colour plate 16**). Another monk is reading prayers from a book and closest to the dying brother are his fellow lay brothers, praying for and consoling him.

It is significant that almost all representations of lay brothers – whether in manuscripts, carvings or glass – come not from the golden age of the institution in the first half of the Middle Ages, but from the second half when their numbers had seriously declined and when, in some regions, they had practically disappeared from the scene. Cistercian historians of the second and third generations recorded the stories and anecdotes glorifying the early days of the Order to instruct and inspire their successors. In the same way, later artists depicted lay brothers in order that knowledge of their holy and austere lives, as well as their enormous contribution to the material prosperity of the Order, would encourage future generations of monks and lay brothers to emulate them.

CHAPTER NINE

THE NUNS

'The observance of the nuns of the Cistercian Order has been multiplied like the stars of heaven and has grown tremendously. The Lord blesses them and says: "Increase and multiply and fill the heavens."'

Jacques de Vitry, *c.* 1221[1]

This famous saying, adapting the words of Genesis, has often been quoted to draw attention to the phenomenal increase in Cistercian communities of women, whereby they greatly outnumbered those of monks in many countries. It is, however, misleading unless qualified by adding that this was not always nor everywhere the case. Whereas the expansion of men's houses reached its peak in the first half of the twelfth century, the growth of women's monasteries was at first very slow but accelerated enormously in the first half of the thirteenth century. In German speaking lands, for example, only fifteen were founded in the twelfth century yet in the next three centuries women's monasteries reached the staggering total of 377.[2] In France there were altogether 153 nunneries, concentrated in the north, east and south, with very few houses in the west,[3] while the English houses numbered only twenty-seven as against some seventy men's houses.[4] Even in distant lands there was a great disparity between the number of men's and women's houses: there were only two Cistercian nunneries in Denmark as compared with eleven men's houses, but in Sweden the women's houses outnumbered those of men by seven to six.[5]

Although the beginning was slow, the twelfth-century monastic revival with its emphasis on an ascetic and solitary way of life was as appealing to women as it was to men, and increasing numbers of them, including the wives and sisters of monks, chose the cloistered life. Among them was St Bernard's sister, Humbeline, who sought refuge at Jully, a Benedictine priory which owed its foundation to Molesme. There she later became prioress. She features in several of the Bernard cycles, her entry as a nun being treated almost as an accompaniment to Bernard's own arrival at Cîteaux. In an alter-piece at Zwettl by Jörg Breu she appears in one of the eight scenes.[6] A fifteenth-century manuscript of the Miroir Historial of Vincent de Beauvais, like that of Zwettl,[7] shows double scenes in which Bernard predominates, erroneously giving the impression that Humbeline's entry to Jully coincided with Bernard's to Cîteaux, but in which, in true medieval fashion, the essential point that Humbeline followed her brother into the religious life is made without too much attention to accurate timing for, in fact, Humbeline did not enter the cloister until much later than her brother.

In a post-medieval oil painting from 1635 entitled 'The Holy Nuns of Cîteaux', Humbeline is depicted as the central character, sitting at the foot of a tree in whose branches are medallions with portrait busts of twenty-five named, mainly thirteenth-century, saints with their attributes.[8] (89) She is portrayed as the spiritual mother of Cistercian nuns and is flanked by three nuns on each side. To her left are Gratia and Maria of Spain, shown with their martyrs' attributes of sword and axe, and Hedwig, the foundress of Trebnitz, with a crown to denote

89 St Humbeline and female saints of the Cistercian Order.

her status, and on the right are Franca, an abbess shown with her crozier, Hildegard of Bingen and Elizabeth of Schönau. The latter two, although closely associated with the Cistercians, were in fact Benedictines and not members of the Order, and yet they are shown in the white Cistercian habit. The same is of course the case with Humbeline, also shown in the Cistercian habit as well as with a crozier, thus erroneously being elevated to an abbess, whereas, as head of Jully, she was only a prioress. Nevertheless, her portrayal in this manner accords with the traditon that she was to be seen in relation to her brother, St Bernard, just as St Scholastica was to St Benedict or St Clare to St Francis. In this way she was later acknowledged as the head of the female branch of the Cistercian Order. The nun kneeling in the bottom left corner of the painting, her hands folded in prayer with her crozier on the ground is Jeanne de Marotte, abbess of La Paix-Dieu, the church of which may be seen in the background.

Within two or three decades of the foundation of Cîteaux communities of women arose, wishing to emulate the way of life of the monks there and, increasingly, groups of nuns that were already in existence wished to become Cistercian. Among these was Tart, founded in 1120 with the daughter of the great benefactress of Cîteaux, Elizabeth of Vergy, as its head and with the active support of Stephen Harding.[9] According to a later abbot of Cîteaux, Guy (1187–1202), the abbey was founded 'by the hands of Lord Stephen, abbot of Cîteaux' for 'nuns living according to the *instituta* of the Cistercian Order' under 'an abbess in the same place according to the prescribed manner (*formam*) of the Cistercian Order'.[10] Tart was dependent on the abbot of Cîteaux and was itself to head a family of nunneries organized on the model of Cîteaux, acting as the 'mother' with the right of visitation and correction, and presiding over an annual chapter of abbesses.

Bernard's involvement with his own rapidly growing filiation of monks and active participation in all major issues of church and state throughout Europe left him little time to devote to the spiritual direction of nuns. Yet, he is known to have had contact with groups of nuns and to have urged them to adopt Cistercian usages. He had, together with three other Cistercian abbots, been consulted by the abbot of Molesme when drawing up ordinances for Jully,[11] and he had played a part in founding at least one convent of nuns – Montreuil-sous-Laon.[12]

There are, as one would expect, quite a number of medieval representations of Bernard with nuns. These do not so much reflect his contribution to the expansion of Cistercian women's houses as pay tribute to the debt the nuns owed to his spiritual teaching. Not surprisingly, Bernard is featured, nimbed and carrying a crozier, blessing three kneeling nuns in white habits with black veils within the initial *P(rima)* from a Cistercian antiphonary written at the end of the twelfth century in what is perhaps the oldest known representation of Cistercian nuns, as well as being the first of Bernard in the extensive collection of the Belgian Royal Library. (90) Although the exact provenance of the manuscript is not known, the red and green initials with fine floral decoration and the habits of the nuns indicate that it comes from a Cistercian nunnery.

91 St Bernard preaching to nuns.

90 St Bernard blessing three nuns.

Two historiated initials from the end of the thirteenth century featuring St Bernard preaching to nuns are of particular interest. In one – from a manuscript of Bernard's sermons also in the Belgian Royal Library – he is shown, at the beginning of his sermon for Easter, in a brown habit, tonsured, nimbed, with a short beard, and sitting on a stool. A crozier is in his left hand, and his right hand is raised in blessing a group of seven kneeling nuns in brown habits and black veils. (91) The other picture – from the Austrian National Library – shows Bernard within the initial *H(odie)* at the opening of his Sermons for Advent. (92) Nimbed and tonsured and wearing a brown habit he holds a crozier in his left hand, his right hand being outstretched to a group of seven sitting nuns, also in brown habits and with black veils. The style of the two manuscripts is very similar and indicates that they come from the same workshop from the diocese of Cambrai, and it is thought that they probably belonged to the famous abbey of Nizelles, near Nivelles in Brabant. As their format is also the same, it may well be that they were originally the summer and winter halves of the same work.

Not all women's houses had their origin either as daughter-houses of Cistercian monasteries or as already existing communities which adopted Cistercian usages. Both the congregations of Savigny and Obazine, which joined the Cistercian Order in 1147, had nunneries attached to their male houses. Obazine had been founded by St Stephen as a double monastery of which Coyroux, whose buildings were some half a mile distant from the men's, was the female component. According to Stephen's Life, 'the holy man governed both men and women, the latter formally forbidden by their Order'.[13] Thus the stumbling block the nuns presented upon affiliation with Cîteaux was acknowledged for, although a number of Cistercian women's monasteries already existed, they did not formally belong to the Order and yet this was not sufficient to prevent the absorption into the Cistercian family and for the continued existence of Coyroux under the umbrella of the abbot of Obazine.

92 St Bernard preaching to nuns.

The nuns are represented as members of the Obazine monastic family on the tomb of St Stephen in the abbey church dating from *c.* 1280. (**93**) They are shown in the fifth of the six trifoliate arcades behind the Virgin and Child, Stephen and the abbots of the daughter-houses, the monks and the lay brothers (*see* 27).

In the words of Stephen's Life the founder decided 'by a very firm ordinance' that the nuns were to live there in the strictest enclosure, making sure that they were not accessible.[14] The ingenious arrangement whereby the nuns received what they needed without having contact with the outside world is described in detail in the Life. At the exit of the cloister there was a corridor with a door at each end. The key to the outer door was kept by an aged and trusted brother porter. He placed the nuns' provisions, bread, wine, herbs, and wood, in the corridor, locked the outer door which he knocked with a stick to notify the portress who would then open the inner door to remove the provisions. Other monks were responsible for the spiritual direction of the nuns – the *cura monialium* – saying Mass, hearing confessions, holding chapters and preaching on certain days. The nuns' own lay brothers took care of a multitude of menial tasks and manual labour outside the enclosure, thus allowing the nuns to pursue their religious duties uninterrupted.

This almost total dependence of the nuns on monks for their material as well as spiritual needs is perhaps the greatest distinguishing feature between the two branches of the Order. The obligation of deferring to their male counterparts imposed a restriction on them which circumscribed their ability to retain what may be called a fully Cistercian character. The limitations imposed on women by society inevitably resulted in their lives being very different from that of the monks.

As far as their material welfare is concerned, the nuns had not always been dependent on the monks. Manual labour formed an essential part of the monastic life as laid down in the Rule, and its restoration was one of the main planks in the Cistercian reform. At first the nuns interpreted this in the same

93 Nuns from Coyroux on the tomb of St Stephen of Obazine.

way as the monks to mean agricultural labour. According to the monk
Herman,

> Having spurned linen garments and cloaks in order to wear only tunics of
> wool, they are not content to spin and sew, as is proper for women, but
> they work the land, and penetrating into the forests with axe and mattock
> in hand, they uproot brambles and thorn-bushes and so gain their food in
> silence and in the assiduous labour of their hands.[15]

In the Life of Ida of Nivelles we read that she had gone with a group of nuns from
their abbey of La Ramée to one of the granges where they remained for more than
eight days to gather the harvest in the fields.[16] This was not to last, however, and
we have, unfortunately, no medieval representations of nuns doing field work.
Manual labour outside the cloister was inconsistent with the demands of strict
enclosure, the insistence on which was a recurring theme of General Chapter
statutes.[17] In 1242 it was decreed that nuns should not speak with outsiders
except through a window fitted with bars.[18] In German speaking lands the
separation was enforced by the distinctive nuns' choir or *emporium* which was set
at a higher level than the rest of the single vessel chapel from which it was thus
separated.[19] Furthermore, the incentive to direct cultivation, represented by the
earlier tithe exemption on lands tilled by the Cistercians themselves, had been
withdrawn by the Fourth Lateran Council in 1215, and as most nunneries were
founded after that date the privilege from which the Cistercians had previously
benefited no longer applied.[20] Their income consisted now largely of rents; the
nuns concentrated on inside work and they became content to 'spin and sew',
and, also unlike the monks, they devoted themselves to the education of girls.

A number of factors make generalizations about the women's houses of the
Order either dangerous or misleading. Partly because of the absence of the
Cistercian system of government based on annual visitation and attendance at
General Chapter at Cîteaux there was a much greater divergence between
nunneries than existed among monasteries for men. This reflects itself in their
origin, their size and wealth, their obscurity or lack of it, their architecture, their
siting, their composition, the variety in their form of dress, and their relationship
with bishops and with the Order. Some houses were fully incorporated into the
Order and answerable to an abbot, usually of a neighbouring monastery, known
as the Father Immediate or Father Abbot. Some placed themselves under the
spiritual direction of a Cistercian abbot without formally belonging to the Order.
Yet others merely followed Cistercian usages but remained under the jurisdiction
of their bishop. The fully fledged Cistercian monasteries were abbeys, while
others often remained mere priories. Some were small, poor, and remote with
survival one of the main preoccupations while others, owing their origin to noble
and sometimes royal benefactors, were rich and magnificent. Unlike the men's
houses, they were not always in remote areas and some were even situated on the
outskirts of important cities, like Paris, Laon, Cologne, Koblenz, Bamberg,
Rostock and Vienna.

Perhaps the most privileged nuns' monastery of all was that of Sancta Maria Regalis at Las Huelgas on the outskirts of Burgos, founded in 1187 by Alphonsus VIII of Castile near the king's summer residence. He had already endowed three men's houses: Bonaval (1164), Matallana (1174) and Oliva (1175).[21] He did so on 'the insistence of his most serene wife', Elinor Plantagenet, daughter of Henry II of England and Eleanor of Aquitaine, perhaps following her mother's example in endowing the great abbey of Fontevraud. The nuns, who were the first to cross the Pyrenees, came from Tulebras, founded in Navarre in 1157, a daughter of Lum-Dieu (Fabas) in the diocese of Comminges, itself a daughter of Tart, under their abbess, Dona Missol. The abbess of Las Huelgas had very extensive powers. She was described as 'lady, prelate, superior, legitimate spiritual and temporal administrator of the monastery' as well as the large number of daughter-houses in Castile over whose General Chapters she presided together with their dependent churches and villages. Las Huelgas was subject to the visitation of the abbot of Cîteaux who was described as 'the very own father' (*proprius pater*) of Las Huelgas and the monastery as his 'special daughter' (*specialis filia*), in line with the description of Tart as Stephen Harding's 'very own daughter' (*propria filia*).[22] As such the abbess was of course obliged to comply with the regulations laid down by the General Chapter of Cîteaux, but her powers were nevertheless so extensive that it was said that should the pope ever consider marriage he could do no worse than to choose the abbess of Las Huelgas![23]

The foundation scene is depicted in a carving on the western gable end of the lid of the tomb of Alphonsus which, with that of Elinor beside it, is in a place of honour in the nuns' choir facing the high altar. (**94**) Here, in accordance with the wish expressed in the foundation charter, the Divine Office has been chanted in the presence of the earthly remains of the founders for eight centuries down to our own day. Alphonsus is shown crowned, with long curly hair and a beard, and seated on his throne dressed in a tunic and cloak. With his right hand he presents a roll of parchment from which the royal seal hangs, the foundation charter, to the abbess kneeling on the right, Dona Missol. Another nun kneels behind her, and two more nuns kneel behind the king on the left. The tombs were placed in the new church when this was completed in 1279 and the dedication ceremony took place on 4 September in the presence of the king's granddaughter, Berenguela, who had taken the veil. The front of the king's tomb is decorated with a castle which formed his coat of arms while that of Elinor bears the three crowned lions of the House of Plantagenet.

Another royal foundation where it seemed as if the prayers of the nuns carried special weight with God was the abbey of Notre-Dame la Royale de Maubuisson founded in 1236 by Blanche of Castile. Blanche was the daughter of the founders of Las Huelgas, Alphonsus VIII and his queen, Elinor, the wife of Louis VIII of France who died in 1226, and the mother of another great benefactor of the Cistercians, Louis IX (St Louis). When she died in 1252, she chose to be buried at Maubuisson having previously taken the veil. The scene is depicted as a detail

94 Tomb of Alphonsus VIII with the foundation scene of Las Huelgas.

of a magnificent full-page miniature in a late medieval Life of Saint Louis: *Livre des faits de monseigneur saint Louis*.[24]

Another nuns' monastery which owed its existence to princely patronage was Trebnitz, founded in 1203 as the first Cistercian nunnery in Silesia. With four daughter-houses, it played an important part in the expansion of Cistercian women's houses in eastern Europe. Just as King Alphonsus had founded Las Huelgas 'on the insistence of his wife', Trebnitz arose on the initiative of a woman, St Hedwig of Andechs, duchess of Silesia, the cost being borne by her husband, Duke Henry II. In 1225 Caesarius of Heisterbach referred to Hedwig as 'a woman who was praiseworthy in every respect', and when she died in 1243 she was buried in the nuns' church at Trebnitz near where she had chosen to live as a widow. Her sanctity was marked in a Life written by the Cistercian, Englebert, a monk from Leubus (Lubiaz) whose abbot was responsible for Trebnitz. In 1267 she was canonized. A number of further biographies which became known as *legenda sanctae Hedwigis* were written at Leubus. These formed the basis for the so-called *Hedwig Codex* commissioned by Hedwig's great-great grandson, Duke Ludwig I of Leignitz and Brieg in 1353. It was written in the ducal court atelier by Nicolaus Pruzie ('the Prussian') and copiously illustrated in watercolour and pen. In addition to the Hedwig cycle, the manuscript also contains the Homilies of St Bernard with illustrations of Bernard (*see* 18).

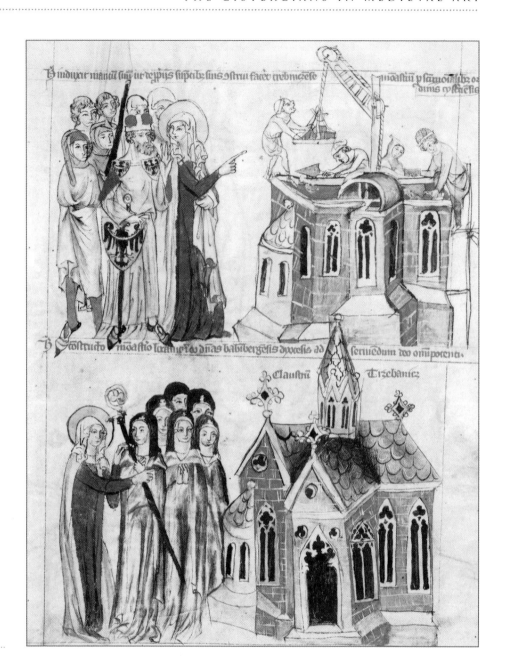

95 St Hedwig and the
building of Trebnitz.

One folio contains two separate scenes recording the foundation of the
monastery. (95) Above, in a rare picture of a nuns' abbey church under
construction, Hedwig is seen turning to her husband and pointing to the building
work in progress. The caption tells us that 'she prevailed upon her husband to
build the monastery at Trebnitz for nuns of the Cistercian Order from his own
means'. The fuller legend elaborates:

According to information from the master of works, the costs of this
undertaking amounted to approximately 30,000 marks; for the walls without
the roof – which was made of lead and still stands to this day – alone were
evaluated at about 20,000 marks. . . . On the advice of his wife, the holy

Hedwig, Duke Henry richly endowed the monastery when it was completed and provided it with revenues sufficient for the support of one thousand persons and for the ongoing management of a hospice and hospital.[25]

Below, Hedwig escorts the nuns, led by their abbess carrying a crozier, to their completed church. The caption reads, 'The monastery having been built she installs the nuns from the diocese of Bamberg so as to serve God in that place'. The nuns came from the monastery of St Theodore in Bamberg, itself a daughter-house of the oldest Cistercian nunnery in Germany, Wechterswinkel (founded

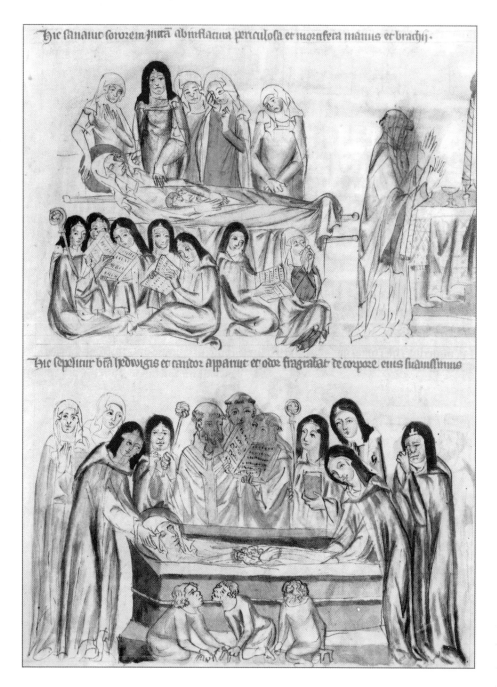

96 Hedwig heals Sister Jutta and the burial of Hedwig.

1144),[26] where Hedwig's sister was a nun and where her brother was made bishop the same year as the nuns left for Trebnitz. In common with many representations of Cistercian nuns, the Trebnitz sisters are wearing grey habits and black veils, but an unusual feature is the white crosses on the front of the veils.

Another scene shows Hedwig with her husband and children, one of them being Gertrude who was abbess of Trebnitz during 1232–68 and who is depicted in the Cistercian habit and carrying a crozier.[27]

In another double illustration the captions inform us that, 'She heals Sister Jutta from a dangerous and possibly fatal tumour of the hand and arm' (above) and, 'Here Blessed Hedwig is buried and a bright light appeared and a very sweet odour issued from her body' (below). (96) The healing scene takes place in the context of a Mass being offered by a tonsured priest wearing chasuble and maniple at an altar upon which are placed a chalice and lighted candle. A group of nuns, with their abbess carrying a crozier, is sitting on the floor singing from choir books. In the burial scene, Hedwig is being placed in a tomb by the sisters with their abbess carrying a crozier and a book. In the centre the celebrant, tonsured and wearing a chasuble, is sprinkling the body with holy water and reading prayers from an open book held for him by a monk assisted by another monk. The officiating priest is quite likely Abbot Günther of Leubus who, as father-abbot of Trebnitz, is featured together with Hedwig in another illustration in which he is described as her confessor.[28] Strange dwarf-like creatures (perhaps pall-bearers) are crouching on the ground, perhaps waiting for their services to be required again.

Two examples, one celebrating the dedication of the church and the other a narrative foundation picture, are parallels to those found at the men's houses of Marienstatt (see 11) and Maulbronn and served the same purpose of reminding members of the communities of their glorious past, as well as testifying to the crucial role played by noble and royal ladies in the history of the Cistercian women's houses.

In 1221 nuns from the abbey of Wöltingerode near Goslar under their abbess, Eviza, settled at Nienhausen on land given to them by Count Palatine Henry, the son of Duke Henry the Lion and his wife Agnes of Meissen and Landsberg, on whose initiative the nuns moved to Wienhausen some years later. Agnes died there in 1266 and chose to be buried in the church. Shortly after the completion of the new buildings in 1308 a painting, described as a 'pictorial dedication document', was commissioned to commemorate the event.[29] (97) Two metres high, it covers the wall of the upper west cloister walk at a place that every sister passed when going from choir to the refectory. Above, Mary and Child are seated on a throne accompanied by the abbey's secondary patron saint, Alexander. Below, the foundress, Agnes (*Agnes ducissa*) presents her foundation to Mary, and Abbess Margareta II von Schöningen (1302–17) (*Margareta abbatissa*) and Provost Dietrich von Prome (1307–16) (*Thidericus prepositus*) offer up the new Gothic red-brick building. The painting helped to perpetuate the memory of the monastery's origin as well as of those who had been

97 Wall painting showing
foundation of Wienhausen.

responsible for its continued well-being, and at the same time acted as a reminder
that Mary was the principal patron of the abbey and of the whole Order.

The other painting records the beginnings of yet another royal foundation,
that of the monastery of the Holy Cross in Rostock in 1270 by Queen Margareta
of Denmark in fulfilment of a vow and named after the relic she donated and
which had been presented to her by the pope.[30] It is approximately nine metres
long and formerly hung on the west wall of the church. Although it is only from
the sixteenth century and is no great work of art, it is almost certainly modelled
on an earlier picture and is of great historic interest. It is probably no coincidence

98 Donor nun in scene of the anointing of Christ's body.

99 Nun from Wienhausen in pointed veil with cross.

that late medieval nuns living at a time when they were no longer able to rely on their earlier security of a place in society felt the need to remind themselves of their golden past.

The Trebnitz illustrations and the Wienhausen and Rostock paintings demonstrate two things. First, that the greater divergence that existed between the women's houses as compared with those of men also expressed itself in the variety of their form of dress. Whereas white habits with black veils were the norm, the use of brown and grey was also fairly common and seems to have been even more widespread than among monks. Peculiarities of detail include the rosary carried by the nuns of Wienhausen and Rostock, the white veils of the Wienhausen and Rostock nuns, and the white crosses on the veils at Trebnitz. A further change between the earlier and later Middle Ages may be seen at Wienhausen. In a square diagonally mounted stained glass panel from c. 1330 – one of a cycle featuring the Passion – the white lifeless body of Christ is being placed in the grave by Simon of Cyrene and Joseph of Arimathea, predominantly red and yellow, the two colours repeated in the two Marys behind and contrasted with the strong blue background. The scene is witnessed by the figure of a small kneeling donor nun in a white habit and veil but without the cross, her hands raised up in prayer. (98) This contrasts with the habit of a nun illustrated in the Wienhausen Processional from c. 1500, the most richly decorated of all the manuscripts belonging to the large group of Lüneburg nunneries. The illumination is clearly provincial in character and was probably carried out in the monastery's scriptorium. The nun at the foot of one folio wears a striking pointed veil and, like the Trebnitz and Rostock nuns, she has a cross at the front, but instead of this being white on black it is red on white. (99) Similar pointed veils with red crosses appear in a number of manuscripts from the other Lüneburg Cistercian nunnery, Medingen. In some of the earlier manuscripts, from before 1478, the veil takes the more conventional round shape but still has a red cross whereas in manuscripts known to be later than 1494 the veil is pointed as at Wienhausen.[31] It is possible that the same change took place at Wienhausen during this period. In one of the manuscripts some of the nuns have crosses while others do not. The latter have been interpreted as lay sisters or conversae, but they may equally well be novices. The crosses were not a peculiarity of Cistercian nuns, but their use was widespread in northern Germany among nuns of other Orders as well. It is of particular interest as a precursor of the later distinctive Bridgettine headdress consisting of a linen band around the veil with a further band from front to back and another from side to side forming a cross. At the five intersections, four around the head and one on top, were small crosses representing the five wounds of Christ.[32]

Secondly, these pictures tell us the extent to which the nuns relied on men for their material well-being. Strict enclosure dictated their dependence on men, sometimes known as prior and sometimes as procurator or, as at Wienhausen, as provost, to administer the estates, collect rents and look after their business and legal affairs. Their importance, sometimes only marginally secondary to that of the abbess, may be seen by the inclusion of Provost Dietrich in the Wienhausen painting, and the tonsured figure behind Queen Margareta in the Rostock painting probably held the same office there.

The nuns' spiritual welfare – the *cura monialium* – was in the hands of the father-abbots. They were responsible for visitation, for presiding at the election of abbesses and for receiving the nuns' professions. An early fourteenth-century picture in another manuscript, an account in verse of the foundation of the monastery of Les Prés at Douai in Flanders, illustrates one of the duties being performed by the abbey's father-abbot. (**100**) At the opening of the poem there is a square miniature divided into four panels. The poem tells of the great length to which the foundress, Frescende, went before she succeeded in establishing her abbey in 1212. She had to undertake three journeys to Rome before she obtained papal approval for her plan. In the top right panel she is shown in a simple white dress with a white wimple as worn by pious women and with a staff in her left hand. The scroll in her right hand no doubt contains the papal bull authorizing the project. In the top left panel is her young travelling companion in a red tunic with a staff and accompanied by a donkey. Below, an abbot is shown placing a black veil on the head of a kneeling nun in a white habit and with her hands folded in prayer. Behind her are two other nuns similarly clad with the black veils floating above their heads. Two round arches above and a bell in the centre indicates that the ceremony is taking place in the church. The abbot, nimbed and carrying a crozier in his left hand, is wearing a chasuble and maniple and standing by an altar upon which a chalice is placed, telling us that the clothing ceremony is performed within a celebration of the Eucharist.

100 Foundation picture of Des Prés.

Like so many nunneries in Flanders and the Low Countries Les Prés had its beginning as a community of Beguines. It probably became Cistercian after Frescende's return from Rome in 1221 when the three de la Halle sisters, Sainte, Rose and Fulcede, who headed the founding community received the habit. The abbot of Vaucelles acted as their father-abbot, and it is he and the three sisters who are featured in the illustration. In the right-hand panel the three sisters, wearing white habits and black veils, are seen sitting, each with a book on her knees and within three Gothic arches separated by slender columns. The scene appears to be set in the cloister. The first abbess, Elissent d'Assonville, as well as the chaplain, came from the monastery of de la Brayelle d'Annay, probably appointed by the father-abbot. Chaplains appointed were normally Cistercian priests, chosen by the father-abbot to celebrate Mass and hear the nuns' confessions.

For other duties the nuns, like the monks, were dependent on the services of a bishop even if they were incorporated into the Order and therefore not subject to episcopal jurisdiction. Two almost contemporary historiated initials illustrate the dedication of the churches of two women's monasteries from opposite ends of Europe. One, dating from *c.* 1280, is from the summer part of the Osek Lectionary, so called because the manuscript was deposited at this Cistercian monastery before the war, but also known as the Lectionary of Arnoldus Misnensis, although it originally came from the nunnery of Marienstern near

101 Dedication of
Marienstern Church.

Kamenz in Saxony, founded in 1248.[33] (**101**) Within the initial *Q(uociens)* and
under three round arches surmounted with curious towers, a mitred bishop,
wearing alb, chasuble and dalmatic, is sprinkling holy water on the newly built
church using a large bunch of hyssop which he replenishes from the aspergillum.
This is carried by a tonsured monk in a white habit who is accompanied by a
group of monks, also tonsured and in white.

The other, showing the dedication of the church of the nunnery of Beaupré
near Grammont in Belgium, is featured in the famous Antiphonary from that
abbey from 1290. (**102**) This may have been written at Cambron whose abbot
was responsible for Beaupré. Within the initial *O(rnaverunt)* a bishop, in alb,
chasuble, dalmatic and mitre, holds a crozier in his left hand while blessing a
group of four nuns with his right hand. He is attended by four clerics, one
holding a book while another carries an aspergillum containing holy water. The

nuns are shown kneeling through the half-open door of a trifoliate porch of a magnificent Gothic church. An unusual feature worth noting is the coronets around their white veils, no doubt worn to celebrate the occasion. This may correspond to the 'crowns and veils', referred to by Caesarius of Heisterbach when the bishop of Livonia consecrated a group of nuns, another special occasion.[34] The dedication of a church was an important event which was solemnly commemorated annually.

102 Dedication of Beaupré Church.

Las Huelgas, Maubuisson, Trebnitz, Wienhausen and Rostock were not the only Cistercian women's monasteries which enjoyed royal or noble patronage or where the foundresses or benefactresses or their immediate families took the veil and sometimes served as abbesses. The relatively large number of extant representations of such personages in medieval art of course greatly outnumber those of abbesses and nuns of the multitude of modest foundations. Although it is true that by and large the nuns came from a higher level of society than the monks, the nobility are nevertheless greatly overrepresented in Cistercian iconography, and one must guard against concluding that nuns were recruited exclusively from the ranks of the nobility or the well-to-do middle classes.

Nevertheless, the names of the many abbesses reveal their noble status. In some cases, especially in Germany, belonging to the higher echelons of society was almost a precondition for entry into the Cistercian novitiate. Some very fine grave monuments make this point. At Himmelkron near Bad Bernech (fd 1280), the tombstone of Abbess Agnes, Countess of Orlamünde, who died in 1354 shows her with a crozier in the left hand and a book (the Rule) in the right.[35] A carving of a young nun in the abbey church of Sonnefeld (fd 1260, incorporated into the Cistercian Order 1262), whose abbesses always belonged to the nobility, is considered to be one of the finest in Franconia.[36] It dates from 1363 and is of Sister Anna von Henneberg who died aged only eighteen. On account of the value of her dowry she was referred to as the second foundress of the monastery.

A magnificent effigy in white marble from the second half of the fourteenth century features Jeanne de Flandre, the benefactress of Le Sauvoir-sous-Laon who died in 1333. (103) She was the wife of Enguerrand IV, lord of Coucy and Saint Gobain, after whose death she entered the monastery of which she subsequently became abbess. Her feet resting on two lions, she wears the Cistercian habit with hands folded in prayer, and her rank is underlined by the crozier under her left arm.

In some cases the office of abbess seems to have been the exclusive preserve – almost the fief – of an influential family, negating the Cistercian principle of the heads of houses being chosen by free election. One of the oldest preserved tombstones in Spain is that of Abbess Eldiarda d'Anglesola who ruled as abbess at Vallbona from 1246 to 1258, and who is buried in the chapter house. Three subsequent members of the family served as abbesses at Vallbona: Bianca (1294–1328), Berenguera (1348–77) and Sibil (1379–92).

In Sweden the nunneries were to a large extent the preserves of the nobility and even royalty for whom a religious vocation was not always the primary consideration. Here, as elsewhere, they sometimes fulfilled a particular role in the

103 Effigy of Abbess
Jeanne de Flandre.

structure of society whereby they offered an acceptable refuge for members of
the higher social strata. The oldest, Vreta, was founded *c.* 1162 by King Karl
Sverkersen (1161–7) with the king's sister as the first abbess.[37] Another wealthy
nunnery founded in the twelfth century as a Benedictine monastery moved to Sko
in 1235. It is referred to in a papal bull as Cistercian in 1244.[38] An early

sixteenth-century incised grave stone over two abbesses is known from an eighteenth-century drawing.[39] The inscription around the edge reads:

> This stone covers the bones of two abbesses. Strangely they were both called Helena. Their names were as dear to us as music. The first buried lies to the right, the other on the left.

An abbess is shown under a trifoliate arch supported by two columns. In her left hand she has a crozier, in her right an open book with the legend, 'Have mercy on me, O God, according to your word' (Ps. 50). The two may have been Elin Filipsdotter who was abbess in 1457 and Elin Pedersdotter who is mentioned as abbess in 1508.

The rapid rise in women's houses that occurred in Brabant in the first half of the thirteenth century is described by Jacques de Vitry in the following words:

> Virgins throng there, widows hasten there and married women, with the husbands' consent, renounce the bonds of the flesh to fly to spiritual nuptials. Nuns, leaving behind their former monastery and habit eagerly seek the advantage of a more perfect life and a more austere way. Noble and powerful ladies of the world, abandoning earthly possessions and vast domains, prefer to live humbly and hidden in the house of God rather than dwell in the tent of sinners. Virgins of distinguished birth refuse the alliances offered them, and, far from their noble family, despising the delights of a seductive world, rejecting costly garments and adornments, in poverty and humility, are wed to Jesus, the spouse of virgins.[40]

The spread of Cistercian nunneries was not confined to Brabant and the Low Countries. A large number of foundations were made in the Rhineland where many of the stories in the *Dialogue on Miracles* by Caesarius of Heisterbach are set. One of these, that of the custodian Beatrice from an unnamed monastery, was so powerful that a number of versions found their way into later collections of Marian miracle stories.[41] Unable to resist the advances of a cleric, Beatrice went to the altar of Mary to whom she surrendered her keys before leaving. After a few days she was abandoned by the cleric and, being ashamed to return to the monastery, she gave herself up to a life of shame. After fifteen years she returned to enquire of the porter whether he knew Beatrice who had once been the custodian. To her surprise he answered that she was an 'honourable and saintly lady'. As she was about to leave again, she saw Mary who told her that she had fulfilled her duties during her long absence, and she ordered Beatrice to return to her place and do penance for 'none knows of your sin'. Beatrice then made known to her confessor all that had happened and returned to her duties. The story appears in a later poem in Middle Dutch, and in a manuscript of this from 1374 Beatrice, dressed in a grey habit with a black veil, is shown within the initial *V(an)* kneeling before Mary and Child.[42] (104) According to this version Beatrice had given birth to two sons whom she left in the care of a Cistercian abbot who saw to it that they became good monks:

104 Beatrice the Sacristan.

105 Beatrice leaves her
monastery.

In habits grey he dressed the two
Into virtuous men they grew.

The story is also illustrated in an early fourteenth-century manuscript, the
masterpiece of English illumination known as Queen Mary's Psalter, so called
because it was given to the queen in 1553 by a customs officer who had
prevented it from going abroad, and it remained with her as a cherished
possession. It excels both in the number and the beauty of its coloured
miniatures and tinted drawings. Among the latter is a series illustrating thirty-six
different miracles of the Virgin. Two of the drawings feature the story of
Beatrice. Interestingly, they are not accompanied by any text which suggests that
such stories were too familiar to need any. The first shows Beatrice, on the left,
within the architectural setting of the church kneeling before the statue of Mary.
On the right she is pictured riding away from the monastery accompanied by the
cleric. (105) On the following page Beatrice is shown confessing all to her
abbess.[43] Such stories were didactic, and the message was the boundless mercy of
God and the power of Mary's intercession.

Two parallel stories from Spain feature Cistercian nuns being chastised for
planning to elope with a man and their subsequent repentance. One of them is
found in the *Cantigas* [Poems] *de Santa Maria*, a collection of over 400 Marian
miracles and hymns in verse made by King Alfonso X (1252–84), some of which
he may have written himself. It tells of a nun who, like Beatrice, takes leave of
the image of Mary before her departure. The image weeps, but the nun
perseveres undeterred and, when she reaches a life-sized Cross, the figure of

Christ wrenches one of his arms from the Cross and strikes her, driving the nail through her cheek. The nun repents and the king adds that he visited the monastery to verify the story. Another version appears in the *Castigos e documentos para bien vivir* (Counsel and instrument for right living) written by Alfonso's son, Pancho IV, for his son Fernando. In this, as Mary asks the nun why she is planning to desert her Son for the devil, Christ tears himself away from the Cross and pursues the fleeing nun through the church, strikes her and drives a huge nail through her cheeks. She falls to the floor unconscious, is saved by the nuns and subsequently repents. Christ returns to the Cross to which he is fastened as before except for the hand which struck the nun and whose nail pierced her cheeks. In the *Cantigas* scene the image of Mary and Child is placed on an altar under one pointed arch, and Christ on the Cross is depicted under another arch, the two separated by a slender column. (**106**) The nun is shown kneeling before Mary, but with her head turned the other way towards Christ who, still hanging on the Cross, is seen striking her. The illustration in the *Castigos* is very much cruder and more violent. (**107**) Christ has left the Cross, huge nails piercing his bleeding feet and left hand, while the nail from his right hand is shown transfixing both sides of the nun's cheeks from which blood gushes. These gory details are omitted from the altogether more sophisticated *Cantigas* illustration. Compared with the story of Beatrice the accent in these Spanish examples is on the deterrent rather than on the forgiving nature of God.

106 Christ chatises the errant nun.

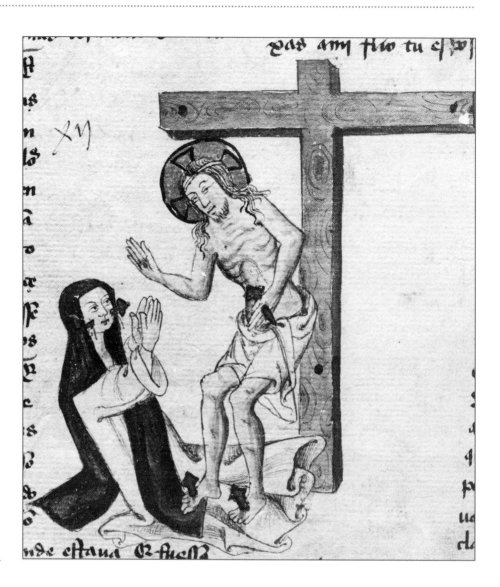

107 Christ strikes the eloping nun.

Further afield, many new monasteries were established as a result of the initiative and active participation of powerful abbots, among them Eberhard of Salem (1191–1240) who alone was responsible for six women's monasteries in Upper Swabia.[44] In the thirteenth century six nunneries were subject to the rule of the abbot of Eberbach, and by 1500 this had grown to sixteen, including three in the city of Mainz.[45] The link between Eberbach and its dependent women's monasteries is well documented by a manuscript from one of these. Dated *c.* 1260 it has a historiated initial depicting a nun – probably the abbess of one of the Eberbach nunneries thought to be either Altmünster or Dalheim which became Cistercian in 1243 and 1265 respectively – and a monk who probably represents the scribe who wrote it in the Eberbach scriptorium.[46] This is one of a number of examples of books for the use of nuns written at men's houses.

Another is the magnificent Beaupré Antiphonary written three decades later (*c.* 1290) by a monk scribe who probably came from Beaupré's mother house of Cambron. At the beginning of the third volume the Visitation is depicted within the initial *A(ntequam)* below three cusped and pointed arches. Mary and Elizabeth are accompanied by a slightly smaller nun in a grey habit with a black veil. In the ornamental bar in the lower margin a tiny monk is seated in a small Gothic niche writing at a desk. **(108)** His identity as the scribe is revealed by the scroll: 'I am John who wrote this book.'

A much later example is that of the Antiphonary from 1516 written by two named monks from Altzelle and illuminated by a third for the nuns of Marienstern.[47] The lower margin of the opening folio depicts Abbot Martin von Lochau of Altzelle (1493–1522), under whose rule the scriptorium became the most important in Saxony, and the abbess of the dependent monastery of Marienstern, Elizabeth von Temnitz (1515–23), for whom the manuscript was produced.

108 Scribe of Beaupré antiphonary.

These examples reflect the disparity between the far more restricted educational opportunities of nuns as compared with those of monks, many of whom received much of their education before entering the novitiate. The nuns' book collections were smaller: in a study of 153 French Cistercian nunneries books are only known to have existed in 46, and only a very small number of scribes are known.[48] The accent was largely on liturgical and devotional works with less of intellectual content, and the proportion of vernacular books was greater than was the case with the monks.

An altogether different impression is gained from a manuscript of a *Liber Usuum* (Book of Usages) from a Cistercian women's house in north-western Germany dated *c.* 1215. This contains an important and very rare, perhaps unique, representation of a nun scribe (**colour plate 17**). Next to a golden initial *I*, a nun in a grey habit with a black veil is depicted sitting on a stool writing in an open book with her right hand and holding a knife in her left. This corroborates the pictorial evidence we have from the three founding nuns of Notre-Dame des Prés in the cloister each holding a book (*see* 100) that nuns could and did read; that nuns were involved in copying books which we know from the Life of Beatrice of Nazareth who, as a young nun, was sent to La Ramée to learn to copy manuscripts and whose own words survive;[49] and that some houses had scriptoria, for example Wöltingerode in the early Middle Ages and Wienhausen later.[50]

The famous saying that Cistercian nunneries multiplied 'like the stars of heaven' originally referred to the foundation or affiliation of seven nunneries in the diocese of Liège in quick succession. Among them were two that were to play an important part in the religious women's movement, Aywières and La Ramée. Another was Florival, founded by the father of Beatrice of Nazareth, one of the greatest thirteenth-century mystics.[51]

Some of these new houses had formerly been Benedictine or Augustinian, while others had their origins as beguinal societies – loosely knit groups of religious women – *mulieres sanctae*.[52] The Cistercian abbey of Villers played a central role in the absorption of these into the Cistercian Order and in the foundation of other Cistercian nunneries. Under the leadership of a succession of great abbots, Villers, and to a lesser extent Aulne, took a keen interest in the formation of Cistercian nunneries.⁵³ One of them, Walter of Utrecht (1214–21) was said to be 'burning with divine love and completely absorbed in God and desired nothing so much as to draw men to the monastic life and founded convents for women'. A number of laymen also contributed to the growth of women's houses. Among them was the father of Beatrice of Nazareth, the wealthy burgher Barth de Vleeschouwer, whose four daughters became Cistercian nuns. After the death of his wife Barth himself joined the monastery as a lay brother. The nuns also counted princes among their benefactors, including Henry II of Brabant and Gerard, count of Looz, the founder of the great abbey of Herkenrode. Most important of all, however, was Jeanne of Flanders, (not to

109 Nun kneeling at the foot of the Cross.

be confused with the benefactress of Le Sauvoir-sous-Laon of the same name), who endowed three nunneries and was the benefactor of altogether fifteen, and her sister who founded two houses, including Flines in 1234. Jeanne of Flanders, who died in 1244, is commemorated in a thirteenth-century manuscript from Marquette as 'our dearest mother'. A full-page miniature has a Crucifixion scene with a small nun in a brown habit and black veil kneeling at the foot of the Cross with hands folded and eyes looking upwards in adoration. (109) Christ hangs on the Cross, his side pierced and with blood gushing out, and in lieu of the crown of thorns he wears a green headband. He is cross-nimbed and he is flanked by Mary and John, each with an orange nimbus. The background is rose and squared, the border gold with an inner patterned border in rose and blue with orange corners. Like the window from Wienhausen (see 98), the picture affirms one of the characteristics of the nuns' spirituality of the time, a special devotion to the Passion of Christ.

The same is even more compellingly expressed in a remarkable and highly expressionistic, almost modern, representation of the Crucifixion, in which St Bernard and a nun are witnessing the terrible scene (colour plate 18). This is not encumbered by the presence of Mary and John or the usual crowd but shared by the two figures alone. They kneel at the foot of the Cross, both grasping the legs of Christ and the Cross with two hands. The hanging cross-nimbed head of Christ and the bright red body and torrents of blood streaming out from all over, are in keeping with the ecstatic visions of the Crucified associated with mystics like Saint Lutgard of Aywières, who may possibly be the nun represented in the picture. The highly expressive figures, boldly drawn, contrast with the crude crozier which Bernard is too preoccupied to be carrying, but which is there to identify the figure of the saint. The drawing is from the first half of the fourteenth century and is thought to be a devotional picture from a Cistercian nunnery in the Lower Rhine.

St Lutgard (1182–1246) is known to us through the Life written by the Dominican, Thomas of Cantimpré, which is one of the outstanding biographies of the thirteenth century.[54] After twelve years at the distinguished Benedictine abbey of Sint-Truiden, Lutgard joined a small and poor community which a few years later was incorporated into the Cistercian Order and subsequently moved to Aywières. Leading a deeply spiritual life centred on a devotion to the suffering of Christ and to the Eucharist, Lutgard was also known for her understanding and deep compassion for ordinary people to many of whom she is known to have offered substantial help, even though she was herself afflicted by blindness for the last eleven years of her life. Her only lament was, however, that she would not be able to see her spiritual friends any more. Through her fasting and sacrifice she became a powerful advocate. Thomas tells of her persistent prayers which even helped an abbot and Pope Innocent III in purgatory, and freed others from their temptations. Shortly before Easter 1246 Christ and Mary appeared to Lutgard to tell her that she would soon die, and two weeks before her death, Mary and John the Baptist appeared to her and repeated the message. Her friend, the abbot of Afflighem, visited her some days before she died. As death

110 St Lutgard on her
deathbed.

approached, her countenance was very beautiful and she opened her eyes and in the midst of singing her soul flew heavenward. By common consent she was buried in the church by the abbey's father-abbot of Aulne.

The scene of Lutgard's deathbed is depicted in a manuscript of a rhymed version of her Life written in Middle Dutch *c.* 1274 at the Benedictine abbey of Afflighem by the monk William who later became abbot of Sint-Truiden. (**110**) Nimbed and with hands folded, Lutgard lies in the church within a Gothic arch surrounded by eight nuns, one of whom is carrying a processional cross and another, the abbess, a crozier. In the centre an open book from which the abbess is reading prayers is held by two nuns. Lutgard and the nuns are dressed in grey habits with black veils and white wimples. Another picture shows William in a black habit kneeling with folded hands within a trifoliate arch.[55] Above, a nimbed Lutgard is leaning out of a Gothic door to heaven held open on each side by two angels, and she places a crown on the scribe's head.

A rare document of great importance highlights the role of Herkenrode in the development of eucharistic devotion and especially in the veneration of the Host. The abbey was founded in 1182 and the nuns given permission to wear the Cistercian habit during the abbacy of Guy of Cîteaux (1187–1202) although it was not incorporated into the Order until 1217, when it was placed under the abbot of Clairvaux. Herkenrode is known to have possessed a monstrance made in a Paris goldsmith's workshop around 1268, and as such was one of the first churches to have owned this liturgical article designed for the exposition of the Blessed Sacrament not many years after the feast and its rite had been introduced. There arose a cult of the miraculous Host which gave rise to pilgrimages and processions which endured until the French Revolution and formed the basis for the abbey's thriving economy. In connection with this, Pope Urban V granted a plenary Indulgence on 16 April to all the faithful who took part in these events.

A procession of the Blessed Sacrament, emanating from the church contained within the initial *U(niversis)*, is depicted at the top of the document, a papal Indulgence (**colour plate 19**). It represents a unique pictorial record of the composition of a Cistercian women's house, and perfectly demonstrates the dependence of the nuns on the services of others. The procession is led by an acolyte carrying the aspersorium containing holy water, followed by two young men with banners, another two with candles, then two young ladies in lay dress – perhaps novices – behind whom comes the community represented by six nuns in grey habits with black veils followed by their abbess carrying a crozier. She is accompanied by a man who may be the prior or provost, and followed by two bearded men with fringed hair dressed in habits – lay brothers. Finally, the celebrant carrying the monstrance with the Host is flanked by two other clerics and covered by a baldachin carried by four lay men.

The splendour of the glass from Herkenrode, fortunately still extant as it was removed after the suppression in 1793 and installed in the Lady Chapel of Lichfield Cathedral, is evidence of the abbey's continued prosperity. In the lower left corner of twelve windows an abbess in white with a yellow crozier

111 Donor nuns from
Herkenrode.

112 Donor abbess with
St Bernard.

kneels with two white nuns behind her, also kneeling. (**111**) The panel to the
left contains the arms of Abbess Beatrice de Lobosh, who died in 1371 and
under whom the papal Indulgence was granted, with a crozier and the church
in the background. The kneeling abbess may represent her or Mathilde de
Lexhy during whose term of office the window was commissioned, as
indicated by the date of 1532 inscribed on a prominent red cartouche above
the abbess.

Another window in an English church, the parish church of Ashtead in
Surrey, is glazed with glass from Herkenrode. It consists of three panels with
the principal scene the Crucifixion and with three smaller panels below. On the
right is a nun with a crozier, wearing a white habit with a black veil and
kneeling at a prie-dieu upon which is an open book. (**112**) Below is a shield of
arms which refers to three abbesses of the Lexhy family who ruled the house:
Gertrude (d. 1519), Mathilde (d. 1548) and Aleyde (d. 1561). Behind the

abbess is the nimbed and tonsured figure of
St Bernard in a white habit, carrying a book and
crozier under his left arm and supporting the
abbess with his right hand. He is identified by the
small dog at his feet, one of his attributes. The
abbess is thought to be Mathilde de Lexhy and
the window to have originated from the private
chapel of the abbesses of Herkenrode.

The spirituality contained in the written sources
dealing with Cistercian nuns is very much reflected
in their iconography. The place of the humanity of
Christ as well as devotion to Mary owed much to
the teaching of St Bernard as did the frequent use
of bridal imagery based largely on his Sermons on
the Song of Songs. Furthermore, Bernard himself
had an honoured place in their cult.

In a stained glass panel from the nunnery of
Heiligkreuztal a small figure of a nun dressed in a
pale brown habit is seen kneeling, hands folded in
prayer and glancing upwards at the feet of a
disproportionately larger figure of the Virgin and
Child. (**113**) This forms part of the great east
window consisting of forty sections in three rows:
in the lowest is this panel of the Virgin and that of
women saints, then male saints, and in the top
row St Peter and St Paul and two martyrs. The
nun is identified as Elizabeth von Stepheln by the
inscription behind her. She was abbess from 1305
to 1312 and the window was probably commissioned by her before her death in 1312 but may
not have been completed before 1320. It was
probably the work of an atelier at Konstanz.

In a full-page miniature from a sermon
collection of St Bernard dating from *c.* 1300 the
central figures are Mary, nimbed and crowned,
in a blue tunic and red cloak, with cross-nimbed
Child in a grey tunic, his right hand raised in
blessing, on her knees. (**114**) Mary is seated on
an elaborate throne under a round trifoliate
arch. On the right is a tonsured and nimbed St
Bernard with a short beard, in a dark brown
habit and holding a crozier in his right hand and
a book in his left. His gaze is fixed on the Child.
On the left is a small figure of a kneeling Cistercian nun gazing upwards at
Mary and the Child. She is dressed in a brown habit with black veil and white

113 Abbess Elizabeth von
Stepheln of Heiligkreuztal.

114 Mary and Child with
St Bernard and a Cistercian
nun.

wimple, and her hands are raised up in adoration. The artist has chosen to
represent the figures in three quite distinct scales in order of their importance
in what was quite normal medieval practice: largest are the central characters,
then Bernard, and smallest the kneeling nun.

CHAPTER TEN

GOD'S WORK –
OPUS DEI

'They [The Cistercians] *celebrate the Divine Office with such solemnity and devotion that you would imagine that their voices were mingled with those of the angels. With psalms and hymns and spiritual canticles they invite all men to the praise of God in imitation of the angels.'*

Stephen of Tournai (+1203)[1]

'Mary is the mould, the model, the mirror, and the example of a way of life worthy of God. It is beyond our power to say anything worthy of her, since whatever we say is far below the praise that is due to her.'

St Bernard[2]

The *Opus Dei* – the Work of God – forms the primary and distinctive occupation of monks, the essential core of the monastic life around which all other activities revolve. The pre-eminence of 'the solemn praises that are daily offered to God in the oratory' was assertively defined by St Bernard in these words, 'By our Rule we must put nothing before the Work of God'.[3] It may indeed be said to constitute the very *raison d'être* of monasticism itself.

The catchphrase *par excellence* of the Cistercian founding fathers was a return to the sources, right back to the fountainhead (*fontes*), and this applied specially to matters liturgical.[4] St Benedict devoted twelve chapters in the Rule to the composition and manner of celebrating the eight canonical hours.[5] Seven of these were celebrated in the daytime, for 'The prophet saith: *"seven times a day have I given praise to thee"*. (Ps. 118:164) We shall observe this sacred number of seven, if we fulfil the duties of our service in the Hours of Lauds, Prime, Terce, Sext, None, Vespers, and Compline'. In addition the monks were to rise at night to render praise, for 'of the Night Office the same prophet saith: *"At midnight I rose to give praise to thee"*.' (Ps. 118:62)[6] According to the Rule, all 150 psalms were to be recited in the course of each week, and as a number of these were recited daily, the weekly total was approximately 250. Psalms 148, 149 and 150 were, for example, recited daily at the end of Lauds, terminating with the last words of the last psalm: 'let everything that has breath praise the Lord.'(Ps. 150:6)

115 King David and a
kneeling monk.

The psalms may be said to form the kernel of the Offices. A manuscript dated
c. 1270 from the Silesian abbey of Lubiaz (Leubus) has a picture of King David
playing the harp in the centre of the initial *A(d te levavi)*, the opening words of
Psalm 24: 'Unto thee, O Lord, do I lift up my soul.' (**115**) The initial is formed
by tendrils emanating from the mouth of a monster at the top and framed within
a square border. On the right is a small tonsured figure of a kneeling monk, his
hands raised up and pointing to the words of the psalm, thus indicating that he is
lifting up his soul in praise.

Accretions to the liturgical service as celebrated at Cluny included a great increase in the number of psalms recited, several new offices, the celebration of a great many saints' days, as well as additional masses, litanies and processions. These were all stripped away and replaced by a liturgy that conformed to the simplicity and poverty which characterized the Cistercian reform in all its aspects and to what St Benedict had laid down in the Rule.[7]

Writing at the end of the twelfth century, Conrad of Eberbach noted that,

> both as regards the way and the order of the service of God they decided from the very outset to observe in everything the traditions of the Rule, removing entirely and rejecting all additions to the psalms, prayers, and litanies which less discreet fathers had added of their own accord.[8]

This could be and was interpreted as implying that the Cistercians attached less importance to the liturgy but having decided that they would live by the labour of their own hands, this return to primitive simplicity was in fact an absolute necessity in ensuring their survival. Conrad goes on to say that, aware of human frailty, they thought the Cluniac liturgy more dangerous as its multiplicity leads to an 'altogether tepid and negligent recitation, not only by the indifferent but also by the zealous'.

Cistercian literature abounds in stories of how God rewards those who sing with devotion and punishes those who do it neglectfully. A whole chapter is devoted to such anecdotes in the *Exordium Magnum*.[9] Most common of all are those relating to somnolence at vigils, not surprisingly a relatively common occurrence. It was the cantor's responsibility to see to it that the monks stayed awake.[10] One monk was so irate at being reprimanded that he left the church and returned to the dormitory only to become the prey of demons.[11] The devil was behind all temptations; he was there, often in a number of guises, encouraging distraction and accidie, lack of perseverance, and creating occasions for sin, and he was there in full force at night when the monks were at their most vulnerable.

Caesarius of Heisterbach tells of a monk who had difficulty in getting up for vigils but who was cured when he realized that an unknown voice from under the bed urging him to stay was that of the devil. Another monk saw the devil in the form of a serpent sitting on the back of a lay brother who was asleep in choir. Yet another lay brother had his eyes closed by a cat when he was giving way to sleep in choir. As soon as the cat placed its paws on the brother's eyes, he began to yawn. A monk who fell asleep in choir was struck in the face by the devil with a wisp of straw. Yet another was so prone to falling asleep that he rarely opened his mouth during the psalms. He was surrounded by demons in the form of hogs who fed on the husks that fell from the monk's mouth and which signified the words of the psalms robbed of all goodness.[12]

Conrad of Eberbach recounts the vision of a monk, Christian, who saw the monks in choir surrounded by a great light while saying the Office and above whom there was an angelic choir.[13] St Bernard is said to have had a vision of an

116 St Bernard's vision at
the night office.

angel with a thurible incensing the brothers in choir, but passing over those who
were negligent or asleep.[14] The story from the *Exordium Magnum* that has most
frequently been represented in the Bernardine iconography, however, is that of
St Bernard's vision of angels surrounding the monks during vigils and recording
their varying degrees of devotion by writing in gold, silver, ink or water.[15] It forms
the subject of one of the early sixteenth-century stained glass panels from the
Altenberg cloister. (**116**) The choir at Clairvaux is depicted with three cowled and
tonsured monks on either side of the stalls and the high altar in the background.
Furthest left is Bernard, nimbed and holding his crozier, and with an aspersorium of
holy water before him. In the front of the other five monks are five kneeling angels,
each with a scroll on which their decision is recorded in one of the four media.
While four of them have their heads bowed and are clearly writing, the fifth – the
one facing the monk opposite St Bernard – is looking up and her scroll is blank.

St Bernard's views on the chant, parallel to his more famous opinions on the
visual arts contained in the *Apologia*, are contained in a letter in which he reveals
his objections to some of the current practices, his likes and dislikes:

If there is to be singing, the melody should be grave and not flippant or uncouth. It should be sweet but not frivolous; it should both enchant the ears and move the heart; it should lighten sad hearts and soften angry passions; and it should never obscure but enhance the sense of the words. Not a little spiritual profit is lost when minds are distracted from the sense of the words by the frivolity of the melody, when more is conveyed by the modulations of the voice than by the variations of the meaning.[16]

Very much the same sentiment is contained in St Aelred's *Mirror of Charity* in which he asked himself,

what are we doing, I often wonder, with the thunder of organ music, the clash of cymbals, and elaborate part-settings for different voices? We hear monks doing all sorts of ridiculous things with their voices, plaguing us with womanish falsettos, spavined bleating and tremelos. I myself have seen monks with open mouths, not so much singing, as doing ludicrous feats of breathing, so that they looked as if they were in their last agony or lost in rapture.[17]

He goes on to say that organ music may impress simple folk, but that it would make them laugh and that they would be 'more likely to think that they are watching a stage play than praying in church'.

Although the use of organs was at first forbidden, they were gradually introduced and, ironically, the earliest extant organ music, from *c.* 1350, comes from a Cistercian monastery, Robertsbridge in Sussex.[18] Meaux in Yorkshire is known to have had an organ in 1396, and the General Chapter sanctioned the use of an organ at Schöntal in Württemberg in 1486.[19] A Cistercian monk playing the organ is already featured in the magnificent Antiphonary from the Flemish nuns' abbey of Beaupré from 1290 which may have been written at the monastery of Cambron (Hainaut).(colour plate 20) He is depicted within the initial *I(ntende)* from the hymn for Vespers on Christmas Day sitting on a faldstool, tonsured and dressed in a white tunic and grey scapular, in front of the organ. This consists of the keys and a series of thirty-five gradated pipes under two trifoliate arches. Behind the pipes the figure of a lay person dressed in red works the bellows with his hands against a gold background. The instrument is operated by the keys being pulled out which lets the air into the pipes from below, and the note thus created is stopped by the keys being pushed back again. The blue of the pipes divides the composition diagonally into two equal halves.

The Cistercians attached the greatest importance to uniformity of practice, at the basis of which lay uniformity of worship, a requirement noted in the earliest documents of the Order:

And because we receive all monks coming from other monasteries into ours, and they in like manner receive ours, it seems proper to us and it is, furthermore, our will that all our monasteries have usages in chanting and all the books necessary for day and night offices and the celebration of Masses similar to the usages and books in use at New Monastery; that there may be no discord in our daily actions, but that we may all live together in the bond of charity under one rule and in the practice of the same usages. [20]

This was reiterated in greater detail in the earliest statutes:

It is not permissible to have different books; missal, gospel book, book of epistles, book of collects, gradual, antiphonary, rule, book of hymns, psalter, lectionary, calendar, they must all be everywhere the same.[21]

Uniformity was further guaranteed by the General Chapter decree that all monasteries were to have the same book of usages. In a number of stages a collection of regulations concerned with all aspects of monastic life emerged in the form of the *Ecclesiastica Officia*. [22] The first 52 of its 121 chapters deal with the Church's year and general liturgical concerns, followed by regulations regarding the Mass (53–66), then prescriptions as to the daily schedule (67–85), and the remainder (86–121), cover a variety of topics, ranging from the reception of guests, including that of their bishop, the care of the sick, the burial of the dead, to the various officials of the monastery.

Fourteen chapters in the *Ecclesiastica Officia* regulated the Mass. Perhaps the oldest representation of a Cistercian celebrating Mass is that of St Bernard in the Missal from the Austrian abbey of Zwettl dated *c.* 1175/6 which adorns the beginning of the Canon (*see* 17). A manuscript from the Franconian abbey of Heilsbronn dated *c.* 1260 has two historiated initials featuring monks saying Mass. It is a Gradual, the book containing the chant of the Proper of the Mass, the sections of text that vary with the season or the feast. The large opening initial *A(d te levavi animam meam)* from the first Sunday in Advent, the beginning of the Church's year, is formed by a complex design of interlacing foliated tendrils within a stepped frame. (**117**) At the top an oval medallion contains an image of God the Father. In the middle two circular medallions formed by the tendrils contain the Virgin and Child and Christ the Man of Sorrows, and the traditional symbols of the four evangelists are depicted in four smaller medallions above and below. At the bottom two further small medallions, one on each side, contain pictures of two monks dressed in blue chasubles with grey stoles celebrating the Eucharist, each attended by a kneeling monk in a grey habit. A more detailed version of the same scene is portrayed in the other initial – *D(omine ne longe)*, the opening words of the Introit for Palm Sunday. (**118**) Here the priest, in a red chasuble, is seen at the Elevation of the Host with the chalice placed on the altar; above the altar is the blessing hand of God. He is assisted by two monk acolytes in grey habits.

The same opening initial *A(d te levavi)* in another, almost contemporary, manuscript of the Gradual from Zwettl has yet another scene of the Mass being celebrated (**colour plate 21**). According to an inscription it was written by a German monk, Gottfried von Neuhaus, from south-east Bohemia in 1268. This

118 Elevation at Mass with a nimbed celebrant.

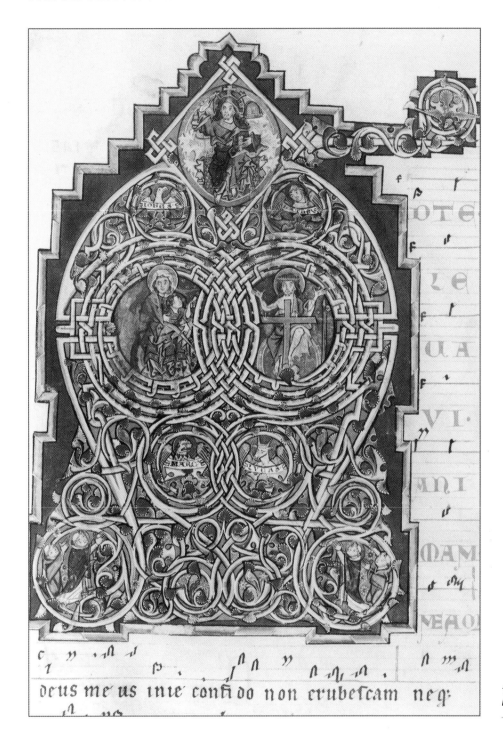

117 Monks celebrating Mass.

time the letter is formed by a dragon. In the upper half a tonsured priest in a red chasuble is depicted before the altar at the Elevation of the Host. Behind him a kneeling monk is ringing a bell. Below, a group of seven monks, four in black and three in white, form the *schola* in choir before an open Gradual on a lectern with the words *Ca(n)ta(te) fortiter* – their instruction for singing loudly and clearly.

119 Monks at Mass.

A similar scene is enacted in one of the nine carved capitals from the Polish abbey of Kołbacz dated *c.* 1330–40. (**119**) Here the Chalice, surmounted by the Host, is placed on the altar which is covered with a cloth. A tonsured monk, his hands clasped in prayer, kneels in adoration. Behind him a monk with his hood above his head is swinging a thurible, while another monk on the other side holds up an open book – a Missal or Gradual.

As is to be expected, portrayals of monks in choir are sometimes to be found in Antiphonaries, the choir books containing the chants for the Divine Office. Like the Gradual, they usually consist of several volumes divided between the days of the week (Temporal) and the feasts of saints (Sanctoral). Because of the cost of producing books, they were of a size, with large notation and text, which enabled groups of monks to share one book. This may be clearly seen in an Antiphonary dated *c.* 1300 from Morimondo in Lombardy, founded in 1133/4 as a daughter-house of Morimond (Haute-Marne). (**120**) The initial *A(ngelus)* from the feast of Easter occupies three quarters of the folio and is formed by interlacing foliage with lions' masks and grotesques. The upper half has nine tonsured monks in grey cowls in an architectural setting which represents either the church or perhaps the choir stalls. The monks are all looking in the same direction and concentrating on a large open book on a lectern. The lower half is badly damaged. Similarly, three singing monks are depicted within the initial *C(antare)* from Psalm 97 in a richly decorated Bible from Heisterbach dated *c.* 1240 as one of ninety-six miniatures. (**121**) The monks are sharing an open Antiphonary displaying the text *Alleluia letamini in Domino*. Representations of monks are also sometimes to be found in Lectionaries, the books which contain biblical readings and patristic homilies

120 Group of monks singing from an antiphonary.

for the Night Office and are usually in two parts, winter and summer. As we have seen, three of these are to be found in the Marienstern Lectionary (*see* 5, 19, and 101).

Although exemption from the jurisdiction of the local bishop was one of the privileges the Cistercians came to enjoy in the course of the second half of the twelfth century, it was nevertheless important for them to maintain friendly relations.[23] They depended to a large extent on his goodwill, for they were not only required to have his consent to found a monastery in his diocese, but they were also obliged to turn to him to perform episcopal functions like ordinations and the dedication of churches. The reverence to be shown to bishops is indicated in the chapter in the *Ecclesiastica Officia* which deals with the procedure to be followed when they visited monasteries.[24] It is perhaps what lies behind a late thirteenth or early fourteenth-century carving of a roof boss from the former nave of Abbey Dore in Herefordshire, the only daughter-house of Morimond in England. (**122**) A tonsured monk with hands clasped is kneeling in homage before a figure in a chasuble and amice who appears to have had a mitre and whose left arm, which may have held a crozier, is broken off. It is unlikely that he represents an abbot who would probably not have been mitred, and as he appears to have long hair and not a tonsure it is almost certainly a bishop before whom the monk is kneeling.

We have already seen pictures of bishops performing the dedication of the churches of two nuns' abbeys, those of Marienstern and Beaupré (*see* 101 and 102).

121 Three singing monks.

A comparable image, contained within the initial *D* in an early fourteenth-century Gradual, depicts the Dedication of the church of Vauclair (Aisne), founded in 1134 from Clairvaux. (**123**) In a scene very similar to that of the two other examples, a bearded figure in a chasuble and mitre is seen sprinkling the church with an aspergillum in his right hand. In his left hand he holds a crozier. He is assisted by a tonsured monk in a white habit who holds an aspersorium containing holy water.

The *Ecclesiastica officia* also makes provision for the confession of monks.[25] A carving of a corbel from the second half of the fifteenth century from Cadouin (Dordogne) depicts two tonsured monks, one of them with his hands folded, and the other – the confessor – with his right hand placed on the penitent's head in absolution. (**124**)

The role that the cult of Mary played in the devotional life of the Cistercians is well known, as is the contribution of St Bernard to this. The part Bernard played

122 Cistercian monk
kneeling before a bishop.

was immortalized by Dante in the Divine Comedy (Paradise, Canto 31) where
Bernard introduces Beatrice to Mary with the words:

> And from Heaven's Queen, whom fervent I adore,
> All gracious aid befriend us; for that I
> Am her own faithful Bernard.[26]

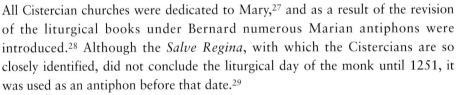

123 Dedication of
Cistercian church by a
bishop.

124 Confession scene on a
carved corbel.

All Cistercian churches were dedicated to Mary,[27] and as a result of the revision of the liturgical books under Bernard numerous Marian antiphons were introduced.[28] Although the *Salve Regina*, with which the Cistercians are so closely identified, did not conclude the liturgical day of the monk until 1251, it was used as an antiphon before that date.[29]

Sculptures were originally forbidden in Cistercian churches,[30] but statues of the Virgin were gradually introduced. Perhaps the earliest, and certainly one of the finest, was that from Fontenay (Côte-d'Or) from the late thirteenth century. Later, all monasteries would have had a statue to which the community turned during the singing of the *Salve Regina* at the end of Compline. There is a statue in the church at Cadouin with the tiny figure of Abbot Peter de Gaing who died in 1486 kneeling at Mary's feet. (**125**) At the same time as honouring Mary, the donor has seen to it that he himself was commemorated. The statue, which bears traces of polychrome, was badly damaged in the Wars of Religion but was restored in 1891.

A late fifteenth-century abbot of Cîteaux, Jean de Cirey (1476–1501), described the Cistercian Order as Mary's 'very own family', its 'patroness,

125 Abbot at the feet of the Virgin.

protectress, and advocate': 'she came in person to console, instruct, help, and direct them.'[31] According to Conrad of Eberbach, her powers of intercession were without limit. He claims, for example, that even if the Devil and Judas followed the observance of Cîteaux in humility and in its entirety they would have no cause for despair: 'the Virgin, by her mercy, would save them!'[32]

126 Abbot kneeling before the Virgin.

Mary's role as patron has received ample recognition in Cistercian iconography. We have seen examples in the presentation of churches such as in the Marienstatt panel (*see* 11) and the Wienhausen wall painting (*see* 97), as well as an early one in the Cîteaux manuscript of St Stephen Harding offering up a model of his church to Mary (*see* **colour plate 5**). She is depicted as the intercessor of the Obazine community on the tomb of St Stephen of Obazine (*see* 27), as well as in a number of images testifying to the devotion towards her of nuns (*see* 97, 104, 113, and 114) and of lay brothers (*see* 88 and **colour plate 15**).

Others include a late thirteenth or early fourteenth-century carved boss from Abbey Dore which may have come from the former stone vault of the presbytery. (**126**) An abbot with his crozier is kneeling before a seated Virgin and Child. There is a similar carving from Eberbach in Germany dated *c.* 1380, but of a simple monk and not an abbot. (**127**) It was formerly in the cloister under a canopy of two trifoliate arches and near the chapter house where the monks would pass it daily on their way between chapter and church. Locally it has traditionally been considered to depict St Bernard, but as the figure of the monk is neither nimbed nor carries a crozier, it must be seen as representing the community and as a reminder of Mary's role as the special patron of the Order. Yet another example, but in a different and highly unusual medium, comes from the monastery of Dargun in Mecklenburg. (**128**) It consists of two principal and three secondary reliefs in terracotta from the late fifteenth century.[33] They were formerly set into the wall of one of the southern brick pillars of the nave of the church. The larger of the two main reliefs is of a crowned Virgin standing with Child, while the smaller represents a tonsured and cowled monk with hands folded and kneeling before the Virgin. Below the two are three very small reliefs with pictures of animals. The composition is most unusual in that no other pair of figures is to be found in northern Germany. As can be seen in the illustration, each figure consisted of a number of blocks of clay with its shape formed by modelling with a wooden stick. Other reliefs at Dargun – those of the pillar bases in the choir and transept – were produced by impression using a mould. The Dargun reliefs have to be seen in the context of the terracotta reliefs which flourished in the southern Baltic area from around 1300 until the Renaissance and spread as far as Estonia.

Another most unusual and fine example of Cistercian reverence for and devotion to Mary is a presentation image of the scribe and perhaps also author of a manuscript from Eberbach dated *c.* 1330[34] (**colour plate 22**). A kneeling monk, tonsured and wearing a bluish grey cowl with the hood partially over his head, is depicted in the lower margin presenting his book to the nimbed Virgin in the right-hand margin. She is receiving it with her right hand while she is carrying the Christ Child in her left hand. Although the figures are somewhat clumsily drawn and unnaturally elongated with the heads too small in relation to the body, there is a sweetness and gentleness in Mary's face which is accentuated by the soft colouring and by the way she is concentrating on her Child in an exchange of glances. It is reinforced by their heads almost touching and the Child's gentle tugging at the pale rose cloak over His mother's green robe with

127 Monk kneeling before the Virgin.

128 Reliefs of the Virgin
and kneeling monk.

his right hand. The message of the image is further enhanced by the spontaneous, almost naive, text with which it is surrounded. Encircling the Virgin and Child are the words of the Salutation of the Angel, the *Ave Maria*, and the name of the monk scribe or author appears above his head as 'Gisilbertus'. He may be the monk of that name who appears as a doctor of canon law in an entry from about the same time in the abbey's cartulary. Then his words follow:

> O, my most clement Mother
> Queen of heaven, Virgin Mary,
> I beg you to take my soul
> into your most holy safe-keeping
> that you may guard the punishment due to my guilt according to your kindness and my needs. Amen.

Then, above the picture of the Virgin and Child an exchange between them:

> Although my first-born, you are to me a Father
> And you, Mother, to me a daughter.

The manuscript is an otherwise unknown canon law treatise which partly deals with the relative merits of marriage and virginity, a subject which naturally leads the mind to the most perfect of virgins, Mary, and explains the last section of text:

> She was the first who vowed herself totally to Virginity.
> Because she offered this new type of gift she was worthy to
> be honoured with the new and unheard of Gift.

As we have seen, when Benedict XII instituted the conventual seal for the Cistercians in 1335 it was decreed that it should be round, made of copper, and bear an image of the Virgin.[35] One of the forms that this came to take was that of Our Lady of Mercy – what the Germans call the *Schutzmantelmadonna* – that is Our Lady of the Protecting Mantle, one of the most popular medieval images of Mary and one that probably originated with the Cistercians.[36] It is based on a story made famous by Caesarius of Heisterbach in the early thirteenth century but had already appeared in an earlier English manuscript of Marian Miracles and been repeated in a collection of *exempla* from the Cistercian abbey of Beaupré (Oise) dated *c.* 1200.[37] In a vision the terrified monk who could find no Cistercians in heaven was comforted when Mary opened her cloak and revealed an 'innumerable multitude of monks, lay bothers, and nuns' of the Order.[38] The oldest is from a manuscript from Lubiaz (Leubus) dated *c.* 1300 with monks on one side and lay brothers on the other (*see* 79). It was already incorporated into the design of the conventual seal of the nuns' abbey of Beaupré (Hainaut, Belgium, not to be confused with the men's house above) the year this was introduced (1335), occurs again in *c.* 1350 in that of Cercamp (Pas-de-Calais), in the nuns' abbey of Ste-Marie-de-Bilohe (Ghent) *c.* 1360, and in the seal of the Definitors of the Order the same year.[39] It also occurs in the conventual seal of Esrum in Denmark. (**129**) An impression of the seal is found attached to a document from 1374 in which the monks committed themselves to anniversary

129 Conventual seal of
Ersum Abbey.

Masses for Queen Helvig, the mother of Queen Margrete I. She died that year
and was buried in the abbey church. The seal was used regularly in documents
up to the Reformation in 1536. The Virgin holds up her cloak with her right
hand while the Child standing on her knee holds it up on the other, with the
cloak protecting the two kneeling monks on each side.

The best known image of Our Lady of Mercy, however, is that of the early
sixteenth-century painting from the nuns' house of Flines (Nord) attributed to
Jean de Bellegambe (*c.* 1470–1535). (**130**) A crowned Virgin sits on a throne
with a delicately traceried back. Her voluminous cloak is held up by two angels.
Beneath it, on one side, is a nimbed and tonsured monk carrying a crozier –
St Bernard – with a large group of monks, all of them in white cowls. On the
other, a community of nuns, in white habits and black veils, is headed by the
donor, Ysabel de Maléfiance, and not the abbess, Jeanne de Boubais, whose
portrait appears on the reverse in a scene of the Last Judgment.

130 Our Lady protecting
the Order of Cîteaux.

It was the principal occupation of the monks, the Work of God, which
determined their place in the hierarchical structure of society and which enabled
them to bestow on their contemporaries the benefits which were so richly
rewarded in material terms. The idea of the reciprocity of services, in which
spiritual resources were exchanged for material protection, formed the basis of
the relationship between the monks and the outside world. The first obligation of
a monastery was to pray for the soul of the founder, but the greatest benefit the
Cistercians were able to bestow was undoubtedly that of the right of burial. The
dangers to monastic discipline inherent in this was recognized early, and the

practice was originally forbidden, but pressure on the monks soon led to an
exception being made for kings and queens, archbishops and bishops.[40] The rule
was further relaxed in 1157 when the burial of founders was allowed.[41] To be
granted a final resting place in the sacred environment of a Cistercian abbey,
surrounded by the prayers of the monks, seemed almost like being offered a
passport to paradise. Many of the greatest houses owed much of their success to
their association with a powerful founder and their ability to retain the goodwill
of his successor. Founders and their families and descendants were usually buried
in the presbytery, and many of the most important abbeys contained tombs and
effigies commemorating their patrons. We have already seen iconographic
evidence of the interdependence of the highest civil authority with the pinnacle of
spiritual force as represented by the Cistercians. It appears in the use to which
the Esrum seal was put, as well as in examples from the royal abbeys of Las
Huelgas (*see* 94) and Poblet (*see* 74).

131 Carving of kneeling
monk.

Images of monks at prayer on grave monuments are there as a reminder of
their constant intercession on behalf of their benefactors. An example of this
from Cadouin (Dordogne) may be seen in a thirteenth-century carving in low
relief of a monk kneeling with hands folded before a prayer book placed on a
lectern. (**131**) Another common form was small images of praying monks
surrounding the principal figure of the person commemorated. An incised effigy
of a layman from Vaux-de-Cernay (Seine-et-Oise) dated 1302 has two small
kneeling monks reading from prayer books at the feet of the figure.[42]

The best example, however, of the relationship between a patron and the
Cistercians and the way in which this found expression in Cistercian
iconography is that of the crusader king of France, Louis IX, who became St
Louis following his canonization in 1260.[43] He inherited his devotion to the
Cistercians from his mother, Blanche of Castile, whose father had been a great
supporter of the Cistercians and the founder of Las Huelgas (*see* 94), while she
herself founded Maubuisson (Val d'Oise) where she chose to be buried. Louis
was the benefactor of the Cistercians at Lys (Seine-et-Marne) and Chaalis (Oise),
but he is best known for his own royal abbey of Royaumont (Seine-et-Oise)
which, according to his Life, he himself helped to build:

> As the monks, following the custom of their Order of Cîteaux, went out to
> work after the hour of Terce carrying stones and mortar to the place where
> they were building a wall, the blessed king took the stretcher and, going in
> front with a monk behind, carried it full of stones.[44]

He had a room prepared for him overlooking the church, and whenever he could
he was present at the monastic Office, attended chapter and ate in the refectory
at the abbot's table. Such was his love for the monks that he would have liked to
have assumed the habit himself. But instead he was obliged to take the cross, and
he went on his way fortified with the prayers of the whole Order, granted by the
General Chapter in 1245.[45] He took with him a Cistercian, Odo of Châteauroux,
a monk and abbot of Grandselve (Haute-Garonne) according to some,

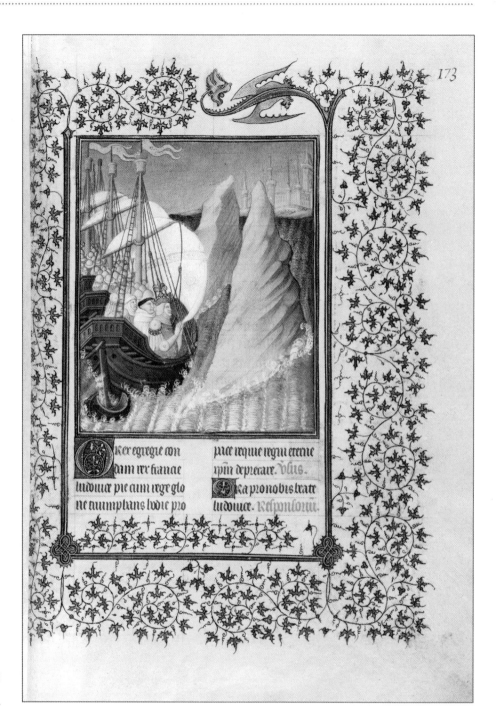

132 St Louis, King of
France, and Cistercian Papal
Legate.

Ourscamp (Oise) to others. Odo had been appointed legate in 1245 and had
consecrated the Sainte-Chapelle in 1248. He is depicted in a wonderful miniature
by Pol, Jean and Herman de Limbourg in *The Belles Heures of Jean, Duke of
Berry*, from *c.* 1406–9. (**132**) The royal fleet had left Cyprus in May, 1249, and it
is shown approaching Dalmietta in early June. The town was captured and the
Great Mosque turned into a cathedral dedicated to Our Lady, but in a
subsequent siege the king was captured. He was forced to seek favourable terms

133　Monk on the tomb of
Prince Louis of France.

before being freed and allowed to return to France. Louis is depicted on his ship wearing a plumed crown, kneeling in prayer before landing. Immediately behind him is the tonsured figure of Odo who stands out in his white habit. He is followed by the queen and the royal troops. After their return the General Chapter ordered all priests of the Order to say three Masses for the king.[46]

Louis had already chosen Royaumont as the family's burial place during his lifetime. He buried his brother there the year the church was consecrated, his daughter Blanche aged three in 1243, his son Jean in 1248, his son Louis aged sixteen in 1259, and after his own death two of his grandchildren were also buried there. The enamel plates on top of the tombs of Blanche and Jean consist of their effigies flanked by four small figures of monks carrying prayer books.[47] The sides of the stone tomb of Louis consist of a series of trifoliate arches supported by columns and resembling a cloister. (133) Within each is the figure of a tonsured monk walking while reading from a book. The background is of blue glazed tiling. Such images were a reminder of the obligation the monks had undertaken as a reward for the pious act of the founder and his descendants.

CHAPTER ELEVEN

MANUAL LABOUR –
LABOR MANUUM

'My dear friend, it is impossible to describe the impression produced on the mind by the sight of these men [Clairvaux monks] when engaged at work, or when on the way to or from the scene of their labours. Everywhere it can be seen that they are led, not by their own spirit, but by the spirit of God. For they accomplish every action with such tranquillity of mind, such unalterable serenity of expression, such beautiful and edifying order that, although they work extremely hard, somehow they always seem at rest and never show signs of fatigue, no matter how heavy their toil.'

Peter de Roya, *Letter*[1]

When the Cistercians restored manual labour to the monastic horarium they were reverting to the Benedictine ideal of a balanced life of prayer, study and work. It formed one of the main planks in the Cistercian reform and may be seen both as an essential means of subsistence following the rejection of the traditional income from rents, tithes and the possession of churches and at the same time a way of salvation. It formed an essential part of the monastic life laid down in the Rule: 'Idleness is the enemy of the soul. The brethren, therefore, must be occupied at stated hours in manual labour,' and only if this is observed are they truly monks 'when they live by the labour of their hands, like our father and the apostles'.[2]

The importance attached to self-sufficiency through manual labour expressed itself in the agricultural and horticultural imagery in many early Cistercian texts. The founder of the first German abbey, Kamp, expressed the wish 'to insert spiritually into the garden of our church some branches of the new plantation of Cîteaux'.[3] Referring to the decline of the Danish monastery of Sorø under black monk rule its Cistercian chronicler recorded its transformation from a 'desolate' state from which 'by divine ordinance it was to be handed to other farmers, who would make it bear fruit'. The patron of another monastery in Denmark, Øm (*Cara Insula*), Bishop Svend of Århus, was urged to 'take on a small flock as a painstaking shepherd and provide it with pasture, so that the first bud of the Order in his diocese might grow and reach maturity'.[4]

134 Cîteaux monk reaping corn.

Sometimes the involvement of the monks in farm work was carried to such lengths that they had no time for contemplation. John of Ford refers to monks so absorbed by field work that they forgot about the spiritual welfare of their brethren and of themselves: 'They labour with such great sweatings of their brow to bring forth from the earth bread that will perish, that they have no energy left for the bread which does not perish but endures to life everlasting.'[5]

Pre-dating these and all other literary references to manual labour, however, were the five historiated initials with genre scenes of monks at work in two of the four volumes of the commentary of St Gregory the Great on the Book of Job dated 1111. Together with a full-page opening miniature and twenty-eight other initials containing highly imaginative scenes of human and animal struggle, mostly not related to the text, they have been described as 'no less important in the art of the twelfth century than Cistercian architecture is for the history of Gothic Art'[6] and are not surprisingly the most commonly reproduced Cistercian manuscript images. In addition to the scenes of monks at work are three of lay workers, one of a youth threshing, his contorted figure and the flail he wields ingeniously forming the initial *S*, one of two men picking grapes and one of cloth-making with two men folding some cloth and a third carding some wool.[7]

They remind us that the *Exordium Parvum* had made provision not only for lay brothers but also for hired workers without whose help 'they would be unable to observe fully the precepts of the Rule'.[8] Even if, as has been claimed, the source for the Cîteaux pictures was Anglo-Saxon calendar scenes, they nevertheless provide us with a unique insight into daily life at the 'new plantation' of Cîteaux.

One of the Cîteaux scenes represents the archetypal agricultural activity of harvesting corn. (134) On the right the curved figure of a tonsured monk in a tattered brown tunic and scapular holds some of the standing corn with his left hand while in the process of cutting it with a sickle in his right hand. On the left some of the corn has been left standing in the form of a curve, and with a cornflower blue background and a bound sheaf on the right behind the monk the highly original composition forms a most successful and easily recognizable initial *Q(ui)*. The object hanging from the monk's belt is probably a case containing a stone with which to sharpen his sickle.

Many of the early Cistercian recruits came from the upper social strata, and the idea of such young men being engaged in menial tasks then normally performed by serfs was considered revolutionary and attracted much comment. According to Ordericus Vitalis, 'many noble warriors and profound philosophers have flocked to them . . . and have willingly embraced the unaccustomed rigour of their life'.[9] The critic of the Cistercians, Walter Map, marvelled at the way they lived 'like the apostles by the work of their own hands' although he claimed that it was not to be so for long.[10] One of St Bernard's novices, Peter de Roya, made the point that 'some of these evangelical poor' have been noblemen or bishops, or been distinguished for their learning, who when 'in the garden with a hoe, in the meadows with fork and rake, in the fields with a sickle, in the woods with an axe', to judge from their outward appearance, seem to 'have renounced the use both of speech and understanding', the scorn of men.[11]

At first all monks, including abbots, were required to share in the field-work. Anecdotes about St Bernard and St Aelred at work were perhaps primarily intended to convey the idea that they were both in poor health, but at the same time there is the underlying notion that because of their social background they were not conditioned to hard physical work. Aelred's biographer says that 'weak though he was in body . . . he did not spare the soft skin of his hands, but manfully wielded with his slender fingers the rough tools of his field-tasks to the admiration of all'.[12] The *Vita Prima* has the story of St Bernard's distress at not being able to keep up with his brethren in the fields. One day at harvest time he was struggling but was forced to give up. His abbot, Stephen Harding, noticed his plight and ordered him to rest. He fell on his knees and, through divine intercession, he was able to continue and take his full share in the work.[13]

The scene formed part of several of the late medieval Bernard cycles. Among them is that of the harvest on one of the eight panels from the Jörg Breu retable at Zwettl, each of which represents a different episode in the life of St Bernard. (135) Painted on fig wood, *c.* 1500, four of the panels may be seen when open and four when closed. The retable was commissioned by Abbot Wolfgang Örtl

135 St Bernard praying alongside the reapers.

136 St Bernard at prayer
during harvest.

(1495–1508) for use in his private chapel and is now in the abbey church. A
nimbed St Bernard in a black cowl with the hood over his head is shown in
prayer with his hands folded and looking up to heaven while four monks in
white tunics and black scapulars with the hoods over their heads are busy cutting
the corn with sickles and gathering it into sheaves. At Bernard's feet is a tiny
white dog which appears in seven of the eight panels, one of the attributes
associated with Bernard. It alludes to the story in the *Vita Prima* of his mother's
dream, when expecting, that she would bear a puppy who would 'become the
guardian of God's household' and 'bark on its behalf at the great enemies of the
faith'.[14]

The other harvest scene portraying early Cistercian field-work is in the form of a
rectangular panel of stained glass from the nuns' abbey of St Apern in Cologne,
dated *c.* 1525. (**136**) Here a nimbed and tonsured St Bernard in a white tunic and
black scapular is kneeling with hands folded at a small Marian wayside shrine with

the words of his prayer on a scroll before him: 'Lord, give me the grace to learn how to harvest.' At his feet is his scythe. Four tonsured monks in similar habits are at work, two of them scything and the other two gathering the corn into sheaves. The abbey buildings are in the background. The cloister at Altenberg had a panel with almost the identical scene which was made in the same Cologne workshop. Instead of being rectangular it was contained within a pointed arch; Bernard was portrayed without halo, and there were five and not four monks at work.[15]

137 Monk fishing.

Other aspects of manual labour also found their way into Cistercian iconography. One of the early Cîteaux initials from the *Moralia* refers to domestic work: two monks folding linen form the initial *M*. Their grey and brown habits have been repainted at a later date and the contour retouched.[16]

Another important part of the monastic economy was fishing and fisheries, both for their own consumption which in the later medieval period was greatly increased by grants of pittances – the pious gifts by which the monks received extra food – and to supplement their income. The Cistercians were well known for their expertise in water management, and they also used the plentiful supply of water in canals and reservoirs surrounding their monasteries for fishponds. A historiated initial *D* in a Psalter from the Austrian Heiligenkreuz, dated the first quarter of the thirteenth century, contains a fishing scene drawn in red and black ink. (137) The lower half within the initial represents water on which a boat is paddled by a lay worker. In the water are four fish. To the left of the initial a tonsured monk in tunic and scapular has a rod and line in his right hand with which he is catching one of the fish. In his left hand is a basket containing a fish he has already caught. A late medieval painted panel from Bebenhausen in Württemberg contains a small fishing scene. (138) The principal theme of the painting is the *Amplexus* – Christ descending from the Cross to embrace St Bernard – with the kneeling donor abbot, all in the setting of the abbey with the buildings in the background and the adjacent pond with the monks fishing. By the time this was painted in about 1500, the monastic economy had long been transformed from one based on the direct labour of the monks to one in which they relied on rents for their livelihood. This small vignette transmits the idea that the monks here fishing were not engaged in an activity essential to their subsistence, but in a leisure pursuit of a recreational nature.

The economy of the monastery and its estates and granges, as well as the supervision of lay brothers, was the responsibility of the cellarer. The material well-being of the community depended on his stewardship. The importance St Bernard attached to the office may be seen by the choice of his brother, Gerard, as cellarer at Clairvaux. His duties were succinctly outlined by Bernard in the lament upon his brother's death when he said,

did anything ever escape the skilled eye of Gerard in the buildings, in the fields, in gardening, in the water systems, in all the arts and crafts of the people of the countryside? With masterly competence he supervised the masons, the smiths, the farm workers, the gardeners, the shoemakers and the weavers.[17]

138 Monks fishing at
Bebenhausen.

Evidence of the status of the office is to be found at Dundrennan in Galloway
where the cellarer, Patrick Douglas, who died in 1490, is commemorated on a
grave slab. (139) He is depicted in a frontal position in low relief, dressed in a
voluminous cowl and with his hands folded in prayer. The chalice and service
book above his head refer to his priestly rank.

A successful term in office as cellarer frequently led to election as abbot.[18]
One of these was Abbot Johannes Zenlin of Tennenbach in Breisgau (founded

1158 from Frienisberg), author of the abbey's property register, one of the oldest records of the possessions of a monastery, who had been cellarer before being elected abbot in 1337. In true Cistercian fashion it meticulously records all the belongings of the abbey, its granges, houses, meadows, forests, mills, fisheries, etc. The opening folio has two magnificent historiated initials in gold with red outline and surrounded by filigree decoration (**colour plate 23**). Above the initial O (*Dee paratum sit opus*) there is a most unusual representation of the Trinity in the upper half, and below are the kneeling figures of St Benedict in dark bluish grey and St Bernard in pale bluish grey, both nimbed, tonsured and carrying croziers. The Trinity consists of an abnormally large one-eyed dove representing the Holy Spirit with its wings enveloping the Father and the Son on either side and with two beaks pointing left and right. All three are cross-nimbed. The text gives the date as 1346 and is the abbot's prayer – 'Although lacking in goodness but faithful to the Order' – he prays that his work may be pleasing to God and he invokes the intercession of the two saints. The lower initial S(*cripturus igitur possessiones*) contains a kneeling abbot, tonsured and with a crozier, with the legend 'Frater Jo(hannes) Zenli Abbas', and below a unique scene in Cistercian iconography: a seated monk, tonsured and in a grey habit, is writing in an open book – perhaps the manuscript itself – placed on a lectern in front of him. He is identified as 'Frater Jo(hannes) Meig(er)', probably the abbot's successor as cellarer or possibly the scribe and illuminator of the manuscript. In front of him are two standing figures, a bearded lay brother with the distinctive fringe and wearing a grey habit who is accompanied by a peasant with a stick. The lay brother may be one of the grange masters reporting to his cellarer who is recording what is being said.

139 Grave slab of Patrick Douglas, cellarer at Dundrennan.

So far two of the five historiated initials in the *Moralia* with monks at work have been referred to. It is no coincidence that the other three refer to monks cutting down trees. Cîteaux was described as a 'place of horror and vast solitude', a commonplace description borrowed from Deuteronomy and later applied to other Cistercian sites. Although the earliest Cistercian documents referred to the predilection for remote and desolate places,[19] recent research has shown that the majority were on the margins of already settled lands as opposed to totally untilled areas.[20] Cîteaux and many other monasteries were, nevertheless, in forest areas as witnessed by Ordericus Vitalis when he said that 'they have built monasteries with their own hands in lonely, wooded places',[21] and the need for clearing is amply revealed by the three images.

One of the three *Moralia* initials, the large I(*ntellectus*) depicting a monk felling a tree at the top of which a novice has been deputed the more onerous task of lopping branches, has already been mentioned (*see* 45). The safety of the novice as the monk progresses inevitably springs to mind and reveals a sense of humour on the part of the artist that also characterizes the other scenes. The monk has the same object hanging from his belt as the harvesting monk, and is probably used for sharpening his axe.

The other very realistic woodcutting scene is of two monks splitting a log lying on the ground which forms another initial Q(*uia*) (**colour plate 24**). The two curved figures are tonsured and wearing tattered brown tunics and scapulars and socks in numerous folds. The smaller monk has an axe with a red handle placed on the log while the larger one wields a hefty mallet. The top of the branch forms the tail of the Q. The third initial is of yet another Q(*via*). It is badly defaced and has therefore rarely been reproduced.[22] It represents two monks again forming the curve of the main body of the letter. One is plump, the other thin. They are wearing tunics with darker scapulars and are warming themselves by the fire. One of them is drying a shoe by the fire while the other shoe with long laces rests on the log behind him which, once again, forms the tail of the initial.

Cutting down trees also forms the subject of the central panel of the miniature depicting the foundation of the 'four branches from the Cistercian root' in the *Commentary on the Apocalypse* written *c.* 1243 (*see* **colour plate 6**). The note in the left margin above the picture reads, 'Here is the monastery of Cîteaux whose brothers are engaged in manual labour', represented here by six figures wielding silver axes with grey handles. The one on the left with his axe over his shoulder appears to have finished work and is about to leave while the five others are in the process of cutting down one of the three small green trees. A closer look reveals that three of them are tonsured – in other words monks. The one on the left appears to be bearded and may therefore be a lay brother, while the remaining two are not and probably represent hired labourers. If this interpretation is correct, we have here the three elements of the Cistercian workforce: monks, lay brothers and hired workmen. The artist has chosen the central panel to make an important statement underlining two of the principal characteristics of the Cistercian reform: the restoration of manual labour as an integral part of the monastic life and the institution of the lay brotherhood coupled with the need for outside assistance.

Timber yielded firewood for the kitchen and the calefactory, material for fencing and charcoal, but its chief use was in building. There was an ancient tradition for the active involvement of monks in the construction of their own oratories and homes. St Benedict had acknowledged the presence of craftsmen in the monastic community when he said in the *Rule*: 'If there be craftsmen in the monastery, let them practise their crafts with all humility.'[23] The purity and austerity of their early architecture and the remarkable degree of uniformity in the plan (now known as the 'Bernardine' plan) which was represented in every corner of Europe are of course the outcome of a number of factors, but one of these was undoubtedly the role the monks themselves played as their own architects and craftsmen.

According to the Cistercian constitution no new abbey was to be founded 'without the prior construction of such places as an oratory, a refectory, a dormitory, a guest-house, and a gate-keeper's cell, so that the monks may immediately serve God and live in a religious discipline'.[24] Such rudimentary buildings were made of wood and, as the quotation implies, were built for the monks and not by them. In some cases, however, the monks may have been involved themselves. The chronicle of the Danish abbey, Øm, records how, after four years at an unsuitable site, they moved in 1172 to their new home 'having themselves first erected houses, or rather huts'.[25] And at Rievaulx in Yorkshire they 'set up their huts near Helmsley . . . by a powerful stream called the Rie'.[26] The monks whom St Bernard had sent as an advance party 'to investigate the situation carefully and report back to me faithfully' (as Bernard said in a letter)[27] may have played some part in the erection of the 'huts'.

A number of General Chapter statutes refer to monks engaged in building work. Among these are two from 1157, one reminding monks that such involvement did not excuse them from attending offices in choir, and the other restricting monks and lay brothers to work only for their own abbeys or other monasteries of the Order, and not for outsiders.[28]

A detail in one of the sixteenth-century glass panels from Altenberg, the one depicting Stephen Harding commissioning St Bernard to found Clairvaux, has a detail of the building of Clairvaux (*see* 22). Stephen points with his left hand to the new monastery which is shown in the process of being built on the right of the picture. The scene is accurate to the extent that lay workers and not monks are depicted, but it anticipates the later stone buildings. In the foreground are some dressed stones; mortar is being prepared and transported to the site to be hoisted up to a mason working on a scaffold.

The early wooden buildings soon became too small for the growing communities. At Cîteaux their replacement began some six years after the original settlement. At Clairvaux the ever-increasing number of monks made the enlargement an urgent necessity. At first Bernard was opposed on account of the expense, but at the prospect of having to turn postulants away he relented and offers of help poured in. In the words of the *Vita Prima*, 'Abundant supplies of building material were brought, and the monks supplied the labour themselves'.[29]

140 The monk Rosen Schöphelin.

141 Prior Walther.

142 Carving of lay brother.

In England the Meaux Chronicle records how the abbot himself, Adam, took charge of replacing the building in which the monks had chanted and slept with a new one which consisted of a dormitory below and an oratory above.[30] Adam had already had a hand in replacing the original buildings at Kirkstead, Woburn and Vaudey while still a monk at Fountains and before be became abbot of Meaux. It is noteworthy that at this early date it was not unusual for an abbot to be involved as master mason. Other abbots who are known to have participated in the construction of their abbeys were Robert of Newminster and Dan Alexander of Kirkstall.

Adam had probably learnt his craft from one of the three of Bernard's monks known to have been actively engaged as master builders, either as planners and architects or as master masons. The most distinguished of these was Geoffrey of Ainai who was responsible for the second church at Clairvaux, and who is described in the *Vita Prima* as having built a number of monasteries.[31] An experienced and elderly monk, he was sent to Fountains in Yorkshire in 1133 to instruct the monks who had settled there from the Benedictine abbey in York in Cistercian observance, and at the same time he was responsible for laying out the new buildings.

The second was Achard, described as the 'initiator and builder of several monasteries'.[32] Such was his skill that he was sent to Himmerod in Germany to oversee the construction of the monastery there.[33] The third was Robert who was sent to Ireland to help build Mellifont. Bernard wrote to Archbishop Malachy asking him to 'help him [Robert] in the buildings and other things necessary for the well-being of your house'.[34]

Evidence in the form of architectural sculpture underlines the contribution of monks and lay brothers as builders. At Maulbronn in Württemberg, for example, the part played in the building of the west cloister walk in the early fourteenth century is commemorated by two corbels. One of them is the tonsured head of the monk Rosen Schöphelin, the master of the works whose name is inscribed and alluded to by the three carved roses above the head. (140) The other is that of Prior Walther, also tonsured, under whom the cloister was built. (141) His name is recorded in the inscription which states that he was responsible for the completion of the building. He is probably the Prior Walther mentioned in a document from 1303.

The carving of a bust forms a round boss in the north transept of the abbey church of Salem. (142) It is of a bearded figure with straight-cut hair and with the hood drawn up behind the head. It is thought to be that of a lay brother master builder dated *c.* 1320. Another lay brother from Salem is known to have been responsible for the building of the tower at Bebenhausen in the fifteenth century.[35] As we have seen, other carvings of lay brothers from Spain and Ireland (*see* 85) may represent lay brothers who had a hand in the building of their abbeys. The carving of a bearded head covered by a hood on a capital in the fourteenth-century cloister at Flaran (Gers) may represent another. (143)

The church at Maulbronn was rebuilt in Gothic style shortly after 1420. The master builder is known to have been the lay brother, Berthold, who is represented in a corbel in the north transept of the church. (**144**) He is bearded with his hand covered by his hood and is shown in a crouching position, his left hand on his knee, and in his right hand he holds a stonemason's hammer, the symbol of his craft.

These examples support the theory that the Cistercians were extensively engaged in building operations, at least in some parts of Europe. Their involvement may have been largely in a supervisory capacity with most of the physical work carried out by lay masons and carpenters, but often it was the result of a joint venture. There are a couple of remarkable iconographic examples which bear witness and pay tribute to the cooperative achievement of lay brothers and professional masons. A circular boss in the chapter house at Sulejów in Poland shows four primitively carved bearded heads. (**145**) Two of them have the very pronounced fringed hair characteristic of lay brothers while the others do not. This may represent two lay brothers and two professional masons. One of them is thought to be Simon, a lay brother from Tuscany, whose 'portrait' in the form of a carved corbel of a bearded head with straight-cut hair is found in the refectory of another Polish abbey, Wachock, and whose signature is found there (the inscription F. SIMON appears on the façade of the church) and at another Polish abbey. He headed a group of Italian craftsmen associated with the construction of the famous abbeys of Fossanova, Casamari and San Galgano and who were active in Poland between 1217 and 1239 where they were responsible for building four monasteries, Wachock, Koprzywnica, Sulejów and Jedrzejów.[36]

Another example of cooperation with lay craftsmen is provided by a corbel in the cloister at Pforta in Thuringia. The corbel has two heads, one with long curly hair and a beard, clearly a layman, and the other a typical lay brother with a neat beard and fringed hair. (**146**) A carving of three heads from the thirteenth century (?), which was formerly in the west wall of the nave at Villelongue (Aude) but whose original location is not known, is further evidence of monastic and lay cooperation. One is of a tonsured monk while the two others with long hair are hired workmen. (**147**)

Cistercians are also known to have been involved with the production of bricks and tiles. A number of kilns have been found close to their abbeys.[37] The use of floor tiles in Cistercian abbeys was extensive, and a wealth of material has survived.[38] The commonest designs were geometric patterns akin to those found in Cistercian capitals and corbels as well as in the characteristic grisaille windows. Other designs include foliage, floral patterns, animals, heraldry and heraldic beasts, and initials, whereas figural scenes are rare. There are, however, a number of examples from the Flemish Les Dunes, among them rare late thirteenth-century tiles portraying monks and lay brothers.[39] Les Dunes is known to have had tile makers among its lay brothers and a tile works at the neighbouring grange of Bogaerde. Also known for its extensive use of tiles was the English abbey of Warden in Bedfordshire. A tile fragment from there has part of a bearded head covered by a hood and may represent a lay brother.[40]

143 Carving of monk's head.

144 Carving of Brother Berthold.

145 Carving of four heads.

146 Carving of lay brother
and hired worker.

147 Carving of monk and
lay helpers.

There are only a few pictures which show the building of Cistercian abbeys. Although they mostly portray twelfth-century scenes, they are all late medieval. This, however, scarcely affects the accuracy of what they portray as there was only little advance in building techniques in the Middle Ages. However, the two best known, showing the building of the two German abbeys of Maulbronn and Schönau, are highly inaccurate in that the former portrays exclusively monks at work, while the bustling activity shown in the Schönau pictures is monopolized by lay brothers. An example from a third abbey, Neuberg in Austria, is more convincing in that it depicts both monks and lay workers.[41]

The Maulbronn building scene is part of a triptych painted in oil on wood in 1450 known as the Foundation Panel. It forms the outer side of the left wing. (**148**) Its original location is not known nor the purpose for which it was painted, but an account in German of the foundation of the monastery on another part of the triptych suggests that it was intended for lay people, even for lay brothers. It depicts seven tonsured monks in white tunics and black scapulars at work building the nearly completed church. In the background one monk is shown in a treadmill which operates a hoist; another monk on the roof is receiving a bucket of mortar. In the middle of the picture a monk, sitting on a stool with a square at his feet, is dressing a stone; left of him mortar is being prepared, while on the other side a stone is being measured. In the foreground two carpenters are at work.

Two out of ten pen and ink drawings from around 1600 show scenes of the building of Schönau. The drawings represent two cycles: the lay brother revolt

148 Monks building
Maulbronn.

under Abbot Gottfried (*see* 84) and the life of Saint Hedwig to which the
building scenes belong. They were probably copied from the glass which was
installed in the refectory in the late fifteenth century. One of them shows the
building operation in great detail. (**149**) Altogether twenty lay brothers are
shown at work. In the distance stones are being extracted from the quarry and
dressed; a wagon with a team of four oxen is carting the stones down to the site
while another is returning empty for another load. Two brothers are carrying
mortar on a ladder to the roof where others are receiving a large stone brought
up by hoist. In the foreground two brothers are moving a stone, three are mixing
mortar, two others are dressing stones, while yet another is having a rest and
drinking from a bottle. At his feet is a flagon which he has tied to a pole so as to
cool it in the stream. Another brother is crossing the stream carrying a long rule
and a square. Another square and template hang on the wall.

CONSTRVXERE DOMVM CONVERSI SCHONAVIENSEM
QVOS PIVS INDVXIT RELIGIONIS AMOR.

149 Building Schönau.

In the second Schönau drawing the church has been completed and work is in progress on the east range adjoining the north transept of the church.[42]

These are all interesting examples of the spirit of revival which prevailed in the late Middle Ages. It expressed itself in an interest in the pioneering days of the Order which they sought to emulate. By looking back with pride to the times when monks immersed themselves in hard physical labour they hoped to be able to regain some of the primitive zeal that had been eroded with the passage of time.

CHAPTER TWELVE

SACRED READING –
LECTIO DIVINIA

'Blessed is the servant who being intent on his spiritual reading and devoted to his meditation, takes care to collect this wheat. Then he will feast on the book of Holy Law which the Lord God has given, and it will fill his stomach.'

John of Ford (+1214)[1]

The two main characteristics of Sacred Reading are contained in this quotation from John of Ford in one of his commentaries on the Song of Songs written to complete the series originated by St Bernard and continued by Gilbert of Hoyland. First, at its core was Scripture and the works of the Fathers, themselves largely meditations on this. Second, as an exercise that was specifically monastic, it differed fundamentally from profane reading. Elsewhere, John of Ford speaks of gathering for ourselves honey from the beautiful flowers of the meadow from which it is possible 'by holy meditation, to extract an imperishable glory', for something of the glory of the Lord is reflected in even the most insignificant flower.[2] From this the true meaning of *lectio* may be gleaned: derived from the Latin verb 'lego' it does *not* mean so much to 'read' as 'to gather' or 'to collect'.[3] Just as the bee collects nectar from the flowers it visits, the monk in his meditative *lectio* gathers wisdom from the written word. The further allegory with eating is in the tradition of the Fathers who speak of 'ruminating' and 'chewing', almost in the sense of chewing the cud. A slow process which was originally carried out aloud, it enabled the reader to extract all goodness from the spiritual food and thus 'fill his stomach'. Its purpose was least of all to entertain, nor was it chiefly to inform, and it was even more than to edify: it was to open the reader to the saving grace of the Spirit and the effect was, according to John of Ford, being 'endowed thereby with insight'.[4] The *Lectio Divina* should be a reading with the heart, a listening which turns to prayer, the listening which St Benedict refers to in the opening words of his Rule: 'Listen carefully . . . with the ear of the heart.'[5]

Lectio Divina was specifically the private reading for which stated hours were allotted in the Rule and which took place mainly early in the day between Vigils and Lauds.[6] A carving from the cloister at Eberbach, close to the chapter house,

150 Bearded monk
reading.

of a bearded and hooded monk surrounded by foliage and holding an open book
provides an example of this. (**150**) Another hooded monk with a book is
featured on a corbel on the outside wall of the Royal Palace at Poblet. (**151**) Both
carvings are from the fourteenth century.

Apart from private *Lectio*, readings took up as much of the monastic day as
any other activity. There were scriptural readings at Mass and the main Offices,
the Rule was read at chapter, one of the monks read to the community at meals,
which were otherwise taken in silence, and, as prescribed in the Rule, the
Collationes of Cassian or other edifying works were read daily before Compline.[7]
This took place in the north cloister walk, therefore also known as the collation
gallery. Here, at Cadouin (Dordogne) a fifteenth-century carving of two monks
holding up an open book – an invitation to reading – may allude to this
ceremony. (**152**)

Monks were as immersed in words as most people today are in the images of
the mass media, and the possession of books at a time when they were rare and
exceedingly costly was a *sine qua non* for a monastic community. When St
Robert returned to Molesme the monks at Cîteaux were allowed to keep a
'certain breviary . . . until the feast of St John the Baptist so that they may copy
it'.[8] Within a short time the chant was revised and a magnificent Bible and
Gregory's *Moralia* were produced in the scriptorium. The earliest statutes
prescribed which books each monastery was to possess and in order to ensure
the unity of the Order stipulated that they were everywhere to be the same.[9] A
wonderful example of the importance the Cistercians attached to the possession
of books, and the way they managed to combine the spiritual with the practical,
is contained in the account of the move from Varnhem in Sweden of 'twenty-two

151 Monk reading.

monks and a larger number of lay brothers with their chalices, books, silver, vestments, and cattle' following their persecution there to Vitskøl in Denmark.[10]

Making and copying books were among the most important monastic occupations. Their production, from the rearing of animals for their skins, to the preparation of parchment, to the actual writing and illuminating, and finally to their binding, formed a major part of the manual labour for which the Cistercians were renowned. Apart from the churches they built, their manuscripts form the only part of their handiwork that has survived. Without them we would not have any of the wonderful works of art that emanated from Cîteaux and the other scriptoria. Worse still, we would have lost the works of St Bernard and the other Cistercian Fathers, and much of the history of the Order, based as it is on the writing and diffusion of Cistercian manuscripts, would no longer be known.

152 Two monks holding a book.

The importance of books has already been extensively demonstrated by a large number of images: we have seen abbots portrayed for their commissioning of books (*see* 61 and **colour plate 5**), examples of a nun and a lay brother as scribes (*see* 82 and **colour plate 17**), of a monk acting as a scribe for nuns (*see* 108), of books in use at Mass and the Offices (*see* 17 and 90), of abbots carrying a copy of the Rule (*see* 39 and 68), which, together with the crozier, was an attribute of abbots, of St Bernard writing and teaching (*see* 18 and **colour plate 7**), of St Bernard with the recipients of his books (*see* 12), of William of St Thierry writing the Life of Bernard (*see* 21), and of St Aelred, Baldwin of Ford and Caesarius of Heisterbach as authors (*see* **colour plate 10**, 32, and 47).

Accomplished copyists and illuminators were greatly valued, and many are known by name. They include seventeen from Grandselve (Tarn-et-Garonne) in the period 1150 to 1229, eight from Clairmarais (Pas-de-Calais) from Peter who died *c*. 1175 to the sixteenth century, and ten from Bonnemont (Haute-Garonne) from the mid-twelfth to the mid-thirteenth century, one of whom became abbot.[11] Several of the early abbots in Scandinavia are remembered as skilled scribes. The first abbot of Varnhem in Sweden, Henry (1150–8), who came from Clairvaux, is said to have copied missals. At Øm (*Cara Insula*) in Denmark Abbot Bo (1262–3) was, according to the Chronicle, 'not only a good copyist, but also a painter as well as being endowed with artistic talent in a number of fields', and Abbot Peder Pape (*c*. 1278) 'was a good copyist, skilled at dictating and illuminating'.[12]

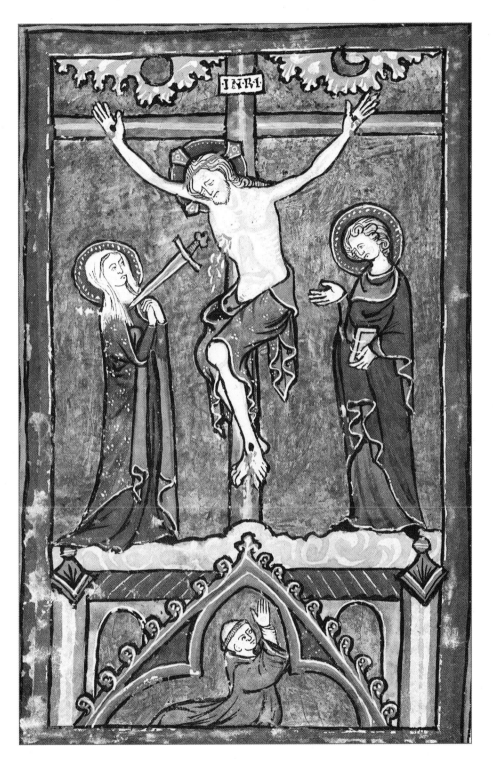

153 Scribe kneeling in Crucifixion scene.

The copying of books was a costly and laborious task. Many skins were required to produce just one book. Small letters and the standard use of contractions were a means of minimizing the number of folios. A scribe's daily output was in the region of four to six pages, and the copying of a whole Bible would take a scribe between one and two years.[13] At the important scriptorium at Stična (Sitticum) in Slovenia there was an exceptionally fast scribe, Engilbert, who copied ten pages in one day.[14] The main scribe and illuminator there was Bernard who may have come from Alsace and brought with him manuscripts which he copied at Stična. Having completed a manuscript it is not surprising that the scribe made a point of requesting the prayers of the reader either by way of a text or an image. Bernard inscribed one of his manuscripts thus: 'To the reader: Bernard, the least of Christ's monks. Whenever you read this which I have written, please remember my travail and endeavour to support me with your prayers.'[15] The half figure of a tonsured monk pointing to an illegible scroll within the initial *P(ost)* is thought to be a self-portrait of another scribe from Stična known as the Augustine Master because of his St Augustine manuscript in which he portrayed his abbot who commissioned him (*see* 61).[16]

Another form of commemorating the work of a scribe was by his portrayal in a secondary position to the dominant religious scene. The small kneeling figure of a tonsured monk, with his hands raised in prayer within the architectural setting of a trifoliate arch, which takes up approximately a quarter of a full-page Crucifixion scene, almost certainly represents a scribe. (**153**) The manuscript is a Missal from the first half of the fourteenth century. It probably comes from the scriptorium of Himmerod in the Rhineland but it may have been intended for the use of nuns as it includes the rite for the reception of nun novices.

The request for the prayers of the reader by the scribe of the Bible from Kamp in the Lower Rhineland was inserted by him at the end of the first volume of his work: 'Whenever you read this book, pray for the monk of Kamp, Rutger von Berke, who wrote it in the year of Our Lord 1312 under the Lord Arnold von Sittard, abbot of this monastery.'[17] At the beginning of the Preface on Kings by Jerome, Rutger is portrayed writing within the initial *V(iginti duas)* (**colour plate 25**). Tonsured and wearing a brown habit with his hood partially over his head, he is shown sitting on a high chair under a trifoliate arch supported by two columns and surmounted by pinnacles. Before him is an open book which lies on a board supported by a hinged rod which makes it possible to remove the board and place it behind the seat. On the side of the seat are two ink horns, one each for black and red ink. Rutger holds a pen in his right hand and a knife in his left. The knife served the threefold purpose of sharpening the pen, erasing any errors and holding down the wavy parchment, thus ensuring the evenness of the writing.

Examples of both forms of commemorating a scribe – his portrayal in a religious scene relating to the text and showing him at work – are known from the Franconian abbey of Ebrach. At the same time as Rutger was copying the Bible at Kamp, another monk was engaged in the same work in the Ebrach scriptorium. Some years earlier he had copied a Gradual. An inscription in this tells us that it was written in 1303 by Brother Sifridus Vitulus (meaning calf in Latin), and the same manuscript contains a historiated initial *M(ichi autem)* in which a monk identified as Brother Sifridus is kneeling before St Andrew whose cross is in part made up of the central column of the initial.[18] At the end of the Bible, which he wrote in 1315, there is a humorous self-portrait in which Sifridus, again identified by an inscription, has portrayed himself as a calf in a cowl sitting at a desk writing within an imaginary architectural setting of three round arches supported by two columns and surmounted by three turrets.(**colour plate 26**) At his feet is a hybrid creature, a smaller calf with a human head and torso, who is handing an ink horn to the scribe.

An earlier version of a monk at work copying comes from the important scriptorium at Heiligenkreuz in Austria. A fine drawing in red and black ink from the third quarter of the twelfth century has a tonsured monk sitting at a desk within the initial *D(um)*. (**154**) He is writing with a pen in his right hand and supporting the parchment with a curved knife in his left hand. As we have seen, the portrayal of scribes in manuscripts with pen in one hand and a knife in the other is quite standard. Unusually, this way of writing is also clearly depicted in a fourteenth-century carved corbel of a cowled figure, now headless, but with the hands holding pen and knife on the writing surface still intact. (**155**) It is from the east cloister walk at Eberbach in Rheingau.

Although monasteries had for centuries been the sole repositories of learning, following the revival of the twelfth century they were gradually superseded as places of education by the cathedral schools, out of which the nascent universities grew. At first the Cistercians ignored the challenge which this and the emergence of the mendicant friars presented, but in the long run their uncompromising attitude was untenable.[19] Regular observance was based on the maintenance of a minimum standard of education, a prerequisite which was not always present,

154 Scribe from Heiligenkreuz.

155 Carving of a scribe.

especially in remoter abbeys, and following the election of the English abbot of Stanley, Stephen of Lexington, to the abbacy of Clairvaux action was taken when he founded the College of St Bernard in Paris in 1245 with the approval of the pope and the General Chapter.[20] A number of other regional *studia* were founded, and the importance of organized studies was reinforced by the constitution *Fulgens sicut stella* of the Cistercian pope, Benedict XII (*see* 35), when all smaller monasteries were obliged to send monks to any *studium* and larger ones to Paris.

Among the *studia generales* that had been set up prior to the reforming activities of Benedict XII was the college at Oxford, established when monks from Thame founded Rewley Abbey in 1281 to serve all English Cistercian abbeys. It was later replaced by the College of St Bernard which, following the Dissolution, became the present-day St John's College. All that remains of medieval Rewley in what is now central Oxford is a piece of wall and a doorway, but a few miles north of the city there is a memorial to the Cistercian presence in Oxford in the form of two figures of kneeling monks in white habits in the tracery lights of a window in the parish church of Yarnton. (**156**) Dated *c.* 1400–20, the glass is of high quality and, most unusually, forms part of the original glazing and is still *in situ*. The two monks are almost certainly the donors of the window, and their identity as monks of Rewley may be deduced from the fact that the manor of Yarnton was granted to Rewley in 1294 and that the parish church was appropriated to the abbey. The window provides us with a rare visual testimony to the intellectual pursuits of the Cistercians in the later Middle Ages.

156 Two Cistercian scholars.

CHAPTER THIRTEEN

EDIFICATION, ENTERTAINMENT, EXPOSURE

'Oh! let us never, never doubt
What nobody is sure about!'

Hilaire Belloc[1]

Numerous examples of the 'obscene monkeys, savage lions, unnatural centaurs' condemned by St Bernard, the 'cranes and hares, darts and does, ravens and magpies' mocked by St Aelred, and the 'centaurs with quivers, headless men grinning, the so-called logical chimaera, the fabled intrigues of the fox and the cock, monks playing the pipe' ridiculed by Adam of Dore, are all to be found in the historiated initials of the early Cîteaux manuscripts.[2] This is hardly surprising. Although known in ancient Egypt and Mesopotamia, deformed monsters also occur in the prophetic and apocalyptic texts with which the monk-artists at Cîteaux would have been steeped.[3] Animals were thought of as being ruled by the base senses, and creatures which were part man and part beast contained within them the tension which characterizes the human condition. One of the scenes in the *Moralia* manuscript involving hybrids is of particular interest, for one of the combatants is tonsured and therefore clearly represents a monk.[4] The upper curved part of the initial *P* is formed by a large red dragon biting a centaur, the human upper part of which is a monk defending himself by catching hold of the dragon's neck and wielding a sword with which he is about to slay the dragon. The scene is one of a violent spiritual struggle between the forces of evil in the form of the dragon and the hybrid condition of fallen man who, despite his imperfections, has it in his power to triumph.

Images of similar spiritual struggles are replicated in a sculptural form in the fourteenth-century cloister at Villelongue (Aude). Here the elegant slender double columns are surmounted by capitals featuring a wealth of carved fig, vine and ivy leaves among which are hidden scenes of grotesque combat. At the centre of one capital is the head of a lion carved upside down and clutching in its mouth the tails of two winged griffons, one of them with the head of a monk with his hood over his head and the other that of a wolf. (157) The other side of the same capital has a large tonsured head, also carved upside

157 Head of monk with body of winged griffon.

down, and biting the tails of two winged griffons, thus symbolizing good overcoming evil. (158) The meaning of the monk-griffon having his tail bitten by a lion is more puzzling but, as it is located near the door to the refectory, it could perhaps be an allegory of gluttony and a warning to the monks in the same way as was perhaps the case with one of the cloister carvings at Cadouin (Dordogne) (*see 57*).

Greed was the vice with which the monks were most commonly associated. In the twelfth-century beast-epic, Ysengrinus the wolf-monk was driven by the urgings of his belly which had doubled since he became a monk.[5] He was, admittedly, a Cluniac, but the Cistercians did not escape criticism, both St Bernard and Eugenius III being among the poet's main objects of attack. Greed was a common subject of early Cistercian stories although it was frequently confused with legitimate hunger. Caesarius of Heisterbach tells of a lay brother, for example, who fell asleep during Mass and

> began to gnaw with his teeth the wood on which he was lying prostrate, the devil making him think that he was chewing flesh; and the grinding of his teeth was as the sound of a mouse breaking through the shell of a nut. . . . Thus the enemy tries to deceive in sleep those religious whom he cannot entrap with gluttony when awake.[6]

158 Head of monk with tails of griffons in his mouth.

One of the most popular medieval characters, Reynard the Fox, makes an appearance in Ysengrinus. He features frequently in misericords, wall paintings and marginal illustrations in manuscripts, preaching to geese and fowl, sometimes dressed as a friar or mitred bishop.[7] Such examples, and

numerous others in the margins of manuscripts, testify to
the way in which medieval man juxtaposed the sacred and
the profane, a way which modern observers may find quite
shocking. Humour and satire were thought quite
compatible with religious devotion, and grotesques
mingled happily with sacred texts. The fox, being cunning
and sly, was a great favourite with satirists. St Bernard
also made a number of references to foxes. According to
him there were three kinds: flatterers, detractors and
seducers of the spirit, 'who are skilled and practised in
representing evil in the guise of good'. He also described
them as heretics who were to be caught by arguments,
exposed and brought back to the true faith.[8] The way in
which foxes were portrayed in a variety of guises in the
margins of manuscripts is therefore quite understandable.
More puzzling, however, is the appearance of a fox
dressed as a monk in a Cistercian church. A carving in red
sandstone from the third quarter of the fourteenth century
at Amelungsborn in Lower Saxony, in one of the partitions
between the three seats of the sedilia, has a standing fox
with a bushy tail between its legs and dressed in a hooded
cowl. He holds a book and is preaching to a group of
geese at his feet. (159) What can this mean? It may
represent a symbol of a cunning misuse of spiritual power,
a warning against false preachers to those naive enough to
be deceived by a heretic dressed as a monk. Or it could
possibly be an example of something good: just as 'the
lion will lie down with the lamb' in the messianic era, so
the fox will read to geese instead of ravaging them. In the
particular setting of a Cistercian church, however, it does
seem an enigma. Perhaps it is best not to be too subtle and to admit, in the
words of the eminent art historian, Emile Mâle, that 'symbolism occupies a
great enough place in medieval art without us trying to look for it where it is
not'.[9]

159 Carving of fox in
monk's habit.

Less ambiguous than this example of impersonation and the strange
contorted configurations of animal, human and hybrid forms locked in mortal
combat are the more straightforward representations of monks in struggle
with the devil, a theme familiar in Cistercian *exemplum* literature. A
thirteenth-century Gradual from Lubiaz (Leubus) has an initial P(*uer natus est
nobis*) whose main motif is a Nativity scene but which also contains a tiny
image of a monk who takes hold of the mouth of a monster, signifying the
triumph of good over evil.[10] Significantly, a similar scene is depicted in an
understated, almost imperceptible, detail in a fourteenth-century manuscript
of the *Dialogue on Miracles*. It forms part of the upper flourish of the initial
C containing an image of Caesarius of Heisterbach (*see* 48). A tonsured head

160 Monster perched on the head of a monk.

appears within the smaller initial *A(nno)* and a closer look reveals a monster looking at the monk and with its hind legs perched on the monk's head. (**160**) The monster has a long foliate tail. This vignette recalls the story in the *Dialogue*, for example, of a vision of demons in the form of apes and cats sitting on the shoulders of monks on their way to church which caused the monks to imitate the frivolities of the demons. There were others 'before whom great and hideous dogs went in such a way that the chains which could be seen round their necks also passed round the necks of the monks, and by them they were dragged to share in the gambols of the devils'.[11] The story had its desired effect, for it caused Caesarius' novice to remark how man often gives the devil the opportunity for temptations, to which Caesarius readily concurred.

The devil was particularly active when the monks were at prayer. On another occasion, demons so thronged the choir that the brothers broke down in the psalm and peace was only restored when the demons departed.[12] A devil is depicted attacking a monk during Mass in a carved capital dated *c.* 1330–40 from the Pomeranian abbey of Kołbacz (Kolbatz). (**161**) One side depicts a Mass scene (*see* 119); on the other a naked devil with long ears pointed downwards holds his tail with his left hand while grabbing hold of the hood of a monk kneeling in prayer before an open book. In a similar cowardly attack from the

161 Monk attacked by the devil.

162 The devil attacks a monk from behind.

back a winged devil with long pointed ears is depicted in the margin of a thirteenth-century manuscript from Dore in Herefordshire. Here the devil is again catching hold of a monk's hood from behind, this time using a long rod with a hook. (**162**) The monk is seated and in conversation with a layman. Such portrayals of the devil in a monastic context as 'a fisher of men' is not uncommon: it occurs in a fifteenth-century Flemish drawing of monks in a boat being plucked out by devils on the shore using rods, and in another from *Le Pèlerinage de la Vie Humaine* Guillaume de Degulleville meets Satan engaged in fishing with a rod and nets.[13]

Small images of the heads of monks, either as a planned integral part of the overall design such as within a historiated initial, or as a casual afterthought in the margin, are not uncommon in Cistercian manuscripts. We have already seen the self-portrait of the lay brother scribe from the Flemish abbey of Ter Doest (*see* 82). Other examples include tiny tonsured heads in the flourish of two historiated initials in an early thirteenth-century manuscript from Cîteaux.[14] A caricature of a monk's head in profile forms part of the *N* of the magnificent illuminated initial *A(ngelus)* in the late thirteenth-century Beaupré Antiphonary. (**163**) The head is clearly tonsured, is very toothy and with a pronounced stubbly beard. A not dissimilar strange cartoon of a monk in profile makes up the initial *P(anem)* in a late medieval Gradual from Cadouin (Dordogne). (**164**) The same manuscript contains two further caricatures of monks.[15] A tonsured and bearded head in a frontal position neatly fills the initial *O(nus)* in a manuscript from the Franconian abbey of Heilsbronn. (**165**)

Other representations are more in the nature of spontaneous jottings, the product of daydreams, almost doodles or even graffiti. They include a marginal drawing full of character in a canon law manuscript from Vauclair (Aisne). It is

163 Caricature of a monk's head in Beaupré antiphonary.

164 Caricature of monk's head from Cadouin Gradual.

165 Head of a monk with initial.

166 Caricature of monk in profile.

167 Caricature of two monks from Fountains.

of a hooded monk with a long nose and a prominent chin. (166) The Victorian antiquary, J.R. Walbran, sketched caricatures of two monks which he found in a medieval manuscript from Fountains in Yorkshire. (167) It has not been possible to locate this manuscript, and it may therefore be lost. He noted that the drawings show that the abbey was 'occasionally tenanted by men not wholly deficient in sarcastic and graphic power of expression'. Caricatures of monks were not confined to manuscripts. At Cleeve in Devon a crude profile head of a tonsured monk reminiscent of the Fountains caricatures is painted on the wall in the gallery north of the Painted Chamber. (168) He may be the 'Thomas' whose name appears nearby in two places, and was perhaps the artist of the wall paintings in the adjacent chamber.

Just as many representations of monks in medieval manuscripts are visual parallels to the themes in Cistercian *exempla* and thus didactic in character, others adorning the margins of secular manuscripts were of a satiric or even burlesque nature.[16] Many of the *fabliaux* illustrations were fiercely anti-clerical, and much of the criticism was directed at monks. The same theme found its way into popular legends. Stories of the escapades of demons within the cloister may have a common ancestry with the *exempla* which were an aid to preaching and, like the Germanic cobalts or goblins of pagan times, they specialized in tricks which were mischievous rather than evil and which tended to be played on those who deserved them.

Among them was the fifteenth-century legend of the devil in the guise of Brother Rus from Esrum in Denmark which has parallel counterparts from both Saxony and England and which may have its origin in milder thirteenth-century versions. He is best known, however, in the form presented in the 1555 printed edition as part of the anti-monastic propaganda of the recently introduced Lutheran Reformation. He entered the monastery as a cook's assistant. After a quarrel with his superior he gained promotion by disposing of him in a large boiling kettle, as illustrated in a woodcut from a 1515 edition. (169) He was expert at preparing sumptuous dishes and for smuggling women into the abbey, and as a reward he was invited to join the community. He caused much discord, and some of the versions have him making clubs with which to arm the monks and hurling a wooden bench at his fellow monks. The scene is depicted in the lower half of the illustration.

Another legend in a Cistercian setting is that of the rogue jester Till Eulenspiegel (Owlglass). The text which illustrates one of his pranks explains how he came to enter the monastery of Mariental near Brunswick: 'Now having spent a lifetime crisscrossing the land Eulenspiegel had become old and weary and was smitten with massive remorse. He decided that he wanted to enter a monastery there to complete his time in poverty and serve God to the end of this life.' (170) The story goes back to the fourteenth century and is an amalgam based on two historical characters. Eulenspiegel was made doorkeeper and given orders by the abbot only to let in every fourth person lest the monastery should grow poor having to provide for too many mouths to feed. This he fulfilled so faithfully that he even refused entry to the monks themselves. He was removed

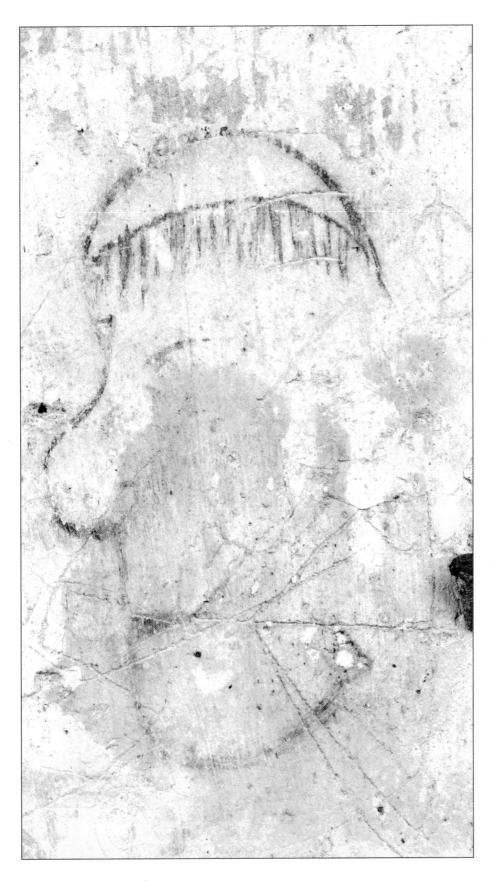

168 Caricature of a monk's head from Cleeve.

169 Legend of Brother Rus.

and given the task of checking the attendance at night office. He broke a few steps of the wooden staircase and recorded the number of those who fell by a cut on a tally stick which he handed to the abbot. A woodcut from the 1515 edition printed in Strassburg shows the monks tumbling down with Eulenspiegel behind them with crossed arms. The original character is more in line with the ancient cobalt tradition, but in the later Middle Ages there was a transformation of the goblin figure with his relatively harmless pranks giving way to events of a diabolical nature. Like Brother Rus, the Mariental legend was adapted as part of the Reformation polemic. The goblin was equated with the devil and some of the features from the Danish legend, including the club motif and boiling a person alive, found their way into the story of Till Eulenspiegel.

A satirical woodcut from 1521 by Sebald Beham – one of the three so-called 'godless artists from Nuremberg' because of the polemical nature of their work – depicts the three vices for which the monks were accused in the later Middle

170 Legend of Till Eulenspiegel.

171 The hunting of monks
and priests.

Ages: Pride, Luxury and Avarice are represented by three women tugging at the
hood of a monk while a peasant, supported by Poverty, is pulling him by the hair
and thrusting a book representing the true Gospel into his mouth.[17] The same
artist has illustrated a Reformation Pamphlet dated 1526 entitled 'The Papacy
and its Adherents'.[18] It consists of seventy-three woodcuts showing the dress of
the different ranks of the church hierarchy and of religious orders accompanied
by a short text. The 'Bernardine Order' is represented by a cowled monk with
the text: 'The holy man St Bernard first founded this order. His rule has sustained
many people so that the devil may hold sway over them for they have thought up
much wickedness and made poor people entirely into fools.'

Contemporary with these is a large woodcut in four parts by Erhard Schön
entitled 'The Hunting of Monks and Priests'. (171) Priests, monks and friars are
depicted in a clearing in a wood surrounded by a fence being chased by devils
with spears and clubs. One of them is on horseback, another is using hounds, yet
another is preventing an escape over the net. They are driving the clerics towards
the mouth of hell in which the pope is enthroned as Antichrist. Some of the
clerics are accompanied by their concubines, including the Cistercian at the
centre of the picture in the background who is holding the hand of a woman.

The most powerful indictment against the monks for incontinence, however, is in a full-page miniature in a Hussite propaganda manuscript dated 1490–1510. (**172**) The Hussites had destroyed some thirty Cistercian monasteries in Bohemia, Moravia and Silesia.[19] The Jena Codex contains eighty-eight full-page pictures by a number of hands. Together with the text it contrasts the simplicity and poverty of the early church with the corruption of the medieval church, the suffering of

172 The monastery garden.

the martyrs with the luxury of the pampered cardinals, and the purity of the true Christian with the depravity of the monk. One of the illustrations is entitled 'The Monastery Garden'. It shows two trees with a monk and a nun embracing in the centre. On the top of one tree, shaken by a nun, is the forbidden fruit of two monks. A third is on his way down with a nun ready to catch him. The scene is reversed on the other side: here two nuns are at the top of the tree being shaken by a monk, and a third nun is on her way down, a monk preparing to catch her. The monk in the centre and the one falling from the tree on the left are clearly Cistercians. The text is partly in Czech, partly in Latin. One scroll has, 'Many humans take spiritual risks – they are damned by God' and, at the bottom in both languages, 'Where there is incense and litigation [that is in monasteries] there is no child's play'.

Although these pictures do not, of course, present an objective view, arguing that there is no smoke without a fire, they cannot be altogether dismissed. Decline in discipline was the inevitable corollary of loosening ties with Cîteaux, which in turn resulted from a growth of nationalism and was eventually to lead to the fragmentation of the Order into congregations. And yet, paradoxically, the period immediately preceding the extinction of monasticism in large parts of Europe showed signs of energy and renewal following the dark years of the fourteenth century. Cîteaux was ruled by one of its great abbots, Jean de Cirey (1476–1501), who prepared for the troubled times that lay ahead by editing a complete collection of the Order's privileges (*see* 9) and who was described as 'the column which prevented the ruin of Cîteaux'.[20] In England the decades before the Dissolution were marked by much building activity, for example at Cleeve, Forde and Fountains under a succession of great abbots, including John Darnton (*see* 76) and his successor, Marmaduke Huby. According to David Knowles the Cistercians were 'better organized, better disciplined, and more firmly tied to the foreign centre of authority than has hitherto been realized'.[21] In Germany, the marvellous glass from Altenberg (*see*, for example, 12 and **colour plate 16**) testifies to a vitality and faith in the future at variance with the storm that was looming on the horizon.

Sometimes the Cistercians were the victims of political events. A Scandinavian example followed the atrocities known as the 'Bloodbath of Stockholm' when Christian II of Denmark, having failed in his attempt to gain the Swedish throne, paused at the Cistercian abbey of Nydala and, in return for the hospitality received, pillaged the monastery, desecrated the church, and murdered the abbot and five of his monks. The scene is depicted in a detail from King Gustav Vasa's 'Reformation Plate', an engraving from 1676 copied from the original commissioned in 1524 shortly after the event by the Swedish king. (**173**) It shows the monks being thrown into the nearby lake with the church in the background.

Even today the Cistercians are not immune from the traumas and currents of the times. The same forces of evil are still at play. On 21 May 1996 seven French monks from the abbey of Our Lady of Atlas in Algeria were assassinated for their monastic way of following Christ according to the Rule which, in the words

173 The murder of monks at Nydala in Sweden.

of William of Malmesbury, was promulgated to 'call wayward nature back to reason'.[22] Although decimated by religious wars and the secularization following the Enlightenment, the Cistercians survive today as the heirs of generations of men and women in pursuit of an ideal above themselves, and are still now witnesses to this in a greater part of the world than ever before.

174 A present-day
Cistercian – New Melleray,
Iowa, USA.

NOTES

PREFACE

1. William of Malmesbury 1968, 351.
2. Chibnall 1969–80, 4:310–11.
3. Chibnall 1969–80, 4:327. For the construction of the three churches, see Aubert 1947, 1:191, 182, and 158 respectively.
4. There are many fine examples, the more recent ones beautifully produced with many colour illustrations. The classical study (Hümpfner, 1927), however, has only two examples from manuscripts out of a total of ninety-six, and both are late medieval. The work covering Spain (Durán, 1990) has only two illustrations from the thirteenth century, the rest being later. An Italian study (Dal Prà, 1991) deals with examples from the fifteenth to the seventeenth century. A study of the Bernard cycles (Paffrath, 1984) is inevitably confined to later material, mostly post-medieval. A more recent work by the same author (Paffrath, 1990), however, covers much of the earlier German material as well as later medieval examples of paintings of the Italian school.
5. *Apologia* 29; trans. Matarasso, 1993, 57.
6. Rudolph, 1990.
7. For legislation on art and architecture, see Norton, 1986.
8. Reuterswärd, 1986, 99.
9. For this and other examples of illumination at Clairvaux, see Dodwell,1954, 109.
10. James, 1951, 141.
11. For the use of glass in Cistercian cloisters, see Hayward, 1973.

CHAPTER ONE

1. Philip of Harvengt, *De institutione clericorum*, 4:125, PL 203:836–7; trans. Constable 1985, 43.
2. Dt 32:10; *Exordium Cistercii* 1, Bouton & Van Damme, 1974, 111; trans. Lekai, 1977, 443. Also used in the *Exordium Magnum* 1:13, Griesser, 1961, 65.
3. *Exordium Cistercii* 1, Bouton & Van Damme, 1974, 111; trans. Lekai, 1977, 443.
4. *Exordium Parvum* 3, Bouton & Van Damme, 1974, 60; trans. Lekai, 1977, 452.
5. *Exordium Parvum* 1, Bouton & Van Damme, 1974, 57; trans. Lekai, 1977, 451.
6. *Exordium Parvum* 2, Bouton & Van Damme, 1974, 58; trans. Lekai, 1977, 451.
7. Chibnall, 1969–80, 3:338–9.
8. Chibnall, 1969–80, 4:312–3.
9. William of Malmesbury, 1847, 349.
10. PL 182:704.
11. Erlangen, University Library MS 486/2, f. 13r; Lutze 1936, 33–4 and fig. 17; Sprusansky, 74, no. 52, fig. 28.
12. For the iconography of St Benedict, see *Lexikon der Christlichen Ikonographie*, 1968–76, 5:351–64; Batselier, 1980; Stiennon, 1993; and vol. 1 of *Benedictus in de Nederlanden*, 1980.
13. The catacomb fresco is reproduced in colour in Batselier, 1980, 12. For the Civate image, *see* Stiennon, 1993, 155.
14. Rule Prologue, trans. McCann, 1976, 1.

15. Zwettl MS 84, f. 123v; Ziegler, 1985–92, 1:158–67; Winkler, 1923, 13–4.
16. Libor, 1967, 54–6; Rothe, 1968, 197; Bruck, 1906, 86–7, no. 35.
17. Kloss, 1942, 199; Jazdzewski, 1992, 243–5.
18. London, British Library MS Add. 16950, f. 193r; Swarzenski, 1936, 1:114–15.
19. Karlsruhe, Badische Landesbibliothek MS Cod. U H 1, f. 159v; Batselier, 1980, 31; Beer, 1959, 99.
20. Ziegler, 1985–92, 1:158–67.
21. Rule 1, trans. McCann, 1976, 5. The suggestion that the four monks depicted in the Zwettl manuscript are the four kinds described by St Benedict is made in Ziegler, 1985–92, 1:XXX. I am indebted to Fr Hilary Costello for the further identification of the four different kinds.
22. Ziegler, 1985–92, 1:24–6.
23. Jazdzewski, 1992, 246; Kloss, 1942, 198–9.
24. I am indebted to Zuzana Všetčková of the Czech Academy of Sciences for information on the Osek Lectionary.
25. Oxford, Bodleian Library MS Lyell 85, f. 1v; *De praecepto et dispensatione*, SBOp 3:253.
26. PL 185:267.
27. Bernard was frequently described as *vir Dei* in the *Vita Prima*, for example PL 185:274, 275, 277, 278; the same description also occurs in the *Exordium Magnum*, for example in 2:6, Griesser, 1961, 102.
28. Frundt, 1961, 102.
29. Cocheril, 1972, 135–7.
30. Becksmann & Korn, 1992, 227–8. The two saints also appear together in a stained glass panel dated 1547 from the Swiss nunnery of La Maigrauge separated by the arms of Clairvaux, Bernard in white and Benedict in grey, now in the Cleveland Museum of Art. (Zakin, 1995, 179–86).
31. *Liber de Gradibus Humilitatis et Superbiae*, SBOp 3:13–59. For the dating, see, Holdsworth, 1994, 34–9 and 58.
32. Rule 7, trans. McCann, 1976, 16–22.
33. Kline, 1992, 169.
34. Escallier, 1852, 110; this was copied at Anchin *c*. 1165 according to Leclercq (SBOp 3:XXX). The initial *B(ernardus)* is on f. 4v. See also the caption on the reverse of plate 9 in Załuska, 1992.
35. *Sermo 1 In natali Sancti Andreae*, SBOp 5:433.
36. Rule Prologue, trans. McCann, 1976, 4.
37. Aachen, 1980, 421–2 and colour plate 3.

CHAPTER TWO

1. *Exordium Parvum* 12, trans. Lekai, 1977, 456.
2. Quoted in Paulus, 1890, 70. A drawing of the wall painting is facing p. 64.
3. King, 1954, 2; Lekai, 1977, 14.
4. For this, see Lekai, 1977, 11–13.
5. *Exordium Cistercii* 1, trans. Lekai, 1977, 443.
6. *Exordium Parvum* 9, trans. Lekai, 1977, 455.
7. William of Malmesbury, 1847, 350.
8. *Exordium Parvum* 7, trans. Lekai, 1977, 454.
9. *Exordium Parvum* 7, trans. Lekai, 1977, 455.
10. William of Malmesbury, 1847, 350.
11. *Exordium Parvum* 9, trans. Lekai, 1977, 455.
12. *Exordium Magnum* 1:16 and 1:21, Griesser, 1961, 69 and 77; Załuska, 1991, 56–60
13. PL 157:1269–88.
14. Canivez 2:34 (Statute 1224:22).
15. Lekai, 1977, 16–17.
16. The Beaupré collection. For this, see McGuire, 1983, 224.

17. *Pro libro Oisb. scriptore perpetua vita.*
18. PL 185:266.
19. Bouton & Van Damme, 1974, 104–5.

CHAPTER THREE

1. PL 207:303.
2. James, 1931.
3. Kauffmann, 1968, 14–6.
4. James, 1931, 67–8.
5. Kauffmann, 1968, 40.
6. The Latin text is printed in Wachtel, 1955.
7. Wachtel, 1955, 347–9.
8. The notes in the margin are not printed in Wachtel, 1955 but in Leclercq, 1956, 305.
9. Sadly the figure is partly damaged by a dark stain and since the modern re-binding of the manuscript only part of it can be seen properly, the rest of it being hidden in the joint.
10. Auberger, 1986, 25.
11. Lekai, 1977, 463.
12. Knowles, 1940, 213.
13. For this and the evolution of the *Charter of Charity*, see Auberger, 1986, 25–41.
14. The way in which the ideas that led to the *Charter of Charity* were rooted in Stephen Harding's interpretation of the Rule is dealt with in McGuire, 1995, 402-4. Here visitation is interpreted as emanating from the emphasis in the Rule on consultation in the exercise of abbatial authority, and the General Chapter as an extension of the dialogue which took place within the chapter of individual monasteries to that which was to regulate the relationship between all houses of the Order.
15. Leclercq, 1956, 305.
16. King, 1954, 108, 149–53 and 332.
17. For the distribution of monasteries, see Donkin, 1978, 21–9. The total number of houses belonging to each filiation were: Clairvaux 356, Morimond 214, Cîteaux 109, Pontigny 43, and La Ferté 16. The divergence between the character of Cîteaux and Clairvaux forms the thesis of Auberger, 1986; for a summary, see 317–24.
18. Scott & Swinton Bland, 1929, 6.
19. Załuska,1989, 233–4.
20. Mahn, 1951, 148–50.
21. *Exordium Magnum* 1:21–31, 6:10, Griesser, 1961, 77–89 and 365.
22. Knowles, 1963, 100.
23. *Exordium Magnum* 1:27, Griesser, 1961, 84.
24. PL 185:1332; *Exordium Magnum* 1:23, Griesser, 1961, 82.
25. Paffrath, 1984, 52–4.
26. For this, see Pächt, 1962.
27. Lekai, 1977, 451.
28. Auberger, 1986, 31.
29. France, 1992b, 130–2.
30. Cologne, 1974, no. 5, 70.
31. Illustrated in Paulus, 1890, facing p. 64.

CHAPTER FOUR

1. James, 1983, 76.
2. Abbot Geoffrey's Sermon on the anniversary of St Bernard's death; PL 185:576
3. *Vita Quarta* 2:16; PL 185:549.
4. Paffrath, 1990, 44–9; Paris, 1990, 71; Duràn, 1990, ill. 58, 72, 78, 96; Berlioz, 1990, 119.
5. For the satirical literature on St Bernard, see Berlioz, 1993, 211–28.

6. St Bernard as the 'chimaera' of his age is examined in Sommerfeldt, 1987, 5–13.
7. Letter 12 in SBOp 7:62; trans. James, 1953, 49.
8. Letter 48 in SBOp 7:139; trans. James, 1953, 81.
9. Letter 250 in SBOp 8:147; trans. James, 1953, 402.
10. For this, see the chapter, 'The first Cistercian Renewal and a Changing Image of Bernard' in McGuire, 1991, 99.
11. *Exordium Magnum* 2:2, Griesser, 1961, 99.
12. *Vita Quarta* 2:16; PL 185:549.
13. *Vita Prima* 1, 3:7; PL 185:230..
14. *Vita Prima* 1, 12:57; PL 185:258
15. Apocalypse 20:1. Examples include a carved oak statue from the Rhineland, ill. in Paris, 1990, 281, and a Florentine painting dated 1505 in which Bernard is depicted with a small devil on a chain at his feet, ill. in Paffrath, 1990, 50.
16. Réau, 1955–9, 3:1:215. Other examples are found in Paris, BN MS Lat. 10532, f. 330; and Paris, Arsenal MS 438, f. 13.
17. *De Miraculis* 3:2:19, PL 185:1328; *Exordium Magnum* 2:7, Griesser, 1961, 102–3.
18. Paffrath, 1990 gives examples of paintings: no. 15, 55–7; no. 16, 58–9; no. 25, 69; no. 26, 70; of a manuscript: no. 42, 89; and of stained glass: no. 55, 104.
19. Paffrath, 1984, ill. 56 and 57.
20. Duràn, 1990, ills. 72, 74 and 90.
21. *Lexikon*, 1968–76, 5:371–85.
22. For the lactation, see Réau, 1955–9, 3:1:213–5; Berlioz, 1988, 270–83; Dupeux, 1993, 152–65.
23. Illustrated in Paris, 1990, 12 and 23 (detail).
24. Chantilly, Musée de Condé, MS 1078, f. 178r, ill. in Berlioz, 1988, 275.
25. For this, see McGuire, 1991, 196–204.
26. Dupeux, 1993, 157.
27. An example of this is an anonymous Flemish painting from 1470–80 in Antwerp, ill. in Dupeux, 1993, 164.
28. Illustrated in Paffrath, 1990, no. 6, 45 and no. 8, 47.
29. On the *Vera Effigies*, see Quarré, 1954, 342–9; Schmitt, 1990, 151–2; Schmitt, 1992, 639–46.
30. *Vita Prima* 3, 3:1, PL 185:303.
31. *Vita Prima* 1, 3:6, PL 185:306.
32. For example, in the classical Bernardine iconographical study (Hümpfner, 1927) the Clairvaux *Vera Effigies* is followed by six more examples up to the seventeenth century.
33. Examples include colour plate 8, 17, 18, 25 and 39. Many other examples are illustrated in Paris, 1990; 59, 162, 275, 277, 278, 282; Duràn, 1990; 14, 18, 21, 23, 31, 37, 42 and many others; Paffrath, 1990; 40, 46, 52, 60, 91, 94, 96, 117.
34. *Summa Cartae Caritatis* 26, trans. Lekai, 1977, 450.
35. Quarré, 1954, 343, quoting Joseph Meglinger *Descriptio iteneris cisterciensis*, Lucerne, 1667, 164.
36. This carried the inscription: 'The true likeness of Lord Bernard, life size, from the sculpted prototype which is to be found at Clairvaux.' (Quarré, 1954, 343).
37. Réau, 1955–9, 3:1:207–17; *Lexikon*, 1968–76, 5:371–85.
38. A German triptych from *c.* 1500 has an *Amplexus* picture with five mitres at the foot of the Cross (ill. in Paffrath, 1990, 59). One of the Altenberg glass panels now lost showed Bernard refusing the five bishoprics: Genoa (1133?), Chalons (before 1135), Milan (1135), Langres (1138) and Reims (1139). For this, *see* Paffrath, 1984, 126–9. Bernard's second biographer, Arnald of Bonneval, says: 'How many churches destitute of pastors have chosen him for their bishop! . . . All these invitations he disregarded; the honours offered did not appeal to his soul' (*Vita Prima* 2, 4:26; PL 185:283).
39. *Vita Prima* 1, 1:2; PL 185:227–8. For example, a small white dog appears in seven of the eight panels of the Zwettl retable, ill. in Paffrath, 1984, 371–6 and 378.
40. A rare example is in a historiated initial from Stams in Tirol dated 1459, MS 12, f. 19v, ill. in Paffrath, 1990, 93.

41. Letters 284 and 298 in SBOp 8:198–9 and 214; trans. James, 1953, 430–1 and 435–6.
42. Paris, 1990, 265, nos. 183–4.
43. Schmitt, 1990, 149.
44. *Vita Prima* 3, 8:29; PL 185:320.
45. *The Steps of Humility* in SBOp 3:16; trans. Conway, 1980, 28.
46. Illustrated in Paffrath, 1990, 80.
47. Nantes, Musée Dobrée, MS V, f. 1v; ill. in Paris, 1990, 51.
48. Réau, 1955–9, 3:2:610; Lexicon, 1968–76, 6:432.
49. *Vita Prima* 1, 8:42; PL 185:252, referring to 1 Corinthians 12.
50. London, British Library, MS Cleopatra c. XI, f. 75, illustrated in James, 1925, facing p. 6.
51. Luke, 1:26–38.
52. For example, in an Altenberg panel (ill. in Paffrath, 1984, 49), and in a late fifteenth-century manuscript (Paris, BN MS Fr. 245, f. 55r ill. in Paris, 1990, 51).
53. *Vita Prima* 1, 12:57; PL 185:258.
54. Illustrated in Paffrath, 1984, 85.
55. *Vita Prima* 5, 2:14; PL 185:360.
56. Donkin, 1978, 21–9.
57. *Exordium Magnum* 6:10, Griesser, 1961, 366.
58. Knowles, 1940, 228.
59. *Vita Prima* 1, 3:15; PL 185:235; James, 1983, 79.
60. Knowles, 1940, 252.
61. Kelly, 1986, 172–3.
62. Letter 238 in SBOp 8:115–19; trans. James, 1953, 277.
63. John, 1964, 298.
64. Knowles, 1940, 725.
65. Knowles, 1940, 252.
66. Canivez, 1933–41, 1:45 (Statute 1152:1).
67. *Exordium Magnum* 3:7, Griesser, 1961, 162: *post aurea . . . ferrea.*

CHAPTER FIVE

1. Chibnall, 1969–80, 4:325.
2. Foliot, 1967, 148.
3. Canivez, 3:410; trans. Schimmelpfennig, 1993, 339.
4. Letter 106, SBOp, 7:265–6; trans. James, 1953, 156.
5. Rule Prologue, McCann, 1976, 4.
6. Letter 320, SBOp, 8:253–4; trans. James, 1952, 242–3. For a short biographical sketch, see DNB 13:1218–20.
7. Letter 321, SBOp, 8:255; trans. James, 1952, 243–4.
8. The family tree is given in Knowles, 1940, 725.
9. For the complex case, see Knowles, 1963, 76–97.
10. Described in Walbran, 1863, 101.
11. Walbran, 1863, 85.
12. Walbran, 1863, 109: *duces gregis Dominici; ecclesiae columptae; luminaria mundi.*
13. Printed in Hoste & Talbot, 1971, 3–161; an English translation by Elizabeth Connor in Connor & Braceland, 1990.
14. Powicke, 1950, LXV.
15. Powicke, 1950, 25–6.
16. Thus Powicke, 1950, LIX: 'The *Speculum Caritatis* is Aelred's finest work'; Squire, 1969, 27–8: 'As an introduction to Aelred's talents as a writer . . . nothing more complete exists'; and McGuire, 1994, 41: 'The *Mirror of Charity* became the most complete and profound work of Aelred's authorship.'
17. Hoste & Talbot, 1971, 5.
18. For example as the frontispiece in Hoste & Talbot, 1971: 'The only surviving representation of Aelred'; as the frontispiece in Squire, 1969; and in Schneider, 1986, 127.

19. Letter 523, SBOp, 8:486; trans. James, 1953, 246.
20. Leclercq, 1953, 42.
21. Letter 523, SBOp, 8:486; trans. James, 1953, 246.
22. Letter 201, SBOp, 8:60; trans. James, 1953, 339.
23. Knowles, 1940, 240.
24. Walter Daniel, *The Life of Aelred of Rievaulx* in Powicke, 1950, 38.
25. For this, see Mahn, 1951, 141; Squire, 1969, 94; and Powicke, 1950, XLVIII.
26. For Aelred's authorship, see Knowles, 1940, 643–4.
27. Knowles, 1940, 644.
28. For the Battle of the Standard, see Squire, 1969, 73–82; and McGuire, 1994, 68–9.
29. For this, see Squire, 1969, 92–7; and McGuire, 1994, 73–5.
30. In his *Life of Aelred* Walter Daniel said that 'he wrote this at the request of his kinsman Laurence, the Abbot of Westminster, and to please the brethren there serving God'. (Powicke, 1950, 41–2).
31. Squire, 1969, 95; Powicke, 1950, XLVIII. It would have fitted well with the return from the General Chapter at Cîteaux in September. (Knowles, 1940, 263n).
32. Prologue to *Vita S. Edwardi Regis*, PL 195:738–9. The *Life* itself is in PL 195:739–90.
33. We owe the discovery of the two historiated initials and an excellent account of their iconographical significance to Professor Marsha Dutton, to whom I am greatly indebted. It is published in Dutton, 1993 and Dutton, 1994 on which subsequent references are based.
34. Dublin, Trinity College MS 172, p. 22, illustrated in colour in Dutton, 1993, facing 209.
35. King, 1954, 219.
36. *Chronica Albrici* quoted in King, 1954, 340.
37. A translation of this is in Mierow, 1994.
38. Mierow, 1994, 247.
39. One modern scholar argues that to many of Bernard's contemporaries, among whom he includes Otto, Bernard's influence was not as dominant as we have been led to believe. He points to the few references Otto made to him and to the need Otto felt to identify Bernard suggesting that many of his readers might not have heard of him (Phillips, 1992, 39–41).
40. Mierow, 1994, 101.
41. Illustrated in Holzhey, 1924, ill. 14.
42. For short accounts, see DNB 1:952–4, and Knowles, 1940, 316–22.
43. The Benedictine monks who formed the chapter chose the abbot of Battle, but they were overruled by the bishops of the province who opted for Baldwin.
44. Printed in PL 204:402–774.
45. For a biographical sketch, see DHGE fasc. 129–30, col. 862–3. See also, *Lexikon der Christlichen Ikonographie*, 8:606.
46. For the conflict at Grandmont, see Hutchison, 1989, 74–82.
47. Hutchison, 1989, 83.
48. King, 1954, 156; Canivez 1:485 (Statute 1218:3) and 2:477–8 (Statute 1261:12).
49. Bony, 1987, 227. The seal is illustrated as fig. 14, 74.
50. In reality an archbishop, like an ordinary bishop, also carried a crozier and not a cross-staff which was carried in procession before him by his chaplain. In images of archbishops, however, they are commonly depicted carrying this themselves as a kind of shorthand to identification.
51. Bony, 1987, fig. 14, 75.
52. For a biographical sketch, see DHGE fasc. 99, col. 777–80.
53. Smith, 1958, 20.
54. For the Cistercian involvement in the Crusades and Missions, see Lekai, 1977, 52–64.
55. King, 1954, 254–6.
56. King, 1954, 156.
57. Quoted in Lekai, 1977, 56. This is how Caesarius records the event (Book 5, chapter 21): 'When they discovered, from the admissions of some of them, that there were Catholics mingled with the heretics, they said to the abbot, "Sir, what shall we do,

for we cannot distinguish between the faithful and the heretics?" The abbot, like the others, was afraid that many, in fear of death, would pretend to be Catholics, and after their departure, would return to their heresy, and is said to have replied: "Kill them all; for the Lord knoweth them that are His" and so countless numbers in the town were slain.' (Scott & Swinton Bland, 1929, 1:345–6) The words of St Paul are from 2 Timothy 2:19.

58. Letter 241, SBOp, 8:125; trans. James, 1953, 388.
59. Smith, 1958, 16.
60. Smith, 1958, 38.
61. Short notices are in Kelly, 1986, 217–19, and DHGE 8:116–35.
62. DHGE 8:121.
63. Printed in Canivez 3:410–36.
64. Details of the provisions are in Mahn, 1949, 35–59.
65. For the *Benedictina* and its impact, see Schimmelpfennig, 1993, 338–47.
66. See Stürzinger, 1893.
67. For an exhaustive study of Guillaume, see Faral, 1952. For Guillaume in a Cistercian context, see Keenan, 1976, 166–85.
68. Holloway, 1987, 78.
69. Hill, 1858, 5–7.
70. Letter 64, SBOp, 7, 157–8; trans. in James, 1953, 90–1.
71. Quoted in Mahn, 1949, 32–3.
72. Reproduced in Batselier, 1980, 33.
73. It is mentioned in the inventory of the duke's library from 1467.
74. This is how it is described in the exhibition catalogue Edinburgh, 1963, 37 (no. 39).
75. These are depicted in Bruxelles Bibliothèque Royale MS 10176-8 on ff. 2r, 4r and 1v respectively.
76. Illustrated in Stürzinger, 1893, facing pages 2, 338 and 358 respectively.
77. For Lydgate, see Knowles, 1957, 273–5.
78. An illustration of this is in Holloway, 1987, 219.

CHAPTER SIX

1. Powicke, 1950, 10–11.
2. Powicke, 1950, 78.
3. *Exordium Cistercii* 11, trans. Lekai, 1977, 448.
4. Rule 55; trans. McCann, 1976, 60–1.
5. The most exhaustive study of the origin and development of the Cistercian cowl is Gaillemin, 1905, 304–14.
6. Bruyne, 1921, 55–61.
7. Rule 58; trans. McCann, 1976, 64.
8. Rule 58; trans. McCann, 1976, 63.
9. *Exordium Parvum* 15, Bouton & Van Damme, 1974, 77; trans. Lekai, 1977, 459.
10. *Apologia* 10:25, SBOp 3:102; trans. Matarasso, 1993, 54.
11. *Exordium Magnum* 1:20, Griesser, 1961, 75.
12. Letter 1, SBOp 7:9; trans. James, 1953, 8.
13. Letter 1, SBOp 7:10; trans. James, 1953, 8. Contrast this with what Walter Map says: that monks are brought 'indoors in winter cold, to shade in summer heat' (James, 1983, 85).
14. *De vestitu superfluo vel superbo*, SBOp 3:101–2; trans. Matarasso, 1993, 53–4.
15. Illustrated in Dal Prà, 1990, 37 (Fig. 12).
16. Other examples of the primitive cowl may be seen in colour plates 2, 3, 4, 5, 6 & 8.
17. SBOp 3:81; trans. Rudolph, 1990, 81. The description of St Bernard in the *Ysengrinus* is in Mann, 1987, 15.
18. Letter 1, SBOp 7:1–11; trans. James, 1953, 1–10.
19. Quoted in Hufgard, 1987, 72.
20. PL 185:1344–5.

21. PL 185:1346.
22. Wilmart, 1940, 63.
23. Wright, 1872, 1:85.
24. James, 1983, 101–3.
25. Hockey, 1975, 219.
26. Gaillemin, 1905, 311–12.
27. Illustrated in Wetesko, 1991, 115.
28. For other examples, see Duràn, 1990, 37 and 43, and Paffrath, 1990, 96 and 120.
29. For a discussion of this and the dating, see Constable, 1967, 2:116, 270–3.
30. Constable, 1967, 1:287.
31. Constable, 1967, 1:368.
32. Henriquez, 1630, 253.
33. Othon, 1933, 108.
34. Chibnall, 1969–80, 4:325, 311.
35. PL 203:836.
36. James, 1983, 85.
37. Powicke, 1950, 10.
38. Canivez, 1933–41, 1:89 (Statute 1181:11).
39. Among the drawings in the Beaulieu Account Book (London, British Library, Additional MS 48978) are one showing two men in a fulling mill (f. 39v), a lay brother carrying a sack of wool (f. 41v), and one of two men cutting what is either cloth or parchment (f. 43r).
40. Chibnall, 1969–80, 4:327.
41. Canivez, 1933–41, 3:423.
42. Charles Oursel refers to the 'primitive habit' which was grey or brown before the white was adopted. (Oursel, 1960, 27) Although this has been challenged, claiming that the colour is the result of later overpainting and that the only untouched picture is of the white monk prostrate at the feet of an angel (Davidson, 1987, 67, note 63), the only reference in the later most thorough studies by Yolanta Załuska to any subsequent retouching refers to only one historiated initial (the *M* in MS 170, f. 20, where the habits of the two monks have been repainted a darker grey and brown and the outline retraced in black) and not to any of the other scenes of monks at work (Załuska, 1989, 201).
43. *Dialogue* 3:50; trans. Idung of Prüfening, 1977, 137.
44. France, 1992, 60–2.
45. *Dialogue* 3:46, 48; trans. Idung of Prüfening, 1977, 135, 136.
46. Caniveż 1933–41, 3:326 (Statute 1312:6), and 3:517 (Statute 1350:3).
47. The church has in fact been identified as having been modelled on that of St Servaas in Maastricht. (Kinder, 1991, 206).
48. Quoted in Bruyne, 1921, 57. The origin of the proverb is apparently not known.
49. Rule 1; trans. McCann, 1976, 5.
50. *Dialogue* 3:41; Idung of Prüfening, 1977, 132–3.
51. Gilbanks, 1899, 123–5. The fragments of the abbot's tomb are illustrated facing page 102.
52. These include Heiligenkreuz MSS 66, f. 25v; 224, f. 1v; 226, f. 129v, 146r, 149v; Zwettl MSS 144, f. 26r; 194, f. 3r; Vienna, Nat. Bibl. (Rein) MSS 507, f. 2v; & (Sittich) 650, f. 62r; 758, f. 180r; St-Omer, Bibl. Mun. (Clairmarais) MS 94, f. 42v; Brussels, Royal Library (Aulne) MS II 1076, f. 82r.
53. Powicke, 1950, 18.
54. SBOp 6, 2:141.
55. Rule 58; trans. McCann, 1976, 62–4.
56. The details of entry and profession are contained in the *Ecclesiastica officia*, Chapter 102 entitled 'Concerning Novices', Griesser, 1956, 263–5.
57. Aubert, 1947, 1:118–22.
58. Rule 58; trans. McCann, 1976, 64.
59. Letter 1, SBOp 7:7; trans. James, 1953, 6.
60. Compare this with the knight represented in Oursel, 1926, plate 25.
61. *Vita Prima* 1, 4:23–4; PL 185:240.
62. *Vita Prima* 1, 4:20; PL 185:238.

63. *Ecclesiastica Officia* Chapter 102, Griesser, 1956, 264.
64. For example in the 1698 *Rituale*. I am indebted to Fr Chrysogonus Waddell for this information.
65. *Ecclesiastica Officia* Chapter 113, Griesser, 1956, 272–3.
66. Powicke, 1950, 23–4.
67. On Caesarius of Heisterbach, see McGuire, 1980, 167–247.
68. *Dialogus Miraculorum* 4:36; trans. Scott & Swinton Bland, 1929, 1:233.
69. *Dialogus Miraculorum* 1:3; trans. Scott & Swinton Bland, 1929, 1:9.
70. *Dialogus Miraculorum* 12:53; trans. Scott & Swinton Bland, 1929, 2:339.
71. McGuire, 1983a, 47.
72. McGuire, 1983b, 253.
73. *Exordium Magnum* 2:5, Griesser, 1961, 101.
74. Sermon 37:3; PL 184:194.
75. There were, for example, ninety novices at Clairvaux in the time of Bernard: *Exordium Magnum* 6:10, Griesser, 1961, 366.
76. The details of this are given in the *Ecclesiastica Officia* Chapter 102, Griesser, 1956, 263–5.
77. Rule 58; trans. McCann, 1976, 63–4.
78. Illustrated in Dal Prà, 1991, 10.
79. *Vita Prima* 4, 2:10; PL 185:527–8.
80. Sometimes the site dictated that the position of the cloister should be to the north of the church. Examples of this are given in Aubert, 1947, 1:112.
81. Quoted in Aubert, 1947, 1:117.
82. Rule 4; trans. McCann, 1975, 11–14.
83. *Sermones de diversis* 42, SBOp 6, 1:258.
84. Quoted in Camille, 1992, 56.
85. Wilmart, 1940, 63.
86. For these images, see Hamburger, 1990, 45; and Smith, 1996, 3–19.
87. *Exordium Magnum* 3:6, Griesser, 1961, 161.
88. PL 212:758.
89. Aubert, 1947, 2:51–70.
90. *Sermo in sollemnitate apostolorum Petri et Pauli* I, SBOp 5:188–91.
91. Arens, 1982, 7–15; Monsees, 1987, 108.
92. Quoted in Maisières, 1949, 287.
93. Henriquez, 1630, 278.
94. Adhémar, 1974–6, 1:21; Duval-Arnould, 1984, 689–91; Aubert, 1947, 1:340.
95. Letter 441, SBOp 8:419; trans. James, 1953, 517–18.
96. It was already prescribed by St Benedict that a brother should daily 'read the Conferences of Cassian or the Lives of the Fathers, or something else that may edify the hearers'. (Rule 42; trans. McCann, 1976, 48).
97. *Ecclesiastica Officia* Chapter 81, Griesser, 1956, 245–6.
98. Aubert, 1947, 2:22–3.
99. Rule 39–41; trans. McCann, 1976, 45–7.
100. Letter 1, SBOp 7:9; trans. James, 1953, 8.
101. Lekai, 1977, 368–9.
102. Beckford, 1956, 50, 54.
103. Rule 39; trans. McCann, 1976, 46.
104. Jaritz, 1985, 57–8.
105. Illustrated in Oursel, 1926, Plate 23 and Załuska, 1991, Plate 18.
106. *Ecclesiastica Officia* Chapter 85, 'On Shaving', Griesser, 1956, 249.
107. Burchard of Bellevaux, 1985, 117.

CHAPTER SEVEN

1. Trans. from Matarasso, 1993, 196.
2. *Exordium Magnum* 1:27, Griesser, 1961, 84.
3. Rule, chapters 2, 27, 56 and 64; trans. McCann, 1976, 6–9, 36, 61 and 70.

4. Zwettl MS 84, f. 128v; illustrated in Ziegler, 1985–92, 1: colour plate 2.

5. Rule, chapter 1; trans. McCann, 1976, 5.

6. Rule, chapter 64; trans. McCann, 1976.

7. Significantly, he received a biographic notice from the thirteenth-century Cistercian chronicler, Alberic of Trois Fontaines. (Clark, 1992, 8).

8. Clark, 1992, 274–8.

9. The miniature from Les Dunes reflects the work of an artist active in St Omer in the 1150s and whose workshop may also have been responsible for the Clairmarais picture. (Clark, 1992, 63–66).

10. These are listed in the Catalogue of Illuminated Aviary Manuscripts in Clark, 1992, 267–312.

11. Brussels, 1990, 101–2: Heiligenkreuz (MS 226), Zwettl (MS 253), Buildwas (Lambeth Palace MS 107), Aulne (Brussels, Bibl. Royale MS II, 1070), Clairvaux (Troyes, MS 177).

12. Heiligenkreuz MS 226, f. 146. Illustrated in colour in Walliser, 1969, 20.

13. *Exordium Cistercii* 2, trans. Lekai, 1977, 443.

14. Illustrated in Stalley, 1987, 206.

15. Stalley, 1987, 207.

16. Rae, 1966, 71 and Hunt, 1974, 1:179.

17. Others include the grave stones of Abbot Jacques de Beranzy of Orval, Belgium from *c.* 1380 (illustrated in Greenhill 2: Plate 15 a); Abbot Georgius Darabos of Saint Gothard, Hungary from *c.* 1474 (Hervay, 1984, 272); Abbot Johann von Decksprfund of Bebenhausen, Germany from 1460 (Greenhill 2: Plate 34 b); and Abbot Rafal Zaborowita of Wachock, Poland (Greenhill 2: Plate 27 b).

18. Illustrated in Hunt, 1974, 2: Plate 87.

19. The three references are: in *Sermones de diversis* 92 (SBOp 6:1:348), *Sententiae* 81 (SBOp 6:2:118); and Letter 242 (SBOp 8:129).

20. On Cistercian seals, see Heslop, 1986 and Clay, 1928. French seals are catalogued in Douët d'Arcq, 1868, volume 3.

21. Canivez 1:251–2 (Statute 1200:15).

22. Canivez 3:437 (Statute 1335:2).

23. Canivez 3:415 (Statute 1335:9).

24. Heslop, 1986, 278.

25. Illustrated from a print in Heslop, 1986, plate 153.

26. Heslop, 1986, 279–80.

27. For the connection between seal and tomb design, see Butler, 1993, 78–88.

28. Mâle, 1925, 399.

29. Illustrated in Butler, 1993, 243.

30. Illustrated in Aubert, 1947, 1:347.

31. Illustrated in Butler, 1993, 244; and Stalley, 1987, 205.

32. Canivez 1:87 (Statute 1180:5).

33. Canivez 1:145 (Statute 1191:78); 1:172 (Statute 1194:7); and Lucet, 1964, Dist X:33. And yet simple staff slabs were still in use at La Bussière, Ourscamp and Cîteaux in the sixteenth century. (Adhémar, 1974–6, 1:178, 2:11 and 2:90).

34. Bertram, 1976, 17.

35. Schlie, 1896, 516–53.

36. Illustrated in Schlie, 1896, 540, 546 and 543 respectively A similar double grave is known from La Ferté. (Adhémar, 1974–6, 1:142).

37. Illustrated in Stanzl, 1992, 72. There are also two fourteenth-century double slabs each with two staffs with the heads pointing to the right from Ourscamp (Adhémar, 1974–6, 1:145).

38. Illustrated in Norris, 1988, plate 254; and Orval, 1970, 91.

39. Illustrated in Schlie, 1896, ill. 19. Another interpretation of this is that he suffered a violent death. (Schlie, 1896, 541).

40. Illustrated in Coppack, 1993, 67. According to another theory the reason for him not wearing the mitre is that he may have died before he was blessed, but this is unlikely as he is thought to have resigned (Bertram, 1976, 162).

41. The *insignia* are listed and the dates of grants to a number of English black monk houses given in Knowles, 1940, 711–2.
42. I am indebted to Fray Jesús M. Oliver OCist for the information on Poblet.
43. Lekai, 1977, 256.
44. Douët d'Arcq, 1868, no. 8640.
45. Illustrated in colour in Aachen, 1981, colour plate 8 facing p. 256.
46. Knowles, 1959, 32–7.
47. Palmcke, 1956, 82.
48. For this, see France, 1992, 421–2.

CHAPTER EIGHT

1. Burchard of Bellevaux, 1985, 167.
2. On lay brothers in general, see Lekai, 1977, 334–46; Donnelly, 1949; Toepfer, 1983; Ducourneau, 1929, 2:139–201; Leclercq, 1965, 239–58.
3. Auberger suggests that the fact that the figures shown in the manuscript of Gregory's *Moralia* which was completed in 1111 were all monks and featured no lay brothers indicates that these may only have been introduced after this date (Auberger, 1986, 141–2). It seems, however, that they already existed a little earlier during the abbacy of Alberic.
4. *Exordium Parvum* 15, trans. Matarasso, 1993, 7.
5. Aubert, 1947, 2:121–40.
6. *Dialogue* 3:43; Idung of Prüfening, 1977, 133.
7. Burchard of Bellevaux, 1985, 47–150. In the introduction to the critical edition by Giles Constable the text is analyzed and discussed.
8. Burchard of Bellevaux ,1985, 166–7.
9. *Dialogus miraculorum* 7:54; trans. Scott & Swinton Bland, 1929, 1:546.
10. Kloss, 1942, 46 and 200.
11. Baxandall, 1980, 127, 130–1, 292–3, and fig. 72.
12. Ebrach, 1739, 21–2; Wiener, 1985, 272 and 290.
13. Ducourneau, 1929, 2:161–3.
14. Kienzle, 1995, 219–43.
15. Mantour, 1736, 193–232, and ill. plate 12.
16. Bruges, 1981, no. 41, 115; Hoste, 1971, 88 and 142; Lieftinck, 1953, 89.
17. Aubert, 1947, 1:97–8.
18. The drawing is in London, British Library, MS Add. 48978 f. 41v. The text surrounding the drawing is in Hockey, 1975, 219.
19. The fulling mill is on f. 39v.
20. F. 43r.
21. Ducourneau, 1929, 163.
22. James, 1983, 85–6.
23. For an exhaustive survey of the number of monks and lay brothers in different countries and at different periods, see Toepfer, 1983, 53–7.
24. PL 197:263-4; trans. Donnelly, 1949, 27.
25. Batany, 1969, 241–59.
26. Leclercq, 1965, 250.
27. *Exordium Magnum* 5:10, Griesser, 1961, 292–8. Conrad of Eberbach devotes a whole chapter to the conspiracy which he calls 'The danger of the conspiracy'.
28. Illustrated in Becksmann, 1979, plate 20c. The third drawing is shown on plate 20e.
29. Stalley, 1987, 155 and 189.
30. Rae, 1966, 71; Beuer-Szlechter, 1975, 245–6; Hunt, 1974, 1:179.
31. Leclercq, 1965, 240.
32. Roisin, 1947, 32–47.
33. *Exordium Magnum* 3:18, Griesser, 1961, 243–4.
34. He is referred to as a monk in Anderes & Hoegger, 1989, 341; as an abbot in van der Meer, 1965, 306; and as St Bernard in Tobin, 1995, 58.

35. *Dialogus miraculorum* 7: 12 and 13; trans. Scott & Swinton Bland, 1929, 1:469.

36. *Exordium Magnum* 4:13, Griesser, 1961, 238–9. A complete chapter is devoted to the story.

37. A chapter entitled, 'Of the great humility of a certain lay brother' in *Exordium Magnum* 4:19, Griesser, 1961, 244–5.

CHAPTER NINE

1. From his *Historia occidentalis*, in Hinnebusch, 1972, 117.

2. Kuhn-Rehfus, 1995, 135–6. A list of all German houses is given in Schneider, 1986, 710–26, from which the final figure is taken.

3. As listed in Bondeelle-Souchier, 1994, 227.

4. For the English houses, see Nichols, 1995, 49–61.

5. For the Scandinavian nunneries, see France, 1992a, 159–84.

6. For Jully, see Bouton, 1995, 14–15.

7. PL 185:244-5.

8. A key to this and details of the nuns depicted is given in Nichols & Shank, 1995, 2:813–20.

9. On Tart, see Bouton, 1995, 15; Connor, 1995, 38–46; and Degler-Spengler, 1995, 87–8.

10. PL 185:1413–14.

11. Degler-Spengler, 1995, 87–8.

12. Bouton, 1995, 15.

13. Aubrun, 1970, 112–13.

14. Aubrun, 1970, 102–3.

15. PL 156:1001-2.

16. Bouton, 1995, 19.

17. It is mentioned in statutes from 1213, 1214, 1218 and 1219.

18. Canivez, 1933–41, 2:248–9 (Statute 1242:17).

19. For the architecture of the churches of German Cistercian nunneries, see Schneider, 1986, 339–82.

20. Berman, 1993, 25.

21. Dimier, 1954, 10.

22. PL 185:1413-14.

23. Connor, 1995, 32.

24. Colour illustration in Soulier, 1988, 30.

25. Quoted in Hamburger, 1992, 117.

26. Kuhn-Rehfus, 1995, 136. See also the filiation table in Schneider, 1986, 323.

27. MS Ludwig XI 7 (83 MN 126) f. 11r.

28. MS Ludwig XI 7 (83 MN 126) f. 38r.

29. Appuhn 1986, 14–15.

30. Illustrated in Ehlers' & Ende, 10–11 and 40.

31. Uhde-Stahl, 1978, 31–46. The earlier manuscripts with the rounded veil are Copenhagen, Royal Library, MS Thott 120.8, and Hildesheim, Dombibliothek MS J. 29; the later ones with pointed veils are Münster, Staatsarchiv Alterthumsverein MS 301, and Oxford, Bodleian Library, MS lat. lit. f. 4.

32. Kroos, 1973, 117–34.

33. I am grateful to Zuzana Všetečková of the Institute of Art History, Czech Academy of Sciences, Prague, for this information.

34. *Dialogus Miraculorum* 8:80; trans. Scott & Swinton Bland, 1929, 2:82–3.

35. Illustrated in Hotz, 1982, 74.

36. Illustrated in Hotz, 1982, 68.

37. France, 1992a, 171–4.

38. France, 1992a, 172.

39. Illustrated in Gardell, 1945, 2:279.

40. Quotation from Bouton, 1995, 21.

41. *Dialogus Miraculorum* 7:34; trans. Scott & Swinton Bland, 1929, 1:502. See also Swinton Bland, 1928. 43. Among the later versions are London, British Library, MSS Additional 18,929; Add. 33,956; and Egerton 1117, f. 173 (see Ward 1893, 659, 672 and 668).
42. de Moor, 1993, 307–21.
43. London, British Library, Royal MS 2 B VII, f. 219. This is illustrated in Warner, 1912, pl. 232a.
44. Kuhn-Rehfus, 1995, 139–56.
45. Monsees, 1989.
46. For this, see Swarzenski, 1945, 1:103–4, illustrated in Swarzenski, 1945, 2, ill. 257.
47. Rothe, 1968, 226–7.
48. Bondeelle-Souchier, 1994.
49. Roisin, 1947, 61–2. See also, Oliver, 1988, 1:204.
50. Schneider, 1986, 324.
51. Sullivan, 1995, 345–59.
52. For this, see McDonnell, 1954.
53. See Cawley, 1992.
54. For St Lutgard, see King, 1995, 225–53.
55. Copenhagen, Royal Library, MS Ny kgl. Saml. 168, 4°, f. 255r.

CHAPTER TEN

1. PL 211:363.
2. *Sententiae*, SBOp 6:2.
3. Sermon on the Song of Songs 47, SBOp 2:66; trans. Walsh & Edmonds, 1979, 9.
4. For the Cistercian Liturgy, see King, 1955, 62–154; Lekai, 1977, 248–60; Lackner 1970, 1–34.
5. Rule Chapters 8–19; trans. McCann, 1970, 22–32.
6. Rule Chapter 16; trans McCann, 1970, 28.
7. Lackner, 1970, 20.
8. *Exordium Magnum* 1:20, Griesser, 1961, 75.
9. *Exordium Magnum* 5:6, Griesser, 1961, 281–4.
10. *Ecclesiastica Officia* 115, Griesser, 1956, 274.
11. *Liber Miraculorum* 3:4; PL 185:1356.
12. *Exordium Magnum* 4:1, 4:4, 4:4, 4:6; Griesser, 1961, 224, 230, 230–1, 232.
13. *Exordium Magnum* 1:34, Griesser, 1961, 95.
14. *Exordium Magnum* 2:4, Griesser, 1961, 101.
15. *Exordium Magnum* 2:3, Griesser, 1961, 100–1.
16. Letter 398, SBOp 8:378; James, 1953, 592.
17. *Speculum Caritatis* PL 195:571; trans. Webb & Walker, 1962, 72–3.
18. I am grateful to Father Chrysogonus Waddell OCSO to whom I owe this information.
19. King, 1955, 97; Canivez 5:555 (Stat. 1486:89).
20. *Carta Caritatis Posterior* 3, trans. Lekai, 1977, 462.
21. Canivez 1:13 (Statute 1134:III).
22. *Ecclesiastica Officia*; Griesser, 1956, 183–280.
23. For a general treatment of the subject of Cistercian exemption, see Mahn, 1951, 119–55.
24. *Ecclesiastica Officia* Chapter 86, Griesser, 1956, 249–50.
25. *Ecclesiastica Officia* Chapter 70, Griesser, 1956, 234–7.
26. *Divine Comedy*, Paradiso, Canto 31.
27. Canivez 1:17 (Statute 1134:XVIII).
28. Waddell, 1982, 106–7.
29. King, 1955, 112; Canivez 2:361 (Statute 1251:7).
30. *Summa Cartae Caritatis* 26; trans. Lekai, 1977, 450.
31. Quoted in Tissier, 1660, at the beginning of volume 1.
32. *Exordium Magnum* 2:5, Griesser, 1961, 101.

33. I want to thank Christine Kratzke, who is completing her doctoral dissertation at Kiel University on Dargun Abbey, and to whom I owe the information on the Virgin and Monk Relief. For this, see forthcoming Kratzke, 1998, chapter 2.

34. I am most grateful to Professor Nigel Palmer for drawing my attention to this manuscript. He has established the provenance of the mansucript, hitherto unknown, to Eberbach, and I owe the transcription of the text surrounding the image to him, as well as the information as to the scribe and possible author..

35. See chapter 7, note 22.

36. Perdrizet, 1908.

37. For this, see McGuire, 1983, 227–9.

38. *Dialogus Miraculorum* 7:64; trans. Scott & Swinton Bland, 1929, 1:546.

39. Bony, 1987, figs 11, 12.

40. Canivez 1: 47 (Statute 1152:10).

41. Canivez 1: 63 (Statute 1157:63).

42. Illustrated in Greenhill, 1976, 2: Plate 28a.

43. For St Louis and the Cistercians, see Richard, 1983, and Dimier, 1954.

44. Quoted in Dimier, 1954, 57.

45. Canivez 2:289 (Statute 1245:2).

46. Canivez 2:400-1 (Statute 1254:7).

47. Both tombs are illustrated as figs 189, 190 in Adhémar, 1974, 1:42. They are to be found in the collection of Gaignières drawings in the Bodleian Library, Oxford.

CHAPTER ELEVEN

1. Peter de Roya was one of St Bernard's novices at Clairvaux. The quotation is from a letter to a friend in the world who was provost of the church of Noyon. Quoted in Luddy, 1950, 349–50.

2. Chapter 48, trans. McCann, 1976, 53.

3. Quoted in Constable, 1982, 44.

4. For the Danish examples, see France, 1992, 256.

5. Beckett, 1984, 78.

6. By the distinguished American art historian, Arthur K. Porter.

7. Dijon MS 173, f. 148r; MS 170, 32r; and MS 173, 92v. Oursel wrongly describes the figures in the cloth-making picture as a monk and two lay brothers (Oursel, 1960, 28).

8. *Exordium Parvum* 15, trans. Lekai, 1977, 459.

9. Chibnall, 1969–80, 4:327.

10. James, 1983, 77.

11. Quoted in Luddy, 350.

12. Powicke, 1950, 22.

13. *Vita Prima* 1, 4:24; PL 185:240–1.

14. *Vita Prima* 1, 1:2; PL 185:227–8.

15. Illustrated in Paffrath, 1984, 55.

16. Załuska, 1989, 201 and Załuska, 1991, 58.

17. Sermon 26, SBOp 1:175; trans. Walsh, 1976, 66.

18. Examples from Denmark, for example, in France, 1992, 508, 511, 515.

19. For example in the *Summa Cartae Caritatis*, Lekai, 1977, 448.

20. For this, see Donkin, 1978, 37–51.

21. Chibnall, 1973, 4:327.

22. It is MS 173, f. 167r. An exception is in Davidson 1987, fig. 28. See also, Załuska, 1989, 203–4.

23. Chapter 57, trans. McCann, 1976, 62.

24. *Exordium Cistrcii*, trans. Lekai, 1977, 448.

25. For this, see France, 1992a, 65–6.

26. Powicke, 1950, 12.

27. Letter 92 in SBOp 7:241; trans. James, 1953, 142.

28. Canivez 1:62 & 1:63 (Statutes 1157:29 & 1157:47).
29. *Vita Prima* 2, 5:31; PL 185:285.
30. For the earliest Cistercian buildings in England and their builders, see Ferguson, 1983, 74–86.
31. *Vita Prima* 4, 2:10; PL 185:327.
32. In the *Exordium Magnum* 3:22, Griesser 1961, 201.
33. A whole chapter is devoted to him in the *Exordium Magnum* 3:22, Griesser 1961, 201–2.
34. Letter 357 in SBOp 8:302; James, 1953, 455.
35. Toepfer, 1983, 86.
36. See Białoskórska, 1966, 14–22 where it is also illustrated (Ill. no. 3), and also Białoskórska, 1994, 57-85.
37. In northern Germany and southern Scandinavia Cistercian monasteries were, like other buildings, generally built in brick. For German examples, see Schneider, 1986, 545.
38. See, for example, Norton, 1986, 228–55.
39. Dewilde & Meulemeester, 1991, 7–50.
40. Illustrated in Baker, 1993, fig. 5.
41. Illustrated in Donkin, 1978, facing 171.
42. Illustrated in Aachen, 1981, 431.

CHAPTER TWELVE

1. John of Ford 71:3, trans. Beckett, 1977–84, 5:109.
2. John of Ford 37:3, trans. Beckett, 1977–84, 3:96–7.
3. I am grateful to Fr Hilary Costello for drawing my attention to this and to the quotations from John of Ford. On the *Lectio Divina*, see also Louf, 1983, 74–9.
4. John of Ford 82:1, trans. Beckett, 1977–84, 243.
5. Rule Prologue.
6. Rule Chapter 48, trans. McCann, 1976, 53–4.
7. Rule Chapter 42, trans. McCann, 1976, 48.
8. *Exordium Parvum* 7, Bouton & Van Damme, 1974, 64–5; trans. Lekai, 1977, 454–5.
9. Canivez, 1933–41, 1:13 (Statute 1134:III).
10. France, 1992a, 187.
11. Bondeelle-Souchier, 1991, 126, 83, 35.
12. France, 1992a, 187.
13. Lekai, 1958, 251.
14. Galob, 1994, 32; Galob, 1996, 66–7.
15. Galob, 1994, 30; Galob, 1996, 178
16. Illustrated in Galob, 1994, 74; Galob, 1996, 50.
17. There is a facsimile reproduction of this in Schneider, 1986, 398.
18. Illustrated in Aachen, 1980, 449.
19. For the Cistercian attitude to intellectual activities, see Dimier, 1963, 119–46.
20. For this, see the chapter, 'The Challenge of Scholasticism' in Lekai, 1977, 77–90; also Mahn, 1949, 50–75.

CHAPTER THIRTEEN

1. *More Beasts for Worse Children.*
2. *Apologia* 29, trans. Matarasso, 1993, 57; *Mirror of Charity* 2:24, *Corpus Christianorum Continuatio Medievalis* 1, 99; James, 1951, 141.
3. For images of monsters in ancient art, see Feld, 1990, 41–5.
4. Dijon MS 173, f. 56v. For this, see Rudolph, 1990, 147–8 and ill. 30.
5. The text with translation and a commentary is in Mann, 1987; see also Billy, 1992, 301–28.
6. *Dialogue* 4:82; Scott & Swinton Bland, 1929, 1:285.

7. Randall, 1966, 17–18, also illustrations of examples: plates 197, 199, 202, 203.
8. *Sermon* 65:1 and 64:8, SBOp 2: 172, 170; trans. Walsh & Edmonds, 1979, 178, 175.
9. Mâle, 1984, 52.
10. Illustrated in Libor, 1967, 63.
11. *Dialogue* 5:50; Scott & Swinton Bland, 1929, 1:384.
12. *Dialogue* 5:6; Scott & Swinton Bland, 1929, 1:325.
13. Illustrated in Stürzinger, 1893, facing 358.
14. Dijon MS 4, f. 376, 377 from *c.* 1230–40. F. 376 is illustrated in Załuska 1991, Pl. 70
15. Perigueux, Archives Diocésaines MS CR67, f. 123r, 171r.
16. For this, see Randall, 1966.
17. Dodgson, 1903–11, 1:471; Mencke, 1976, 44; Pauli, 1901, 392.
18. Dodgson, 1903–11, 1:441; Mencke, 1976, 76–7; Pauli, 1901, 398–406; Zschelletzchky, 1975, 140–1.
19. Lekai, 1977, 94.
20. King, 1954, 62–9.
21. Knowles, 1940, 37. There was a similar high level of building activity in Denmark in the years preceding the Reformation. For this, see France, 1992a, 421–2.
22. William of Malmesbury's *Chronicle of the Kings of England.* The translation is from Waddell, 1985, 104.

GLOSSARY

alb – white close-fitting tunic with tight sleeves reaching to the feet. Worn by priest under eucharistic vestments.

amice – rectangular piece of white linen placed on the shoulders over the alb and attached by strings under the arms, crossed behind, brought round and tied at front. A length of embroidered material known as apparel sewn along the edge forms a stiff collar around the back of the neck.

antiphonary or **antiphoner** – book of antiphons or short passages of plainsong introducing a psalm or canticle.

aspergillum or **aspergill** – a brush for sprinkling holy water, originally a bunch of hyssop twigs. From the opening words recited during the sprinkling of holy water before Mass: 'Sprinkle me with hyssop, and I shall be clean.' (Ps 50:7)

aspersorium or **aspersory** – the vessel used for holy water. Sometimes also used to denote the brush for sprinkling holy water.

banderole – a ribbon-like scroll bearing an inscription.

boss – round ornamental carving at intersection in vaulting.

censer – a vessel for burning incense, suspended by chains and swung during services. Also known as thurible.

collation – a reading from St John Cassian's *Collationes Patrum* or Conferences, and later from other edifying texts, instituted by St Benedict before Compline. Took place in north cloister walk, therefore known as the collation gallery.

converse or **conversus** – a lay brother. The plural is *conversi*.

Compline – the seventh and last of the daytime offices said before retiring for the night. From the Latin for 'to complete'.

corbel – a projecting stone bracket, often carved, to support roof timbers or vaulting.

cowl – the distinctive monastic garment worn in choir, chapter and at meals over the tunic and scapular, and in the case of the Cistercians made of undyed wool and therefore whitish. A full cloak with wide sleeves and with hood attached. Later versions were made in two parts.

crozier or **crosier** – the staff shaped like a shepherd's crook and carried by bishops and abbots as a symbol of the pastoral nature of their office.

dalmatic – a wide-sleeved vestment with two vertical orphreys joined by a horizontal one. Worn by deacons and as part of the full eucharistic vestments of a bishop.

filigree – delicate decorated initials in illuminated manuscripts using fine lines speckled with dots of gold or silver.

flourished – initials embellished with flowers and leaves extending into the margins.

Gradual – a book containing the sung parts of the Mass. Originally the antiphon sung between the epistle and gospel as the priest mounted the steps at the altar (*gradus*).

historiated – initials decorated with figures of people or animals.

knop – the protuberance, often decorated, between the volute or upper part of the crozier and the staff itself.

lauds – the first office of the day, sung at dawn. From the Latin *laus*, praise.

maniple – a narrow strip similar to the stole but much shorter and worn by the priest over the left arm near the wrist as part of the eucharistic vestments. Not always visible. Originally a napkin.

miniator – one who illuminates a manuscript.

miniature – from the Latin *minium* – red oxide of lead or vermilion, the decorated initial came to mean any picture in an illuminated manuscript.

nimbed – having a nimb or nimbus – a halo surrounding the head of a saint.

none or **nones** – the fifth daytime office sung originally at the ninth hour of the day (mid-afternoon).

orphrey – an ornamental band on eucharistic vestments, often richly decorated.

pallium – a narrow woollen band placed round the shoulders with a short lappet hanging from front and back and worn over eucharistic vestments. Conferred by the pope on archbishops.

prime – the office appointed for the first hour of the day.

profession – the vows made on the completion of the probationary novitiate and the ceremony marking this; hence 'professed', someone who has taken the religious vows.

retable – a frame enclosing painted or carved panels raised above the back of an altar. From the Latin *retrotabulum* – a panel behind.

scapular – a piece of cloth covering the shoulders and extending in front and behind below the knees and fitted with a hood. Worn for work as a protection for the tunic very much like an apron. The Cistercian scapular is black.

sedilia – a series of three decorated seats made of wood or stone on the south side of the high altar. Used by the priest, deacon and sub-deacon officiating at Mass.

sext – the third of the lesser canonical hours originally belonging to the sixth hour of the day (midday).

stole – a long narrow strip of cloth worn by priests over the shoulders and hanging down in front to below the knees. Often fringed at the ends. Part of the eucharistic vestments worn under the chasuble.

sudarium – a small piece of cloth attached to the top of the crozier to protect it against tarnishing caused by perspiration and to avoid the cold touch of metal. Also known as **vexillum**.

terce or **tierce** – office sung at the third hour of the day (mid-morning).

thurible – a vessel for burning incense. Also known as censer.

trifoliate – consisting of three lobes or trefoils as in a tracery window.

triptych – a set of three painted or carved panels, hinged so as to allow side panels to fold over the central panel. Frequently used as an altar-piece.

tunicle – a wide-sleeved vestment similar to dalmatic but plainer and without the horizontal orphrey. Worn by sub-deacon and as part of the full eucharistic vestments of a bishop.

vespers – the sixth of the canonical hours sung towards dusk – from Hesperus, the evening star.

vexillum – the same as sudarium

vigils – the night office. From the Latin *vigilia*, to watch, watchfulness.

volute – the curved head of a crozier.

LIST OF ILLUSTRATIONS

Dimensions are given in centimetres: height × width × depth

COLOUR PLATES

Between pages 54–5

1   ST BENEDICT'S FOUR KINDS OF MONKS
1173 parchment MS 84 f. 123v (detail)
Prov. Zwettl, Austria – Stiftsbibliothek
Bibl. Ziegler, 1985–92, 1:158–67; Winkler, 1923, 13–14

2   STAINED GLASS OF ST BENEDICT
c. 1340 55.5 × 55
Prov. Kloster Wienhausen, Lüneburg, Germany – south walk of upper cloister
Bibl. Korn, 1975, 26; Becksmann & Korn, 1992, 227–8

3   STAINED GLASS OF ST BERNARD
Same as 2

4   BUST OF CISTERCIAN MONK IN ROCHESTER CHRONICLE
Thirteenth-century parchment drawing in margin MS Nero D II f. 108r (detail) 2.6 × 1.8
Prov. Rochester, England (Benedictine abbey) – London, British Library

5   ST STEPHEN HARDING ABBOT OF CITEAUX
Benedictine abbey of St Vaast Arras *c.* 1125 parchment MS 130 f. 104 23 × 14
Prov. Cîteaux (Côte d'Or), France – Dijon, Bibliothèque Municipale
Bibl. Oursel, 1960, 19; Załuska, 1989, 271–2; Załuska, 1991, 127–9

6   ST STEPHEN HARDING AND THE FIRST FOUR FOUNDATIONS
English thirteenth-century third quarter parchment MS Mm. 5. 31 f. 113r (detail)
Prov. Unknown – Cambridge, University Library
Bibl. Leclercq, 1956, 305; Wachtel, 1955, 347–9

7   ST BERNARD WRITING *THE STEPS OF HUMILITY*
Before 1135 parchment MS Bodley 530 f. 15r (detail)
Prov. Benedictine abbey of St Augustine, Canterbury, England – Oxford, Bodleian Library
Bibl. Leclercq, 1955, 145; Leclercq, 1958, 425–50; *Lexikon*, 1968–76, 5:371–85; Pächt &
Alexander, 1973, 3:11

8   ST BERNARD WRITING INSPIRED BY THE HOLY SPIRIT
Unknown French thirteenth-century second half parchment MS not numbered f. 26r (detail) 1.6 × 1.8
Prov. Unknown – Abbaye Notre Dame de Sept Fons (Allier), France
Bibl. Leclercq, 1953, 227

9   ST BERNARD WRITING
Early thirteenth-century parchment MS Laud Misc 385 f. 41v
Prov. Benedictine abbey of St Augustine, Canterbury, England – Oxford, Bodleian Library
Bibl. Pächt & Alexander, 1973, 3:118

10   ST AELRED OF RIEVAULX FACING ST BERNARD
Before 1174 parchment MS 392 ff. 2v & 3r each folio 32 × 21
Prov. Benedictine abbey of Anchin (Nord), France – Douai, Bibliothèque Municipale
Bibl. Schneider, 1986, 127

11   THE SHEPHERDS AND SHEEP
Saint-Omer workshop *c.* 1200–10 parchment MS 94 f. 48v
Prov. Clairmarais (Pas-de-Calais), France – Saint-Omer, Bibliothèque Municipale
Bibl. Clark, 1992, 63–6; Clark, 1987, 97–110

12   ABBOT ROBERT OF CLAIRMARAIS
Mid-thirteenth-century parchment MS Lat. 174 f. 2v
Prov. Clairmarais (Pas-de-Calais), France – Saint-Omer, Bibliothèque Municipale

Between pages 118–19

13   ABBOT STANTENAT OF SALEM ON A BOAT OUTING
Late fifteenth-century parchment MS Sal. IX d f. 152r (detail)
Prov. Salem, Baden, Germany – Heidelberg, Universitätsbibliothek
Bibl. Aachen ,1981, 590–2; Werner, 1975, 26–31

14   RETABLE FROM ESRUM WITH ABBOT PEDER
1496 North German workshop corpus of carved oak retable
Inv. No. 3724 210 × 265 × 23
Prov. Esrum, Denmark (high altar) – Copenhagen, Nationalmuseet
Bibl. Plathe, 1997, 150–66

15   LAY BROTHER KNEELING BEFORE MARY & CHILD
c. 1280 stained glass diameter 42.5
Prov. Wettingen, Switzerland, cloister north walk
Bibl. Anderes & Hoegger, 1989, 341

16   ST BERNARD AT THE DEATHBED OF A LAY BROTHER
Cologne workshop 1505–32 stained glass panel 73 × 113
Prov. Cloister of Altenberg, Rhineland, Germany – Schloss Stolzenfels, Koblenz, Germany
Bibl. Paffrath, 1984, 206–10

17   NUN WRITING
Lower Rhineland *c.* 1215 parchment MS (detail) 15.5 × 12.5
Prov. Probably nunnery in northwest Germany – private ownership
Bibl. Aachen, 1980, 451–2

18   ST BERNARD AND NUN KNEELING AT THE FOOT OF THE CROSS
Lower Rhineland (?) pen and ink drawing mid-fourteenth century Inv. No. M 340
Prov. Cistercian nunnery Rhineland (?) – Cologne, Schnütgen Museum
Bibl. Aachen, 1980, 571; Cologne, 1968, 66; Dupeux, 1993, 153; Hamburger, 1989, 176

19   PAPAL INDULGENCE FROM HERKENRODE
1363 parchment with 16 seals attached Inv. No. KPL/sd/251 (detail)
Prov. Herkenrode, Limbourg, Belgium – Sint-Truiden, Provinciaal Museum voor Religieuze Kunst
Bibl. Paris, 1990, 58–60; Gent, 1980, 3:59; Henneau, 1990, 192–208

20   CISTERCIAN MONK AT THE ORGAN
Cambron (Hainaut) (?) 1290 parchment MS 761 f. 270v (detail)
Prov. Beaupré, Hainaut, Belgium – Baltimore, The Walters Art Gallery
Bibl. Zwettl, 1981, 399; Randall, 1987, 133

21   MONKS IN CHOIR
1268 parchment MS 400 f. 1v (detail)
Prov. Zwettl, Austria – Stiftsbibliothek
Bibl. Zwettl, 1981, 195–6; Kubes & Rössl, 1979, 45; Buberl, 1940, 209

22   GISILBERTUS HANDS HIS MANUSCRIPT TO MARY
c. 1330 parchment MS Laud Misc. 632 f. 88r (detail)
Prov. Eberbach, Rheingau, Germany – Oxford, Bodleian Library

23   PROPERTY REGISTER OF TENNENBACH
1341–7 parchment MS Cod. Berain 66/8553 f. 1v

Prov. Tennenbach, Breisgau, Germany – Karlsruhe, Generallandesarchiv
Bibl. Weber, 1969; Aachen, 1980, 482; Schneider, 1986, 454; Paffrath, 1990, 86; Beer, 1959, 105

24   TWO MONKS SPLITTING A LOG
1111 parchment MS 170 f. 59r 7 × 9 (detail)
Prov. Cîteaux (Côte d'Or), France – Dijon, Bibliothèque Municipale
Bibl. Oursel, 1926, 30, 71; Oursel, 1960, 28; Załuska, 1989, 200–3; Załuska, 1991, 58; Davidson, 1987, 48–68; Hufgard, 1987, 69–80; Pächt, 1986, 59

25   SCRIBE FROM KAMP
1312 parchment MS Diez C. f. 64 f. 1v
Prov. Kamp, Rhineland, Germany – Berlin, Staatsbibliothek zu Berlin Preussischer Kulturbesitz
Bibl. Aachen, 1980, 572–4; Schneider, 1986, 422

26   SELF-PORTRAIT OF SCRIBE SIFRIDUS VITULUS (CALF)
1315 parchment MS Cod. Guelf. 131 f. 317r
Prov. Ebrach, Franconia, Germany – Wolfenbüttel, Herzog-August-Bibliothek
Bibl. Milde, 1972, 144; Schneider, 1986, 414–15

BLACK AND WHITE PHOTOGRAPHS

1   ST BENEDICT AND HIS RULE
1173 parchment MS 84 f. 123v (detail)
Prov. Zwettl, Austria – Stiftsbibliothek
Bibl. Ziegler, 1985–92, 1:158–67; Winkler, 1923, 13–14

2   ST BENEDICT INSTRUCTING A YOUNG MONK
Benedictine abbey of Posa mid-thirteenth-century parchment MS 15 f. 113r (detail) 13.4 × 11.8
Prov. Altzelle, Saxony, Germany – Zisterzienserinnenabtei St Marienthal, Saxony, Germany
Bibl. Libor, 1967, 54–6; Rothe, 1968, 197; Bruch, 1906, 86–7

3   ST BENEDICT WITH YOUNG DISCIPLE
c. 1270 parchment MS IF 411 f. 82r (detail) 7.5 × 8.1
Prov. Kamenz, Silesia, Poland – Wroclaw (Breslau), University Library
Bibl. Jazdzewski, 1992, 246; Kloss, 1942, 199

4   ST BENEDICT WITH HIS RULE
1173 parchment MS 10 f. 46r (detail)
Prov. Zwettl, Austria – Stiftsbibliothek
Bibl. Ziegler, 1985–92, 1:24–6

5   ST BENEDICT TEACHING
1280–90 parchment MS Osek 76 (Lectionary winter part) f. 184r (detail)
Prov. Marienstern nunnery, Saxony, Germany – Prague, National Library
Bibl. Všetečková, 1996, 219–23

6   CARVING OF ST BENEDICT AND ST BERNARD ON CHOIR STALLS
c. 1310 oak 135 × 87
Prov. Doberan, Mecklenburg, Germany (choir stalls)
Bibl. Fründt, 1987, 22; Erdmann, 1995, 38, 54

7   JACOB'S LADDER WITH ST BENEDICT AND ST BERNARD
c. 1165 parchment MS 372 f. 100r (detail)
Prov. Benedictine abbey of Anchin (Nord), France – Douai, Bibliothèque Municipale
Bibl. Escallier, 1852, 110; SBOp 3:XXX; Leclercq, 1953, 42; Leclercq, 1955, 146; *Bernard de Clairvaux*, 1992, text on reverse of pl. 9

8   POPE HANDING CHARTER TO CISTERCIAN FOUNDING FATHERS
1491 wood engraving in Peter Meglinger *Collecta privilegiorum ordinis cisterciensis*
Prov. Dijon (Côte d'Or), France – Dijon, Bibliothèque Municipale

9   POPE HANDING BULLS TO TWO ABBOTS
Mid-fourteenth-century (after 1342) parchment MS 598 f. 1r (detail)
Prov. Cîteaux – Dijon, Bibliothèque Municipale
Bibl. Załuska, 1991, 233–4

10   ST STEPHEN HARDING REPRIMANDS ST BERNARD
Cologne workshop 1505–32 stained glass 65 × 73
Prov. Altenberg, Rhineland, Germany (cloister) – St Mary's Church, Shrewsbury, England
Bibl. Paffrath, 1984, 53–4; Paris, 1990, 284–6

11   MARIENSTATT FOUNDATION PANEL
Cologne 1324 parchment on wood Inv. no. 235 79.5 × 56.5
Prov. Marienstatt, Rhineland, Germany – Bonn, Rheinisches Landesmuseum
Bibl. Düsseldorf, 1880, 323–5; Cologne, 1974, 70; Cologne, 1982, 251–3

12   ST BERNARD AND THE RECIPIENTS OF HIS BOOKS & LETTERS
Cologne workshop 1505–32 stained glass 87 × 100
Prov. Altenberg, Rhineland, Germany (cloister) – St Mary's Church, Shrewsbury, England
Bibl. Paffrath, 1984, 213–14; Paris, 1990, 284–5, 291–2; Cowen, 1985, 178; Hunt, 1951, 12–19

13   ABBOT (ST BERNARD ?) WITH DEVIL ON CHAIN
Second half fifteenth-century sandstone carving 22 × 27
Prov. Cadouin (Dordogne), France (north cloister walk)
Bibl. Delluc, Lagrange, & Secret, 1990, 110

14   CHRIST EMBRACING ST BERNARD
First half fourteenth-century Upper Rhine parchment MS Cod. U. H. 1 f. 195r (detail)
Prov. Wonnental abbey of nuns, Breisgau, Germany – Karlsruhe, Badische Landesbibliothek
Bibl. Aachen, 1980, 569–71; Anderes & Hoegger, 1989, 260–1

15   'VERA EFFIGIES' OF ST BERNARD
Late sixteenth early seventeenth-century Burgundy oil on wood 65 × 50
Prov. monks' refectory, Clairvaux (Aube), France – Cathedral Treasury, Troyes (Aube), France
Bibl. Quarré, 1954, 342–9; Paris, 1990, 282–3; Schmitt, 1990, 151–2; Schmitt, 1992, 640–57

16   STATUE OF ST BERNARD
c. 1350 red sandstone
Prov. Amelungsborn, Lower Saxony, Germany (Celebrants' Sedilia)
Bibl. Paffrath, 1990, 115

17   ST BERNARD CELEBRATING MASS
1175–6 parchment MS 194 f. 3r (detail)
Prov. Zwettl, Austria – Stiftsbibliothek
Bibl. Ziegler, 1985–92, 2:251–9; Paffrath, 1990, 78; Buberl, 1940, 202

18   ST BERNARD WRITING AND TEACHING HIS MONKS
1353 Parchment MS Ludwig XI 7 (83 MN 126) f. 167r 33.8 × 24.5
Prov. Silesia, Poland (Court Atelier of Ludwig I of Liegnitz and Brieg) – The J. Paul Getty Museum,
Malibu, California
Bibl. Gottschalk, 1967, 61–161; Paffrath, 1990, 87

19   ST BERNARD TEACHING MONKS
c. 1280–90 parchment MS Osek 76 (Osek Lectionary, summer part) f. 184v 122 × 82
Prov. Marienstern nunnery, Saxony, Germany – formerly Prague, National Library – now lost
Bibl. Všetečková, 1995, 219–23; Všetečková, 1996, 285–300

20   ST BERNARD THE TEACHER
End of twelfth-century parchment MS MSB f. 1r (detail)
Prov. Unknown, but probably Cistercian abbey, possibly German or Flemish – Mount Saint Bernard
Abbey, Leicestershire, England
Bibl. Morson, 1954, 30–4, 214–21; Leclercq, 1953, 43

21   ST BERNARD AND WILLIAM OF ST THIERRY
c. 1180 parchment MS 144 f. 26r (detail)
Prov. Zwettl, Austria – Stiftsbibliothek
Bibl. Ziegler, 1985–92, 2:117–24; Leclercq, 1953, 45; Piazonni, 1993, 3–18

22   STEPHEN HARDING COMMISSIONS BERNARD TO FOUND CLAIRVAUX
Cologne workshop 1505–32 stained glass panel 65 × 84
Prov. Altenberg, Rhineland, Germany (cloister) – St Mary's Church, Shrewsbury, England
Bibl. Paffrath, 1984, 58–60; Paris, 1990, 284–5, 287; Hunt, 1951, 14

23   ST BERNARD ON HIS SICK BED
Cologne workshop *c.* 1525 stained glass panel 90 × 80
Prov. Nunnery of St Apern, Cologne, Germany (cloister) – Cologne Cathedral
Bibl. Paffrath, 1984, 84–90; Paris, 1990, 284–5; Rode, 1974, 164, 167

24   THE BURIAL OF ST BERNARD
Twelfth to thirteenth-century parchment MS Arsenal 268 f. 2v 7.5 × 5.3 (detail)
Prov. Benedictine abbey of Saint-Martin des Champs, Paris, France – Paris, Bibliothèque de l'Arsenal
Bibl. Martin, 1885, 1:156–7; Leclercq, 1953, 44

25   ST BERNARD AS FOUNDER OF CLAIRVAUX
Late fourteenth-century (?) sandstone with traces of polychrome 80 cm high
Prov. Clairvaux (Aube), France, tomb of St Bernard (?) – Bar sur Aube, Bibliothèque Municipale
Bibl. Paris, 1990, 274

26   ST BERNARD AND POPE EUGENIUS III
Late twelfth early thirteenth-century parchment MS Clm 7950 f. 2v
Prov. Kaisheim, Bavaria, Germany – Munich, Bayerische Staatsbibliothek
Bibl. Strange, 1930, 277–81; Paffrath, 1990, 76; Munich, 1960, 14; Leclercq, 1953, 43

27   TOMB OF ST STEPHEN OF OBAZINE
c. 1280
Prov. Obazine, abbey church
Bibl. Aubert, 1947, 1:342–3; Réau, 1955–9, 3:1:458–9; Texier, 1852; Barrière, 1977

28   PSALTER WITH MEMBERS OF DIVERSE RELIGIOUS ORDERS
Fourteenth-century parchment 27 × 18 MS 76 f. 90v
Prov. English (Oxford ?) for use in diocese of Exeter, England – Cambridge, Sidney Sussex College
Bibl. James, 1895, 56–60; Sandler, 1986, 94

29   MONKS AT THE DEATHBED OF ARCHBISHOP HENRY MURDAC OF YORK
c. 1421 York School of Glass Painting n. VII, 10 c
Prov. York Minster, St William's Window (north choir transept)
Bibl. Fowler, 1875, 198–348; Knowles, 1951, 148–61

30   ST AELRED THE HISTORIAN KNEELING BEFORE KING HENRY II
Mid-fourteenth-century English parchment MS 172 p. 21 (detail) 8.6 × 8.9
Prov. Whalley, Lancashire, England (?) – Dublin, Trinity College
Bibl. Colker, 1991, 1:319; Dutton, 1993, 209–30; Dutton, 1994

31   OTTO OF FREISING MONK AND BISHOP
End thirteenth century stained glass
Prov. Heiligenkreuz, Austria, Lavatorium
Bibl. Frodl-Kraft, 1972, 113, 120; Mierow, 1994

32   BALDWIN OF FORD, ARCHBISHOP OF CANTERBURY
End twelfth beginning thirteenth century parchment MS 200 f. 1r (detail) 6 × 5.7
Prov. Christ Church, Canterbury, England – Cambridge, Corpus Christi College
Bibl. James, 1912, 484

33   ST WILLIAM OF BOURGES
1215–20 stained glass

Prov. Bourges Cathedral (ambulatory window on far right)
Bibl. Martin & Cahier, 1841–4, 2:283–6; Quiévreux, 1942, 255–75

34   FOLQUET OF MARSEILLE
Northern Italy, probably Padua, late thirteenth-century parchment MS 819 f. 55 (detail)
Prov. Unknown – New York, The Pierpont Morgan Library
Bibl. Huot, 1992, 3–24

35   POPE BENEDICT XII
1341 Marble half-figure by Paul of Siena
Prov. Entrance to Nave of St Peter's, Rome – Crypt of St Peter's
Bibl. Mann, 1928, 137–8; Daumet, 1896, 293–7

36   GUILLAUME DE DEGULLEVILLE
c. 1400 French (Paris ?) parchment MS 10176-8 f. 1 23 × 15
Prov. Unknown – Brussels, Bibliothèque Royale Albert Ier
Bibl. Edinburgh, 1963, 37; Delaissé, 1956, 233–50

37   MONK (STEPHEN HARDING?) AT THE FEET OF AN ANGEL
1111 parchment MS 170 f. 6v (detail)
Prov. Cîteaux (Côte d'Or), France – Dijon, Bibliothèque Municipale
Bibl. Oursel, 1926, 71; Załuska, 1989, 200–3; Załuska, 1991, 58; Załuska, 1992, 274

38   WALL PAINTING OF CISTERCIAN MONK
c. 1410–25
Prov. Sorø, Denmark (abbey church, north pillar of nave)
Bibl. Saxtorph 1967, 182

39   ST BERNARD WITH DISCIPLES
c. 1500 parchment MS 74 f. 243r (detail)
Prov. Baudeloo, Flanders, Belgium – Gent, Universiteitsbibliotheek
Bibl. Masai, 1952, 279–84; Leclercq, 1953, 43

40   ST BERNARD WITH HIS MONKS AT CLAIRVAUX
Fifteenth-century parchment MS Yates Thompson 32 (Burgundy Chronicle) f. 9v
20.9 × 14.9
Prov. Burgundy – London, British Library
Bibl. Kinder 1990, 206

41   CARVING OF NAKED MONK
Fourteenth-century carving on capital
Prov. Maulbronn, Württemberg, Germany (west cloister walk)
Bibl. Paulus, 1890, 61

42   CARVING OF MONK'S HEAD, TILTY
Fourteenth-century carving
Prov. Tilty, Essex, England (gatehouse chapel, celebrants' sedilia)

43   CARVING OF MONK'S HEAD, HOLMCULTRAM
Early sixteenth-century carving at end of red sandstone block 41 × 168 × 20
Prov. Holmcultram, Cumbria, England

44   HISTORIATED INITIAL FROM PSALTER
First quarter thirteenth century parchment MS 66 f. 41r (detail) 7.6 × 10.9
Prov. Heiligenkreuz, Austria – Stiftsbibliothek
Bibl. Walliser, 1969, 41; Schneider 1986, 435

45   MONK AND NOVICE FELLING A TREE
1111 parchment MS 173 f. 41r (detail) 22 × 7
Prov. Cîteaux (Côte d'Or), France – Dijon, Bibliothèque Municipale
Bibl. Oursel, 1926, 30, 71; Oursel, 1960, 28; Załuska, 1989, 203–4; Pächt, 1986, 59; Hufgard, 1987, 69–80; Davidson, 1987, 48–68

46   ST BERNARD REPRIMANDED BY ST STEPHEN HARDING
Cologne workshop *c.* 1525 stained glass 90 × 80
Prov. Nunnery of St Apern, Cologne (cloister) – Cologne Cathedral
Bibl. Eckert, 1953, 66; Rode, 1974, 166; Paffrath, 1984, 53–4

47   CAESARIUS OF HEISTERBACH AS MASTER OF NOVICES
First half fourteeth-century parchment MS C 27 f. 1r (detail)
Prov. Altenberg, Rhineland, Germany – Düsseldorf, Universitäts- und Landesbibliothek
Bibl. Aachen, 1980, 362, 435–6; Beitz, 1926, 92; Gattermann, 1989, 46

48   CAESARIUS OF HEISTERBACH KNEELING BEFORE CHRIST
First half fourteenth-century parchment MS C 27 f. 2r (detail)
Prov. Altenberg, Rhineland, Germany – Düsseldorf, Universitäts–und Landesbibliothek
Bibl. Aachen, 1980, 435–6

49   PROFESSION OF NOVICES BY ST BERNARD
Second half fifteenth century wall painting
Prov. Chapel of St Bernard, Pamparato, Cuneo, Italy
Bibl. PL 185:527–8; Dal Prà, 1990–91, 2:27–8

50   ST BERNARD IN THE CHAPTER HOUSE
Just after mid-fifteenth century in Jean Fouquet's, *The Hours of Etienne Chevalier* parchment MS fr.
71 f. 36 16 × 12
Prov. Chantilly, Musée Condé
Bibl. Réau 1955–9, 3:1:215; Schaefer, 1972, no. 40; Paris, 1990, 71

51   ST BERNARD PREACHES TO THE CONVENT
Cologne workshop *c.* 1525 stained glass 65 × 89
Prov. Altenberg, Rhineland, Germany – Cologne, Schnütgen Museum
Bibl. Paffrath, 1984, 202–5; Paris, 1990, 284–5

52   TOMB OF BLESSED GOBERT D'ASPREMONT
Early thirteenth century restored twentieth century
Prov. Villers, Brabant, Belgium (east cloister range)
Bibl. Maisières, 1949, 285–90; Pineault & Coomans, 1994, 132–3; Arens 1982, 7–15

53   THE CONTEMPLATIVE AND THE ACTIVE LIFE
First half thirteenth century parchment MS 226 f. 129v 17 × 26.5
Prov. Heiligenkreuz, Austria – Stiftsbibliothek
Bibl. Walliser, 1969, 41; Clark, 1992, 283; Zwettl, 1981, 242–3

54   ABBOT OF CADOUIN AND HIS MONKS
Second half fifteenth century 54 × 49 (group of figures)
Prov. Cadouin (Dordogne), France (north cloister walk)
Bibl. Aubert, 1947, 2:20–2; Delluc, Lagrange, & Secret, 1990, 100–1, 110

55   CORBEL OF MONK WITH FLASK OF WINE
Fourteenth century
Prov. Santes Creus, Catalonia, Spain (west cloister walk)

56   CORBEL OF MONK BREAKING BREAD
Fourteenth century
Prov. Santes Creus, Catalonia, Spain (west cloister walk)

57   CORBEL OF MONK EATING
Second half fifteenth century 39 × 45
Prov. Cadouin (Dordogne), France (east cloister walk)
Bibl. Delluc, Lagrange, & Secret, 1990, 118

58   THREE MONKS FROM ALCOBAÇA
Portuguese school 1470–80 detail from polyptych of the altar of St Vincent painted by Nuno
Gonsalves Inv. no. 1363 207 × 60.5
Prov. St Vincent de Fora, Lisbon – Lisbon, Museu Nacional de Arte Antiga

59   MONK BEING GIVEN TONSURE
c. 1220–30 parchment MS Cotton Cleopatra C XI f. 27v (detail) 2.6 × 2.5
Prov. Abbey Dore, Herefordshire, England – London, British Library
Bibl. Morgan, 1982, 106–7; Southern, 1969, 93

60   THE WHEEL OF FALSE RELIGION
Early thirteenth-century parchment MS 226 f. 149v 22 × 15.5
Prov. Heiligenkreuz, Austria – Stiftsbibliothek
Bibl. Walliser, 1969, 41–2; Caviness, 1983, 113–14

61   ABBOT FOLKNAND OF STICNA
c. 1180 parchment MS 650 f. 62r (detail)
Prov. Stična (Sittich, Sitticum), Slovenia – Vienna, Nationalbibliothek
Bibl. Galob, 1994, 27–9; Hermann, 1926, 287–90

62   TOMBSTONE OF AN ABBOT OF SAVIGNY
Late thirteenth early fourteenth-century limestone
Prov. Savigny (Manche), France – Parish Church of Savigny-le-Vieux

63   CARVING OF AN ABBOT, KILCOOLY
c. 1450–1520
Prov. Kilcooly, Ireland (beside doorway between transept and sacristy)
Bibl. Stalley, 1987, 194–5

64   CARVING OF AN ABBOT, JERPOINT
c. 1390–1400
Prov. Jerpoint, Ireland (cloister)
Bibl. Stalley, 1987, 155, 189

65   GRAVE SLAB OF ABBOT WILLIAM HALFORDE OF BORDESLEY
Late fifteenth century
Prov. Unknown – Parish Church, Hinton-on-the-Green, Worcestershire, England
Bibl. Greenhill, 1976, 1:98, 2:1

66   ABBOT WALTER CLIFTON OF WARDEN
Late fourteenth-century stained glass panel measures 115 x 46
Prov. Old Warden Parish Church, Bedfordshire, England
Bibl. Marks, 1986, 225–7; Marks, 1976, 179–84, 229–33

67   ST BERNARD WITH SIX MONKS
c. 1180 MS theol. lat. f. 347 fol. 1v (detail)
Prov. Benedictine abbey of Liesborn – Berlin, Staatsbibliothek zu Berlin Preussischer Kulturbesitz
Bibl. Brandis, 1975, 84; Paffrath, 1990, 83; Leclercq, 1953, 41

68   ABBATIAL SEAL FROM LES DUNES
Used by the abbots second half of twelfth century, example from 1171 Inv. Dunes No. 462
Prov. Les Dunes, Flanders – Bruges, Grootseminarie
Bibl. Nerom, 1992, 5–27

69   ABBATIAL/COMMON SEAL FROM GRACE DIEU
Thirteenth to early fourteenth-century impression from brass matrix 4.9 × 2.8
Prov. Grace Dieu, Gwent, Wales – Cardiff, National Museum of Wales
Bibl. Williams, 1987, 148

70   TOMB OF ABBOT DOMENEC PORTA OF POBLET
Early sixteenth century 219 × 85
Prov. Poblet, Catalonia, Spain (chapter house)

71   GRAVESTONE OF ABBOT JOHANN BECKER OF DARGUN
Late fifteenth century 228 × 125
Prov. Dargun, Mecklenburg, Germany
Bibl. Schlie, 1896, 44, 549; Schlegel, 1980

72   EFFIGY OF THE ABBOT OF DUNDRENNAN
Thirteenth century 204 × 48
Prov. Dundrennan, Scotland
Bibl. Richardson, 1964, 66

73   CARVING OF MONKS ON TOMB OF JOANA D'AMPURIAS
Mid-fourteenth century
Prov. Poblet, Catalonia, Spain (abbey church)

74   KING ALPHONSE OF ARAGON WITH CISTERCIAN MONKS
c. 1420 parchment MS Rothschild 2529 f. 444v (detail) 5.2 × 5.3
Prov. Poblet, Catalonia, Spain, Paris – Bibliothèque Nationale
Bibl. Porcher, 1950; *Manuscrits Enluminée*, 1982, 107

75   ABBOT CHRISTIAAN DE HONDT OF LES DUNES
c. 1499 Right-hand panel of diptych by Bruges Master Inv. no. 256 31 × 14.5
Prov. Les Dunes, Flanders, Belgium – Antwerp, Koninklijk Museum voor Schone Kunsten
Bibl. van Os, 1994, 78–81

76   CARVING OF HEAD OF ABBOT JOHN DARNTON OF FOUNTAINS
Late fifteenth century
Prov. Fountains, Yorkshire, England (south wall of Nine Altars' Chapel)
Bibl. Reeve, 1892, 11–12; Coppack, 1993, 68

77   LAY BROTHERS ON TOMB OF ST STEPHEN OF OBAZINE
c. 1280
Prov. Obazine (Corrèze), France (abbey church, tomb of St Stephen – detail)
Bibl. Aubert, 1947, 1:342–3; Réau, 1955–9, 3:1:458–9; Texier, 1852; Barrière, 1977

78   OUR LADY PROTECTING THE CISTERCIAN ORDER
1491 Wood Engraving in Peter Meglinger, *Collecta Privilegiorum ordinis cisterciensis*
Prov. Dijon (Côte d'Or), France – Dijon, Bibliothèque Municipale

79   OUR LADY OF MERCY WITH CISTERCIAN MONKS AND *CONVERSI*
c. 1320–30 parchment MS IF 413 f. 145r (detail) 13 × 12
Prov. Lubiaz (Leubus), Poland – Wroclaw, University Library
Bibl. Kloss, 1942, 46, 200; Paris, 1990, 272

80   EFFIGY OF A LAY BROTHER FROM POBLET
Last third fourteenth century
Prov. Poblet, Catalonia, Spain (east cloister walk next to the day stairs)

81   LAY BROTHER KONRAD TEUFEL FROM EBRACH
Mid-fourteenth-century effigy from engraving in *Brevis Notitia Monasterii B.V.M. Ebracensis Sac.
Ordinis Cisterciensis in Franconia.* (Rome, 1739)
Prov Ebrach, Franconia, Germany (abbey church before entrance to sacristy)
Bibl. Brevis Notitia, 1739, 21–2; Wiener, 1985, 263–353

82   A CARICATURE OF HENRY, LAY BROTHER SCRIBE FROM TER DOEST
End thirteenth century parchment MS 13 f. 180v (detail)
Prov. Ter Doest, Flanders, Belgium – Bruges, Openbare Bibliotheek
Bibl. Hoste, 1993, 88, 143; Bruges, 1981, 115; Lieftinck, 1953, 46–8, 89

83   LAY BROTHER FROM BEAULIEU
Second half thirteenth century parchment MS Add. 48978 f. 41v (detail)
Prov. Beaulieu, Hampshire, England – London, British Library
Bibl. Hockey, 1975, 3–4

84   LAY BROTHERS AT SCHÖNAU DISOBEY THEIR ABBOT
Early sixteenth-century pen and ink drawing Kapsel 1532 Blatt 202
Prov. Schönau, Hesse, Germany – Nuremberg, Germanisches Nationalmuseum
Bibl. Aachen, 1980, 426–8; Becksmann, 1979, 222

85   CARVING OF A LAY BROTHER
c. 1390–1400
Prov. Jerpoint, Ireland (cloister)
Bibl. Stalley, 1987, 155, 189; Hunt, 1974, 1:179; Rae, 1966, 71

86   LAY BROTHER WITH ST HEDWIG
1353 parchment MS 83 MN 126 (Ludwig XI 7) (Life of St Hedwig of Silesia) f. 46v (detail) 34.1 × 24.8
Prov. Court Atelier of Ludwig I of Liegnitz and Brieg, scribe Nicolaus of Prussia – J. Paul Getty Museum, Malibu, California
Bibl. Gottschalk, 1967, 118

87   LAY BROTHER FROM DOBERAN WITH THE DEVIL
1280–1300 oak carving overall height 92 (lay brother 71) × 66
Prov. Doberan, Mecklenburg, Germany (choir stalls abbey church)
Bibl. Schneider, 1986, 497; Gloede, 66–8; Erdmann, 1995, 36, 48

88   LAY BROTHER KNEELING BEFORE MARY
First quarter thirteenth century parchment MS 20 f. 168 (detail) 10.7 × 9.5
Prov. Heiligenkreuz, Austria – Stiftsbibliothek
Bibl. Walliser, 1969, 40; Winkler, 1923, 17

89   ST HUMBELINE AND FEMALE SAINTS OF THE CISTERCIAN ORDER
1635 oil on canvas 180 × 127
Prov. Jehay-Bodegnée, La Paix Dieu Nuns' Abbey – Kerniel, Priory of Mariënlof, Belgium
Bibl. Gent, 1980, 167–9; Hogenelst & Oostrom, 1995, 134; Nichols & Shank, 1995, 813–20

90   ST BERNARD BLESSING THREE NUNS
End twelfth century parchment MS 268 f. 86r (detail)
Prov. Unknown, probably abbey of nuns – Brussels, Bibliothèque Royale Albert Ier
Bibl. Brussels, 1990, 57; Leclercq, 1953, 41

91   ST BERNARD PREACHING TO NUNS
c. 1290–1300 parchment MS 1787 f. 8r (detail)
Prov. Nizelles Nuns' Abbey, Nivelles, Brabant, Belgium – Brussels, Bibliothèque Royale Albert Ier
Bibl. Brussels, 1990, 57; Leclercq, 1953, 41; Pächt & Thoss, 1983, 162–4

92   ST BERNARD PREACHING TO NUNS
c. 1290–1300 parchment MS S. n. 12771 f. 1r (detail)
Prov. Nizelles Nuns' Abbey, Nivelles, Brabant, Belgium – Vienna, Nationalbibliothek
Bibl. Pächt & Thoss, 1983, 162–4

93   NUNS FROM COYROUX ON THE TOMB OF ST STEPHEN OF OBAZINE
c. 1280 detail of tomb
Prov. Obazine (Corrèze), France (abbey church)
Bibl. Aubert, 1947, 1:342–3; Réau, 1955–9, 3:1:458–9; Texier, 1852; Barrière, 1977

94   TOMB OF ALPHONSUS VIII WITH FOUNDATION SCENE OF LAS HUELGAS
1279
Prov. Las Huelgas, Burgos, Spain (abbey church, nuns' choir)
Bibl. de la Cruz, 1991, 30–3

95   ST HEDWIG AND THE BUILDING OF TREBNITZ
1353 parchment MS 83 MN 126 (Ludwig XI 7) (Life of St Hedwig of Silesia) f. 56r 34.1 × 24.8
Prov. Court Atelier of Ludwig I of Liegnitz and Brieg, scribe Nicolaus of Prussia – J. Paul Getty Museum, Malibu, California
Bibl. Gottschalk, 1967, 118; Hamburger, 1992, 108–34

96   HEDWIG HEALS SISTER JUTTA & BURIAL OF HEDWIG
1353 parchment MS 83 MN 126 (Ludwig XI 7) (Life of St Hedwig of Silesia) f. 87r 34.1 × 24.8
Prov. Court Atelier of Ludwig I of Liegnitz and Brieg, scribe Nicolaus of Prussia – J. Paul Getty Museum, Malibu, California
Bibl. Gottschalk, 1967, 132

97   WALL PAINTING SHOWING FOUNDATION OF WIENHAUSEN
Early fourteenth century height 200 cm
Prov. Kloster Wienhausen, Lüneburg, Germany (west walk of upper cloister)
Bibl. Appuhn, 1986, 14–5, 21

98   DONOR NUN IN SCENE OF THE ANOINTING OF CHRIST'S BODY
c. 1330 stained glass 51 × 51
Prov. Kloster Wienhausen, Lüneburg, Germany (south walk of upper cloister)
Bibl. Korn, 1975, 28; Becksmann & Korn, 1992, 226–7; Aachen, 1980, 540–1

99   NUN FROM WIENHAUSEN IN POINTED VEIL WITH CROSS
Second half fifteenth century parchment MS Processional f. 18v (detail)
Prov. Kloster Wienhausen, Lüneburg, Germany – Wienhausen, Archives
Bibl. Uhde-Stahl, 1978, 47–50; Appuhn, 1986, 53

100   FOUNDATION PICTURE OF DES PRES
Early fourteenth-century MS Saint-André f. 3r (detail)
Prov. Notre-Dame des Prés, Douai, France – Notre-Dame de la Plaine, Saint-André, Lille
Bibl. Delmaire, 1979, 331–51; Bondeelle-Souchier, 1994, 251–2

101   DEDICATION OF MARIENSTERN CHURCH
c. 1280–90 parchment MS Osek 76 (Osek Lectionary – summer part) f. 251r (detail)
Prov. Marienstern Nuns' Abbey, Saxony, Germany – formerly Prague, National Library – now lost
Bibl. Všetečková, 1995, 219–23; Všetečková,1996, 285–300

102   DEDICATION OF BEAUPRE CHURCH
1290 from diocese of Cambrai (Cambron ?) parchment MS W. 750 (Beaupré Antiphonary Vol. 1)
f. 90r (detail)
Prov. Beaupré near Grammont, Belgium – Baltimore, The Walters Art Gallery
Bibl. Calkins, 1983, 237; Randall, 1987, 133

103   EFFIGY OF ABBESS JEANNE DE FLANDRE
Second half fourteenth century white marble height 180 cm
Prov. Le Sauvoir-sous-Laon (Aisne), France – Laon, former Premonstratensian abbey church of Saint-Martin
Bibl. Paris, 1968, 84

104   BEATRICE THE SACRISTAN
1374 parchment MS 76 f. 74v (detail)
Prov. Unknown, Netherlands – The Hague, Koninklijke Bibliotheek
Bibl. de Moor, 1993, 306–21; Swinton Bland, 1928, 43

105   BEATRICE LEAVES HER MONASTERY
Early fourteenth century MS Royal 2 B VII (Queen Mary's Psalter) f. 218v 5.5 × 10.8 (detail)
Prov. Unknown, England – London, British Library
Bibl. Swinton Bland, 1928, 43; Warner, 1912, 43–5

106   CHRIST CHASTISES THE ERRANT NUN
Second half thirteenth century MS T.I.1 ('Cantigas de Santa Maria' by Alfonso X) Cantiga 59 panel 3 (detail)
Prov. Unknown, Spain – Madrid, El Escorial, Library
Bibl. Keller & Kinkade, 1984, 52–5

107   CHRIST STRIKES THE ELOPING NUN
1293 MS 3995 f. 74v (detail)
Prov. Unknown, Spain – Madrid, Biblioteca Nacional
Bibl. Keller & Kinkade, 1984, 52–5

108   SCRIBE OF BEAUPRE ANTIPHONARY
1290 from diocese of Cambrai (Cambron ?) parchment MS 761 (Beaupré Antiphonary Vol. 3) f. 1 (detail)
Prov. Beaupré near Grammont, Belgium – Baltimore, The Walters Art Gallery
Bibl. Calkins, 1983, 235; Büttner, 1983, 206

109   NUN KNEELING AT THE FOOT OF THE CROSS
Thirteenth-century parchment MS 99 f. 5v 13.8 × 10. 9

Prov. Marquette (Nord), France – Cambrai, Bibliothèque Municipale
Bibl. Bondeelle-Souchier, 1994, 298; Leroquais, 1934, 1:189

110   ST LUTGARD ON HER DEATHBED
c. 1274 parchment MS Ny kgl. Saml. 168 4° f. 254v
Prov. Benedictine abbey of Afflighem, then abbey of Rookloster – Copenhagen, Royal Library

111   DONOR NUNS FROM HERKENRODE
1532–59 stained glass
Prov. Herkenrode, Limbourg, Belgium – Lichfield Cathedral, England
Bibl. Bemden & Kerr, 1986, 192–7

112   DONOR ABBESS WITH ST BERNARD
Mid-sixteenth-century stained glass
Prov. Herkenrode, Limbourg, Belgium (probably private chapel of abbess) – Church of St Giles,
Ashtead, Surrey, England
Bibl. Bemden & Kerr, 1986, 215–17

113   ABBESS ELIZABETH VON STEPHELN OF HEILIGKREUZTAL
Early fourteenth-century stained glass
Prov. Heiligkreuztal, Swabia, Germany
Bibl. Wentzel, 1958, 190–4; Becksmann, 1967, 84–6

114   MARY & CHILD WITH ST BERNARD AND A CISTERCIAN NUN
c. 1300 parchment MS W 255 f. 1v full-page miniature 33 × 24
Prov. Heisterbach (?), Rhineland, Germany – Cologne, Historisches Archiv
Bibl. Swarzenski, 1936, 1:19, 95; Leclercq, 1953, 227; Aachen, 1980, 369; Paffrath, 1990, 76, 85;
Dupeux, 1993, 153

115   KING DAVID AND A KNEELING MONK
c. 1270 parchment MS IF 411 f. 2r (detail) 14.3 × 11.8
Prov. Lubiaz (Leubus), Poland – Wroclaw, University Library
Bibl. Kloss, 1942, 199; Jazdzewski,1992, 246

116   ST BERNARD'S VISION AT THE NIGHT OFFICE
Cologne workshop 1505–32 stained glass 63 × 89
Prov. Altenberg, Rhineland, Germany (cloister) – St Mary's Church, Shrewsbury, England
Bibl. Paris, 1990, 284–5, 291; Paffrath, 1984, 195–6

117   MONKS CELEBRATING MASS
After 1253 parchment MS 113 f. 3r (detail) 24 × 13.4
Prov. Heilsbronn, Bavaria, Germany – Erlangen, Universitätsbibliothek
Bibl. Aachen, 1981, 567–9; Lutze, 1936, 47–8; Swarzenski, 1935, 1:150–1

118   ELEVATION AT MASS WITH NIMBED CELEBRANT
After 1253 parchment MS 113 f. 57r (detail) 4.6 × 4.9
Prov. Heilsbronn, Bavaria, Germany – Erlangen, Universitätsbibliothek
Bibl. Lutze, 1936, 47–8; Swarzenski, 1935, 1:150–1

119   MONKS AT MASS
c. 1330–40 Gotland limestone carving Inv. no. MNS/Szt. 143 56 × 53 × 37
Prov. Kołbacz, Pomerania, Poland – Szczecin, Muzeum Narodowe
Bibl. Białoskórska, 1995, 645–6

120   GROUP OF MONKS SINGING FROM AN ANTIPHONARY
c. 1300 before 1318 parchment MS CFM 6 f. 1v (detail) 17.4 × 13.5 (whole initial)
Prov. Morimondo, Lombardy, Italy – Cambridge, The Fitzwilliam Museum
Bibl. Wormald & Giles, 1982, 1:11–14

121   THREE SINGING MONKS
c. 1240 parchment MS Theol. Lat. F. 379 f. 247v (detail) 6 × 5.5
Prov. Heisterbach, Germany – Berlin, Staatsbibliothek zu Berlin Preussischer Kulturbesitz
Bibl. Swarzenski, 1935, 1:91–5

122 CISTERCIAN MONK KNEELING BEFORE A BISHOP
Late thirteenth early fourteenth-century limestone carving 54 × 34
Prov. Abbey Dore, Hereford, England – Hereford, Cathedral Treasury

123 DEDICATION OF CISTERCIAN CHURCH BY A BISHOP
Fourteenth-century parchment MS 232 f. 39r
Prov. Vauclair (Aisne), France – Laon, Bibliothèque Municipale
Bibl. Calkins, 1983, 234–8

124 CONFESSION SCENE ON CARVED CORBEL
Second half fifteenth century limestone carving 29 × 30
Prov. Cadouin (Dordogne), France (north cloister walk)
Bibl. Delluc, Lagrange, & Secret, 1990, 109

125 ABBOT AT THE FEET OF THE VIRGIN
Late fifteenth century restored nineteenth century – part of statue of Mary with traces of polychrome
40 cm high (Virgin 170 cm high)
Prov. Cadouin (Dordogne), France (abbey church)
Bibl. Delluc, Lagrange, & Secret, 1990. 105–6.

126 ABBOT KNEELING BEFORE THE VIRGIN
Late thirteenth early fourteenth-century limestone carving
Prov. Abbey Dore, Hereford, England (boss from former presbytery vault)
Bibl. Paris, 1990, 271; Coldstream, 1986, 152

127 MONK KNEELING BEFORE THE VIRGIN
c. 1380 limestone carving 37 × 93 × 70
Prov. Eberbach, Rheingau, Germany (entrance to chapter house) – Eberbach, abbey museum
Bibl. Aachen, 1981, 551; Schneider, 1986, 162

128 RELIEFS OF THE VIRGIN AND KNEELING MONK
Fifteenth-century terracotta reliefs – Virgin: 103 × 43 Monk: 60 × 37
Prov. Dargun, Mecklenburg, Germany – Dargun, Parish Church
Bibl. Schlie, 1896, 537; Kratzke, 1998, chapter 2

129 CONVENTUAL SEAL OF ESRUM ABBEY
1374 seal impression in green wax – Inscription: S. CONVENTUS MONASTERII BEATE MARIE
DE ESROM seal in use until 1536
Prov. Esrum, Denmark – Copenhagen, Royal Archives
Bibl. Petersen, 1886, 37; *Diplomatarium Danicum* 3:9:338

130 OUR LADY PROTECTING THE ORDER OF CITEAUX
1506–9 Painting on wood attributed to Jean Bellegambe Inv. No. 408
Prov. Flines (Nord), France – Douai, Musée de la Chartreuse

131 CARVING OF KNEELING MONK
Thirteenth-century carving in low relief 67 × 58
Prov. Cadouin (Dordogne), France (north transept of church)

132 ST LOUIS, KING OF FRANCE, AND CISTERCIAN PAPAL LEGATE
c. 1406–9 French, Paris parchment Pol, Jean, & Herman de Limbourg *The Belles Heures of Jean, Duke of Berry* 23.8 × 16.8
Prov. New York, Metropolitan Museum of Art, Cloisters Collection

133 MONKS ON THE TOMB OF PRINCE LOUIS OF FRANCE
Second half of thirteenth-century carving
Prov. Royaumont (Seine-et-Oise), France – Abbey of Saint-Denis, Paris

134 CITEAUX MONK REAPING CORN
1111 parchment MS 170 f. 75v (detail) 6.5 × 10.5
Prov. Cîteaux (Côte d'Or), France – Dijon, Bibliothèque Municipale
Bibl. Załuska, 1989, 200–3; Załuska, 1991, 58; Oursel, 1926, 30, 71; Oursel, 1960, 28; Davidson, 1987, 46–68; Hufgard, 1987, 69–80

135   ST BERNARD PRAYING ALONGSIDE THE REAPERS
1500 Zwettl retable panel painted on fig wood by Jörg Breu 74 × 74
Prov. Zwettl, Austria (abbot's chapel) – Zwettl, abbey church
Bibl. Zwettl, 1981, 743–5; Buberl, 1940, 80; Kubes & Rössl, 1979, 7–14; Paffrath, 1984, 421

136   ST BERNARD AT PRAYER DURING HARVEST
Cologne workshop *c.* 1525 stained glass 90 × 80
Prov. Cologne, women's abbey of St Apern – Cologne, Cathedral
Bibl. Paffrath 1984, 55–7

137   MONK FISHING
First quarter thirteenth century parchment MS 66 f. 25v 7.5 × 9.3
Prov. Heiligenkreuz, Austria – Stiftsbibliothek
Bibl. Walliser, 1969, 40

138   MONKS FISHING AT BEBENHAUSEN
c. 1500 Painted panel – detail of abbot kneeling at scene of *Amplexus*
Prov. Bebenhausen, Württemberg, Germany

139   GRAVE SLAB OF PATRICK DOUGLAS, CELLARER AT DUNDRENNAN
Late fifteenth-century grave slab carved in low relief 169 × 84
Prov. Dundrennan, Scotland
Bibl. Greenhill, 1976, 1:98

140   THE MONK ROSEN SCHÖPHELIN
Early fourteenth-century carved corbel 56 × 48
Prov. Maulbronn, Württemberg, Germany (west cloister walk)
Bibl. Paulus, 1890, 60–1

141   PRIOR WALTHER
Early fourteenth-century carved corbel 56 × 40
Prov. Maulbronn, Württemberg, Germany (west cloister walk)
Bibl. Paulus, 1890, 60–1; Gerstenberg, 1966, 87; Dörrenberg, 1938, 11

142   CARVING OF LAY BROTHER
c. 1320 carved boss
Prov. Salem, Baden, Germany (abbey church)
Bibl. Dillmann & Schultz, 1989, 29

143   CARVING OF MONK'S HEAD
Fourteenth-century carved capital
Prov. Flaran (Gers), France (cloister)

144   CARVING OF BROTHER BERTHOLD
After 1420 carved corbel
Prov. Maulbronn, Württemberg, Germany (north aisle of church)
Bibl. Paulus, 1890, 68; Gerstenberg, 1966, 34

145   CARVING OF FOUR HEADS
Thirteenth-century carved boss
Prov. Sulejów, Poland (chapter house)
Bibl. Białoskórska, 1966, 20

146   CARVING OF LAY BROTHER AND HIRED WORKER
Carved corbel
Prov. Pforta, Thuringia, Germany (parlour)
Bibl. Hirschfeld,1933, 111

147   CARVING OF MONK AND LAY HELPERS
Thirteenth-century (?) carving 25 × 55
Prov. Villelongue (Aude), France (proprietor's dining room, formerly west wall of nave above west
door – original position ?)
Bibl. Chauvin, 1992, 2:353–5

148   MONKS BUILDING MAULBRONN
1450 part of triptych painted oil on wood
Prov. Maulbronn, Württemberg, Germany – Maulbronn, Evangelisches Seminar
Bibl. Aachen, 1980, 601–4

149   BUILDING OF SCHÖNAU
c. 1600 pen and ink drawing Kapsel 1532 Blatt 196
Prov. Schönau, Hesse, Germany – Nuremberg, Germanisches Nationalmuseum
Bibl. Aachen, 1980, 423–4, 430–2

150   BEARDED MONK READING
Fourteenth-century limestone carving 42 × 68
Prov. Eberbach, Rheingau, Germany (east cloister walk near chapter house) – Eberbach, abbey
museum

151   MONK READING
End fourteenth century carved corbel
Prov. Poblet, Catalonia, Spain (outside wall of Royal Palace)

152   TWO MONKS HOLDING A BOOK
Second half fifteenth century carving 72 × 50
Prov. Cadouin (Dordogne), France (north cloister walk)
Bibl. Delluc, Lagrange, & Secret, 1990, 111

153   SCRIBE KNEELING IN CRUCIFIXION SCENE
First half fourteenth century parchment MS lat. quart. 718 f. 7v 21.5 × 14.5
Prov. Himmerod, Eifel, Germany – Berlin, Staatsbibliothek zu Berlin Preussischer Kulturbesitz
Bibl. Berlin, 1988, 160

154   SCRIBE FROM HEILIGENKREUZ
Third quarter twelfth century parchment MS 224 f. 1v (detail) 7 × 8
Prov. Heiligenkreuz, Austria – Stiftsbibliothek
Bibl. Walliser, 1969, 31

155   CARVING OF SCRIBE
Fourteenth-century carved corbel
Prov. Eberbach, Rheingau, Germany (east cloister walk)

156   TWO CISTERCIAN SCHOLARS
c. 1400–20 stained glass
Prov. Yarnton Parish Church, Oxfordshire, England
Bibl. Newton, 1979, 224–5; Marks, 1986, 224

157   HEAD OF MONK WITH BODY OF WINGED GRIFFON
Fourteenth-century limestone carving 28 × 65
Prov. Villelongue (Aude), France (south cloister walk)
Bibl. Chauvin, 1992, 2:309; Lignon & Padelier-Schlumberger, 1973, 490

158   HEAD OF MONK WITH TAILS OF GRIFFONS IN HIS MOUTH
Fourteenth-century limestone carving
Prov. Villelongue (Aude), France (south cloister walk)
Bibl. Chauvin, 1992, 2:315

159   CARVING OF FOX IN MONK'S HABIT
Third quarter fourteenth century red sandstone carving
Prov. Amelungsborn, Lower Saxony, Germany (church)
Bibl. Heutger, 1968, 36

160   MONSTER PERCHED ON THE HEAD OF A MONK
First half fourteenth century parchment MS C 27 f. 2r (detail)
Prov. Altenberg, Rhineland, Germany – Düsseldorf, Universitätsbibliothek
Bibl. Aachen, 1980, 435

161   MONK ATTACKED BY THE DEVIL
c. 1330–40 Gotland limestone carving Inv. No. MNS/Szt. 143 56 × 53 × 37
Prov. Kołbacz, Pomerania, Poland – Szczecin, Muzeum Narodowe
Bibl. Białoskórska, 1995, 645–6

162   THE DEVIL ATTACKS A MONK FROM BEHIND
c. 1220–30 parchment MS Cotton Cleopatra C XI f. 25r (detail) 2.6 × 4.8
Prov. Abbey Dore, Herefordshire, England – London, British Library
Bibl. Morgan,1982, 106–7

163   CARICATURE OF MONK'S HEAD IN BEAUPRE ANTIPHONARY
1290 Cambron (Hainaut) (?) MS W 759 f. 3v (detail)
Prov. Beaupré nuns' abbey, near Grammont, Belgium – Baltimore, The Walters Art Gallery
Bibl. Calkins, 1983, 235; Randall, 1987, 133

164   CARICATURE OF MONK'S HEAD FROM CADOUIN GRADUAL
Fourteenth/fifteenth-century parchment MS CR 67 f. 97r (detail) 5.3 × 6.3
Prov. Cadouin (Dordogne), France – Perigueux, Archives Diocésaines

165   HEAD OF MONK WITHIN AN INITIAL
c. 1230 parchment MS 62 f. 94v (detail)
Prov. Heilsbronn, Franconia, Germany – Erlangen, Universitätsbibliothek
Bibl. Lutze, 1936, 16

166   CARICATURE OF MONK IN PROFILE
Fourteenth-century parchment MS 391 f. 142r (detail)
Prov. Vauclair (Aisne), France – Laon, Bibliothèque Municipale

167   CARICATURE OF TWO MONKS FROM FOUNTAINS
Drawing copied from Fountains manuscripts now lost (?)
Prov. Fountains, Yorkshire, England
Bibl. Walbran, 1862, 90

168   CARICATURE OF MONK'S HEAD FROM CLEEVE
Wall painting approx. 10 × 5
Prov. Cleeve, Devon, England
Bibl. Park, 1986, 208

169   LEGEND OF BROTHER RUS
1515 woodcut
Prov. Strassburg, France
Bibl. France, 1992a, 412–3

170   LEGEND OF TILL EULENSPIEGEL
1515 woodcut
Prov. Strassburg, France
Bibl. Hucker, 1988, 151–67; Ranke, 1983, 538–55

171   THE HUNTING OF MONKS AND PRIESTS
c. 1524 woodcut by Erhard Schön 37.6 × 49.2
Bibl. Dodgson, 1903–11, 1:498; Mencke, 1976, 115; Pauli, 1901, 463; Röttinger, 1925, 124

172   THE MONASTERY GARDEN
1490–1510 parchment MS IV B 24 f. 73r
Prov. Bohemia – Prague, Národní Muzeum Library
Bibl. Bohatec, 1970, 189

173   THE MURDER OF MONKS AT NYDALA IN SWEDEN
1676 copied from 1524 original (now lost) – detail from engraving of King Gustav Vasa's
'Reformation Plate' by Dionysius Padt-Bugge
Bibl. France, 1992a, 427–9

174   A PRESENT-DAY CISTERCIAN – NEW MELLERAY ABBEY, IOWA, USA

ACKNOWLEDGEMENTS

Permission to reproduce has kindly been given by the following (numbers in bold refer to colour plates):

Zisterzienserstift Zwettl, Austria col. pl. **1**, col. pl. **21**, 1, 4, 17, 21; Klosterarchiv Wienhausen, Germany, photograph Wolfgang Brandis col. pl. **2**, col. pl. **3**, 97, 98, 99; by permission of the British Library, London col. pl. **4**, 40, 59, 83, 105, 162; Dijon, Biblothèque Municipale col. pl. **5**, col. pl. **24**, 9, 37, 45, 134; by permission of the Syndics of Cambridge University Library col. pl. **6**; Oxford, Bodleian Library, col. pl. **7**, col. pl. **9**, col. pl. **22**; Abbaye Notre-Dame de Sept Fons, Dompierre-sur-Besbre, photograph Roger Cambray col. pl. **8**; Douai, Bibliothèque Municipale col. pl. **10**, 7; Saint-Omer, Bibliothèque Municipale col. pl. **11**, col. pl. **12**; Heidelberg, Universitätsbibliothek col. pl. **13**; Copenhagen, Nationalmuseet col. pl. **14**; Inventarisation der Aargauischen Kunstdenkmäler, Switzerland col. pl. **15**; Dr Heinz Martin Werhahn, Aachen col. pl. **17**; Cologne, Rheinisches Bildarchiv col. pl. **18** (courtesy Schnütgen Museum), 44, 48, 51, 114, 137, 160; Provincie Limburg, Provinciaal Centrum voor Cultureel Erfgoed, Rijkel, Belgium col. pl. **19**; Baltimore, The Walters Art Gallery col. pl. **20**, 102, 108, 163; Karlsruhe, Generallandesarchiv col. pl. **23**; Berlin, Staatsbibliothek zu Berlin Preussischer Kulturbesitz col. pl. **25**, 67, 121, 153; Wolfenbüttel, Herzog-August-Bibliothek col. pl. **26**; Zisterzienserinnenabtei St Marienthal, Ostritz, Germany 2; Wroclaw, University Library 3, 79, 115; Prague, Czech Academy of Sciences, Institute of Art History 5, 19, 101; Sonia Halliday Photographs 10, 12, 22, 116; Bonn, Rheinisches Landesmuseum 11; Karlsruhe, Badische Landesbibliothek 14; The J. Paul Getty Museum, Malibu, California 14, 18, 86, 95, 96; Mount Saint Bernard Abbey, Leicestershire 20; Cologne, Dombauverwaltung Köln 23, 46, 136; Paris, Bibliothèque de l'Arsenal 24; Bar sur Aube, Bibliothèque Municipale 25; Munich, Bayerische Staatsbibliothek 26; by permission of the Master and Fellows of Sidney Sussex College, Cambridge 28; reproduced by kind permission of the Dean and Chapter of York 29; The Board of Trinity College Dublin 30; Vienna, Bundesdenkmalamt 31, 135; The Master and Fellows of Corpus Christi College, Cambridge 32; The Conway Library, Courtauld Institute of Art 33, 66 (courtesy Professor Richard Marks); New York, The Pierpont Morgan Library 34; Vatican, Fabrica di San Pietro 35; Brussels, Bibliothèque Royale Albert Ier 36, 90, 91; Karsten Duus Jørgensen 38; Gent, Universiteitsbibliothek 39; Dr Ulrich Knapp 41, 144; Düsseldorf, Universitäts und Landesbibliothek, on loan from City of Düsseldorf 47; Fr Goffredo Viti OCist, Certosa di Firenze, photograph L. Pellegrini 49; Photographie Giraudon, courtesy Musée Condé, Chantilly 50; Dr Thomas Coomans 52; Zisterzienserstift Heiligenkreuz, Austria 53, 60, 88, 154; Lisbon, Museu Nacional de Arte Antiga 58; Vienna, Österreichischen Nationalbiblothek 61, 92; Dr Roger Stalley 63; Dublin, Department of Arts, Culture & the Gaeltacht 64, 85; Bruges, Grootseminarie 68; by permission of the National Museum of Wales 69; Photohaus Eschenburg 71; Paris, Bibliothèque Nationale 74; Antwerp, Koninklijk Museum voor Schone Kunsten 75; English Heritage 76, 168; Bruges, Openbare Bibliothek 82; Nuremberg, Germanisches Nationalmuseum 84, 149; Dr Marie-Elizabeth Henneau 89; Notre-Dame de la Plaine, Saint-André, Lille 100; The Hague, Koninklijke Bibliotheek 104; Madrid, Patrimonio Nacional 106; Madrid, Biblioteca Nacional 107; Cambrai, Mediathèque Municipale 109; Copenhagen, Royal Library 110; Dr Richard Ingle 111; Corpus Vitrearum Medii Aevi Deutschland 113; Erlangen, Universitätsbibliothek 117, 118, 165; Szczecin, Muzeum Narodowe 119, 161; Cambridge, The Fitzwilliam Museum 120; by kind permission of the Dean and Chapter of Hereford, photograph Gordon

Taylor 122; Laon, Bibliothèque Municipale 123, 166; Copenhagen, Rigsarkivet 129; Douai, Musée Beaux-Arts 130; New York, Metropolitan Museum of Art, Cloisters Collection 132; Landesedenkmalamt Baden-Württemberg 138, 142; Dr Krystyna Białoskórska 145; Professor Rainer Oefelein 146; Karlsruhe, Landesbildstelle 148; Fr Jesús M. Oliver OCist, Poblet Abbey 151; Perigueux, Archives Diocésaines 164; London, British Museum 171; Prague, Národnì Muzeum Library 172; Stockholm, Royal Library 173; Cistercian Publications, Kalamazoo, Michigan 174.

Other photographs are by the author.

BIBLIOGRAPHY

ABBREVIATIONS

PL = Migne, J.P. 1844–64. *Patrologiae cursus completus, series latina* 221 vols. Paris. SBOp = Leclercq, Jean, Talbot, C.H., & Rochais, H.M. ed. 1957–77. *Sancti Bernardi Opera* 8 vols. Rome. DHGE = *Dictionnaire d'Histoire et de Géographie Ecclésiastique*. DNB = *Dictionary of National Biography* CF = *Cistercian Fathers Series*. CS = *Cistercian Studies Series*.

Exhibition Catalogues are listed under the city where the exhibition was held.

Aachen. *Die Zisterzienser*, Katalog zur Ausstellung des Landschaftsverbandes Rheinland, Rheinisches Museumsamt, Brauweiler, Cologne, 1980

Adhémar, Jean. *Les Tombeaux de la Collection Gaignières*, 3 vols, Paris, 1974–6

Anderes, Bernhard & Hoegger, Peter. *Die Glasgemälde in Kloster Wettingen*, 1989

Appuhn, Horst. *Einführung in die Ikonographie der Mittelalterlichen Kunst in Deutschland*, Darmstadt, 1979

——. *Kloster Wienhausen*, Wienhausen, 1986

Arens, Fritz. 'Das Nischengrab in der Ostecke des Kreuzgangs in Zisterzienserklöstern', *Mélanges à la Mémoire du Père Anselme Dimier*, ed. Benoit Chauvin, Arbois, 1982, 3:5:7–15

Auberger, Jean-Baptiste. *L'Unanimité Cistercienne Primitive: Mythe ou Réalité?*, Achel, 1986

Aubert, Marcel. *L'Architecture Cistercienne en France*, 2 vols, Paris, 1947

Aubrun, Michel. *Vie de Saint Etienne de Obazine*, Clermont Ferrand, 1970

Baker, Evelyn. 'The Warden Abbey Pavements: Fine Art on a Floor', *Studies in Cistercian Art and Architecture*, 4, ed. Meredith Parsons Lillich (CS 134) Kalamazoo, Michigan, 1993, 59–77

Barrière, Bernadette. *L'Abbaye Cistercienne d'Obazine en Bas-Limousin*, Tulle, 1977

Batany, J. 'Les Convers chez quelques Moralistes des XIIe et XIIIe Siècles', *Cîteaux* 20, 1969, 241–59

Batselier, P. ed. *Benedictus Pater Europae*, Antwerp, 1980

Baxandall, Michael D.K. *The Limewood Sculpture of Renaissance Germany*, 1980

Beckett, Wendy Mary, trans. *John of Ford On the Song of Songs*, 7 vols, (CF 29, 39, 43–47) Kalamazoo, Michigan, 1977–84

Beckford, William. *Excursion à Alcobaça et Batalha* (with text in English and French), Lisbon, 1956

Becksmann, Rüdiger. *Die Architektonische Rahmung des Hochgotischen Bildfensters*, Berlin, 1967

——. *Die Mittelalterlichen Glasmalereien in Baden und der Pfalz*, (CVMA Deutschland 2), Berlin, 1979

—— & Korn, Ulf-Dietrich. *Die Mittelalterlichen Glasmalereien in Lüneburg und den Heidenklöstern* (CVMA Deutschland 7: Niedersachsen Teil 2) Berlin, 1992

Beer, Ellen J. *Beiträge zur oberrheinischen Buchmalerei*. Basel & Stuttgart, 1959

Beitz, Egid. *Caesarius von Heisterbach und die Bildende Kunst*, Augsburg, 1926

Bemden, Yvette vanden & Kerr, Jill. 'The Glass of Herkenrode Abbey', *Archaeologia* 108, 1986, 189–226

Berlin. *Glanz Alter Buchkunst – Mittelalterliche Handschriften der Staatsbibliothek Preussischer Kulturbesitz*, Exhibition Catalogue, 1988

Berlioz, Jacques. *Saint Bernard en Bourgogne – Lieux et mémoire*, Dijon, 1990

——. 'Saint Bernard dans la littérature satirique, de Ysengrinus aux Balivenes des courtesans de Gautier Map', *Vies et Légendes de Saint Barnard de Clairvaux*, ed. Patrick Arabeyre, Jacques Berlioz, et Philippe Poirrier, 1993, 211–28

Berman, Constance H. 'The Economic Practices of Cistercian Women's Communities', *Studiosorum Speculum*, Studies in Honor of Louis J. Lekai, ed. Francis R. Swietek & John R. Sommerfeldt (CS 141) Kalamazoo, Michigan, 1993, 15–32

Bernard de Clairvaux – Histoire, Mentalités, Spiritualité. Colloque de Lyon – Cîteaux – Dijon, Paris, 1992

Bertram, Jerome. *Lost Brasses*, Newton Abbot, 1976

Beuer-Szlechter. 'Contribution à l'Iconographie de Saint Bernard', *Cîteaux* 26, 1975, 241–54

Białoskórska, Krystyna. 'L'abbaye cistercienne de Wachock', *Cahiers de Civilisation Médiévale* 5, 1962, 335–5

——. 'Polish Cistercians Architecture and Its Contacts with Italy', *Gesta* 5, 1966, 14–22

——. 'La Fabrique du Maître Simon et son Activité en Pologne dans la première moitié du XIIIe Siècle', *Arte medievale* 2, Serie Anno 8, no. 1, tome 2, 1994, 57–85

——. 'Le Caractère et les Idées du Décor sculpté architectonique des Monastères Cisterciens Polonais du XIIIe Siècle et sa position en regard des traditions et de la Spiritualité de l'Ordre', *La vie quotidienne des moines et chanoines réguliers au Moyen Age et Temps modernes* (Actes du Premier Colloque International, Wroclaw 1994), 1995, 615–49

Billy, Dennis J. 'The *Ysengrinus* and the Cistercian-Cluniac Controversy', *American Benedictine Review* 43, 1992, 301–28

Bohatec, Miloslav. *Illuminated Manuscripts*, Prague, 1970

Bondeelle-Souchier, Anne. *Bibliothèques Cisterciennes dans la France Médiévale*, Paris, 1991

——. 'Les Moniales Cisterciennes et leurs Livres Manuscrits dans la France d'Ancien Régime', *Cîteaux* 43, 1994, 193–337

Bony, Pierre. 'An Introduction to the Study of Cistercian Seals', *Studies in Cistercian Art and Architecture* 3, ed. Meredith Parsons Lillich (CS 89), Kalamazoo, Michigan, 1987, 201–40

Bouton, Jean de la Croix & Van Damme, Jean-Baptiste. *Les plus anciens textes de Cîteaux*, Achel, 1974

Brandis, Tilo ed. *Zimelien – Abendländische Handschriften des Mittelalters aus den Sammlungen der Stiftung Preussischer Kulturbesitz*, Berlin-Wiesbaden, 1975

Bruch, Robert. *Die Malereien in den Handschriften des Königreichs Sachsen*, Dresden, 1906

Bruges. *Vlaamse kunst op perkament. Handschriften en miniaturen te Brugge van de 12de tot de 16de eeuw*, Gruuthusemuseum Exhibition Catalogue, 1981

Brussels. *Manuscrits Cisterciens de la Bibliothèque royale de Belgique*, ed. Thérèse Glorieux-De Gand, Exhibition Catalogue, 1990

Bruyne, D. de. 'Note sur le Costume Bénédictine Primitif', *Revue Bénédictine* 33, 1921, 55–61

Buberl, Paul. *Die Kunstdenkmäler des Zisterzienserklosters Zwettl*, Baden bei Wien, 1940

Büttner, F.O. *Imitatio Pietatis*, Berlin, 1983

Burchard of Bellevaux, (Burchardi, ut videtur Abbatis Bellevallis). *Apologia de Barbis*, ed. Giles Constable (Corpus Christianorum Continuatio Medievalis 62), Turnhout, 1985

Butler, Lawrence. 'Cistercian Abbots' Tombs and Abbey Seals', *Studies in Cistercian Art and Architecture* 4, ed. Meredith Parsons Lillich (CS 134), 1993, 78–88

Calkins, Robert G. *Illuminated Books of the Middle Ages*, London, 1983

Camille, Michael. 'Seeing and Reading: Some visual implications of medieval literacy and illiteracy', *Art History* 8, 1985, 26–49

——. *The Image on the Edge – The Margins of Medieval Art*, London, 1992

Canivez, J.-M. *Statuta Capitulorum Generalium Ordinis Cisterciensis ab anno 1116 ad 1786*, 8 vols, Louvain, 1933–41

Caviness, Madeline H. 'Images of Divine Order and the Third Mode of Seeing', *Gesta* 22, 1983, 99–120

Cawley, Martinus. 'Four Abbots of the Golden Age of Villers', *Cistercian Studies Quarterly* 27, 1992, 299–327

Chauvin, Benoît. *Pierres . . . Pour l'Abbaye de Villelongue, Histoire et Architecture*, 2 vols, Pupillin, 1992

Chibnall, M. ed. and trans. *The Ecclesiastical History of Orderic Vitalis*, 6 vols, Oxford, 1969–80

Clark, Willene B. 'Three Manuscripts for Clairmarais: A Cistercian Contribution to Early Gothic Figure Style', *Studies in Cistercian Art and Architecture* 3, ed. Meredith Parsons Lillich (CS 89) Kalamazoo, Michigan, 1987, 97–110

——. *The Medieval Book of Birds. Hugh of Fouilloy's Aviarium*, Brighamton, New York, 1992

Clay, C. 'The Seals of the Religious Houses of Yorkshire', *Archaeologia* 78, 1928, 1–36

Cocheril, Maur. *Notes sur l'Architecture et le Décor dans les Abbayes Cisterciennes de Portugal*, Paris, 1972

Coldstream, Nicola. 'Cistercian Architecture from Beaulieu to the Dissolution', *Cistercian Art and Architecture in the British Isles*, ed. Christopher Norton & David Park, Cambridge, 1986, 139–59

Colker, Marvin L. *Trinity College, Dublin. Descriptive Catalogue of the Mediaeval and Renaissance Latin Manuscripts*, 2 vols, Aldershot, 1991

Cologne. *Das Schnütgen Museum – eine Auswahl*, Cologne, Exhibition Catalogue, 1968

——. *Vor Stefan Lochner*, Exhibition Catalogue, 1974

——. *Rheinisches Landesmuseum Bonn – Gemälde bis 1900*, Exhibition Catalogue, 1982

Connor, Elizabeth. 'The Royal Abbey of Las Huelgas and the Jurisdiction of its Abbesses', *Cistercian Studies Quarterly* 23, 1988, 128–55

—— & Braceland, Lawrence C. trans. *Aelred of Rievaulx: The Mirror of Charity and Spiritual Friendship*, (CF 17) Kalamazoo, Michigan, 1990

Constable, Giles ed. *The Letters of Peter the Venerable*, 2 vols, Harvard, 1967

——. 'Renewal and Reform in Religious Life', *Renaissance and Renewal in the Twelfth Century*, ed. Robert L. Benson & Giles Constable, Oxford, 1982

Conway, Ambrose trans. *Bernard of Clairvaux Treatises 2 – The Steps of Humility and Pride*, (CF13A) Kalamazoo, Michigan, 1980

Coppack, Glyn. *Fountains Abbey*, London, 1993

Cowen, Painton. *A Guide to Stained Glass in Britain*, London, 1985

Dal Prà, Laura. *Bernardo di Chiaravalle nell'arte Italiana*, Milan, 1990

——. *Iconografia di San Bernardo di Clairvaux in Italia*, II.1 La Vita (Biblioteca Cisterciensis 8/2 Corpus Iconographicum Bernardinum), Rome, 1991

Daumet, Georges, 'Le Monument de Benoit XII dans la Basilique de Saint-Pierre', *Mélanges d'Archéologie et d'Histoire* 16, 1896, 293–7

Davidson, C. Treat. 'Sources for the Initials of the Cîteaux *Moralia in Job*', *Studies in Cistercian Art and Architecture* 3, ed. Meredith Parsons Lillich (CS 89) Kalamazoo, Michigan, 1987, 46–68

Delaissé, L.M.J. *La miniature flamande à l'époque de Philippe le Bon*, Milan, 1956

Delluc, Brigitte & Gilles, Lagrange, Jacques, & Secret, Jean. *Cadouin – Une aventure cistercienne en Périgord*, Le Bugue, 1990

Delmaire, B. 'Deux Recits Versifiés de la Fondation de l'Abbaye des Prés a Douai', *Revue du Nord* 241, 1979, 331–51

Dengler-Spengler, Brigitte. 'The Incorporation of Cistercian Nuns into the Order in the Twelfth and Thirteenth Century', *Hidden Springs*, ed. John A. Nichols & Lillian Thomas Shank (CS 113A) Kalamazoo, Michigan, 1995, 85–134

Dewilde, M. & Meulemeester, J. de. 'Van abtswoning tot monnikenverblijf – Een bouwhistorische en archeologische benadering an O. L. V. Ten Duinenabdij to Koksijde', *De Duinen – Bulletin van het wetenschappelijk en kultureel centrum van de Duinenabdij en de Westhoek* 21, 1991

Dillmann, Erika & Schultz, Hans-Jürgen. *Salem*, Salem, 1989

Dimier, Anselme. *Saint Louis et Cîteaux*, Paris, 1954

——. 'Les premiers cisterciens étaient-ils ennemis des études?', *Los Monjes y los Estudios*, IV Semana de Estudios Monásticos, Poblet, 1963, 119–46

Dodgson, Campbell. *Catalogue of Early German and Flemish Woodcuts in the Department of Prints and Drawings*, 2 vols, London, 1903–11

Dodwell, C.R. *The Canterbury School of Illumination 1066–1200*, Cambridge, 1954

Dörrenberg, Irmgard. *Das Zisterzienserkloster Maulbronn*, 1938

Donkin, R.A. *The Cistercians: Studies in the Geography of Medieval England and Wales*, (Pontifical Institute of Mediaeval Studies: Studies & Texts 38), Toronto, 1978

Donnelly, James S. *The Decline of the Medieval Cistercian Laybrotherhood* (Fordham University Studies: History Series 3), New York, 1949

Douët d'Arcq, Louis Claude. *Collection des Sceaux*, Vol. 3 Paris, 1868

[Ducourneau], Othon. 'De l'institution et des us des convers dans l'ordre de Cîteaux', *Saint Bernard et son temps*, 1929, 2:139–201

Düsseldorf. *Ausstellung der kunstgewerblichen Alterthümer*, Exhibition Catalogue, 1880

Dupeux, Cécile. 'Saint Bernard dans l'iconographie médiévale: l'example de la lactation', *Vies et Légendes de Saint Bernard de Clairvaux* ed. Patrick Arabeyre, Jacques Berlioz et Philippe Poirrier, 1993, 167–72

Durán, Rafael M. *Iconografía Española de San Bernardo*, Poblet, 1990

Dutton, Marsha L. 'Aelred Historien: deux nouveaux Portraits dans un Manuscrit de Dublin', *Collectanea Cisterciensia* 55, 1993, 209–30

——. 'Ælred, Historian: Two Portraits in Plantagenet Myth', *Cistercian Studies Quarterly* 29, 1994, 112–43

Duval-Arnould, Louis. 'Quelques Inscriptions Funéraires de l'Abbaye de Longpont', *Mélanges à la Mémoire du Père Anselme Dimier*, ed. Benoit Chauvin, Arbois, 1984, 2:4:661–91

Ebrach. *Brevis Notitia Monasterii B.V.M. Ebracensis Sac. Ordinis Cisterciensis in Franconia*, Rome, 1739

Eckert, K. *Sankt Bernhard von Clairvaux Glasmalereien aus dem Kreuzgang von Altenberg bei Köln*, Wuppertal, 1953

Edinburgh. Treasures of Belgian Libraries National Library of Scotland. Exhibition Catalogue, 1963

Edmonds, Irene M. & Walsh, Kilian. *Bernard of Clairvaux On the Song of Songs 3* (CF 31), Kalamazoo, Michigan, 1979

Ehlers, Ingrid & Ende, Horst, *Zum Heiligen Kreuz*, Rostock, (no date)

Erdmann, Wolfgang. *Zisterzienser-Abtei Doberan,* Königstein in Taunus, 1995

Escallier, E.A. *L'Abbaye de Anchin 1079–1792,* Lille, 1852

Faral, Edmond. 'Guillaume de Deguieville, Moine de Chaalis', *Histoire Littéraire de la France 39,* 1952, 1–132

Feld, Helmut. *Der Ikonoklasmus des Westens,* London, 1990

Ferguson, Peter. 'The First Architecture of the Cistercians in England and the work of Abbot Adam of Meaux', *Journal of the British Archaeological Association* 136, 1983, 74–86

Foliot, Gilbert. *The Letters and Charters of Gilbert Foliot,* ed. Z.N. Brooke, completed by A. Morey & C.N.L. Brooke, Cambridge, 1967

Fowler, James. 'On a Window representing the Life and Miracles of S. William of York, at the North End of the Eastern Transept', *The Yorkshire Archaeological Journal,* 1875, 198–348

France, James. *The Cistercians in Scandinavia* (CS 131), Kalamazoo, Michigan, 1992a

——. 'The Cistercian Foundation Narratives in Scandinavia in their wider Context', *Cîteaux* 43, 1992b, 119–60

Frodl-Kraft, Eva. *Die Mittelalterlichen Glasgemälde in Niederösterreich* 1 (CVMA Österreich vol. 2), Vienna, Cologne, Graz, 1972

Fründt, Edith. *Das Kloster Doberan,* Berlin, 1987

Gaillemin, Symphorien. 'Simples Notes sur la Coule Cistercienne', *Cistercienser-Chronik* 17, 1905, 304–14

Galob, Nataša. *Stiski rokopisí iz 12 stoletja – Codices Sitticenses saeculi XII* (with German translation) Llubljana, 1994

——. *Twelfth-Century Cistercian Manuscripts – The Sitticum Collection,* London, 1996

Gardell, Sölve. *Gravmonument från Sveriges Medeltid,* 2 vols, Stockholm, 1945

Gattermann, Günter ed. *Kostbarheiten aus der Universitätsbibliothek Düsseldorf,* Wiesbaden, 1989

Gent. *Benedictus en zijn Monniken in de Nederlanden,* Centrum voor Kunst en Cultuur Sint-Pietersabdij Gent, 3 vols, Exhibition Catalogue, 1980

——. *Bernardina en Cisterciensia in de Universiteitsbibliothek,* Leesboek ed. Guido Hendrix, Rijksuniversiteit, Exhibition Catalogue, 1990

Gerstenberg, Kurt. *Die Deutschen Baumeisterbildnisse des Mittelalters,* Berlin, 1966

Gertz, M.C. ed. *Scriptores Minores Historiae Danicae Medii Aevi* (Selskabet for Udgivelse of Kilder til Dansk Historie) vol. 2, Copenhagen, 1917–22

Gilbanks, G.E. *Some Records of a Cistercian Abbey – Holmcultram, Cumberland,* London, 1899

Gilyard-Beer, R. 'The Graves of the Abbots of Fountains', *The Yorkshire Archaeological Journal 59,* 1987, 45–50

Gloede, Günter. *Das Doberaner Münster,* Berlin, no date

Gottschalk, Joseph. 'Die älteste Bilderhandschrift mit den Quellen zum Leben der hl. Hedwig', *Aachener Kunstblätter* 34, 1967, 61–161

——. *Hedwig von Schlesien – Botin des Friedens,* Freiburg in Breisgau, 1982

Grabar, André & Nordenfalk, Carl. *Romanesque Painting from the Eleventh to the Thirteenth Century,* Lausanne, 1958

Greenhill, F.A. *Incised Effigial Slabs,* 2 vols, London, 1976

Griesser, Bruno. 'Die Ecclesiastica officia Cisterciensis Ordinis', *Analecta Sacri Ordinis Cisterciensis* 12, 1956, 153–288

——. ed. *Exordium Magnum Cisterciense sive Narratio de Initio Cisterciensis Ordinis,* Rome, 1961

Hamburger, Jeffrey. 'The Visual and the Visionary: the Image in late Medieval Monastic Devotions', *Viator* 20, 1989, 161–82

——. *The Rothschild Canticles,* New Haven & London, 1990

——. 'Art, Enclosure and the Cura Monialium: Prolegomena in the Guise of a Postscript', *Gesta* 31, 1991, 108–34

Hayward, Jane. 'Glazed Cloisters and their Development in the Houses of the Cistercian Order', *Gesta* 12, 1973, 93–109

Helyot, P. *Histoire des Ordres Monastiques,* vol. 5, Paris, 1718

Henneau, Marie-Elizabeth. *Les cisterciennes du pays mosan, moniales et vie contemplative à l'époque moderne,* Brussels-Rome, 1990

Henriquez, Crisostomo. *Menologium Cisterciense,* Antwerp, 1630

Hermann, H.J. *Die deutschen Romanichen Handschriften* (Beschreibendes Verzeichnis der Illuminierten Handschriften in Österreich 2), Vienna, 1926

Hervay, Terenc L. *Repertorium Historicum Ordinis Cisterciensis in Hungaria,* Rome, 1984

Heslop, T.A. 'Cistercian Seals in England and Wales', *Cistercian Art and Architecture in the British Isles,* ed. Christopher Norton & David Park, Cambridge, 1986, 266–83

Heutger, Nicolaus C. *Das Kloster Amelungsborn in Spiegel der Zisterziensischen Ordensgeschichte,* Hildesheim, 1968

Hill, Nathaniel. *The Ancient Poem of Guillaume de Guileville entitled le Pèlerinage de l'Homme compared with the Pilgrim's Progress of John Bunyan*, London, 1858

Hinnebusch, Frederick, ed. *Jacques de Vitry: Historia occidentalis*, Freiburg i. U., 1972

Hirschfeld, Werner. *Zisterzienserkloster Pforte, Geschichte seiner romanischen Bauten und ein älteres Westwerk*, Berlin, 1933

Hogenelst, Dini & Oostrom, Frits van. *Handgeschreven Wereld*, Amsterdam, 1995

Holdsworth, Christopher. 'The early writings of Bernard of Clairvaux', *Cîteaux* 45, 1994, 21–61

Holloway, Julia Bolton. *The Pilgrim and the Book – a Study of Dante, Langland and Chaucer*, New York, 1987

Holzhey, Karl. 'Babylonisches bei Otto von Freising', *Wissenschaftliche Festgabe zum Zwölfhundertjährigen Jubiläum des Heiligen Korbinian*, ed. J. Schlecht, Munich, 1924

Hoste, Anselm. *De Handschriften van Ter Doest*, Steenbrugge, 1993

—— & Talbot, C.H. ed. *Aelredi Rievallensis, Opera Omnia 1* (Corpus Christianorum, Continuatio Medievalis 1), Turnhout, 1971

Hucker, Bernd Ulrich. 'Eulenspiegel in der Zisterzienserabtei Mariental', *Das Zisterzienserkloster Mariental bei Helmstedt 1138–1988*, ed. Christof Römer, Munich, 1988

Hümpfner, T. *Ikonographie des heiligen Bernhard von Clairvaux*, Augsburg, 1927

Hufgard, M. Kilian. 'An Inspirational and Iconographic Source for the Early Cistercian Miniatures', *Studies in Cistercian Art and Architecture* 3, ed. Meredith Parsons Lillich (CS 89), 1987, 69–80

Hunt, J. Eric. *The Glass in St Mary's Church Shrewsbury*, Shrewsbury, 1951

Huot, Sylvia. 'Visualization and Memory: the Illustration of Troubadour Lyric in a Thirteenth-Century Manuscript', *Gesta* 31, 1992, 3–24

Hutchison, Carole A. *The Hermit Monks of Grandmont* (CS 118), Kalamazoo, Michigan, 1989

Idung of Prüfening. *Cistercians and Cluniacs* (CF 33), Kalamazoo, Michigan, 1977

Järitz, Gerhard. 'The Standard of Living in German and Austrian Cistercian Monasteries of the Late Middle Ages', *Goad and Nail* (Studies in Cistercian History 10, CS 84) Kalamazoo, Michigan, 1985, 56–70

James, B. Scott, trans. *The Letters of St Bernard of Clairvaux*, London, 1953

James, M.R. *A Descriptive Catalogue of the Manuscripts in the Library of Sidney Sussex College Cambridge*, Cambridge, 1895

——. *A Descriptive Catalogue of the Manuscripts in the Library of Corpus Christi College Cambridge*, Cambridge, 1912

——. *The Apocalypse in Art*, London, 1931

——. 'Pictor in Carmine', *Archaeologia* 94, 1951, 141–66

——. ed. & trans. *Walter Map De Nugis Curialium – Courtiers' Trifles*, revised by C.N.L. Brooke & R.A.B. Mynors, Oxford, 1983

Jazdzewski, Konstanty Klemens.*Lubiaz – Losy i kultura unysłowa slaskiego opactwa Cystersow (1163–1642)*, (with German summary 242–5) Wroclaw, 1992

Kaftal, G. *Iconography of the Saints in the Painting of North West Italy*, Florence, 1985

Kauffmann, C.M. *An Altar-piece of the Apocalypse from Master Bertram's Workshop in Hamburg*, London, 1968.

Keenan, Joseph M. 'The Cistercian Pilgrimage to Jerusalem in Guillaume de Deguileville's *Pèlerinage de la Vie Humaine*', *Studies in Cistercian History* 2, ed. John R. Sommerfeldt (CS 24) Kalamazoo, Michigan, 1976

Keller, John E. & Kinkade, Richard P. *Iconography in Medieval Spanish Literature*, Lexington, Kentucky, 1984

Kienzle, Beverley M. 'The Tract on the Conversion of Pons of Leras and the True Account of the beginning of the Monastery of Silvanès', *Cistercian Studies Quarterly* 30, 1995, 219–43

Kinder, Terryl N. 'Les églises médiévales de Clairvaux – Probabilités et fiction', *Histoire de Clairvaux*, Actes du Colloque Juin 1990, Bar-sur-Aube, 1991, 205–29

King, Archdale A. *Cîteaux and her Elder Daughters*, London, 1954

——. *Liturgies of the Religious Orders* London, New York, Toronto, 1955

King, Margot H. 'The Dove at the Window: The Ascent of the Soul in Thomas de Cantimpré's Life of Lutgard of Aywières', *Hidden Springs – Cistercian Monastic Women*, ed. John A. Nichols & Lillian Thomas Shank (CS 113A), Kalamazoo, Michigan, 1995, 225–53

Kirschbaum, E. & Braunfels, W. See *Lexikon*, 1968–76

Kline, Francis. 'Saint Bernard and the Rule of Saint Benedict: an Introduction', *Bernardus Magister*, ed. John R. Sommerfeldt (CS 135), Kalamazoo, Michigan, 1992, 169–83

Kloss, Ernst. *Die Schlesische Buchmalerei des Mittelalters*, Berlin, 1942

Knowles, David. *The Monastic Order in England*, Cambridge, 1949

——. *The Religious Orders in England*, vol. 2, Cambridge, 1957

——. *The Religious Orders in England*, vol. 3, Cambridge, 1959

——. *The Historian and Character*, Cambridge, 1963

Knowles, J.A. 'Technical Notes on the St William Window in York Minster', *The Yorkshire Archaeological Journal* 37, 1951, 148–61

Korn, Ulf-Dietrich. *Kloster Wienhausen – Die Glasmalereien*, Wienhausen, 1975

Kratzke, Christine. *Das Kloster Dargun in Mecklenburg-Vorpommern*, Kiel, 1998

Kroman, Erik ed. *Danmarks Middelalderlige Annaler*, Copenhagen, 1980

Kroos, Renate. 'Der Codex Gisle', *Niederdeutsche Beiträge zur Kunstgeschichte* 12, 1973, 117–34

Kubes, Karl & Rössl, Joachim. *Stift Zwettl*, St Pölten-Wien, 1979

Kuhn-Rehfus, Maren. 'Cistercian Nuns in Germany in the Thirteenth Century', *Hidden Springs* ed., John A. Nichols & Lillian Thomas Shank (CS 113A), Kalamazoo, Michigan, 1995, 135-58

Lackner, Bede. 'The Liturgy of Early Cîteaux', *Studies in Medieval Cistercian History presented to Jeremiah F. O'Sullivan* (CS 13), Shannon, Ireland, 1971

Leclercq, Jean. 'Pour l'Iconographie de S. Bernard', *Analecta Sacri Ordinis Cisterciensis* 9, 1953, 40–5, 226–8

——. 'Pour l'Iconographie de S. Bernard', *Analecta Sacri Ordinis Cisterciensis* 11, 1955, 145–6

——. 'Textes et manuscrits cisterciens dans diverses bibliothèques', *Analecta Sacri Ordinis Cisterciensis* 12, 1956, 289–310

——. 'Aspects littéraire de l'oeuvre de Saint Bernard', *Cahiers de Civilisation Médiévale* 1, 1958, 425–50

——. 'Comment vivaient les Frères Convers', *Analecta Cisterciensia* 21, 1965, 239-58

Lekai, L.J. *Geschichte und Wirken der Weissen Mönche*, Cologne, 1958

——. *The Cistercians – Ideals and Reality*, Kent, Ohio, 1977

Leroquais, V. *Les Bréviaires Manuscrits des bibliothèques publiques de France*, vol. 1, Paris, 1934

Lexikon der Christlichen Ikonographie, ed. E. Kirschmann & W. Braunfels, 8 vols, Rome, Freiburg, Basel, 1968–76

Libor, Reinhard Maria. *Ars Cisterciensis. Buchmalereien aus mittel- und ostdeutschen Klosterbibliotheken*, Würzburg, 1967

Lieftinck, G.I. *De librijen en scriptoria der Westvlaamse Cistercienser-abdijen Ter Duinen en Ter Doest in de 12e en 13e eeuw en de betrekkingen tot het atelier van de kapittelschool van Sint Donatiaan te Brugge*, (summary in French), Bruxelles, 1953

Lignon, B. & Pradelier-Schlumberger, M. *Congrès archaeologique de France* 131, 1973

Louf, André. *The Cistercian Way* (CS 76), Kalamazoo, Michigan, 1983

Lucet, B. *La Codification Cistercienne de 1202 et Son Evolution Ultérieure* (Biblioteca Cisterciensis 2), Rome, 1964

Luddy, Ailbe J. *Life and Teaching of St Bernard*, Dublin, 1950

Lutze, E. *Die Bilderhandschriften der Universitätsbibliothek Erlangen*, Erlangen, 1936

Mahn, Jean-Berthold. *Le Pape Benoit XII et les Cisterciens*, Paris, 1949

——. *L'Ordre Cistercien et son Gouvernement*, Paris, 1951

Maisières, Thibaut de. 'La Tombe de Gobert d'Aspremont au cloître de Villers', *Miscellanea Leo van Puyvelde*, Bruxelles, 1949

Mâle, Emile. *L'Art religieux de la fin du Moyen Age en France*, Paris, 1925

——. *Religious Art in France – The Thirteenth Century*, Princeton, 1984

Mann, H.K. *Tombs and Portraits of the Popes of the Middle Ages*, London, 1928

Mann, Jill ed. *Ysengrinus – Text with Translation* (Mittelalterliche Studien und Texte Band 12), Leiden, 1987

Mantour, Moreau de. 'Description Historique des Principaux Monuments de l'Abbaye de Cisteaux', *Histoire de l'Académie Royale des Inscriptions et Belles Lettres* 9, 1736, 193–232

Manuscrits Enluminés de la Péninsule Ibérique dans la Bibliothèque Nationale, Paris, 1982

Marks, Richard. 'Medieval Stained Glass in Bedfordshire', *Bedfordshire Magazine* 15, 1976, 179–84, 229–33

——. 'Cistercian Window Glass in England and Wales', *Cistercian Art and Architecture in the British Isles*, ed. Chrsitopher Norton & David Park, Cambridge, 1986, 211–27

Martin, Arthur & Cahier, Charles. *Monographie de La Cathédrale de Bourges – Vitraux du XIIIe Siècle*, 2 vols, Paris, 1841-4

Martin, Henry. *Catalogue des Manuscrits de la Bibliothèque de l'Arsenal*, vol. 1 (Catalogue Général des Manuscrits des Bibliothèques Publiques de France), Paris, 1885

Masai, François. 'Un Missel Cistercien de Baudeloo', *Scriptorium* 6, 1952, 279–84

Matarasso, Pauline trans. & ed. *The Cistercian World*, London, 1993

McCann, Justin (second edition). *The Rule of St Benedict*, London, 1976

McDonnell, Ernest W. *The Beguines and Beghards in Medieval Culture*, New Brunswick, 1954

McGuire, Brian Patrick. 'Friends and Tales in the Cloister: Oral Sources in Caesarius of Heisterbach's *Dialogus Miraculorum*', *Analecta Sacri Ordinis Cisterciensis* 36, 1980, 167–247

——. 'A Lost Clairvaux Exemplum Collection Found: The *Liber Visionum et Miraculorum* compiled under Prior John of Clairvaux (1171–79)', *Analecta Sacri Ordinis Cisterciensis* 29, 1983a, 26–62

——. 'The Cistercians and the Rise of the Exemplum in Early Thirteenth-Century France: a Revaluation of *Paris BN MS lat. 15912*', *Classica et Mediaevalia* (Societas Danica Indagationis Antiquitatis et Mediiaevi) 34, 1983b, 211–67

——. *The Difficult Saint* (CS 126) Kalamazoo, Michigan, 1991

——. *Brother and Lover – Aelred of Rievaulx*, New York, 1994

——. 'Who founded the Order of Cîteaux ?', *The Joy of Learning & the Love of God, Essays in Honor of Jean Leclercq* (CS 160) Kalamazoo, Michigan, 1995, 389–413

Meer, Frederic van der. *Atlas de l'Ordre Cistercien*, Amsterdam/Brussels, 1965

Mencke, Hermann ed. *Flugblätter der Reformation und des Bauernkrieges*, Leipzig, 1976

Mierow, Charles Christopher trans. & intro. *The Deeds of Frederick Barbarossa and his continuator Rahewin*, Toronto, 1994

Milde, W. *Mittelalterliche Handschriften der Herzog August Bibliothek*, Frankfurt am Main, 1972

Monsees, Yvonne. 'Grabdenkmäler in Kloster Eberbach im Rheingau', *Nassauische Annalen* 98, 1987, 105–22

——. 'Zisterzienserinnenklöster unter geistliger Leitung Eberbachs', *Forschung und Form Kloster Eberbach*, Heft 3, Eltville, 1989

Moor, Geertruida de. 'The Role of the Female Sacristan Prior to Trent', *Vox Benedictina* 10, 1993, 307–21

Morgan, Nigel. *A Survey of Manuscripts illuminated in the British Isles*, vol. 4, Early Gothic Manuscripts 1, 1190–1250, Oxford, 1982

Morson, John. 'A Newly Found Bernardine Manuscript', *Collectanea Ordinis Cisterciensium Reformatorum* 16, 1954, 30–4, 214–21

Munich. *Bayerns Kirche im Mittelalter – Handschriften und Urkunden,* Exhibition Catalogue, 1960

Nerom, Claire van. 'L'abbaye de Dunes au XIIe siècle', *De Duinen – Bulletin du Centre Scientifique Culturel de l'abbaye des Dunes et du Westhoek*, 1992, 22, 5–27

——. 'Cistercian Tiles', *Studies in Cistercian Art and Architecture* 4, ed. Meredith Parsons Lillich (CS 134) Kalamazoo, Michigan, 1994, 45–58

Newton, P.A. *The County of Oxford – a Catalogue of Medieval Stained Glass*, London, 1979

Nichols, John A. & Shank, Lillian Thomas. *Hidden Springs – Cistercian Monastic Women* (Medieval Religious Women Volume 3), 2 books (CS 113), Kalamazoo, Michigan, 1995

Norris, Malcolm. *Monumental Brasses*, 2 vols, London, 1977

Norris, M.W. intro. *Monumental Brasses – The Portfolio Plates of the Monumental Brass Society 1894–1984*, London, 1988

Norton, Christopher. 'Early Cistercian tile pavements' and 'Table of Cistercian legislation on art and architecture', *Cistercian Art and Architecture in the British Isles*, ed. Christopher Norton & David Park, 1986, 228–55, 315–93

Oliver, Judith H. *Gothic Book Illumination in the Diocese of Liège*, Louvain, 1988

Orval. *Orval, neuf siècles d'histoire*, Exhibition Catalogue, 1970

Os, Henk van. *The Art of Devotion in the Late Middle Ages in Europe*, 1994

Othon, J. 'Les Origines Cisterciennes', *Revue Mabillon* 23, 1933, 81–111

Otto of Freising, see Mierow, Charles Christopher

Oursel, Charles. *La Miniature du XIIe Siècle a l'Abbaye de Cîteaux*, Dijon, 1926

——. *Miniatures Cisterciennes (1109–1134)*, Mâcon, 1960

Pächt, Otto. *The Rise of Pictorial Narrative in Twelfth-Century England*, Oxford, 1962

——. *Book Illumination in the Middle Ages*, London, 1986

—— & J. J.G. Alexander. *Illustrated Manuscripts in the Bodleian Library*, vol. 3, Oxford, 1973

—— & Thoss, Ulrike Jenni Dagmar. *Die Illuminierten Handschriften und Inkunabeln der Österreichischen Nationalbibliothek*– Flämische Schule 1, Vienna, 1983

Paffrath, Arno. *Bernhard von Clairvaux – Leben und Wirken – dargestellt in den Bilderzyklen von Altenberg bis Zwettl*, Bergisch Gladbach, 1984

——. *Bernhard von Clairvaux 2*, Bergisch Gladbach, 1990

Palmcke, Robert. *Schulpforte*, Leipzig, 1956

Panofsky, Erwin. *Tomb Sculpture*, London, 1964

Paris. *L'Europe Gothique XIIe – XIVe Siècles – Douzième Exposition du Conseil de l'Europe*, Exhibition Catalogue, 1968

——. *Saint Bernard et le Monde Cistercien*, ed. Lèon Pressouyre & Terryl N. Kinder, Exhibition Catalogue, 1990

Park, David. 'Cistercian wall painting and panel painting', *Cistercian Art and Architecture in the British Isles*, ed. Christopher Norton & David Park, Cambridge, 1986

Pauli, Gustav. *Hans Sebald Beham*, Bremen, 1901

Paulus, Eduard. *Die Cisterzienser-Abtei Maulbronn*, Stuttgart, 1890

Perdrizet, Paul. *La Vierge de Miséricorde*, Paris, 1908

Petersen, Henry. *Danske Gejstlige Sigiller fra Middelalderen*, Copenhagen, 1886

Phillips, Paschal. 'The Presence – and Absence – of Bernard of Clairvaux in the Twelfth-century Chronicles', *Bernardus Magister*, ed. John R. Sommerfeldt (Cistercian Studies Series 135), Kalamazoo, Michigan, 1992, 35–53

Piazonni, Ambrogio M. 'Le premier biographe de Saint Bernard, Guillaume de Saint-Thierry', *Vies et légendes de Saint Bernard*, ed. Patrick Arabeyre, Jacques Berlioz et Philippe Poirrier, 1993, 3–18

Pineault, Jacques & Coomans, Thomas. 'Le "Soleil de Villers", Cycle Iconographique Cistercien du XVIIe Siècle', *Cîteaux* 45, 1994, 121–53

Plathe, Sissel F. 'Altertavlen i Esrum klosterkirke', *Bogen om Esrum Kloster* ed. Søren Frandsen, Jens Anker Jørgensen, & Chr. Grom Tortzen, Frederiksborg, 1997, 150–66

Porcher, Jean. *Le Bréviaire de Martin d'Aragon*, Paris, 1950

——. *French Miniatures from Illuminated Manuscripts*, London, 1960

Powicke, F.M. ed. and trans. *The Life of Aelred of Rievaulx by Walter Daniel* (Nelson's Medieval Texts), London, 1950

Quarré, Pierre. 'L'Iconographie de Saint Bernard à Clairvaux et les Origines de la *Vera Effigies*', *Mélanges Saint Bernard*, Dijon, 1954, 342–9

Quiévreux, François. 'Les Vitraux du XIIIe Siècle de l'Abside de la Cathédrale de Bourges', *Bulletin Monumental* 101, 1942, 255–75

Rae, Edwin C. 'The Sculpture of the Cloister of Jerpoint Abbey', *The Journal of the Royal Society of Antiquaries of Ireland* 96, 1966, 71

Randall, Lilian M.C. *Images in the Margins of Gothic Manuscripts*, Berkeley & Los Angeles, 1966

——. 'From Cîteaux Onwards: Cistercian-Related Manuscripts in the Walters Art Gallery', *Studies in Cistercian Art and Architecture* 3, ed. Meredith Parsons Lillich (CS 89), Kalamazoo, Michigan, 1987, 111–36

Ranke, Kurt ed. *Enzyklopädie des Märchens*, vol. 4, Berlin, 1983

Réau, Louis. *Iconographie de l'Art Chrétien*, Paris, 1955–9

Reeve, J. Arthur. *A Monograph of the Abbey of Fountains*, London, 1892

Reuterswärd, Patrik. *The Forgotten Symbols of God* (Stockholm Studies in History of Art 35), Uppsala, 1986

Richardson, James S. *The Medieval Stone Carver in Scotland*, Edinburgh, 1964

Rode, Herbert. *Die Mittelalterlicher Glasmalereien des Kölner Domes*, Berlin, 1974

Röttinger, Heinrich. *Erhard Schön und Niklas Stör – Studien zur Deutscher Kunstgeschichte*, 229 Heft, Strassburg, 1925

Rothe, Edith. *Buchmalerei aus Zwölf Jahrhunderten – die schönsten Illustrierten Handschriften in den Bibliotheken und Archiven in Mecklenburg, Berlin, Sachsen und Thüringen*, Berlin, 1966

——. *Medieval Book Illumination in Europe*, London, 1968

Rudolph, Conrad. *The 'Things of Greater Importance' – Bernard of Clairvaux's Apologia and the Medieval Attitude Toward Art*, Philadelphia, 1990

Sandler, Lucy Freeman. *Gothic Manuscripts 1285–1385*, London, 1986

Saxtorph, N.M. *Jeg ser på Kalkmalerier*, Copenhagen, 1967

Schaeffer, Claude. *Jean Fouquet – The Hours of Etienne Chevalier*, London, 1972

Schlegel, Gerhard. *Das Zisterzienserkloster Dargun 1172–1552* (Studien zur katholischen Bistums – und Klostergeschichte 22), 1980

Schlie, Friedrich. *Die Kunst- und Geschichts-Denkmäler der Grossherzogthums Mecklenburg-Schwerin*, vol. 1, Schwerin, 1896

Schmitt, Jean-Claude. 'Le Culte de Saint Bernard et ses Images', *Le Monde Cistercien*, 1990, 149–63

——. 'Saint Bernard et son image', *Bernard de Clairvaux – Histoire, Mentalités, Spiritualité*, Colloque de Lyon-Cîteaux-Dijon, Paris, 1992, 639–57

Schneider, Ambrosius *et al.* (third enlarged edition). *Die Cistercienser – Geschichte, Geist, Kunst*, Cologne, 1986

Scott, H. von E. & Swinton Bland, C.C. ed. and trans. *The Dialogue on Miracles – Caesarius of Heisterbach*, 2 vols, London, 1929

Smith, Cyril E. *The University of Toulouse in the Middle Ages*, Milwaukee, Wisconsin, 1958

Smith, Susan Warrener. 'Bernard of Clairvaux and the Natural Realm: Images related to the Four Elements', *Cistercian Studies Quarterly* 31, 1996, 3–19

Soulier, Philippe ed. *Histoire et Archéologie à L'Abbaye Royale & Cistercienne de Maubuisson*, Cergy-Pontoise, 1988

Sprusansky, Svetozar. *Das Zisterzienserkloster Heilsbronn und seine Bibliothek – Ausstellung des Landeskirchlichen Archivs*

Squire, Aelred. *Aelred of Rievaulx*, London, 1969

Stalley, Roger. *The Cistercian Monasteries of Ireland*, London & New Haven, 1987

Stantzl, Günther. *Die Klosterruine Disibodenberg* (Forschungsberichte zur Denkmalphlege in Rheinland-Pfalz), 1992

Stiennon, J. 'Quelques réflections sur les moines et la creation artistique dans l'Occident du Haut Moyen Age', *Revue Bénédictine* 103, 1993, 153–68

Strange, Alfred. 'Beiträge zur Kaisheimer Buchmalerei', *Festschrift für Georg Leidinger*, Munich, 1930, 277–81

Stürzinger, J.J. ed. *Guillaume de Deguileville le Pèlerinage de Vie Humaine*, London, 1893

Sullivan, Mary Ann. 'An Introduction to the *Vita Beatricis*', *Hidden Springs* ed. John A. Nichols & Lillian Thomas Shank (CS 113A), Kalamazoo, Michigan, 1995, 345–59

Swartwout, R.E. *The Monastic Craftsman*, Cambridge, 1932

Swarzenski, Hanns. *Die lateinischen illuminierten Handschriften des XIII Jahrhunderts in den Ländern am Rhein, Main und Donau*, 2 vols, Berlin, 1936

Swinton Bland, C.C. ed. *Johannes Herolt called Discipulus – The Miracles of the Blessed Virgin Mary*, London, 1928

Texier, L'Abbé 'La Sculpture au Moyen Age – tombeau de Saint Etienne d'Obazine', *Annales Archeologiques* 12, 1852, 384

Thurn, H. *Die Handschriften der Zisterzienserabtei Ebrach* (Die Handschriften der Universitätsbibliothek Würzburg 1), Wiesbaden, 1970

Tobin, Stephen. *The Cistercians*, London, 1995

Toepfer, Michael. *Die Konversen der Zisterzienser* (Berlin Historische Studien herausgegeben vom Friedrich-Meinecke Institut der Freien Universität Berlin, Band 10), Berlin, 1983

Trout, John M. 'The Monastic Vocation of Alan of Lille', Analecta Cisterciensia 30, 1974, 46–53

Uhde-Stahl, Brigitte. 'Figürliche Buchmalereien in den Spätmittelalterlichen Handschriften der Lüneburger Frauenklöster', Niederdeutsche Beiträge zur Kunstgeschichte 17, 1978, 25–60

Verdon, T.G. ed. *Monasticism and the Arts*, Syracuse, 1984

Všetečková, Zuzana. 'Some Remarks on the Osek Lectionary', *Umeni* 43, 1995, 219–23

——. 'The Cistercian Origin of the Osek Lectionary and the mural Paintings in the Royal Chapel of the Cistercian Monastery in Plasy', *Cîteaux* 47, 1996, 285–300

Wachtel, Alois ed. *Monumenta Germaniae Historica* (Quellen zur Geistesgeschichte des Mittelalters 1), Weimar, 1955

Waddell, Chrysogonus. 'The Reform of the Liturgy from a Renaissance Perspective', *Renaissance and Renewal in the Twelfth Century* ed. Robert L. Benson & Giles Constable, Oxford, 1985, 88–109

Walbran, J.R. *The Shilling Guide to Ripon, Studley, Fountains Abbey, Hackfall, Harrogate etc.*, 8th edition, Ripon, 1862

Walliser, Franz. *Cistercienser Buchkunst – Heiligenkreuzer Skriptorium in seinen ersten Jahrhundert*, Heiligenkreuz, 1969

Walsh, Kilian trans. *The Works of St Bernard – On the Song of Songs 2* (CF 7) Kalamazoo, Michigan, 1976

—— & Edmonds, Irene M. trans. *The Works of St Bernard – On the Song of Songs 3* (CF 31), Kalamazoo, Michigan, 1979

Ward, H.L.D. *Catalogue of Romances in the Department of Manuscripts in the British Museum*, vol. 2, London, 1893

Warner, George, intro. *Queen Mary's Psalter – Miniatures and Drawings by an English Artist of the Fourteenth Century reproduced from Royal MS 2 B. VII in the British Museum*, London, 1912

Webb, Geoffrey & Walker, Adrian trans. *St Aelred of Rievaulx – The Mirror of Charity*, London, 1962

Weber, Max. *Das Tennenbacher Güterbuch (1317-1341)*, Stuttgart, 1969

Wentzel, Hans. *Die Glasmalereien in Schwaben von 1200–1350* (CVMA Deutschland Band 1), Berlin, 1958

Werner, Wilfried. *Cimelia Heildelburgensia – 30 illuminierte Handschriften der Universitätsbibliothek Heidelberg*, Wiesbaden, 1975

Wetesko, Leszek. 'Rekopisy Iluminowane', *Cystersi w Sredniowiecznej Polsce. Kultura i Sztuka*, ed. Krystyn Sobkowicz, Warsaw, 1991

Wiener, Wolfgang. 'Die Ebracher Klosteranlage vor dem barocken Neubau', *Festschrift 700 Jahre Abteikirche Ebrach 1285–1985*, ed. W. Wiener & Gerd Zimmermann, Ebrach, 1985, 263–353

Wiesbaden. *Zimelien – Abendländische Handschriften des Mittelalters aus der Sammlungen der Stiftung Preussischer Kulturbesitz Berlin*, Exhibition Catalogue, 1975

William of Malmesbury. *Chronicle of the Kings of England*, trans. J.A. Giles, London, 1847 (reprinted New York, 1968)

Williams, David H. 'A Catalogue of Welsh Ecclesiastical Seals Part 4: Seals of Cistercian Monasteries', *Archaeologia Cambrensis* 136, 1987, 138–55

Wilmart, André. 'Les Mélanges de Mathieu Precantre de Rievaulx au Début du XIIIe Siècle', *Revue Bénédictine* 52, 1940, 15–85

Winkler, Erich. *Die Buchmalerei in Niederösterreich von 1150-1250*, Vienna, 1923

Wormald, F. & Giles, P.M. *A Descriptive Catalogue of the Additional Illuminated Manuscripts in the Fitzwilliam Museum*, 2 vols, Cambridge, 1982

Wright, T. *The Anglo-Saxon Latin Satirical Poets and Epigrammists of the Twelfth Century* (Rolls Series 59), London, 1872

Załuska, Yolanta. *L'Enluminure et le Scriptorium de Cîteaux au XIIe Siècle*, Cîteaux, 1989

——. *Manuscrits Enluminée de Dijon*, Paris, 1991

——. 'L'Enluminure Cistercienne au XIIe Siècle', *Bernard de Clairvaux – Colloque de Lyon-Cîteaux-Dijon*, Paris, 1992, 271–85

Ziegler, Charlotte ed. *Zisterzienserstift Zwettl – Katalog der Handschriften des Mittelalters*, 3 vols, Zwettl, 1985–92

Zschelletzschky, Herbert. *Die 'Drei Gottlosen Maler' von Nürnberg – Sebald Beham, Barthel Beham, und Georg Pencz*, Leipzig, 1975

Zwettl. *Die Kuenringer – Das Werden des Landes Niederösterreich*, Niederösterreichische Landesausstellung Zwettl, Vienna, Exhibition Catalogue, 1981

INDEX

Colour plate numbers are in **bold** type, black and white illustration numbers in *italics*.

Abbreviations: abb. = abbot or abbess, M = Cistercian monasteries for men, W = Cistercian monasteries for women.

abbots, Cistercian, **11–14**, *61–76*, 99–121
Abelard, 58
Achard, monk at Clairvaux, 200
Adam, monk at Dore, 213
Adam, abb. of Meaux, 200
Aduard, lay brother, 129
Aelred, St, abb. of Rievaulx, **10**, *30*, 53–7, 72, 80, 84, 87, 99, 101, 193, 208, 213; *Life of Edward the Confessor*, *30*, 55–7; *Mirror of Charity*, 37, 53, 57, 173
Agnes of Meissen and Landsberg, 97, 150
Agnes of Orlamünde, abb. of Himmelkron, 155
Alan of Lille, lay brother at Cîteaux, 93, 129
Alberic, St, Siest, abb. of Cîteaux, *8*, 14–16, 20, 79
Albert, abb. of Maulbronn, 25
Alcobaça (M), *58*, 97
Alexander, Franciscan friar, 17
Alexander III, pope, 55
Alexander of Scotland, lay brother, 129
Aleyde de Lexhy, abb. of Herkenrode, 166
Alfonso III of Portugal, 9
Alfonso V of Portugal, 97
Alfonso X, 158–9
Alphonsus II king of Aragon, 64
Alphonsus VIII of Castile, *94*, 146–7
Alphonsus the Magnanimous of Aragon, 74, 118
Altenberg (M), **16**, *10*, *12*, *22*, *47*, *48*, *51*, *116*, *160*, 22–3, 27, 29, 41, 43, 58, 138, 195, 199, 224
Altmünster (W), 160
Altzelle (M), *2*, *3*, *5*, 161; *see also* abb. Martin von Lochau
Amandus Schäffer, abb. of Salem, 119
Amelungsborn (M), *16*, *159*, 33, 215

Amplexus, *13*, 28–9, 31
Anchin, Benedictine abbey, **10**, 7, 9, 37, 53
Angelico de Fiesole, Fra, 26
Arnold, abb. of Morimond, 19
Arnold Amaury, abb. of Cîteaux, 65
Arnulf, lay brother at Villers, 133
Artaud, abb. of Preuilly, 93
Atlas, Our Lady of, (M), 225
Attendorne, von, abb. of Dargun, 112
Augustinian canons, *28*, 49
Aulne (M), 100, 161; *see also* lay brother Simon
Austin friars, *28*, 49
Aywières (W), 161; *see also* St Lutgard

Baldwin, abb. of Ford and archbishop of Canterbury, *32*, 60–1, 64, 208
Balerne (M), *see* abb. Burchard
Barth de Vleeschouwer, father of Beatrice of Nazareth, 162
Beatrice, Cistercian nun, *104*, *105*, 157–8
Beatrice de Lobosh, *111*, 166
Beatrice of Nazareth, 161–2
Baudeloo (M), *39*
Beaulieu (M), *83*, 77, 130
Beaupré (Grammont) (W), **20**, *102*, *108*, *163*, 154–5, 160–1, 173, 177, 184, 217
Beaupré (Oise) (M), 184
Bebenhausen (M), *138*, 195
Beckford, William, 97
Beham, Sebald, 222
Belloc, Hilaire, 213
Benedict, St, **1**, **2**, *1*, *2*, *3*, *4*, *5*, *6*, *7*, 1–11, 22, 33, 69, 82, 101, 105, 141; Rule of, 1–6, 37, 51, 54, 72–5, 79, 82, 84, 91, 95, 96, 97, 99–100, 122, 169–71, 191, 193, 199, 206, 225
Benedict XII, pope, *35*, 50,

66–8, 69, 80, 96, 110–1, 116, 184, 212
Benedictines, *28*, 49, 69
Benedictine nuns, *28*, 49
Berenguela, Spanish princess, 146
Berenguera d'Anglesola, abb. of Vallbona, 155
Bernard, St, of Clairvaux, **3**, **7**, **8**, **9**, **10**, **16**, **18**, *6*, *7*, *8*, *10*, *12–26*, *46*, *49*, *50*, *51*, *67*, *90*, *91*, *92*, *114*, *116*, *135*, *136*, 17–24, 26–49, 57, 58, 68–9, 74, 75, 78, 82, 84, 89, 92, 96, 101, 105, 109–10, 119, 121, 126, 133, 136, 138, 147, 169, 171–2, 174, 178–9, 182, 193–5, 199, 205, 207, 208, 213, 214, 215; and St Aelred, 53–5; and Albigensians, 64–5; and St Benedict, *6*, *7*, 6–11; and Henry Murdac, 50–1; as novice, 85–6; and Cistercian nuns, *90*, *91*, *92*, *112*, *114*, 139, 141, 142–3, 163, 167–8; *Apologia*, 29, 74, 172; *On Precept and Dispensation*, 37; *Steps of Humility and Pride*, 9, 35–7; *Vera Effigies*, *32–5*; *Vita Prima*, 28, 30, 37, 39–44, 49, 54, 193, 199, 200
Bernard, abb. of La Ferté, 19
Bernard, monk at Stična, 210
Bernard Paganelli, *see* Eugenius III
Berthold, lay brother at Maulbronn, *144*, 200
Blanche of Castile, 146, 187
Blanche, daughter of Louis IX of France, 190
Bianca d'Anglesola, abb. of Vallbona, 155
Bo, abb. of Øm, 208
Bonaval (M), 146
Bonnemont (M), 208
Bordesley (M), *see* abb. William Halforde

Boyle (M), 112
Brayelle d'Annay, de la (W), 153
Buildwas (M), 100
Burchard, abb. of Balerne, 6, 16, 122, 124, 130
Byland (M), 111–12, 115

Cadouin (M), *13, 54, 57, 124, 125, 131, 152, 164*, 29, 95–6, 106, 178, 180, 187, 206, 214, 217; *see also* Abbot Peter de Gaing
Caesarius of Heisterbach, *47, 48, 104, 105*, 12, 19, 65, 80, 87–8, 124–5, 131, 133, 147, 155, 157–8, 171, 184, 208, 214, 216
Calixtus II, pope, 16
Camaldoli, 122
Cambron (M), *20, 102, 108, 163*, 154, 160, 173
Cantigas de Santa Maria, 106, 158–9
Carmelites, 28, 49
Carthusians, 122
Casamari (M), 201
Castigos e documentos para bien vivir, 107, 159
Celas (W), 9
Cercamp (M), 184
Chaalis (M), 62, 66, 68, 187; *see also* abb. Gautier de Comte
Charles VI, king of France, 71
Charter of Charity, 12, 18, 173
Chaucer, 69
Christ Church, Canterbury, Benedictine abbey, *32*, 61
Christiaan de Hondt, abb. of Les Dunes, *75*, 119
Christian II, king of Denmark, 224
Cîteaux (M), **5, 24**, *9, 37, 45, 134*, 50, 66, 79, 82, 83, 106, 118, 122, 145, 146, 181, 182, 191–3, 198, 199, 206, 207; foundation of, 1–2, 12–16, 47, 58, 124, 139, 141, 224; and Cistercian expansion, 17–24, 43; *see also* abbs. Alberic, Arnold Amaury, Guy, James of Flavigny, Jean de Cirey, Robert, Stephen Harding, and lay brother Alan of Lille
Clairmarais (M), **11, 12**, 100, 208; *see also* abb. Robert
Clairvaux (M), *15, 25, 40, 50, 51*, 18–20, 27, 33, 43–4, 49, 51, 66, 75, 82, 88, 89, 100, 118, 130, 133, 178, 199, 200, 208; *see also*, abbs. St Bernard, Henry de Marcy,

Jean d'Aizanville and Stephen of Lexington, prior John, and Geoffrey of Ainai
Clare, St, 141
Clarté Dieu, La (M), *95*
Cleeve (M), *168*, 218, 224
Cluny, Benedictine abbey, 74, 77, 82, 171; *see also* abb. Peter the Venerable
Conrad of Eberbach, *see Exordium Magnum*
Conrad III, Emperor, *57*
conventual buildings, Cistercian, 89–98
conversi, see lay brothers
Coyroux (W), 47, 143
croziers, 101–10

Dalheim (W), 160
Dan Alexander, abb. of Kirkstall, 200
Dante, 65, 69, 179
Dargun (M), *71, 128*, 112–5, 182; *see also* abbs. von Attendorne, Gregor of Rostock, Hermann of Riga, Johann Becker, Johann Billerbeck and Johann of Rostock
David, king of Scotland, *54, 55*
Dialogue between a Cluniac and a Cistercian, 80, 83
Dialogue on Miracles, see Caesarius of Heisterbach
diet, the Cistercian, 96–8
Dieter, abb. of Maulbronn, 25
Dietmar, abb. Disibodenberg, 115
Dietrich von Prome, provost at Wienhausen, 97, 150, 153
Disibodenberg (M), 112–5, *see also* abbs. Dietmar and Johannes
Doberan (M), *6, 87*, 6, 33, 105, 135
Doest, Ter (M), *82*, 217; *see also* lay brother Henry
Domenec Porta, abb. of Poblet, *70*, 112
Dominic, St, 133
Dore (M), *59, 122, 126, 162*, 37, 98, 177, 182, 217; *see also* Adam
Dundrennan (M), *72, 139*, 115–6, 196; *see also* Patrick Douglas
Dunes, Les (M), *68, 75*, 100, 110, 118, 201; *see also* abb. Christiaan de Hondt

Eberbach (M), **22**, *127, 150, 155*, 80, 160, 182–4, 205, 211; *see also* Gisilbertus

Eberhard, abb. of Salem, 160
Ebrach (M), **26**, 81, 58, 210–11; *see also* laybrother Konrad Zeuffel and scribe Sifridus Vitulus
Ecclesiastica Officia, 85, 86, 90, 95, 98, 174, 177, 178
Eldiarda d'Anglesola, abb. of Vallbona, 155
Elin Filipsdotter, abb. of Sko, 157
Elin Pedersdotter, abb. of Sko, 157
Eleanor of Aquitaine, 146
Elinor Plantagenet, 146
Elizabeth of Schönau, *89*, 141
Elizabeth von Stepheln, abb. of Heiligkreuztal, *113*, 167
Elizabeth von Temnitz, abb. of Marienstern, 161
Elizabeth de Vergy, 141
Ellisent d'Assonville, abb. of Les Prés, 153
Engilbert, monk at Stična, 210
Englebert, monk from Lubiaz, 147
Enguerrand IV, Lord of Coucy and Saint Gobain, 155
Eskil, archbishop of Lund, 44, 58, 121
Esrum (M), **14**, *129, 169*, 121, 184–5, 187, 218; *see also* abb. Peder Andersen and Brother Rus
Eugenius III, pope, *26*, 17, 27, 45–6, 51–3, 214
Eviza, abb. of Wienhausen, 150
Exordium Cistercii, 1, 13, 72, 101
Exordium Magnum, 14, 21, 28–9, 43, 48–9, 74, 88, 99, 101, 132–3, 138, 171–2, 181
Exordium Parvum, 2, 12, 13, 14, 23, 73, 122, 193

Ferdinand the Catholic, 117
Ferté, La (M), *17*, 19–20, 43, 66, 77; *see also* abb. Bernard
Filippino Lippi, 26
Filippo Lippi, 26
Flaran (M), *143*, 200
Flaxley (M), 112
Flines (W), *130, 163, 185*; *see also* abb. Jeanne de Boubais, nun Ysabel de Maléfiance, and Jean de Bellegambe
Florival (W), 161
Foigny (M), *see* Alexander of Scotland
Folknand, abb. of Stična, *61*, 101–2

Folquet, bishop of Toulouse, *34*, 64–5
Fontainejean (M), 62
Fonte Avellana, 122
Fontenay (M), 43, 180
Fontfroide (M), 64, 66; *see also* Peter of Castelnau
Ford (M), 60–1, 224; *see also* Baldwin and John of Ford
Fossanova (M), 95, 201
Fountains (M), 76, *167*, 50–3, 112, 200, 218, 224; *see also* abbs. Henry Murdac, John Darnton, Marmaduke Huby, Richard, and Thomas Swinton
Francis, St, 5, 69–70, 141
Franciscans, 28, 49
Franciscan nuns, 28, 49, 69–70
Frederick II, German emperor, 17
Frescende, foundress of Les Prés, *100*, 153
Frienisberg (M), 197
Fulcede de la Halle, nun at Les Prés, *100*, 153
Fulgens sicut stella, *see* Pope Benedict XII

Garin, abb. of Pontigny and archbishop of Bourges, 62, 64
Gautier de Comte, abb. of Chaalis, 62
Gerald of Wales, 60
Gerard, count of Looz, founder of Herkenrode, 162
Gerard, St Bernard's brother, 195
Geoffrey of Ainai, monk at Clairvaux, 200
Geoffrey of Auxerre, 26, 28, 31–3, 43
Gertrude, abb. of Trebnitz, 150
Gertrude de Lexhy, abb. of Herkenrode, 166
Gilbert de la Porée, 57–8
Gilbert Foliot, bp. of London, 50
Gilbert of Hoyland, abb. of Swineshead, 88, 205
Gisilbertus, monk at Eberbach, **22**, 80, 182–4
Gobert d'Aspremont, Blessed, monk at Villers, *52*, 93, 115
Godefroid of Arenberg, abb. of Orval, 115
Godfrey, monk at Clairvaux and bishop of Langres, 35
Gottfried, abb. of Schönau, *84*, 132–3, 203
Gottfried von Neuhaus, monk at Zwettl, 174
Goya, Francisco de, 26
Grace Dieu (M), 69, 111
Grandmont, mother-abbey of Grandmontines, 62

Grandselve (M), 65, 208
Gratia, Cistercian saint, *89*, 140
graves, abbots', 70–2, 111–16
Greco, El (Domenico Theocópuli), 26
Gregor of Rostock, abb. of Dargun, 112
Gregory, St, the Great, 6; *see also Moralia in Job*
Günther, abb. of Lubiaz, 96, 150
Günther, bishop of Speyer, 25
Guillaume de Degulleville, 36, 68–71, 217
Guldholm (*Aurea Insula*) (M), 80
Gustav Vasa, king of Sweden, 224
Guy, abb. of Cîteaux, 141, 165
Guy, abb. of Vaux-de-Cernay, 64–5

habit, the Cistercian, 72–82
Hedwig, St, duchess of Silesia, *86*, *89*, *95*, 96, 37, 133–5, 140, 147–50
Heiligenkreuz (M), *31*, 44, *53*, 60, *88*, *137*, *154*, 33, 37, 58–60, 83, 95, 100, 137, 195, 211; *see also* lay brothers Salamon and Werner
Heiligkreuztal (W), *113*; *see* abb. Elizabeth von Stepheln
Heilsbronn (M), *117*, *118*, 165, 174, 217; *see also* abb. Ulrich Kötzler
Heisterbach (M), *114*, *121*, 176; *see also* Caesarius of Heisterbach
Hélinand of Froidmont, 65, 90
Helvig, queen of Denmark, 185
Henry, abb. of St Vaast, 5, 16
Henry, abb. of Varnhem and Vitskøl, 208
Henry, archbishop of Cologne, *11*, 25
Henry, count palatine, 150
Henry, lay brother at Ter Doest, *82*, 129
Henry, lay brother at Himmerod, 138
Henry, prince of France and archbishop of Rheims, 57
Henry de Marcy, abb. of Clairvaux, 64
Henry the Navigator, 98
Henry of Sayn, founder of Marienstatt, *11*, 25
Henry Murdac, abb. of Fountains and archbishop of York, 29, 43, 50–3, 58
Henry II of Brabant, 162

Henry II, king of England, 30, 55–7, 60, 77, 146
Henry II, duke of Silesia, *95*, 147–50
Henry IV, emperor, 57
Herbert of Clairvaux, 21, 23, 28–9, 75
Herkenrode (W), **19**, *111*, *112*, 109, 165–6; *see also* abbs. Aleyde, Beatrice, Gertrude, Mathilde, and Gerard of Looz
Herman, monk, 145
Hermann von Kottenheim, former abb. of Ebrach, 3
Hermann of Riga, abb. of Dargun, 112
Hildegard of Bingen, 131, 141
Himmelkron (W), 155
Himmerod (M), *153*, 200, 210; *see also* lay brother Henry
Hirsau, 122
Holbein, Hans, 26
Holmcultram (M), 43, 83; *see also* abb. Robert Chamber
Honorius III, pope, 52, 62
Huelgas, Las (W), *94*, 146–7, 155, 187; *see also* abb. Missol
Hugh, archbishop of Lyons, 2, 12
Hugh of Fouilloy, 83, *95*, 100–1
Hugh of Macon, abb. of Pontigny and bishop of Auxerre, 19
Humbeline, St, St Bernard's sister, *89*, 139–41
Hussites, *172*, 223–4

Ida of Nivelles, 145
Innocent III, pope, 163

Jacques Fournier, *see* Pope Benedict XII
Jacques de Vitry, 139, 157
James of Flavigny, abb. of Cîteaux, 118
Jean, son of Louis IX of France, *133*, 190
Jean d'Aizanville, abb. of Clairvaux, 33
Jean de Bellegambe, *130*, 126, 185
Jean de Cirey, abb. of Cîteaux, 129, 180–1, 224
Jean Fouquet, *50*, 26, 29, 82, 92
Jean de Montmirail, monk at Longpont, 94
Jeanne de Boubais, abb. of Flines, 185
Jeanne de Flandre, abb. of Le

Sauvoir-sous-Laon, *103*, 115, 155
Jeanne de Flandre, benefactress of Marquette, 162
Jeanne de Marotte, abb. of La Paix Dieu, 89, 141
Jedrzejów (M), 201
Jerpoint (M), *64*, *85*, 105, 133
Jervaulx (M), 112
Joana d'Ampurias, *73*, 117
Jörg Breu, *135*, 139, 193
Johann Becker, abb. of Dargun, 71, 115
Johann Billerbeck, abb. of Dargun, 116
Johann of Rostock, abb. of Dargun, 112
Johannes, abb. of Disibodenberg, 115
Johannes Meiger, cellarer at Tennenbach, **23**, 197
Johannes, Polish monk, 3
Johannes Scharpffer, abb. of Salem, 119
Johannes Stantenat, abb. of Salem, **13**, 119
Johannes Zenlin, abb. of Tennenbach, **23**, 196–7
John II of Portugal, 98
John XXIII, pope, 45
John Bunyan, 69
John Cassian, St, 95, 206
John Darnton, abb. of Fountains, 76, 119–21, 224
John of Ford, 205
John the Hermit, 26
John Lydgate, 71
John, prior of Clairvaux, 88
Jully, Benedictine nuns' priory, 139, 141

Kaisheim (M), *26*, 45, 127
Kamenz (M), *3*, *5*, 101
Kamp (M), **25**, 58, 191; *see also* Rutger
Karl Sverkersen, king of Sweden, 156
Kilkooly (M), *63*, 104–5; *see also* abb. Philip O'Molwanayn
Kirkstall (M), *see* abb. Dan Alexander
Kirkstead (M), 200
Knowles, David, 21, 45, 47, 224
Kołbacz (M), *119*, *161*, 176, 216–7
Konrad Zeuffel, *81*, 129
Koprzywnica (M), 201

Labor Manuum, **23**, **24**, *139–49*, 191–204
Lactatio, 28, 30–1

Langland, 69
Laurence, abb. of Westminster, *30*, 55–6
lay brothers, **15**, **16**, *77–88*, 122–38
Lectio Divina, **25**, **26**, *150–6*, 205–12
Leopold III, duke of Austria, 57
Leubus (M), *see* Lubiaz
Liesborn, Benedictine abbey, 67, 37, 109
Life of Edward the Confessor, *see* St Aelred of Rievaulx
Liffard, lay brother, 129
Longpont (M), *see* Jean de Montmirail
Louis, son of Louis IX of France, *133*, 190
Louis VII, king of France, 57
Louis VIII, king of France, 145
Louis IX (St), king of France, *132*, 147, 187–90
Lubiaz (M), *79*, *115*, 5, 6, 127, 134, 147, 170, 215–6; *see also* abb. Günther and monk Englebert
Lucius III, pope, *9*, 20
Ludwig I, duke of Leignitz and Brieg, 147
Lum-Dieu (W), 146
Lutgard of Aywières, St, *110*, 163–5
Lys (M), 187
Lyse (M), 51

Malachy, St, archbishop of Armagh, 44, 58, 200
Mâle, Emile, 215
manual labour, *see Labor Manuum*
Margreta, queen of Denmark, 151
Margareta von Schöningen, abb. of Wienhausen, 97, 150
Margarete I, queen of Denmark, 185
Maria, Cistercian saint, 89, 140
Marienstatt (M), *11*, 24–5, 124, 150, 182; *see also* abb. Wiegand
Marienstern (W), *5*, *19*, *101*, 6, 38–9, 153–5, 161, 177; *see also* abb. Elizabeth von Temnitz
Mariental (M), 218; *see also* Till Eulenspiegel
Marienthal, St (W), *2*, 3
Marmaduke Huby, abb. of Fountains, 119, 224
Marquette (W), *109*, 163; *see also* Jeanne de Flandre
Martin, St Hedwig's chaplain, 86, 133

Martin of Aragon, 117–8
Martin von Lochau, abb. of Altzelle, 161
Matallana (M), 146
Mathilde de Courtenai, countess of Nevers, 62
Mathilde de Lexhy, abb. of Herkenrode, *111*, 166–7
Matthew of Rievaulx, 75, 90
Maubuisson (W), 146, 155, 187
Maulbronn (M), *41*, *140*, *141*, *144*, *148*, 12, 25, 150, 200–2; *see also* abbs. Albert and Dieter, prior Walther, Berthold, Rosen Schöphelin, and founder Walter of Lomersheim
Meaux (M), 173; *see also* abb. Adam
Medingen (W), 152
Meglinger, Joseph, 33
Mellifont (M), *see* Robert
Menard, abb. of Mores, 29
Michel Erhart, 127
Milo, lay brother uncle of St Bernard, 129
Mirror of Charity, *see* St Aelred of Rievaulx
Missol, abb. of Las Huelgas, *94*, 146
Mogila (M), 77
Molesme, 2, 12–14, 141, 206
Montreuil-sous-Laon (W), 141
Moralia in Job, *45*, *134*, 14, 74–5, 79, 80, 83, 84, 98, 122, 192–3, 195, 198, 206, 213
Mores (M), *see* abb. Menard
Morimond (M), 12, 17, 18–20, 43, 58–60, 66, 176, 177; *see also* abb. Arnold
Morimondo (M), *120*, 176
Murillo, Bartolomé Estebàn, 26

Neuberg (M), 202
New Melleray (M), *174*
Newminster (M), *see* abb. Robert
Nicolas of Villers, abb. of Orval, 115
Nicolaus Pruzie, 147
Nigel Wireker, 77
Nizelles (W), *91*, *92*, 143
novices, Cistercian, 45–9, 84–90
nuns, Cistercian, 17–19, *89–114*, 139–68
Nydala (M), *173*, 224

Obazine (M), *27*, 77, 93, 47, 143, 182; *see also* St Stephen
Odo of Châteauroux, papal legate, *132*, 187–90

Øm (M), 191, 199; *see also*
 abbs. Bo and Peder Pape
Oliva (M), 146
On Precept and Dispensation,
 see St Bernard of Clairvaux
Opus Dei, 20, 21, 22, *115–33*,
 169–90
Orderic Vitalis, 2, 50, 79, 80,
 193
Orval (M), *see* abbs. Godefroid
 and Nicolas of Vilers
Osbert, scribe, 16
Osek (M), 6, 153
Otto, bp. of Freising, *31*,
 57–60, 64

Paix Dieu, La (W), *89*, 140–1;
 see also Jeanne de Marotte
Patrick Douglas, cellarer at
 Dundrennan, *139*, 196
Pancho IV, 158
Perugino, 26
Peder Andersen, abb. of Esrum,
 14, 121
Peder Pape, abb. of Øm, 208
Peter, lay brother, 133
Peter of Castelnau, monk of
 Fontfroide and papal legate,
 64–5
Peter of Celle, 90
Peter the Ceremonious, 117
Peter de Gaing, abb. of
 Cadouin, *54*, *125*, 95, 106
Peter the Great, 117
Peter Meglinger, *8*, *78*, 14–16,
 20
Peter de Roya, 191, 193
Peter the Venerable, abb. of
 Cluny, 79, 81
Pforta (M), *146*, 121, 201
Philip of Harvengt, 1, 79
Philip the Good, duke of
 Burgundy, 70
Paschal II, pope, 12, 14
Philip O'Molwanayn, abb. of
 Kilkooly, 63, 104
Pierre Laurent, *altararius* of St
 Peter's, 68
*Pilgrimage of the Life of Man,
 The*, *see* Guillaume de
 Degulleville
Poblet (M), *70*, *73*, *74*, *80*,
 151, 65, 112, 116–7, 187,
 206; *see also* abb. Domenec
Porta, lay brother William
 Tost, Joana d'Ampurias, and
 Martin of Aragon
Pons, founder of Silvanès, 129
Pontigny (M), 12, 17, 18–20,
 62, 68; *see also* abb. Hugh
 of Macon
Posa, Benedictine abbey, 2
Premonstratensians, 28, 49

Prés, Les (W), *100*, 153, 161;
 see also abb. Ellisent
 d'Assonville, foundress of
 Frescende, and nuns Fulcede,
 Rose, and Sainte de la Halle
Preuilly (M), 93

Rahewin, secretary of Otto of
 Freising, 58
Ramée, La (W), 145, 161
Raymond Berenguer IV, 117
Raymond VI, count of
 Toulouse, 64–5
Rein (M), 83
Revesby (M), 53
Reynard the Fox, 214–5
Rewley (M), *156*, 49, 212
Ribalta, Francisco, 26
Richard, archbishop of
 Canterbury, 17
Richard, abb. of Fountains, 51
Richard I, king of England, 64
Rievaulx (M), 50, 52, 53, 55,
 80, 111, 199; *see also* abbs.
 St Aelred, Matthew, and
 William, and Walter Daniel
 and Walter Espec
Robert, abb. of Clairmarais,
 12, 105–6
Robert, monk at Mellifont,
 200
Robert of Molesme, St, abb. of
 Cîteaux, *8*, 1–2, 12–16, 20,
 101, 124, 206
Robert, abb. of Newminster,
 200
Robert, St Bernard's nephew,
 74, 84
Robert Chamber, abb. of
 Holmcultram, 83
Robertsbridge (M), 173
Rochester, Benedictine abbey,
 4, 12
Rose de la Halle, nun at Les
 Prés, *100*, 153
Rosen Schöphelin, monk at
 Maulbronn, *140*, 200
Rostock (W), 151–2, 155
Royaumont (M), *133*, 187–90
Rule, *see* St Benedict
Rus, legend of Brother, *169*, 218
Rutger, monk at Kamp, **25**,
 210

St Apern, Cologne (W), *23*, *46*,
 136, 22–3, 41, 86
St Augustine, Canterbury,
 Benedictine abbey, **7**, **9**, 35
St Bernard's College, Paris, 66
St Martin de Champs, Paris,
 Benedictine abbey, *24*, 43
St Mary's, York, Benedictine
 abbey, 2, 51, 200

St Theodore (W), 149
St Vaast, Benedictine abbey, 16;
 see also abb. Henry
Ste Marie de Bilohe (W), 184
Sainte de la Halle, nun at Les
 Prés, *100*, 153
Salamon, lay brother prince of
 Austria, 129
Salem (M), **13**, *142*, 118, 119,
 200; *see also* abbs. Amandus
 Schäffer, Eberhard, Johannes
 Scharpffer, and Johannes
 Stantenat
San Galgano (M), 201
Santes Creus (M), *55*, *56*,
 95–6, 116–7
Sauvoir-sous-Laon, Le (W),
 103, 155; *see also* abb.
 Jeanne de Flandre
Savigny (M), *62*, 47, 103, 143
Schleswig, Benedictine abbey,
 80
Schön, Erhard, *171*, 222–3
Schönau (M), *84*, *149*, 132–3,
 202–4; *see also* abb.
 Gottfried
Schöntal (M), 173
Scholastica, St, 141
Schulpforte (M), *see* Pforta
seals, abbatial and conventual,
 68, 69, 110–1
Seligenthal (W), 5, 11
Sept Fons (M), **8**
Sibil d'Anglesola, abb. of
 Vallbona, 155
Sifridus Vitulus, monk at
 Ebrach, **26**, 210–1
Silvanès (M), *see* Pons
Simon, lay brother at Aulne, 133
Simon, lay brother at Wachock,
 201
Simon de Montfort, 65
Sittich or Sitticum, *see* Stična
Sko (W), 156–7; *see also* abbs.
 Elin Filipsdotter and Elin
 Pedersdotter
Sonnefeld (W), 155
Sorø (M), *38*, 75, 84, 191
Stanley (M), *see* Stephen of
 Lexington
Stephen Harding, St, abb. of
 Cîteaux, **5**, **6**, *8*, *10*, *22*, *37*,
 46, 12–16, 18–24, 35, 41,
 83, 86, 89, 92, 101, 129,
 131, 141, 146, 182, 193,
 199
Stephen, St, abb. of Obazine,
 27, *77*, *93*, 47, 115, 122–3,
 143, 182
Stephen of Lexington, abb. of
 Stanley and Clairvaux, 212
Stephen of Tournai, 169
Stična (M), *61*, 83, 101–2, 210;

see also abb. Folknand and scribes Bernard and Engilbert
Sulejów (M), *145*, 201
Svend, bishop of Århus, 191
Swineshead (M), *see* abb. Gilbert of Hoyland

Tart (W), 141, 146
Tennenbach (M), **23**, 196–7; *see also* Johannes Meiger and Johannes Zenlin
Theuley (M), 95
Thomas of Cantimpré, 163
Thoronet, Le (M), 64, 95
Thibault, abb. of Vaux de Cernay, 111
Thomas Swinton, abb. of Fountains
Thurstan, archbishop of York, 2, 50
Till Eulenspiegel, legend of, *170*, 218–22
Tilty (M), *42*, 83
tonsure, the Cistercian, *59*, 82–4
Trebnitz (W), *86*, 95, 96, 133, 147–50, 152, 155; *see also* abb. Gertrude and St Hedwig
Troisfontaines (M), 43
Tulebras (W), 146

Ulrich Kötzler, abb. of Heilsbronn, 3
Urban III, pope, 60
Ursin, St, archbishop of Bourges, 62

Vaast, St, Benedictine abbey, 16
Vallbona (W), 155
Vallombrosa, 122
Varnhem (M), 206–7; *see also* abb. Henry

Vaucelles (M), 131
Vauclair (M), *123*, *166*, 51, 178, 218
Vaudey (M), 200
Vaux de Cernay (M), 111, 187; *see also* abbs. Guy and Thibault
Vera Effigies, see St Bernard of Clairvaux
Victor IV, anti-pope, 55
Villelongue (M), *147*, *157*, *158*, 201, 213–4
Villers, *52*, 131, 161' *see also* lay brother Arnulf, Blessed Gobert, and abb. Walter of Utrecht
Vincent de Beauvais, 139
Vita Prima, see St Bernard of Clairvaux
Vitskøl (M), 206–7
Vreta (W), 156

Wachock (M), 201, *see also* lay brother Simon
Walbran, J.R., 218
Walter of Lomersheim, founder of Maulbronn, 25
Walter Clifton, abb. of Warden, 66, 106
Walter Daniel, 53, 72, 84, 87, 193
Walter Espec, founder of Rievaulx, 55
Walter Map, 26–7, 44, 77, 79–80, 131, 193
Walter of Utrecht, abb. of Villers, 162
Walther, prior at Maulbronn, *141*, 200
Warden (M), 201; *see also* abb. Walter Clifton
Waverley (M), 47, 60
Wechterswinkel (W), 149
Werner, lay brother at

Heiligenkreuz, *88*, 137
Wettingen (M), **15**, 135–7
Wiegand, abb. of Marienstatt, *11*, 25
Wienhausen (W), **2**, **3**, *97*, *98*, *99*, 9, 150–3, 155, 161, 163, 182; *see also* abbs. Eviza and Margareta von Schöningen
William, abb. of Rievaulx, 43, 50, 87
William, Benedictine abb. of Sint Truiden, 165
William Fitzherbert, St, archbishop of York, 51–2
William Halforde, abb. of Bordesley, *65*, 106
William of Malmesbury, 2, 14, 225
William of St Thierry, 21, 23, 28, 37, 39–43, 49, 208
William of Tournai, 6
William, St, archbishop of Bourges, *33*, 62–4
William VIII of Montpellier, 64–5
William Tost, lay brother at Poblet, *80*, 127
Woburn (M), 200
Wöltingerode (W), 150, 161
Wolfgang Örtl, abb. of Zwettl, 193
Wonnental (W), *14*, 5, 29

Ysabel de Maléfiance, nun at Flines, 185
Ysengrinus, 75, 214

Zwettl (M), **1**, **21**, *1*, *4*, *17*, *21*, *135*, 3, 5, 6, 33, 41, 82, 83, 99, 100, 101, 139, 174–5, 193; *see also* abb. Wolfgang Örtl, Gottfried von Neuhaus, and Jörg Breu